Foundations of Education

Third Edition

Foundations of Education

Becoming a Teacher

Paul D. Travers
University of Missouri–St. Louis

Ronald W. Rebore
Special School District
St. Louis County, Missouri

Allyn and Bacon
Boston • London • Sydney • Toronto • Tokyo • Singapore

Senior Editor: Virginia Lanigan
Editorial Assistant: Nicole DePalma
Cover Designer: Susan Harbison
Composition Buyer: Linda Cox
Manufacturing Buyer: Megan Cochran
Marketing Representative: Ellen Mann
Editorial-Production Service: P. M. Gordon Associates
Production Administrator: Deborah Brown

The first and second editions of this book
were published by Prentice-Hall, Inc.

Copyright © 1995 by Allyn and Bacon
A Simon & Schuster Company
Needham Heights, Massachusetts 02194

This text is printed on
recycled, acid-free paper.

Library of Congress Cataloging-in-Publication Data

Travers, Paul D.
    Foundations of education : becoming a teacher / Paul D. Travers.
Ronald W. Rebore. — 3rd ed.
      p.   cm.
    Includes bibliographical references (p.   ) and index.
    ISBN 0–205–16472–2
    1. Teacher—Training of—United States. 2. Education—Study and
teaching—United States. I. Rebore, Ronald W. II. Title.
LB1715.T675 1995
370'.71'0973—dc20   94–22535
                                                                          CIP

Printed in the United States of America

10 9 8 7 6 5 4 3 2 1   99 98 97 96 95 94

*There is no final way to judge
the worth of a teacher
except in terms of the lives
of those taught.*

—Peabody Journal of Education

Contents

Preface

The purpose of the third edition of *Foundations of Education: Becoming a Teacher* is the same as that of the second edition: to help prospective teachers better understand their chosen careers by presenting selected facts, themes, and ideas pertinent to professional education. Through an awareness of the context of education and schooling, future teachers can identify more strongly with teaching as a field of study.

The public schools are in a state of rapid change, shaped largely by powerful national and state forces, and the authors have updated much of the content in various chapters. New information has been added pertaining to teacher supply and demand, community attitudes about education, curriculum trends, as well as representative legal, political, economic, and social changes within the last several years. An annotated bibliography containing thirty-six national reports and studies is also included for those students who want to pursue particular issues more thoroughly.

This textbook is different from most introductory editions because it combines the views of both a public school and a university educator. Ronald Rebore has been a central office administrator in three public school districts for a total of twenty years while Paul Travers has been involved in teacher education in the university for almost thirty years. In an age when the public school and the university must synchronize their efforts, the authors believe their collaboration is one step in that direction.

Prospective teachers need to see connections between preservice study and professional practice. They should consider the major historical, philosophical, political, social, economic, and professional forces which pervade public education. To view these themes from only the vantage point of the university or public school would be incomplete. Theoretical and practical considerations must be fused to give the student a better sense of educational reality. Too often, students do not begin to sense this reality until they enroll in clinical experiences; however, a beginning course can initiate such an awareness by portraying how former educational effort flows into the present.

The content of this text extends over sixteen chapters. The major themes are: (1) the educational heritage; (2) developing an educational viewpoint; (3) curriculum and organization; (4) support, control, and administration of public schools; and (5) the legal and professional status of students and teachers in the public schools.

The authors would like to thank the reviewers of the book: Rudy Tarpley, College of the Southwest; Emma Craig, Louisiana State University; and D. Summers, Lebanon (PA) Valley College.

The authors are especially indebted to Elizabeth Eissler for her competent, patient, and energetic assistance in the preparation of this manuscript. Appreciation is also offered to Bernadette Travers for her comments in regard to the clarity of numerous chapters and to the Rebore family, Sandra, Lisa, and Ronald, Jr., for their sacrifices during the period of research and writing.

P. D. T.
R. W. R.

Chapter 1

Teaching as a Career

This chapter contains information on several themes pertinent to teaching as a career. We hope that by providing a fairly broad context of professional facts and views related to the classroom teacher, we can help the student see better his or her role as a future teacher. Teaching is a very personal and complex process. It is both an art and a science because the teaching process depends partly upon subjective factors and partly upon more objective data about the process of teaching itself. In other words, there is no one ideal or "book model" teacher. This is fortunate, however, because children vary and need to relate to many types of human beings throughout their lives.

The Challenge of Teaching

Teachers, despite differing personality types, must have some common traits. Superior intelligence, compassion, humor, respect for children, and patience are necessary ingredients for good teachers. Given these necessary traits, there is a place for most types of people in the profession. The process of teaching, however, also requires an awareness of such things as child maturation and learning as a psychological phenomenon, as well as the sociological forces at work in and out of the classroom. These are the scientific aspects of teaching. Implementation of these aspects enables teaching methodology to become more predictable irrespective of the teacher's personality. An interest in the teacher as a mature human being and research about the teaching act itself constitute the art and science of teaching.

Historically, the teaching profession had long been afflicted by the influx of men and women who saw teaching either as a steppingstone to something financially better or who did not succeed in their original career choice and selected teaching as an alternative career. Generally speaking, these two types did little for the profession. Teaching children was not a strong motivation for them. It was an incidental aspect of employment. This is not to say that enthusiasm alone makes for effective teaching; rather the desire to work with children must be a prerequisite to everything else.

Fortunately, this is no longer typical. Today, those who choose teaching as a career change are often motivated by a sense of idealism and are good scholars. These people constitute the category of "non-traditional" students on many campuses. It is estimated that almost 20 percent of college students are over 35 years of age.

Future teachers must feel the desire to teach. They must respect childhood as a legitimate stage of growth. They must tolerate individual differences. They must respect cultural, ethnic, racial, and religious variances among children. This should not result in hypocritical behavior, condescension, or false flattery. It means rather an acceptance that all children deserve the opportunity to pursue the same cultural benefits. Respect for children also does not mean one must love all children. It can be difficult to like some children. Respect, however, engenders courtesy, fairness, and the belief that learning is every child's right. Teachers have to work at being tolerant and respectful more than do most professionals because they can be sorely tried by young people. Misbehavior can be too easily equated with lack of personal worth.

The way a prospective teacher learns about his or her potential for becoming a good teacher is twofold: First, the future teacher becomes or stays scholarly. Learning is valued. Reading becomes a part of life in and out of school. Scholarship is thought of as a natural pursuit. Second, the future teacher seeks continual opportunities to work with children in particular and the public in general. Opportunities are sought to tutor and to participate occasionally in community events. In other words, a person does not have to be an expert in numerous intellectual or physical endeavors, but he or she should be interested in helping and influencing others.

Often latent talent emerges when an individual tries to find out if teaching is his or her forte. It is crucial to have such "teaching" contacts long before a major is undertaken in college. The sooner one finds out if it is gratifying to instruct as well as to interact with different age levels, the more productive teacher preparation will be. Nothing is sadder than to see prospective teachers fail because they were unaware that they did not like to be around children or adolescents continually. Social experiences can foster better self-awareness in this regard. Participation in school clubs and related peer activities, sales work, or church involvement are all ways to foster greater awareness about the desire to teach. One should like to be with people and youngsters a great deal. Only varied experiences can indicate competency in interpersonal skills as well as a genuine desire to become a teacher. The prospective teacher who lacks significant social involvement before college graduation may be gambling much on career choice, both in terms of career satisfaction and the welfare of the children to be taught.

Teacher Attributes

Research on the attributes or characteristics of teachers has not been effective in depicting a "book model" teacher against whom all can be compared. No strong connection has yet been shown between successful teachers and single variables such as intelligence, knowledge of subject matter, gender, or voice quality.

Naturally, one would have to infer that a successful teacher at any level must possess above-average intelligence or adequate command of subject matter, but these single traits in themselves are no guarantee of effective teaching or learning. Because so many variables come into play in an effective lesson or unit, teaching and teachers are very difficult to analyze. Successful teachers must be able to perform consistently to be labeled successful. Pupils' attitudes will also greatly influence the effect a teacher has upon the learners. Research traditionally has focused heavily upon teachers themselves but not so much on the atmosphere for learning which enhances a teacher's effort.

If a teacher confronts children who are generally malnourished or who are from homes that do not value the status of the teacher or respect formal education, then successful teaching is made more difficult. Furthermore, if school administrators create a climate of excessive expectations, teachers can be hampered in their efforts. Teachers are affected by dozens of variables. Good teaching is multidimensional. The success of a teacher who is faced with austere working conditions and hostile learners will be relative to those variables. More research is needed on the learner and the conditions for learning. Historically, the teacher was the primary object of analysis, but now the environment itself is crucial to those investigations into effective teaching.

The report of James Coleman and others, *Equality of Educational Opportunity* (1966), rendered a great service by empirically demonstrating what had been believed for years: Social and economic factors mean a great deal in one's quest to achieve. Forces operating outside the school may mean more than those within the school. Educational philosophers had been stating this concept for decades, but it had never been demonstrated by research. The Coleman Report indicated how socioeconomic status affects achievement. The teacher is important as a force in terms of very low class children, but peer group and parental stimuli are also very crucial. Effective teaching is greatly influenced by these variables. The Coleman Report has initiated a host of studies about achievement in regard to socioeconomic factors.

In considering the topic of successful teaching, it is always of interest to cite classical studies on attributes of successful teachers. The literature is replete with such studies, and it may be helpful to mention a few.

The American Council on Education in the late 1950s sponsored a study on characteristics of teachers in order to demonstrate effective and ineffective teaching behaviors. In the study, so-called critical incidences (behaviors that contribute to success or failure in teaching) were cited by a variety of individuals, and their responses were summarized. Numerous generalizations were made in regard to effective and ineffective behaviors of teachers. Conspicuous traits were good humor, enthusiasm, fairness, personable style, organized manner, and an acceptance of student views.[1]

Another celebrated study had been undertaken earlier in regard to what students perceive as desirable qualities in teachers. Over 12,000 letters on "The Teacher Who Has Helped Me Most" were submitted by children and youths across the nation. The findings closely resembled those in later studies in terms of desirable teacher traits. Such items as cooperativeness, kindliness, respect for the learner, and humor all emerged as common traits of good teachers.[2]

One synthesis of research on teacher effectiveness embodied an excellent summary on the characteristics of good teachers. Teachers who are considered effective are human in the fullest sense of the word, They possess humor, fairness, and empathy. They are more democratic than autocratic and are able to relate easily and naturally to students on either a one-to-one or group basis.[3] Flexibility and personalized teaching are extremely crucial to their success. The research, it seems, is important in terms of how the teacher behaves *toward* the student.[4] Effective learning is enhanced by such teacher behavior because it is related to a student's self-confidence.

Presently, research on teacher effectiveness basically focuses on the environment and organization of the classroom. The environment of the classroom includes emotional variables that influence the teacher *and* students. Student self-esteem, sense of well-being, and security, for example, have a great deal to do with increased learning. These emotional characteristics (the affective domain) must be enhanced if academic content or knowledge (the cognitive domain) is to develop. The two domains are inseparable and must be investigated in relationship to each other if educators are to learn more about teaching and learning.

The organization of the classroom comprises such things as the teacher's monitoring students' seatwork and providing feedback immediately, establishing rules which are flexible yet foster orderliness, and encouraging problem solving among all students. Teachers seem to be more successful if they possess managerial skills which stress a work environment; that is, little disruption with much efficiency. Of course, these managerial skills cannot be devoid of the affective factors that personalize instruction. It seems that the more teachers allow student participation in the teaching-learning process, the greater is the degree of achievement.

Research also indicates that teacher effectiveness is directly related to the organization of the classroom as well as to the curriculum, regardless of personality types. In other words, a prospective teacher who feels limited in reference to adequate social skills, for example, can still feel optimistic if certain managerial skills, in combination with other instructional and emotional skills, are acquired. The teacher does not have to feel that success is entirely genetic. The research seems to say that what makes people successful in other endeavors applies also to teachers. The successful teacher is generally enthusiastic, emotionally mature, patient, and fair. He or she likes young people and encourages them to become as self-reliant as possible. Obviously, few teachers can be all things to all people at any given time. Many of the traits described cannot be attained on short notice. It may take a lifetime to accomplish emotional maturity; however, it is the *pursuit* of these admirable traits and behaviors that is important.

A.C. Porter and J. Brophy recently synthesized research on good teaching and cited numerous factors which described effective teachers. These teachers

1. Are clear concerning instructional goals
2. Are knowledgeable about content and appropriate strategies
3. Make efficient use of instructional materials to allow for greater enrichment or clarification
4. Develop an awareness of students' needs and the level of their knowledge
5. Teach metacognitive strategies to their students
6. Develop content built upon cognitive objectives or domains[5]

Recent research indicates that effective teachers engage students actively in learning. This implies that teachers must know what students bring to a learning experience and what they need to learn. This challenge varies from subject to subject.

School organization and effective teaching are critically related: How students are organized for learning; how teachers interact with students; how time is allocated according to material content; and how students are academically assessed are crucial factors in determining the effectiveness not only of learning, but also of teaching. In other words, altering the structure of learning and teaching may have a great influence on the success in both. Current research is focusing on this process.[6]

Preparing for Teacher Employment

School administrators and teacher placement officials are becoming concerned about the balance between the supply of licensed teachers and the demand for them by school districts and private schools. For at least the last decade, the oversupply of teachers for most fields was obvious. With the exception of teachers in mathematics, vocational education, and the natural sciences, most had difficulty finding employment. In the past few years, however, college students have not, in great numbers, considered specialties in crowded teaching fields. Industry has also attracted many teachers with scientific or mathematical skills, partially depleting the teaching ranks. Retirement, including early retirement, has also added to the growing shortage of teachers nationally.

In addition, there is an upswing in the birthrate, which will have an impact upon elementary schools in the ensuing years. The former surplus of teachers has dwindled for various reasons. The upshot is that prospective teachers can feel more optimistic now than previously.

In preparing for a better teaching market, it is important that candidates think early and seriously about the traits school administrators desire in their teachers.

A candidate's academic record, of course, is always basic when considering state requirements and institutional standards. In addition to the academic portfolio, however, lies a more subjective area of preparation or experience in which most school districts expect a degree of competency or exposure. It is an area that focuses on experiences beyond the realm of schooling. Specifically, potential employers are interested in a candidate's professional knowledge and outside interests. These experiences probably have not counted for much credit on a transcript, but in the long run they complement the candidate's study. A successful teacher, it is believed, possesses a good scholastic record and a variety of professional and general interests.

Recently, the authors observed that many students were interested in the types of questions school districts ask potential teachers on their employment applications. As a result, an employment application was obtained from each of the 41 school districts in the St. Louis metropolitan area, which comprises both rural and urban, affluent and poor school districts. Because it is a typical locality, many of the items on the applications are applicable to other locales. The questions extracted pertained to what beginning students should be aware of long before graduation or certification to teach.

The following items revolve around selected concerns cited on those 41 employment applications. The concerns, as mentioned, were selected specifically because of their relevance to what beginning students in education ought to know. The list is slightly altered to fit the purpose of this discussion. The percentage of districts that asked the question is noted in parentheses following the concern, but it is difficult to generalize based upon the percentages. For example, most school district personnel ask philosophical questions in the interview for employment, but evidently not many ask for written philosophies to accompany the application. Most school districts regard a candidate's philosophy of education as important in the selection process, but they expect the candidate to state such beliefs at the interview stage. Keep in mind also that the following excerpts from the applications are only part of what a district wants to know about a candidate:

1. Cite achievement in regard to honors acquired, recognition earned, and commendations received in organizations, especially those of an educational nature. (100 percent)
2. Cite references beyond placement file, which indicate scholarship, teaching ability, or potential for effective teaching. (80 percent)
3. List extracurricular activities that you are willing to sponsor. (66 percent)
4. Responses requested to questions of a philosophical nature, such as "What is the most important experience a student can obtain during his or her formal schooling?" or "How can you influence a child's life?" (Seldom is a written philosophy *per se* requested; however, application and interview questions are often geared toward eliciting such information.) (61 percent)
5. Cite non-teaching work experience. (61 percent)
6. List personal hobbies or activities relevant to your application. (51 percent)[7]

In looking at these concerns, it is apparent that experience is valued, and success both in and out of school is desired. A candidate who possesses a diversity of interests and skills and displays a sense of commitment to teaching as a career has the advantage. This does not imply that success in teaching is perceived to be dependent upon well-balanced interests and activities alone, but rather upon devotion to study in combination with outside interests. Earning high grades is believed to be insufficient in light of the questions found on these applications. Rather, it is the application of knowledge that seems important. For example, school administrators want to know about a candidate's "work or outside educational experiences," or those activities an applicant can "sponsor" or "direct." They also want to know what "personal qualities" the individual possesses that would enhance his or her teaching capability. The major point inferred is this: If the candidate concentrates on self-improvement in various ways in preservice study, the prospect for employment increases appreciably.

The interview itself has no definite pattern among districts. It can be assumed, however, that the interviewer learns of a candidate's values about teaching by means of the application. Activities and experiences cited on the application are excellent vehicles for discussion. Academic credits can be easily ascertained and, of course, they cannot be underplayed; however, more subjective factors usually emerge in the interview.

Some school districts will send pertinent officials, such as a principal or personnel officer, to selected college campuses for initial, short interviews. These officials are not bound by a script, but they often tend to ask why the candidate is interested in teaching, what kind of background the candidate has, and, in particular, why the candidate is interested in their school district. These areas of discussion focus sharply on subjective ideas which reflect personality and character. Other inquiries by the interviewer may center on the candidate's knowledge of curriculum and instruction. If the interviewer is impressed with the candidate, he or she may be invited to pursue further discussion either in the school district's central office or in a selected school in the district.

Some school districts avoid campus visitations, preferring instead to interview only on the basis of "appealing" applications. There are, however, variations to this method of selection. Some personnel directors ascertain basic academic credentials and then invite the candidate to meet with one or more principals or with a team of administrators, faculty, and parents. Impressions are then combined into a profile. Team opinion is a strong factor in the selection process. Video or audio taping a candidate's responses is becoming a tool in some interviews. A candidate's belief system, interpersonal skills, and instructional techniques are increasingly being analyzed by trained interviewers.

Candidates have to be open to any topic of discussion, regardless of the format or style of the interview. School officials usually seek not only specific answers to academic questions but also assurances that the candidate is capable of thinking creatively and possesses self-confidence and poise. Furthermore, proficiency in written communication may be determined during the interview. Even a satisfactory score on an aptitude test may be a requirement for employment.

There is no guarantee that a candidate will gain employment even if he or she is superior in every facet of the interview process. The principal or personnel director may be looking for a certain type of personality to complement that of other faculty and administrators. Regardless, the more informed and articulate a candidate is, the greater is his or her opportunity for employment. Consequently, it is in the candidate's best interest to thoroughly prepare responses to anticipated questions. Practice should not diminish the candidate's sincerity or spontaneity. Rather, it should increase one's confidence to field a variety of questions.

In sum, seeking employment is a very personal pursuit. Candidates who realize this early have the advantage. When prospective teachers learn what school districts expect, they will be better prepared. It is possible for students to practice for the interviews in order to be more articulate about their responses, especially to open-ended questions. This early awareness should benefit the future teacher and those soon to be under his or her direction.

Teacher Supply and Demand

As discussed earlier in this chapter, many public school officials are beginning to feel concerned about the lack of teachers for many educational levels. In the last decade the need for teachers was mainly evident in the natural sciences, mathematics, and vocational education. This need is rapidly broadening to include other specialties. It is difficult to generalize about supply and demand because there are wide variances between rural and urban districts and among geographic regions across the country. Frequently, in one metropolitan area, teachers can successfully seek employment simply by relocating to a more remote school district. One reason why a candidate often remains unemployed is his or her refusal to move or drive to a less desirable locality. Many teachers desire an urban setting; however, positions might be more appealing elsewhere in terms of working conditions or status in the community. Rural schools can offer a "sense of community" often lacking in many urban school districts. Table 1-1 indicates national data concerning teacher employment.

The following figures are also included to indicate that an upswing in enrollment is occurring in the lower grades because of the increased birthrate since 1980. Although this trend will not affect secondary education obviously for years, the enrollment picture and its accompanying effect, teacher employment, are beginning to reflect a better future for public and private schools. Refer to Figures 1-1, 1-2, and 1-3 on projected enrollment trends and Figure 1-4 on estimated demand for new teachers for the next several years.

Is Teaching a Profession?

For decades, educators have been debating whether or not teaching is a profession in the classical sense: Does it reflect high intellectual techniques and render

TABLE 1-1   Teacher Supply and Demand by Field and Region

Regions are coded: 1—Northwest, 2—West, 3—Rocky Mountain, 4—Great Plains/Midwest, 5—South Central, 6—Southeast, 7—Great Lakes, 8—Middle Atlantic, 9—Northeast, 10—Alaska, 11—Hawaii.

5 = Considerable shortage; 4 = Some Shortage; 3 = Balanced; 2 = Some Surplus; 1 = Considerable Surplus

Field	Region											National 1993
	1	2	3	4	5	6	7	8	9	10	11	
Agriculture	3.50	2.50	2.50	2.92	2.43	3.00	3.62	3.50	—	—	4.00	3.03
Art	1.92	2.39	2.00	2.52	2.33	2.23	2.36	1.71	1.38	2.00	3.00	2.25
Bilingual Education	4.17	4.78	3.88	4.20	4.69	3.62	4.19	3.82	3.67	4.00	3.00	4.18
Business	2.40	2.69	2.43	2.36	2.18	2.43	2.37	2.25	2.67	3.00	3.00	2.39
Computer Science	3.44	3.62	3.33	3.62	3.56	3.47	3.23	3.36	2.00	4.00	4.00	3.41
Counselor—Elementary	4.17	3.13	3.67	3.94	3.55	3.00	3.15	2.63	2.00	5.00	5.00	3.31
Counselor—Secondary	4.31	3.19	3.44	3.55	3.35	2.67	3.05	2.50	2.00	5.00	5.00	3.16
Data Processing	4.00	3.50	2.67	3.06	3.25	3.50	3.00	3.00	—	3.00	—	3.17
Driver Education	2.00	2.88	2.00	2.28	2.22	2.25	2.73	2.00	3.00	—	—	2.42
Elementary—Primary	2.47	2.14	2.00	1.62	3.00	2.38	1.50	1.66	1.27	4.00	2.00	1.88
Elementary—Intermediate	2.27	2.33	2.00	1.70	2.95	2.56	1.58	1.77	1.25	4.00	2.00	1.96
English	2.43	3.10	2.70	2.61	2.81	2.51	2.27	2.02	1.58	4.00	3.00	2.44
English as a Second Lang.	4.00	4.44	3.71	4.24	4.06	3.72	3.71	3.31	3.86	3.00	3.00	3.91
Health Education	2.22	2.08	2.75	1.67	1.50	2.28	1.76	1.76	2.25	4.00	3.00	1.89
Home Economics	2.17	2.42	2.33	2.18	2.42	2.75	2.88	2.43	2.00	1.00	4.00	2.49
Journalism	2.25	1.89	2.80	2.69	2.55	2.40	2.39	2.00	—	3.00	—	2.46
Language, Modern—French	3.20	2.53	2.88	3.51	3.45	3.46	2.98	2.82	2.50	4.00	3.00	3.13
Language, Modern—German	2.90	2.53	3.00	3.33	3.45	3.47	3.04	2.83	3.00	4.00	3.00	3.13
Language, Modern—Spanish	3.80	3.47	3.70	3.93	4.14	3.66	3.47	3.23	2.63	4.00	4.00	3.61
Language—Other	4.50	4.00	—	3.25	4.50	3.75	4.29	5.00	3.00	5.00	—	4.04
Library Science	3.75	3.40	3.33	3.52	3.30	3.44	3.43	3.11	3.50	3.00	4.00	3.43
Mathematics	3.40	4.00	3.20	3.43	4.14	3.73	3.23	3.05	2.91	4.00	5.00	3.43
Music—Instrumental	3.06	3.00	3.25	3.23	3.00	2.58	2.81	2.60	2.00	5.00	3.00	2.91
Music—Vocal	3.06	2.56	3.25	3.18	2.90	2.57	2.72	2.41	1.86	4.00	—	2.81
Physical Education	2.00	1.61	1.50	1.37	1.58	1.91	1.55	1.75	1.60	—	3.00	1.61
Psychologist (School)	4.55	3.79	4.43	4.00	3.62	3.29	3.50	3.42	3.67	5.00	—	3.72
Science—Biology	3.13	3.40	2.70	3.22	3.52	3.42	2.98	2.93	3.25	3.00	3.00	3.16
Science—Chemistry	3.60	4.25	3.50	3.77	4.19	3.94	3.63	3.60	3.89	4.00	4.00	3.79
Science—Earth	3.31	3.71	3.00	3.29	3.62	3.41	3.03	3.05	3.00	3.00	4.00	3.24
Science—General	3.00	3.42	2.80	3.21	3.48	3.38	3.00	2.85	3.25	3.00	3.00	3.14
Science—Physics	3.60	4.33	3.44	3.95	4.40	4.21	3.80	3.62	4.13	4.00	4.00	3.93
Science—Other Areas	—	4.00	—	—	4.00	—	3.75	4.00	—	—	—	3.86
Social Sciences	2.00	1.44	1.22	1.46	1.75	1.77	1.58	1.56	1.38	1.00	—	1.58
Social Worker (School)	3.63	3.33	3.40	3.42	3.60	2.75	3.18	2.14	3.50	5.00	—	3.22
Speech	2.75	3.31	2.71	2.68	2.86	3.60	2.63	3.00	4.00	—	—	2.88
Special Ed—Deaf	4.30	4.00	4.75	4.20	4.60	4.46	3.50	3.82	4.00	5.00	4.00	4.17
Special Ed—ED/BD	4.36	4.15	4.14	4.41	4.69	4.59	4.36	4.15	4.14	5.00	5.00	4.39
Special Ed—Gifted	3.55	4.00	4.00	3.80	4.31	4.00	3.54	3.42	3.33	5.00	—	3.80
Special Ed—LD	4.38	4.25	4.50	4.17	4.56	4.37	4.25	4.27	3.89	5.00	5.00	4.29
Special Ed—Mental Hand.	4.33	4.36	4.43	4.05	4.69	4.38	4.07	4.09	3.75	5.00	5.00	4.22
Special Ed—Multi Hand.	4.43	4.64	4.43	4.39	4.73	4.52	4.34	4.10	3.86	5.00	5.00	4.40

Continued

TABLE 1-1   *Continued*

Field	Region 1	2	3	4	5	6	7	8	9	10	11	National 1993
Special Ed—Reading	3.64	3.06	3.88	3.53	4.00	3.80	3.10	2.94	3.00	3.00	—	3.38
Special Ed—Other	—	5.00	—	4.50	4.00	4.00	4.00	3.50	2.00	—	—	3.85
Speech Path./Audio.	4.46	4.23	4.00	4.41	4.41	4.47	4.24	4.09	3.50	5.00	—	4.28
Technology/Industrial Arts	4.50	3.11	2.83	2.91	2.60	3.36	3.26	3.00	2.67	3.00	—	3.09
COMPOSITE	3.37	3.33	3.15	3.26	3.44	3.30	3.13	2.98	2.83	3.87	3.71	3.22
N =	17	21	11	68	21	40	72	50	14	1	1	316

From data supplied by survey respondents. In some instances, the averages are based upon limited input, and total reliability is not assured.

Source: Ginger S. Nicholas, *Association for School, College, and University Staffing,* 1994, 4. Used with permission.

a valuable social service? Early educational pioneers regarded teaching as a profession in an embryonic sense. Horace Mann, Henry Barnard, and Edward A. Sheldon, for example, all thought in the nineteenth century that teaching deserved its place beside the traditional professions of medicine and law. Actually, the latter two professions were academically not much better viewed than teaching as a career. Their prestige was higher, but they, too, were genuinely weak as professions.

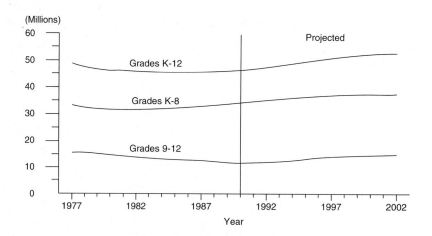

FIGURE 1-1   Enrollment in Elementary and Secondary Schools, by Grade Level, with Projections: Fall 1977 to Fall 2002

Source: D. Gerard and W. J. Hussar, *Projections of Education Statistics to 2002,* Washington, D.C.: National Center for Education Statistics, 1991, 8.

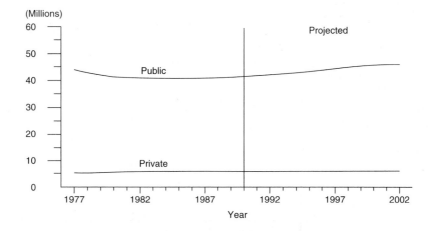

FIGURE 1-2   Enrollment in Elementary and Secondary Schools, by Control of Institution, with Projections: Fall 1977 to Fall 2002

Source: D. Gerard and W. J. Hussar, *Projections of Education Statistics to 2002,* Washington, D.C.: National Center for Education Statistics, 1991, 8.

The history of the National Education Association (NEA) parallels the history of much of American public education and teacher education. The NEA was founded in 1857, and in the inaugural address to its founding members, a leading educator of the time urged the Association to become more professional. Of the

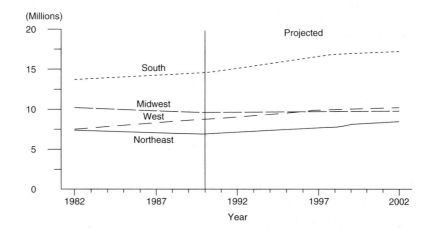

FIGURE 1-3   Enrollment in Grades K-12 in Public Schools, by Region, with Projections: Fall 1982 to Fall 2002

Source: D. Gerard and W. J. Hussar, *Projections of Education Statistics to 2002,* Washington, D.C.: National Center for Education Statistics, 1991, 98.

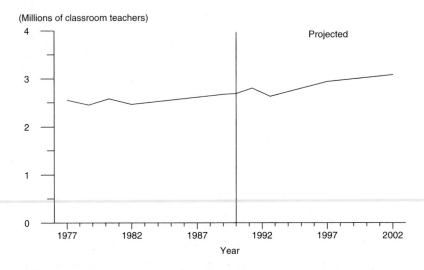

(Millions of classroom teachers)

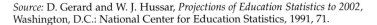

Year

FIGURE 1-4   Need for Public School Teachers to Fall 2002

Source: D. Gerard and W. J. Hussar, *Projections of Education Statistics to 2002,*
Washington, D.C.: National Center for Education Statistics, 1991, 71.

several points stressed, he argued that members consider self-regulation, standards for licensure, and teacher examination as crucial endeavors. These traits
certainly still constitute what is normally professional concern. Sadly, since 1857,
however, teaching personnel in public education—kindergarten through grade
12—have not made great strides to meet the challenges laid down in that inaugural address.

Many educators by modern standards think of a profession in terms of the
following core criteria:

1. Lifelong career commitment
2. Social service
3. Intellectual techniques
4. Code of ethics and
5. Independent judgment relative to professional performance

Most readers would probably agree that prospective teachers are altruistic in
regard to their desire to teach. Teachers leave the profession for reasons of low
income, but they enter for idealistic purpose. The desire to guide children in their
growth and development is a strong motivation to teach. But, in context of the
above criteria, there is much room for debate. Teacher education and the quality
of public school performance are under fire at the moment, so the status of

intellectual techniques, as they apply to teaching in the public school, is open to question.

The authors believe teaching in the public school leaves much to be desired in reference to two other criteria—a code of ethics and independent judgment. The NEA is the only major comprehensive body of public school teachers which embraces a code of ethics. Unfortunately, the NEA Code of Ethics has been little enforced during 60 years of existence. It has been revised six times since 1929, but it is presently not in the national limelight. Most educators strongly believe that if teaching is ever to be considered a true profession, it must have a clearly written, widely applicable code of ethics.

A corollary of this attempt to professionalize teaching by means of a code of ethics is the quest to achieve greater professional independence personally and collectively. A code of ethics can help instill a greater sense of public confidence if the profession monitors itself. In addition, if such public confidence is earned, licensing standards, teacher education, and academic freedom all can be brought under the influence of practitioners themselves. Of course, teaching is unlike any pursuit in the private sector because there are legal and social restrictions imposed upon it.

Teachers in the public schools are legally and financially dependent upon the communities in which they are employed. In other words, they cannot set their own wages or select their own clientele as can doctors or lawyers. Boards of education are the primary agents to set policy, so teachers are truly public employees. These facts, however, do not demean teachers in their quest for higher professional status. Teachers should not compare themselves with the more traditional professions, but rather with the so-called public helping professions such as social work or counseling. Teaching is truly different from most careers, yet it is capable of professional status. An idea often bandied about is that teachers are part of an "emerging" profession, strong in several ways, weak in others.

The NEA considers itself, with its approximate 2 million members, as both an association and a union. The latter term, in recent years, partly characterizes the NEA. Members believe, however, that the scope of the NEA extends far beyond wages, hours, and working conditions; consequently, its vision is both economic and educational. Similarly, the American Federation of Teachers, (AFT) (AFL-CIO), an organization of about 800,000 members, is also concerned about economic and educational goals.

Since its inception in 1916, the AFT has been a union and believes that the term "professional" can be used as a tool to keep teachers from playing an active role in advancing their own political or economic destiny. The AFT makes no apology for being a union. It also, like the NEA, has broader concerns.

Under the aegis of the Carnegie Forum on Education and the Economy, the AFT, NEA, and others are proposing a national teacher board to deal with certification, standards, and ethical behavior. This Board will issue certificates to exemplary teachers in recognition of performance and ability. The NEA also has played a strong role in developing national accreditation standards for teacher education through the National Council for the Accreditation of Teacher Education. The NEA is also, through its negotiated contracts with school boards, beginning to gain a greater voice in policy-making by establishing advisory committees to a number of boards of education. Professionalism now includes involvement of teachers in the formulation of educational policies.

Community Attitudes About Teachers and Teaching

To select teaching as a career is a decision affecting the lives of many people. Children and parents are most directly affected and the well-being of the community, in turn, is enhanced or diminished by the attitude and performance of its teachers.

One of the best tools educators can use to evaluate their status or standing with their constituents is the annual Gallup polls on attitudes toward schools. These educational polls have offered some valuable insights for the last twenty years and, in a sense, have initiated change in public education.

In 1993, the Gallup findings indicated that 47 percent of the public surveyed gave public schools a rating of "A+" "B" (Box 1-1). This rating represented a better view the public had of the schools in 1987. The 1984 and 1985 ratings were much better than those in 1983. Also, Americans tend to rank public schools higher when they know more about them. As shown in Box 1-2, the public ranks financial support, drugs, and school discipline as three major problems facing the nation's schools.

Teacher Compensation

Teachers in the public schools across the nation are generally paid by one of two methods: single salary schedule or merit pay. Most teachers are compensated for their services by the first method. Single salary schedules reflect successful years of teaching and formal education. The schedule is often negotiated between a representative of the board of education, selected administrators in the district, and representatives of the teachers (usually an elected committee). When the board gives its final approval of the proposed salary schedule, the schedule then applies to all teachers in the district from kindergarten through grade twelve. This was not always the case. Until the early 1920s, schedules were often arbitrarily developed by the administrators and board for elementary and secondary teachers separately. Fortunately now, teaching is valued at all levels and rewarded more equitably.

A single salary schedule embodies certain assumptions. First, there is a so-called fixed beginning salary which is usually increased from year to year, but it is labeled "fixed" because it applies to all teachers in terms of their salary. Second,

BOX 1-1   Grading the Public Schools

The 1993 Phi Delta Kappa/Gallup poll registered the largest one-year improvement in the grades given by the public to their local public schools since the question was first asked in 1974. The percentage of respondents awarding A's or B's jumped from 40% in 1992 to 47% in 1993, after nearly a decade of relative stability. College graduates in particular gave high ratings (54% A or B). The question:

Students are often given the grades A, B, C, D, and FAIL to denote the quality of their work. Suppose the *public* schools themselves, in this community, were graded in the same way. What grade would you give the public schools here—A, B, C, D, or FAIL?

Ratings Given the Local Public Schools

	National Totals %	No Children in School %	Public School Parents %	Nonpublic School Parents %
A & B	47	44	56	37
A	10	10	12	5
B	37	34	44	32
C	31	32	28	41
D	11	10	12	9
FAIL	4	4	4	11
Don't know	7	10	*	2

*Less than one-half of 1%.

Ratings Given the Local Public Schools

	1993 %	1992 %	1991 %	1990 %	1989 %	1988 %	1987 %	1986 %	1985 %	1984 %	1983 %
A & B	47	40	42	41	43	40	43	41	43	42	31
A	10	9	10	8	8	9	12	11	9	10	6
B	37	31	32	33	35	31	31	30	34	32	25
C	31	33	33	34	33	34	30	28	30	35	32
D	11	12	10	12	11	10	9	11	10	11	13
FAIL	4	5	5	5	4	4	4	5	4	4	7
Don't know	7	10	10	8	9	12	14	15	13	8	17

Poll respondents were also asked to grade the *nation's* public schools. As has been true in all past years, the "nation's schools" came off a poor second to "local schools" in the current poll. Whereas 47% of the public thought their own schools merit either an A or a B, only 19% awarded these grades to schools of the nation as a whole.

Ratings Given the Nation's Public Schools

	National Totals %	No Children in School %	Public School Parents %	Nonpublic School Parents %
A & B	19	20	19	15
A	2	1	3	6
B	17	19	16	9
C	48	47	49	48
D	17	16	17	15
FAIL	4	4	4	12
Don't know	12	13	11	10

Finally, public school parents were asked to rate the public school attended by their oldest child. Seventy-two percent of these parents gave the school their oldest child attends an A or a B, and among parents whose oldest child is doing above-average academic work the figure rises to 83%. The differences between these grades and the national rankings suggest that the better people know the public schools, the higher their opinion of school quality.

Ratings Given the Schools Attended by Respondents' Children

	1993 %	1992 %	1991 %	1990 %	1989 %	1988 %	1987 %	1986 %
A & B	72	64	73	72	71	70	69	65
A	27	22	29	27	25	22	28	28
B	45	42	44	45	46	48	41	37
C	18	24	21	19	19	22	20	26
D	5	6	2	5	5	3	5	4
FAIL	2	4	4	2	1	2	2	2
Don't know	3	2	*	2	4	3	4	3

*Less than one-half of 1%.

Source: S. M. Elam, L. C. Rose, and A. M. Gallup, "The 25th Annual Phi Delta Kappa/Gallup Poll," *Phi Delta Kappan,* 75 (October 1993): 138–139. Used with permission.

BOX 1-2   Biggest Problems Facing Local Public Schools

In the 25-year history of the Phi Delta Kappa/Gallup education poll, three school problems uppermost in the minds of respondents have been discipline, drugs, and finances. Between 1969 and 1985, discipline was the most frequently mentioned problem each year except 1971, when finances were identified as a major problem by 23% of the public. Drug abuse by students then became the most frequently mentioned problem for six years, 1986 through 1991. In 1992 drugs and lack of proper financial support were each mentioned by 22% of the respondents.

In 1993 lack of proper financial support has clearly emerged as the number one public school problem. Twenty-one percent of poll respondents named it, while 16% cited drug abuse and 15% mentioned lack of discipline. Significantly, the respondents who most clearly recognized the inadequacy of school financing were college graduates, upper-income and professional and business groups, and public school parents.

Concern about the problem of financial support was considerably greater in the West (30%) and the Midwest (30%) than in the South (13%) and the East (15%). In the South and East, concern about drug abuse was mentioned more often (by 18% and 19% respectively) than was lack of financial support.

The question:

What do you think are the biggest problems with which the public schools of this community must deal?

	National Totals %	No Children in School %	Public School Parents %	Nonpublic School Parents %
Standards/quality of education	9	9	8	18
Overcrowded schools	8	6	11	10
Difficulty in getting good teachers	5	4	7	3
Parents' lack of support/interest	4	5	4	3
Integration/ segregation, racial discrimination	4	4	4	4
Pupils' lack of interest, poor attitudes, truancy	4	3	4	4
Low pay for teachers	3	4	3	2
Moral standards, dress code, sex/pregnancy	3	3	3	9
There are no problems	1	1	3	2
Miscellaneous	3	3	2	**
Don't know	14	17	10	16

**Less than one-half of 1%.

The table below shows how public perceptions of the three public school problems most often mentioned have fluctuated over the past decade.

	National Totals %	No Children in School %	Public School Parents %	Nonpublic School Parents %
Lack of financial support	21	19	24	13
Drug abuse	16	17	14	9
Lack of discipline	15	15	15	19
Fighting/violence/ gangs	13	12	14	17

Percentages Mentioning Each Major Problem

	1993 %	1992 %	1991 %	1990 %	1989 %	1988 %	1987 %	1986 %	1985 %	1984 %
Lack of financial support	21	22	18	13	13	12	14	11	9	14
Drug abuse	16	22	22	38	34	32	30	28	18	18
Lack of discipline	15	17	20	19	19	19	22	24	25	27

Authors' note: The 1994 Phi Delta Kappa/Gallup poll (released too late for inclusion in this edition) found "Fighting/violence/gangs" to be the most frequently cited problem.

Source: S. M. Elam, L. C. Rose, and A. M. Gallup, "The 25th Annual Phi Delta Kappa/Gallup Poll," *Phi Delta Kappan,* 75 (October 1993): 139. Used with permission.

there are annual increments that are applicable to all teachers and reflect professional growth in reference to greater levels of education and the increased number of years of successful teaching. Finally, there is a "fixed" maximum or financial lid, which is the top of the salary schedule. Many teachers will reach that maximum dollar amount long before they retire; however, there are so-called longevity increases periodically thereafter.

A number of strengths and weaknesses exist in respect to a single salary schedule. These will be examined in later chapters. Many teachers have long supported single salary schedules because they are uniformly constructed and administered. Teaching is very difficult to define and measure, so the predictability of the schedules has helped to erase bias of all kinds.

Merit pay, or a variation thereof, is the other major means of stimulating instructional quality and financially rewarding teachers for their services. Since the political impetus provided by the 1983 report of the *Nation At Risk,* merit pay has received more attention. Merit schedules have been an occasional method for paying teachers, particularly since World War II, but merit pay has not been accepted widely by teachers because of the difficulty of formulating objective criteria to use in the evaluation process. A lack of confidence by teachers in the evaluators themselves is also an issue. The element of bias is often too difficult to control in the hands of ill-trained evaluators.

Despite widespread teacher apprehension about the application of merit pay, the public strongly desires to reward teachers commensurately with their performance. Arguments for this will be reviewed in later chapters; however, it may be helpful to discuss briefly the structure of a merit pay schedule. Generally, merit pay schedules consist of fewer categories than single salary schedules. Placement is based upon one's competency, overall value to the school, experience, education, and classroom performance. The categories, ideally, are less structured because a teacher can move to a higher category as quality improves. The annual evaluations by the administrator embody about the same criteria as those used for single salary purposes. The evaluations, however, mean more on merit schedules because a teacher may be recommended for a very high raise, for an average raise, or for none at all. On the single salary schedule, unless a teacher is judged very poorly on the basis of evaluation, there is an automatic raise granted. Merit pay raises per year can be as high as $7,000 for some teachers.

Despite fiscal difficulties, more than 20 states in 1994 attempted to implement so-called career ladders, financial incentive plans and teacher mentorship to professionally motivate and sustain teacher productivity. Most incentives encompass meritorious considerations as teachers move from entry-level to higher positions. Improving student achievement by better teacher performance is at the heart of these efforts.

The career ladder in Tennessee is one of the oldest and best such ladders, established in the early 1980s. Teachers in Tennessee are evaluated during their first four years by local school administrators and, if found effective, receive a 10-year professional license. Subsequently, they may seek Career Levels I, II, or III based on experience and successful evaluation as prerequisites for higher levels.

Career Level I is determined by local district evaluation and Career Levels II and III partly or entirely by evaluations of state officials. Salary supplements range from $1000 to $7000 annually based on experience, career level, and positive evaluation.[8]

In sum, when a teacher has met all the necessary criteria at each level of the ladder, then greater remuneration and commensurate instructional leadership become the rule. Inservice involvement, curricular coordination, and instructional initiative all become crucial factors in advancement. It is believed that teachers will be differentiated by effort and ability. As states continue their legislative interest in this career area, professional status will be altered sharply. Tenure may become an artifact because certificates will be commonly renewable and subject to evaluation. Soon, a new era will be upon all public educators. Unfortunately, no easy way exists to define and measure good teaching.

Testing Prospective Teachers

Numerous states are beginning to increase formal requirements for the initial license to teach and are entertaining proposals to test teachers periodically as they apply for a renewal of their licenses. In addition, the American Federation of Teachers is now calling for national entry-level and local board examinations to upgrade teacher selection. Also, the National Education Association is not adverse to entry-level competency testing. Both groups, however, want strong practitioner involvement if such testing develops. Although this latter movement is embryonic and will require much negotiation with all parties to reach a consensus, those people entering the profession will be tested in many states in order to qualify for a license to teach. The public believes overwhelmingly that some type of "state board examination" should exist to test the level of knowledge of those areas one plans to teach before an initial license to teach is awarded. This sentiment is strong at the moment and it parallels the attitude held by other professionals to test their initiates, for example, accountants, optometrists, nurses, lawyers, and doctors.

An example of state interest is the push, particularly in the South, to develop teacher competency examinations ranging from written basic skills tests to systematic classroom observations. Prospective teachers will, in some cases, be required to pass formal tests prior to professional preparation as well as to exhibit specific competencies during student teaching. Such competencies will embody skill in instructional planning, classroom procedures, and interpersonal adeptness.

States will be joined by the institutions of higher learning themselves in this age of testing. Some teacher education programs will embody, perhaps, so-called entrance and exit norm-referenced examinations in addition to the state examination before there is agreement about what tests and when testing should occur.

Some colleges and universities may simply raise their level of percentile rank for admission of prospective teachers. For example, if the institutions expect a minimum score on the Scholastic Aptitude Test (SAT) for the admission of all students, then the minimum score can be higher for prospective teachers. Once admitted, the future teachers will probably be subject to state and institutional minimum requirements, such as a specific cumulative grade point average, increased course requirements in general education and the teaching specialty, as well as greater exposure to children prior to student teaching. A five-year teacher education program is also becoming more of a reality.

Although these endeavors are intended to ensure greater effectiveness in the classroom, some admonitions must be cited in reference to formal testing. The National Teacher Examinations, for example, have been in existence for years and are used occasionally by school districts, universities encompassing teacher education programs, and by thirty states for the initial license to teach. The exam tests literacy in general education and professional knowledge, but it does not predict how well one will teach. Obviously, a future teacher should be knowledgeable in order to inspire his or her students, but such tests should not be ballyhooed beyond their intent.

A new national test is being designed, however, to replace eventually the National Teacher Examinations. This Praxis Series test will be given to prospective teachers at three stages of their preparation and early career. The first part will use a computer to test reading, math, and writing skills during the second year of undergraduate study. The second test will assess proficiency in one's teaching specialty and knowledge of pedagogical principles at the end of teacher training. Beginning teachers will take a third part of the test as to how well they perform in actual classrooms once they have had some supervised experience. This stage will encompass observation and computer simulation. The strength of this national examination is that it is multifaceted and includes clinical performance. Cognitive and affective skills will be assessed.

If competency tests are paper and pencil examinations, they are limited. Such tests may not correlate well with what a prospective teacher was taught in college. The timing of the written test may be too late to screen students effectively, that is, it becomes a "do or die" situation for the student if the test comes at the end of preservice education. Competency tests also do not measure creativity, enthusiasm to teach, as well as the ability to motivate children, all of which are characteristics of effective teachers. Furthermore, many potentially good teachers may fail the test. Written tests, whether they be state mandated or institutionally designed at the local level, should be used judiciously. Literacy is one thing, successful teaching is another. The two concepts are interdependent, obviously, but successful teaching is fostered by much clinical experience with children in order to fuse theory with practice and to refine social and personal skills. The affective domain is crucial. Literacy tests must be viewed in context of this domain.

Many people think that an individual who becomes an education major ultimately teaches in a public or private school for youth from five to 18 years of age. Until 10 or 15 years ago, this was probably true. Before that time, people who earned an education degree and decided not to teach in the conventional way often felt embarrassed and apologetic when they frequently went to industry for a career. Today, this is no longer the case. One can major in education and perform a number of non-school endeavors with the collection of skills acquired in a teacher education program.

Since millions of citizens are now learning in non-school settings, new opportunities are emerging for individuals who desire to teach, but perhaps in a context different from the traditional classroom. The number of adults engaged in learning situations outside a college classroom is impressive. In recent years, 12.4 million individuals were enrolled in college, whereas 46 million people were enrolled in other kinds of educational programs.[9] For example, some top categories in which people were learning a variety of skills were the following: (1) agricultural extension, (2) community organizations, (3) business and industry, (4) professional associations, and (5) city recreation.

The United States has become diversified in how information and skills are conveyed. Schools are part of the learning process, but education generally extends far beyond schooling. People are now commonly pursuing new careers or updating their present skills. They may be also learning nonvocational or career skills simply for personal enrichment. As the median age inches upward, new educational demands will occur, requiring specialists to help learners meet new expectations. Young adults and senior citizens do not want their intellectual needs met only in a college context, which may be too formal or restrictive. In 1992, it was estimated that 19 percent of students in higher education are 35 years of age or older, with 80 percent studying part-time. The implication is that non-traditional students require a variety of times, sites, and learning styles to meet their needs.

Industry is another setting in which "private systems" of education operate. Specialists are hired to write curricula for training programs, to teach the content of those curricula, or to package content in a variety of ways to meet individual learning styles by means of computers and other audio and visual means. Department stores, hospitals, factories, and fast-food chains are but a few examples of sites where formal teaching and learning are underway. The prospective teacher has many options for a career. Physical education, for example, used to be thought of as only a school or community agency specialty. Now, however, recreation, "wellness," and selected lifelong physical activities really have had an impact upon industry. Businesses are beginning to recognize that morale, efficiency, and health costs are all interdependent. Many businesses, sorry to say, are also engaged in the pursuit of literacy because so many employees simply cannot read or write effectively. The 1988, *Training* marketplace listed over 1,000 companies offering such programs as remedial writing and job training skills in over 100

TABLE 1-2   Some Facts About Work Force Profile in Year 2000

- 39 average age
- 15 percent minorities
- 47 percent women
- 20 percent immigrants (minimum projection)
- 63 percent of new entrants will be women

Source: R. T. Jones, "Beyond the College Gates," *Community, Technical, and Junior College Journal* 58 (Dec./Jan. 1987–88), p. 21.

TABLE 1-3   Problems and Challenges Facing Work Force in Years 1990–2000

- Service-producing sector will require post secondary high school skills.
- Training and retraining will characterize the life of every worker.
- Many workers will change jobs five or six times during working life.
- Cognitive and reasoning skills will be at a premium.
- Skill shortage will be acute.
- Intense competition will exist for unskilled jobs.
- Functional illiteracy and job displacement will continue to plague society.
- More jobs than qualified people will exist.
- Machines increasingly will do the jobs of functional illiterates.

Source: W. E. Brock, "Future Shock: The American Work Force in the Year 2000," *Community, Technical, and Junior College Journal* 58 (Feb./Mar. 1987), p. 26.

different educational areas.[10] In other words, an education degree has versatility.

Tables 1-2 and 1-3 cite content that will describe selected occupational patterns, problems, and challenges until the end of the century.

Careers will be in a state of flux in almost all categories. Retraining and updating skills will be common. This state of change necessitates educational activity, both formal and informal. Hence, opportunities for teaching will be at a premium in a variety of ways. Teachers trained in the skills of pedagogy (teaching children and youth) may advantageously "retool" themselves and learn the skills of andragogy (teaching adults). Andragogy is less structured than pedagogy and focuses heavily on individual needs and goals.

Summary

Teaching is both an art and a science. It is a personal art in the sense that skills depend greatly upon personality variables that are too subjective to measure. It is a science in the sense that methods of teaching and the learning environment can be organized on a scientific or objective basis. There is an element of predictability to the procedures used in the instructional process.

Teachers have been studied for decades in regard to selected traits that relate to successful teaching. Traits such as intelligence, knowledge of subject matter, voice quality, and so on, alone have little direct connection in predicting successful teaching; however, combinations of such traits have value. School districts on their employment applications seek to learn about desirable traits that prospective teachers possess. Characteristics such as interests, hobbies, leadership in directing student clubs and activities, and zeal for professional reading and involvement are representative factors school employment officers desire. An academically well-rounded person is very marketable.

Teaching as a career is undergoing change. The public is strongly interested in the manner in which teachers are prepared and compensated. Much of this public attention has been initiated by the plethora of national reports such as *A Nation at Risk* in 1983. As a result, opinion polls have reflected a public desire to pay teachers in a differentiated manner and to upgrade the quality of their selection and performance. The public, however, is supportive of the schools and their teachers.

Since the birth rate is increasing, nursery and elementary schools will benefit from a greater number of children and teachers. A few subject areas in the secondary schools will continue to be difficult to staff because industry is often very appealing to teachers of mathematics, science, or vocational education because of the lucrative salaries they offer. The authors have noted, however, that in the last few years, a greater number of personnel officers have been predicting a "renaissance" in teacher employment for two major reasons: (1) a growing number of preschoolers, and (2) an increasing number of teachers who will retire because of age or financial incentives. Furthermore, in several teaching fields which have been traditionally crowded, the "glut" or surplus is now evaporating. Prospective teachers have not in great numbers majored in these crowded fields, resulting in a better balance of teacher supply and demand.

Another promising trend for teachers is flexibility concerning community and adult education. The entire field of andragogy is growing at a burgeoning rate. Community agencies, industry, labor, and agricultural extension are examples of fields or areas where education is taking place. Traditional schooling is not the only way to meet the needs of citizens involved in a variety of endeavors. Schooling is only a part of lifelong education. There are approximately four times the number of adults engaged in learning in institutions other than a college or university. Some of this learning is formal; some of it is much more casual and highly personal. With some additional study and training, pedagogy can be a springboard to andragogy. Society needs good teachers for all ages. Both the fields of pedagogy and andragogy will continue to be crucial to the national welfare.

Implications for Future Teachers

To become a professional educator, one must be liberally and pedagogically educated. Either category alone is insufficient. A complete teacher-education curriculum takes into account both the university and the social institution in which the teacher will apply his or her knowledge, skills, and understanding—the public school. The authors have included appropriate content to help prospective teachers see the world of teaching from the expectations of both the university and the public school.

Discussion Questions

1. Why do you want to teach? List four or five reasons.
2. What were the major strengths and weaknesses of the "good" and "bad" teachers you have encountered from kindergarten through grade twelve? What can you learn from their teaching styles?
3. What are the scientific aspects of teaching? How do these differ from the traits associated with the art of teaching?
4. What kinds of career opportunities do you think a teacher-education major can pursue other than those in a private or public school?
5. Education is now a topic of national debate. Do you think the recent Gallup polls on education indicate support or loss of confidence in public education? Be specific.
6. Teachers are under scrutiny in relation to their performance and compensation. Should prospective teachers be tested for a license to teach? Should merit considerations also become more common in salary schedules? Why or why not?

Notes

1. David C. Ryans, *Characteristics of Teachers* (Washington, D.C.: American Council on Education, 1960), 82.

2. Paul A. Witty, "The Teacher Who Has Helped Me Most," *NEA Journal* 36 (May 1947): 386.

3. Don Hamachek, "Characteristics of Good Teachers and Implications for Teacher Education," *Phi Delta Kappan* 50 (February 1969): 341–2.

4. William R. Martin, "Teacher Behaviors—Do They Make a Difference? A Review of the Research," *Kappa Delta Pi Record* 16 (December 1979): 48.

5. A. C. Porter and J. Brophy, "Synthesis of Research on Good Teaching: Insights from the Work of the Institute for Research on Teaching," *Educational Leadership* 45 (May 1988): 75.

6. Richard J. Elmore, "Why Restructuring Alone Won't Improve Teaching," *Educational Leadership* 49 (April 1992), 44–48.

7. Paul D. Travers, "Analysis of Teacher Employment Applications," (unpublished) (1991): 2–4.

8. Lynn M. Cornett and Gale F. Gaines, "Reflecting on Ten Years of Incentive Programs," The 1993 Southern Regional Education Board *Career Ladder Clearinghouse Survey*, Atlanta, GA, (April 1994), 1–10, 39–40.

9. Harold Hodgkinson, "What's Right With Education," *Phi Delta Kappan* 61 (November 1979): 162. [In 1980 it was reported that about 62 million adults 25 years of age or older were in a variety of learning situations.]

10. S. B. Merriam and P. M. Cunningham, eds., *Handbook of Adult and Continuing Education,* (San Francisco: Jossey-Bass Publishers, 1989) 281–82.

Recommended Readings

Borich, Gary D. *Effective Teaching Methods.* Columbus, Ohio: Merrill Publishing Company, 1988.

Bracey, Gerald W. "Why Can't They Be Like We Were," *Phi Delta Kappan,* 73 (October 1991): 104–17.

Bracey, Gerald W. "The Second Bracey Report on the Condition of Public Education," *Phi Delta Kappan,* 74 (October 1992): 104–17.

Bracey, Gerald W. "The Third Bracey Report on the Condition of Public Education," *Phi Delta Kappan,* 75 (October 1993): 104–17.

Gage, N.L. "What Do We Know About Teaching Effectiveness?" *Phi Delta Kappan,* 66 (October 1984): 87–93.

Good, Thomas L., Biddle, Bruce J., and Brophy, Jere E. *Teachers Make a Difference.* New York: Holt, Rinehart and Winston, 1975.

Harmon, David. *Illiteracy: A National Dilemma.* New York: The Adult Education Company, 1987.

Hodgkinson, Harold. "What's Right With Education?" *Phi Delta Kappan,* 61 (November 1979): 159–62. and "What's Still Right With Education?" *Ibid* 64 (December 1982): 231–5.

Knowles, Malcolm S., *et.al. Andragogy in Action: Applying Modern Principles of Adult Learning.* San Francisco: Jossey-Bass Publishers, 1985.

Liberman, Myron. *Education as a Profession.* Englewood Cliffs, New Jersey: Prentice-Hall, 1956.

Merriam, Sharon B., and Cunningham, Phyllis M., (eds.), *Handbook of Adult and Continuing Education.* San Francisco: Jossey-Bass Publishers, 1989.

Stellar, Arthur W. *Effective Schools Research: Practice and Promise.* Fastback 276. Bloomington, Indiana: Phi Delta Kappa Educational Foundation, 1988.

U.S. Department of Labor, Bureau of Labor Statistics, *Occupational Outlook Handbook.* Indianapolis, IN: JIST Works, Inc., annual edition.

Chapter 2

American Educational Heritage

Part One

Contemporary American education is rooted deeply in the past. One can trace many modern issues and themes even to the Greeks of the fifth century B.C. For the purposes of this textbook, however, the authors will survey only the American experience. Selected historic themes in this chapter will be cited that have primarily given rise to public education.

The struggle for public education was a long, difficult process. "Universal" education or "popular" education (as public education was referred to historically) means basically three things: schools are tax-supported, secular, and open to all races and creeds. Universal education was nonexistent in early America. This concept did not flourish until the late nineteenth century and, in fact, is still evolving in terms of equal educational opportunity. However, the seeds for free schools were sown in colonial America and took root well in parts of colonial America. Surveying that growth can be beneficial in understanding present educational theory and practice.

The authors will stress the idea of schooling instead of education in this chapter, but the differences between the two concepts should be noted. Today, education is thought of as a broad, comprehensive process of learning and teaching that involves one's entire life. It employs a variety of formal and informal agencies. In other words, education in its broad sense can be a very personal and unstructured process. Learning for its own sake, not only for credits or external reward, usually prevails when one considers the process of education.

Schooling, on the other hand, is much more rigid because it is a formal process that involves a specific time and generally relates to a personal goal. Since most users of this textbook will be involved directly with the process of schooling, the authors will stress formal learning opportunities in American educational history.

The Southern Colonies

Education in the colonial South was truly a reflection of English education in both theory and practice. There was little disagreement between the religious and political intelligentsia in England and America. The Anglican Church was commonly called the Episcopal Church in America. Its attitude was one of indifference in regard to schools for children of all social classes. The Church was sensitive to the poor, but education was not its basic duty. It was the duty of the family, not the Church, to educate. Schools, however, were established by the Anglican Church in America under the aegis of the Society for the Propagation of the Gospel. These schools existed for almost the entire eighteenth century and accommodated poor and orphan children of different races. When England fell into political disfavor in America, so did this society, which died in 1799.

Apprenticeship, voluntary and involuntary, is seen by some as one of the most effective agencies of elementary schooling in early America. Apprenticeship grew out of the European guild system of the Middle Ages and was transplanted totally to all the colonies. Apprenticeship normally meant that poor boys and girls about age seven could be assigned to craftsmen or families for a period of approximately seven years; however, they could be technically apprenticed until adulthood—21 years of age. The legal document for this assignment was called an indenture of apprenticeship. In England, this entailed the responsibilities of teaching a vocational skill and a religiously moral viewpoint. In America, the teaching of reading, writing, and a vocational skill was undertaken. Religious morality was still a goal to be instilled, but as in England, it was conveyed rather haphazardly.

In England, apprenticeship meant vocational training, but in America, it also eventually meant rudimentary elementary education. In the South, principally Virginia and the Carolinas, apprenticeship served as the only significant training lower-class children received. In a sense, these children were economic slaves for whom food, lodging, and training were provided by the town's craftsmen. Frankly, illiteracy was rampant throughout most of colonial America, so one has to keep in mind that basic reading and writing skills were not of high quality. Throughout the South, academic skills for most children were upgraded in the late colonial and early national periods.

Apprenticeship, as an embryonic form of elementary education, was important because it was often compulsory, involved boys and girls for a long period of time, and eventually evolved to include reading and writing skills as part of the indentures of apprenticeship. Girls were given educational opportunities, though minimal, that they scarcely had elsewhere. In the South, apprenticeship took on a significant meaning because it was virtually the only educational opportunity the poor had.

Education in the South for middle and upper-class youth (primarily boys) was implemented chiefly by tutoring. Geographically, it was impractical to build schools conveniently located for everyone. Plantations were so vast that it was more practical to import tutors of Latin and Greek from Europe and New England. Diaries published by tutors indicate that culture was in full flower in numerous places throughout the South. Consequently, this form of education was a primary vehicle for boys of the upper classes to prepare for William and Mary, Oxford, Cambridge, or the University of Paris. Years of preparation were necessary to learn Latin and Greek because the admission test at any college or university in that period chiefly involved a knowledge of Latin prose and verse and a knowledge of Greek nouns and verbs. Only a tutor could direct this classical learning, since formal schools as such were rare. Tutors were "schools" for the rich.

The South lagged far behind other regions of colonial America in relation to colleges and universities. William and Mary (1693) was the only colonial college south of the Potomac River until the late eighteenth century. This fact did not indicate an unconcern for formal education; rather, it indicated that southern boys went abroad for higher education. This was the pattern for well over a century. Girls and boys received basic skills in Latin and Greek from tutors, but boys attained the more thorough Latin immersion. Boys then spent a few college years in England and later in France studying the classics to become ministers, lawyers, or men of commerce, coming back eventually to the South to constitute the social elite.

The irony that only one university existed in the South for almost a hundred years is that the public state university owes its origins to this region. This story is partly a result of an intense political struggle. Southern leaders like Thomas Jefferson were growing uneasy about youth going abroad to study and, consequently, becoming vulnerable to European temptations. Jefferson felt that gambling, drinking, and womanizing would create a distaste for life at home. Political implications were also embodied in Jefferson's fears. If youth were to be future leaders, it would be better to educate them at home. Political infatuation with foreign ideas could be disastrous for the welfare of the nation.

This strong sentiment helped to stimulate Jefferson and fellow Republicans elsewhere to seek partial control of William and Mary and other colonial colleges. These men believed that private, religiously dominated, classically oriented schools should be converted into public institutions. The curriculum, therefore, would be broadened to allow more people to attend and to avail themselves of practical as well as classical studies. An idea had reached its time, but not without great resistance. Many people wanted more colleges and more responsiveness on the part of the original private colleges to the public will. A long struggle ensued.

Two state universities were chartered in the late eighteenth century in Georgia (1785) and North Carolina (1789).[1] The real growth of the state university, however, occurred in the nineteenth century after the famous Dartmouth College Case (1819). Republicans in the various state legislatures tried to gain partial control of private Federalist boards of trustees by placing *ex officio* members such as governors of the state on the boards in order to wrest control away from private interests. The struggle ensued in state after state and culminated in the U.S. Supreme Court as the so-called Dartmouth College case. The context of this case entailed the issue of whether or not a contract established prior to the Constitution was valid. Charters issued to private colleges were valid contracts and were seen as such in 1819 by the U.S. Supreme Court. In other words, the Republican crusade to remake the prestigious private colleges into public institutions was struck down by the high Court.[2]

Partially as a result of this judicial action, the states set about to create new state universities, for example, the University of Virginia. Private colleges now had a legal right to exist and were thrown into competition with new, similar public institutions. The South played a role in the nurturing of these state universities. These public institutions would have developed despite the Dartmouth College Case, but the U.S. Supreme Court provided a strong impetus for growth.

The South, as best represented by Virginia and the Carolinas, was a center for learning and culture even though this was limited to the few—namely, white wealthy males. For the majority of the populace, vocational training was the rule of thumb. The assumption that pervaded life in the South was that education was a family matter. The church and political officials felt indifferent to crusading for formal educational opportunities. It was a matter of family initiative, not paternalism on the part of the "state" or the church. One could be illiterate and still receive salvation if he or she followed the ritual of the Anglican or Episcopal Church. There was no religious zeal to learn how to read.

Politically, there was no major southern strife with England. Youth went abroad to study and returned home to assume positions of leadership. Not until the end of the eighteenth century did differences erupt; then youth studied in France. With such religious and political compatibility, the South would develop differently from the middle and New England colonies. Private education in the South would evolve from the practice of tutoring. A strong military tradition would emerge in military academies, which enrolled wealthy boys who then assumed positions of political influence.

Given an economic system predicated on human bondage, education was seen by many at that time as best centered in the hands of the leaders. If the poor, enslaved, women, or religiously different received formal educational opportunities, political and social upheaval might occur. The elite would lose control; therefore, the best educational policy was an exclusive policy. The elite believed they should perpetuate their class only and not allow education to be an avenue of vertical mobility. Public education here would find little soil for germination until well into the nineteenth century. Free, open, and non-religious schools were not part of the southern fabric. Culture was common only to the few. It would be left to other geographic areas to develop the concept that all children should be taught to read and write. Religious motivation, not a sense of social concern, would stimulate the mission to foster skill in reading. The major educational contribution, then, which emerged from the South was a strong enthusiasm for private schools. Education was valued by those in social and political control, but it was a family matter, not a church or "state" concern. In fact, compulsory schooling did not become a reality in the South until the twentieth century, almost 50 years later than the first attendance law in the North. It should be pointed out, however, that geography played a part in this slow pace to require children to attend school. When people lived in compact communities, as they did more often in northern towns, schooling was seen as more convenient. Add to this phenomenon a religious need to teach reading and one gets, as a result, a more aggressive educational policy. This was the attitude of most Protestant groups outside the South. This does not imply, however, that people outside the South were more democratic. They were not. They simply employed other reasons for establishing schools.

The Middle Colonies

One often thinks of Pennsylvania when colonial education is discussed in early America. In that colony the religious influence was strong but extremely fragmented, which was not the case, for example, in Massachusetts or Virginia. Pennsylvania settlers were quite different from those farther north and south. Their religious (and political) view reflected an educational outlook that contrasted sharply with other settlers.

Probably, the major reason for the diversity throughout the Middle Colonies was the variety of religious groups found in the area: Quakers, Moravians, Mennonites, Amish, Anabaptists, Scotch Irish Presbyterians, Catholics, Lutherans, Muggletonians, Dutch Reformed, Anglicans, and Calvinists. What many groups had in common was a fierce independence. They fled Europe because of religious persecution and certainly did not want to find themselves under the thumb of local authorities. Their belief was that the less cooperation with secular authorities, the better. This attitude is still somewhat true today. Many religious groups thought cultural integrity would weaken if their children would have to attend town schools.

The only other characteristic many of these groups shared was that they were Protestant, but they read the various versions of the New Testament in their native language. Being Protestant is where their commonality generally stopped. These people were mainly of German, French, Dutch, Swedish, Bohemian (Czech), English, Scotch, and Irish descent. Since they did not necessarily trust each other politically or religiously, they could not negotiate differences to support a common school system. They also did not want to surrender rights which might compromise their independence. Many religious groups still feel this way.

The upshot of this fierce independence was the parochial school. The curriculum paralleled that of the parochial schools in Europe. There were no grades, (rather levels), and no kindergartens. Kindergartens were a Prussian contribution that evolved in the nineteenth century. The language of the school was the vernacular, that is, the language of that particular nationality. English as a language was a rarity. The various church leaders wanted to perpetuate their faith in the native tongue. Consequently, mistrust was aggravated because communication was almost nonexistent, especially in rural areas.

It is small wonder that public education would be resisted and not take root. Tax support, secular control, and a religiously pluralistic student population all were alien ideas in the Middle Colonies. Family and parochial school education prevailed—this meant what we think of today as elementary education, certainly not beyond grade eight. Secondary education was not considered to be necessary because only those who were to become ministers needed to study beyond the rudiments of reading and writing. Most people, it was believed, only needed to read the New Testament to work out their salvation. Parochial schools could fulfill that need.

This kind of religious independence was considered and reinforced by the U.S. Supreme Court in 1972 in the famous *Wisconsin* v. *Yoder* case. An Amish community in Wisconsin refused to comply with state officials concerning compulsory school attendance to age sixteen. The Amish people were fearful of the local high schools. If students got a taste for cars and other inimical pleasures, a disrespect might ensue for the religious and agricultural lifestyle. This religious community also felt that family education in the community was a form of vocational education and constituted what youth needed. The Supreme Court agreed and based its decision in part on 300 years of Amish religious tradition. The Court believed age 14 was the upper age limit that could be applied to the Amish concerning compulsory school attendance.

One can quickly feel uneasy about the judicial exception when one thinks of all the groups seeking similar requests. The Court, however, emphatically stressed the long religious heritage of the Amish as a major factor. Whimsical scruples about compulsory attendance would not be taken seriously in the courts. It is easy, though, to see the relationship between the religious struggle of the eighteenth century and the judicial concerns in the *Yoder* case.

A parallel of this struggle to remain free of compulsory school attendance laws because of religious beliefs is the quest by many parents today to educate their children at home. The underlying reason is a matter of control. Who has the constitutional right to educate—the parents or the state?

Apprenticeship was another agency of education in the big cities of the Middle Colonies such as Philadelphia, New Amsterdam (New York), and Baltimore. Destitute children were given minimal vocational training, some moral training, and eventually a little reading and writing. Again, as in the South during the colonial period, it was about the only educational exposure most children received. Pauper children were apprenticed to craftsmen like cobblers, printers, silversmiths, blacksmiths, and candlemakers for a period of time. These vocational skills enabled some children to survive.

Benjamin Franklin's Academy

One of the chief contributions of the Middle Colonies was Benjamin Franklin's Academy. Franklin published his "Proposals Relating to the Education of Youth in Pennsylvania" in 1749.[3] The inherent ideas in this document, however, had little effect upon educational opportunity until well into the nineteenth century. In fact, Franklin died in 1790 thinking few people really cared about his educational scheme. The real value of Franklin's ideas during the colonial period concerned the basic matter of educational opportunity. Not many people had access to schools, tutors, or even family instruction. Franklin wanted to broaden the curriculum for a greater number of youth who never had an opportunity to study for a career or even to become literate.

The educational climate in which Franklin found himself was restrictive. Latin grammar schools and colleges catered to the wealthy. Franklin was born poor, one of thirteen children, and had little opportunity for school of any kind. Apprenticeship was his only hope. He resented that only the well-to-do could ever consider a school such as Harvard. When he joined his half-brother on the *New England Courant* and wrote about the immorality of Harvard students, he was probably expressing an attitude of resentment that he was unqualified economically and socially to attend Harvard. He was bitter that formal education at the time was for the few.

When Franklin settled in Philadelphia, he became heavily involved in the newspaper business as well as in politics, civic, and scientific endeavors. By the time he wrote his "Proposals" in 1749, he was somewhat of a literary figure because of his *Poor Richard's Almanac*. He collaborated to found the American Philosophical Society and the *Junto*, which considered civic and political questions. He was becoming a nationally prominent person and his ideas on education would have a wide appeal. A rising middle class was attracted to his plans on education.

Franklin gathered 24 of the wealthiest people in Philadelphia and organized on an ecumenical basis a board of trustees; he was its first president. In six years, however, he was ousted because the board thought he was too radical. The board thought he moved too far away from the classics as the basis of the curriculum and too far away from religion as an organizing force for study. Franklin was not really anti-humanism or anti-classics, or even anti-religion; rather, he was opposed to a monopoly of one study or viewpoint at the expense of another. He wanted no one religious denomination or curriculum to prevail in his Academy; this liberal view got him into trouble.

Franklin's Academy was by no means the first of its kind. It was the first semi-public school encompassing a broad curriculum for students of different needs. Business, surveying, and navigational academies existed for 50 years before Franklin offered his ideas, but they were mainly "for profit" schools. Franklin was indebted to John Locke, the English humanist and educator who had lived about a century earlier. Locke was a Puritan who founded an academy because he dissented religiously and educationally from the Anglican Church. Franklin was even more radical than Locke because his educational scheme was more vocational and career oriented than Locke's.

Franklin's background had a lot to do with his philosophy of education. He was born a Presbyterian but later wrote that he could not accept such orthodox views. He became a Deist; he believed in creation and judgment, but personal intervention by a supreme being seemed too remote for him. He rejected original sin and innate depravity. Like Locke, Franklin believed in human potential for good or bad behavior; the environment made the difference. The educational implication of this viewpoint would have a profound effect upon Franklin's educational outlook. It ran counter to educational theory and practice in most schools throughout the colonies. His attitude toward students was greatly tempered by his religious view. Franklin was not irreligious. He would not join forces to attack religion. He hated intolerance bred by denominational smugness, and he did not want any one religious view to dominate the curriculum.

The Academy divided its curriculum into three departments: English, mathematics and sciences, and classical studies. Franklin wanted the first two departments to garner the most attention and eventually blossom into higher education—the University of Pennsylvania. He also envisioned a university to complement his Academy. Time would prove that the last department, classical studies, would prevail and become the core of the new university. Franklin was disappointed; however, the state universities of the nineteenth century would eventually incorporate much of his thinking about the curriculum. He was simply ahead of his time by a few decades. Most of what he advocated philosophically made very good sense in decades to come.

The crux of his "Proposals" was his viewpoint that since art is long and time is short, the "most useful and the most ornamental studies" should constitute the curriculum. If one views the Latin grammar schools as the alternative to the Academy, then one can see how liberal Franklin was. In the Latin grammar school, wealthy boys were allowed to enter at about age seven and stay until about age 15. They studied Latin prose and verse, Greek nouns and verbs, some catechism, slight mathematics and science, and philosophy. In other words, if a boy did not desire to become a minister, lawyer, doctor, or man of business, then there was no future for him in a Latin grammar school. Latin was the language spoken because it was the only language used in higher education. It had to be learned fluently.

Franklin believed that this classical curriculum was no longer appropriate for all youth. A growing middle class was becoming weary of limited access to career opportunities. Increased trade with western Europe, an expanding frontier, and new business opportunities began to have an effect upon education. A greater number of people began to agitate for a more practical curriculum. Franklin felt that pulsation and believed the time was ripe for educational reform, especially at the secondary school level.

The "Proposals" embodied a plethora of subject matter. The backbone of the subject matter focused on communication skills, the social and natural sciences in an applied fashion, and languages for pragmatic purposes. The curriculum was a radical departure from the classical humanist positions which dominated secondary education for over six centuries. Franklin gave a new status to studies that traditionally had to be learned incidentally (by personal initiative) or outside the limit of formal education.

English, as a major study suggested by Franklin, was really an innovation. The language conventionally spoken in so-called secondary schools was Latin. Latin was the language of scholarship, of the Anglican and Catholic Churches, of legal contracts and trade, and the mark of culture. The vernacular, one's native language, was not the language of the secondary school. The vernacular was spoken in primary or elementary schools and usually denoted lower prestige. Latin was for the few, the wealthy, and the academically capable. Schools historically had been classified by language, not by age. One could be age 13 in a vernacular school (elementary) or be age eight in a Latin grammar school (secondary). Age was irrelevant at that time as a criterion for organizing schools.

Franklin in his Academy made English the medium of instruction. It was the required language of all, irrespective of career goals. He chose English essayists such as Alexander Pope as models for clarity. He stressed understanding and communication as the basis for English study. Students wrote letters to each other and composed speeches. They critiqued letters and essays. Franklin's motivation was to promote not only clarity of thought and expression but also political cohesiveness. Language diversity was common in the Middle Colonies, which was bad politically if one desired unity of purpose. Franklin wanted to mold a new generation on the basis of a common language.

After the study of English was begun, the students (boys only, of course) could study Latin and Greek if they desired to enter the legal, ministerial, or medical profession. If they wanted, for example, a business career, the students could study Spanish, French, or German. French also could be chosen if law was a career choice. Only English was required of all students.

History, previously a Saturday afternoon avocation at Harvard, was another key subject of Franklin's curriculum. He thought the subject could tie past with present, could show examples of personal and collective morality and immorality, and could offer direction to those who took it seriously. Ancient history was the only study of history in the Latin grammar schools. Classicists believed all important history ended with the fall of Rome in the fifth century. Franklin and other realists, however, believed that contemporary history was as important as ancient history. The study was to be given much emphasis in his curriculum.

The other social sciences (history can be classified in the fields of the humanities or social sciences) Franklin considered important were economics, political science, and anthropology (ancient customs). Each subject had to have practical value in terms of a vocation or to the learner personally. Political science, for example, was a crucial study for the aspiring politician, as economics was for the man of commerce.

The natural sciences were quite interesting as discussed by Franklin. Biology undergirded the study of horticulture; chemistry was the basis of pharmacology;

physics was the foundation of engineering; and astronomy was the prerequisite to navigation as a career. Once the student selected a career, his curriculum would be laid out for him. An activity orientation made the knowledge useful. Experimental farming, for example, put to test those concepts studied in the Academy. Even the library was considered as much a collection of objects (a laboratory) as it was a collection of books.

Good health, both community and personal, was a goal of Franklin's. Biology, chemistry, and physical education lent themselves to a better understanding of more healthful living. Franklin wanted students to embrace physical activities such as swimming, track events, wrestling, and boxing. He preferred all students to be involved, not just a talented few.

Business studies were also crucial to Franklin's list of studies. Accounting, basic arithmetic, a legible hand, commercial art, and bookkeeping were vital subjects for some students. Actually there were prototype business academies in existence already, but they were "for profit" institutions. Franklin wanted to make his Academy more public in scope. Tuition would still be charged; however, some public funds would supplement the program.

The Academy, as Franklin envisioned it, incorporated several germane parallels to present theory and practice. Related subject matter was closely integrated or correlated: mathematics and science; political science, geography, and logic; history and chronology; biology and horticulture; and so on. Today, in some schools, American history and American literature combine to become American studies. Similarly, ecology is fused with the natural sciences.

Another parallel to modern thinking was Franklin's view on religion. As mentioned earlier, he was not irreligious, but he wanted no one denomination to monopolize the curriculum. Franklin liked the Judaic-Christian values, but in a generic sense. He wanted these ethical tenets to permeate the curriculum because the students would hold various religious views. His 13 virtues could meet the "acid test" of appropriate values for a pluralistic setting. His virtues of silence, temperance, sincerity, tranquility, justice, moderation, humility, chastity, order, resolution, industry, frugality, and cleanliness all had pertinence regardless of one's particular denominational view. He practiced what he preached; he checked one virtue daily for a week, and at the end of 13 weeks he would repeat the process. The U.S. Supreme Court today is still struggling with the appropriate place for religion in the curriculum. Franklin believed in moral education, which has yet to be resolved in public schools in terms of consensus.

Franklin was an environmentalist. A child, he believed, was born with the potential for goodness or badness. The setting and its stimuli were crucial to maturation. Nurture was as critical as nature. As previously stated, Franklin was indebted to Locke for this view. When one thinks of the history of school discipline in America, Franklin's ideas become radical notions. Certainly, in modern educational circles, a good learning environment is of unquestioned value. Positive reinforcement is, at least in theory, subscribed to strongly.

A chief purpose of learning in Franklin's Academy was the concept of usefulness. Franklin was a utilitarian, a pragmatist. He wanted knowledge to be of value to the individual. When a boy entered his academy at about age seven, he eventually selected a curriculum which led to a career—medicine, theology, engineering, business, surveying, and so on. He remained in school until roughly age 15 and had little selection or election of subjects once a career was chosen. In modern terms, this variety of liberal and vocational subject matter is called a comprehensive curriculum.

Franklin died in 1790 believing his work had been sabotaged by a conservative board of trustees. He had been fired by that board. Yet his views prevailed in the nineteenth century, proving that some time must pass before new theory becomes practice or commonplace. The Academy became the dominant secondary school of the nineteenth century, replacing the Latin grammar school and waiting only to be replaced at the end of the century by the public high school (which also has an interesting past).

Franklin's accomplishments are important because he changed the direction of formal education. He broke from a single curriculum of the classics, and he breached the denominational hold on education. He was a moral secularist and pragmatic educator. And his contribution to education was profound.

The Middle Colonies also spawned a number of embryonic colleges, mainly religious seminaries, but also those embodying liberal education. Such present universities as Princeton, Rutgers, Pennsylvania, and Columbia were products of the early effort to train ministers.[4] One exception, however, was the University of Pennsylvania, which was in large measure a much more secular school in its founding even though it eventually fell under the influence of tradition and the Anglican Church. Franklin wanted this school to be more egalitarian, practical, and attuned to American needs. Its founding was a departure from the tradition of higher education in both Europe and America.

Harvard was the model for all higher education in the colonies and was a transplant of the European view of scholarship. The colleges in the Middle Colonies followed the lead of Harvard, but the University of Pennsylvania was different. The Scottish influence was felt more at Pennsylvania than elsewhere. The Rev. William Smith, Scot educator and collaborator with Franklin in establishing this college, employed some modern methods, such as student election of courses. Scotland was an advanced nation in terms of higher education (medicine, for example) and its impact was felt at the University of Pennsylvania.

The Middle Colonies, in summary, made a number of contributions to American education. Because of the acute differences among religious sects in this area, church and state issues were dominant. These are yet to be resolved and are largely national questions. Parochial schools, the logical result of such differences, have taken deep root in American soil today and offer parents alternatives to public schools. Colleges in this region are some of the most prestigious in the world. Religious diversity spawned a number of schools, mainly religious seminaries, which evolved into exemplary private colleges and universities.

Despite Franklin's efforts, one cannot find in the Middle Colonies a widespread concern to offer free secular schools open to all. Religious and political variety, in part, prevented popular education. There was suspicion of the "state" or political powers, resulting in nonpublic education. A sad commentary, too, is that had the Dutch been allowed by the British to continue their fine educational effort in New Netherland (New York), they would have been an educational model in regard to compulsory schooling. In 1664, however, the English assumed control and imposed their will, educationally as well as politically.

The New England Colonies

Education as it evolved in America owes much of its existence and success to the Puritans of Massachusetts and Connecticut. These settlers were by no means more democratic than settlers farther south; but because of their religious cohesion, geographic compactness, and political zeal, they stimulated an educational interest that gave rise to schools everywhere. Much of what is taken today as commonplace in American educational theory and practice is owed to the New England colonists of the seventeenth and eighteenth centuries. For example, the small school district as a form of organization, the financial means of local school support, and the local board of education are all contributions which the New Englanders have made to American education.

Religion was the force behind educational activity in Massachusetts and Connecticut. The Separatists and Puritans believed strongly that schools should be the handmaiden of the Congregational Church. Salvation depended on one's ability to read the New Testament in English. Predestination was a common belief, and the ability to read was a possible sign of that selection. Illiteracy was a symptom of eternal damnation. The clergy were no longer the intermediary between God and the people. The onus of salvation was on the shoulders of every person. Therefore, reading was crucial and practical. It even had some secular value to the colonists, but its religious value was paramount. Consequently, one of the first priorities of the settlers was to imbue parents and craftsmen with the idea that reading skills must be instilled early in a child's life so that he or she could "understand the principles of religion and the capital laws of the country."

Two early laws of the Massachusetts General Court in the seventeenth century were significant to the evolutionary development of formal schooling. The first law in 1642 was a brief requirement that parents and master craftsmen must teach their offspring and apprentices the necessary skills of reading and writing to enhance two purposes—religious understanding and civic responsibility. The law was based on the English Poor Relief Law of 1601, which was purely a vocational training law. The Puritans, however, added academic ingredients to the vocational aspect of the English law. For the first time in an English-speaking society a requirement was enacted to instill reading and writing. This was a radical departure from tradition because education in England was purely a family matter, not a function of church or state. The 1642 law in Massachusetts was enforced by censure, fines, or even reassignment of children. Church elders technically became school officials in surveying communities to implement the law.

One major problem arose in requiring parents and craftsmen to comply with the spirit of the 1642 legislation. If most people were illiterate, how could they teach children to read and write? This law was negative legislation. Teachers were not available. Harvard had been founded six years earlier, but its purpose was not to prepare teachers. Consequently, a more positive approach had to emerge which would assist the citizenry to fulfill their educational, religious, and civic responsibilities.

On the heels of the 1642 legislation came the "Old Deluder Satan Act," as the Puritans called it. This legislation that was passed in 1647 was intended to help parents and craftsmen meet their obligations by requiring that communities of 50 families or more hire an elementary teacher and communities of one hundred families or more hire a Latin grammar school teacher. The Puritans assumed that the ability to search the Scripture in English would thwart missionaries of the Anglican or Catholic Churches, who would "delude" the unlearned with their frequent use of Latin. Illiteracy would keep the populace in a vulnerable state. Therefore, the way to overcome Satan and his use of Latin was to read English fluently.

The 1647 legislation became the educational model for almost all subsequent legislation in the colonies. It was honored, however, more by neglect than by observance because communities usually ignored the act. The Massachusetts court fined such communities for noncompliance, but often the fines were too small to make a difference. The precedent, however, was set that the "state" could assist parents and craftsmen in fulfilling their educational obligations. This idea spread rapidly throughout the colonies.

The acts of 1642 and 1647 were of extreme significance and have relevance to contemporary education. These acts were the first educational laws in an English-speaking society. In practice the laws were difficult to enforce, but the precedent they set for subsequent legislation was momentous. In theory several consequences can be noted that are pertinent to modern times. First, it can be inferred that the Puritans believed that the welfare of their political society depended upon a literate citizenry. The fact that "understanding the capital laws of the country" could be fostered by a knowledge of reading attests to that belief. No peoples before the Puritans except the Jews of the first century or the Germans of the sixteenth century could claim the distinction of seeing the political value of a literate society. The American Founding Fathers and early nineteenth century politicians and educators hammered away at this theme. The Puritans were not concerned about education for social mobility, but they thought that at least those who participated in political decisions ought to be able to read and write.

No one would deny the benefits of reading and writing, but today perhaps too much social value is given to schooling. Schooling has been seen in recent decades to be a panacea for all social ills. When America fell behind the Soviet Union in the space race after the launching of Sputnik in 1957, improved schooling was seen as the answer. The National Defense Education Act of 1958 in part advanced scholarship in the foreign languages, the sciences, and mathematics. The gifted, it was believed, could close the space gap if given proper education.

President Lyndon Johnson's "War on Poverty" was mainly prosecuted through the Elementary and Secondary Education Act of 1965. Normal children from low-income families who were academically behind would be given preferential treatment by dollars spent and services provided. While few would not support giving children an academic boost, the hope that more money spent per child would greatly solve the problem of poverty proved to be a romantic notion. Poverty is multifaceted and has to be approached from that standpoint.

Too often moral questions about society are reduced to educational remedies. Can voluntary prayer in the school do much to offset moral deterioration outside the school? Maybe it can help, but the point is that often education is politically seen as the nostrum for social ills. Can school busing for racial desegregation enhance equality of educational opportunity if better housing and employment opportunities are not enacted? Unlikely, but it is easier to attack or fault the schools than legislatures, public opinion, or private industry. Although schools mirror the will of society, they too often bear the brunt of the social or economic breakdown of other institutions.

A major principle that emerged from the Puritan legislation of 1642 and 1647 was the premise that education is a parental duty. The Puritans did not hold the church or government responsible for educational opportunity, but rather the parents or master craftsmen (guardians). Parents could be admonished or fined, and craftsmen could lose their apprentices if reading and writing were neglected. This principle has too often been forgotten because it is easy to think that parents or guardians play a secondary role in providing educational opportunity. They are the primary agents.

This notion of parental duty was a novel idea in the seventeenth century. Few societies before had put much emphasis on the obligation of parents to teach their children reading and writing skills. Historically, it was more of a moral obligation, rather than a legal one. The Puritans made schooling both a moral and legal duty.

The issue of parental responsibility has created quite a division of thought about where the real authority lies in providing and controlling schooling. Some parents do not comply with compulsory school attendance laws because of neglect, disdain for public schools, or religious scruples. Compulsory attendance laws date only from the mid-nineteenth century. The Puritans, however, gave birth to the idea that parents were legally responsible for providing education; and when parents delegated this duty to teachers and boards of education, attendance became mandatory.

Another relevant principle which emerged from these New England laws was the belief that the government (the Massachusetts Court, later the state) can set minimum standards and the required number of years of education, but not the kind of school a child attends. The 1647 legislation laid down the premise that elementary and secondary schooling was necessary, but attendance was not required. The parent, or tutor if desired, could perform the task of teaching the child at home. The implication is that private education is legitimate as long as minimum standards and the extent of education are met. This belief has been tested over the decades, with the result that the type or kind of school a child attends is a parental choice as long as compulsory attendance is fulfilled. This point has been partially breached in terms of religious scruples. In a U.S. Supreme Court case, *Wisconsin* v. *Yoder*, the Court allowed an Amish sect to comply with compulsory attendance to age fourteen only, instead of age 16. Generally speaking, compliance is obligatory until age sixteen.

The last major principle inherent in the 1647 legislation was that the property of the inhabitants "in general" should be the basis for the salary of the elementary and secondary school teachers. The battle over property as the principal means of school support at the local level has always been a heated one. Those who own property realize that as costs increase for education so will their individual burden of taxation. The Puritans knew it, and so do property owners today. Property taxes are not popular in any age. The spirit of taxation was initiated principally by the Puritans, although it would take 200 years to blossom into practice. (In a later chapter, the strengths and weaknesses of real property as a means of support for schools at the local level will be discussed.) The Puritans, in theory at least, realized that fixed property was necessary in relation to schools.

Another major contribution of the New England settlers to higher education was the founding of Harvard (1636) and Yale (1701). Harvard in particular was a model for almost all colleges in colonial America. It was founded to train ministers for the Congregational Church as well as to serve as a transmitter of the cultural heritage. Yale, slightly more conservative at the time, was established to instill in prospective ministers a more traditional and literal interpretation of Scripture. Harvard became the more influential model in higher education.

Latin was the medium of instruction. No boy began his studies in the only curriculum available, the classics, unless he spoke and wrote Latin fluently. Greek was considered as less important than Latin, but Greek nouns and verbs were memorized. Latin was the key to scholarship, the stamp of a cultured man, and the language of contracts and other legal documents. It was also necessary for religious study. For three or four years, boys studied one subject a day per quarter on a yearly basis. For well over a century, this was the kind of curriculum that monopolized higher education.

The school that prepared boys for Harvard or Yale was the Latin grammar school. Over a period of seven or eight years, usually until age 15, boys immersed themselves in classical study in order to gain admittance to Harvard or Yale. A boy usually went to grammar school; however, a tutor could substitute for the Latin grammar school, since compulsory attendance was not an issue. The most famous Latin grammar school, the Boston Public Latin Grammar School (1635) is still in existence; it prepares boys mainly for the Ivy League schools.

Apprenticeship in New England was a serious program, especially for children of very poor parents. It was, in a sense, a prototype system of elementary education because at least destitute children learned to read and write. They also learned something of a trade under the tutelage of a master craftsman. The program was often compulsory for seven years, but it could extend until adulthood for both males and females. The Puritans were concerned that all children should learn to read at least minimally in order to read the Scriptures and related religious material, and apprenticeship education was the key to ensuring that such literacy would be attained. Both laws of 1642 and 1647 were instrumental in putting educational meaning into apprenticeship legislation.

Some mention should be made of the New England dame school, a transplanted English school. The dame school was a nursery and primary school for boys and girls. Usually a semiliterate female would offer in her home rudimentary instruction in reading, writing, and some Latin for boys who were interested in going to the Latin grammar school at age seven or eight. This early school enrolled children from ages three to seven and played a more valuable role than often cited. Girls got a beginning opportunity for schooling, and childhood was at least seen by many New Englanders as a time to undertake education. Unfortunately, the "dame" who taught this school frequently maintained a subsistence standard of living. Her livelihood depended on a few pennies per child.

In considering formal education throughout colonial America, we cannot take much pride in an abundance of educational materials. Textbooks were rare. Children learned to read primarily on imported adult "readers." Gradedness or classification of materials by age was a nonexistent idea until the nineteenth century. No written tests existed. No one thought it was important to fit the curriculum to the child's needs. If a child could not adapt to adult materials, then it was too bad for the child. In addition, a teacher was a "hearer of recitation." Some famous educational materials of this period survived. *The New England Primer* was a commonly used small book of rhyming couplets accompanied by rough illustrations to convey the alphabet and moral messages. The Psalter focused on the Book of Psalms, whereas the hornbook embodied the alphabet, the

In Adam's Fall
We finned all.

Thy Life to mend,
This Book attend.

The Cat doth play,
And after flay.

A Dog will bite
A Thief at Night.

An Eagle' flight
Is out of fight.

The idle Fool
Is whipt at SchooL

A colonial reader
(*New York Public Library Picture Collection*)

vowels, and usually a prayer such as the Lord's Prayer. The hornbook was made of a transparent cow horn covering a sheet of paper tacked to a paddle. In a sense, it was like a small rectangular ping-pong paddle which could be hung from the neck. Eventually, it evolved into a multipaged book composed of heavy paper and called a battledore. Textbooks for children were yet to emerge.

Summary

Education in colonial America meant opportunity when based primarily on wealth, religious preference, and the student's gender. Much of the opportunity for education was limited to the very few. A democratic attitude was not yet fused with educational theory and practice. Education, in other words, was not seen as a tool for personal and professional advancement, nor even for religious salvation, in some parts of colonial America. Education was seen as a necessary part of one's formative years, mainly in colonial New England. Education here was practical because if one could read and write, his or her salvation was more attainable.

What the Puritans instituted was not very radical in terms of structure or organization. What was radical was their attitude that all should be able to read for religious purposes. Their two very important laws of 1642 and 1647 served as models for theory and practice in the ensuing decades.

The southern colonies believed that schooling was a private matter. The church and secular authorities did not advocate tax-supported schools for all. Such educational opportunity was left to later generations. Culture flourished in this region, but it was limited to the upper class.

Benjamin Franklin's "Proposals" were novel for the period because he desired a more practical curriculum for a rising middle class growing weary of the classics. He steered education toward practical studies. His ideas bore fruit in the nineteenth century, for his Academy served as a transition between the Latin grammar school and the public high school. American education was now rapidly evolving toward greater independence from European thought.

Implications for Future Teachers

Public education is fraught with a sense of "presentism." Often, "old wine" is repackaged in "new bottles" and marketed as something novel. To reduce this human tendency to seek panaceas, it is important for prospective teachers to have a sense of how the past underlies the present. To see most innovations in public schools as ideas that have historical roots is an important insight. For example, much concern currently centers on character education and appropriate values. To realize that this topic has been a struggle for centuries is to improve its chances for implementation because successes and mistakes from the past can be analyzed.

The public school teacher who sees his or her labors as a continuation of previous effort to improve society is mature. The university and the school district need each other to prepare and sustain the successful teacher. Despite technologies and innovative strategies, no substitute for the teacher exists in the education of young people.

Discussion Questions

1. Discuss the differences between schooling and education in American society. How has educational opportunity broadened or increased since colonial times?
2. What is an historic definition of universal education? Has this definition been rare? Discuss its implications.
3. Contrast some educational similarities and differences among the three broad, geographic regions of colonial America. What parallels do you see to schooling today?

Notes

1. Edgar W. Knight and Clifton L. Hall, eds., *Readings in American Educational History* (New York: Appleton-Century-Crofts, 1951), 192–96, 200–201.

2. Donald G. Tewksbury, *The Founding of American Colleges and Universities before the Civil War: With Particular Reference Bearing upon the College Movement* (New York: Bureau of Publications, Teachers College, Columbia University, 1932), 150.

3. See David B. Tyack, *Turning Points in American Educational History* (Toronto: Blaisdell Publishing Co., 1967), 50–82. A good discussion of Franklin's views. See also Robert Ulich, *History of Educational Thought* (New York: American Book Co., 1950), 225–42.

4. Frederick Rudolph, *The American College and University: A History* (New York: Vintage Books, 1962), 3–22.

Recommended Readings

Bailyn, Bernard. *Education in the Forming of American Society: Needs and Opportunities for Study.* New York: W. W. Norton, 1962.

Best, John H., ed. *Benjamin Franklin on Education.* New York: Teachers College Press, Columbia University, 1962.

Butts, R. Freeman, and Lawrence A. Cremin. *A History of Education in American Culture.* New York: Holt, Rinehart and Winston, 1953.

Cremin, Lawrence A. *American Education: The Colonial Experience, 1607–1783.* New York: Harper and Row, 1970.

Good, Harry, and James Teller. *A History of American Education.* 2nd ed. New York: Macmillan Co., 1973.

Jernegan, Marcus Wilson. *Laboring and Dependent Classes in Colonial America, 1607–1783.* New York: Frederick Ungar, 1960.

Knight, Edgar W., and Clifton L. Hall. *Readings in American Educational History.* New York: Appleton-Century-Crofts, 1951.

Pulliam, John D. *History of Education in America.* 6th ed. New York: Merrill, 1994.

Rippa, S. Alexander. *Education in a Free Society: An American History.* 7th ed. New York: Longman, 1992.

Spring, Joel. *American Education.* 6th ed. St. Louis: McGraw-Hill, Inc., 1994.

The American School, 1642–1993. 3rd ed. St. Louis: McGraw-Hill, Inc., 1994.

Tyack, David B. *Turning Points in American Educational History.* Toronto: Blaisdell Publishing Co., 1967.

Chapter 3

American Educational Heritage
Part Two

The late colonial period gave rise to a converging interest in educational opportunity. Benjamin Franklin, as discussed earlier, desired a new curriculum at the secondary level that was more responsive to economic and other practical needs. Politicians were voicing the need for education for a literate citizenry. The Continental Congress was trying to induce families to move westward from the east coast by offering land for both settlement and schools, and state universities were beginning to develop in the South. Educational materials were also growing in abundance. Spellers, geographies, arithmetic texts, readers, and history books were more in demand.

Land Ordinances

One of the monumental federal programs prior to the Constitutional Convention was the passage of land ordinances by the Continental Congress in 1785 and 1787. These laws had widespread effects; educationally, they prompted residents to take an interest in public education and assume the responsibility for it thereafter. Originally, land, which is now partially the states of Minnesota, Wisconsin, Michigan, and Ohio, was rectilinearly divided into six-mile squares and further subdivided into thirty-six one-mile squares. Each six-mile square was called a township and each one-mile square a section. A section contained about 640 acres. In each township, at least one section had to be reserved for the support of schools. The school could be anywhere in the township, but the income generated, usually from Section 16, supported a "little red schoolhouse." This school was at first organized by levels and, because of English grammar, it became known as a grammar school. Later, the school was organized to include grades one through eight.

Several fundamental principles came out of these ordinances. Freedom of religion, no slavery, eligibility for statehood, right of trial by jury, and the right of *habeas corpus* were all ensured. Residence was established in lieu of ownership of property as a criterion for voting. One still had to be white, 21 years of age, male, and reside for a period of six months (or less, later on) to be eligible to vote; however, democracy was emerging. Education would prosper eventually because there would be a clamor for tax-supported schools by those who had previously owned little property and, consequently, never had much voice about educational policy.

In over 30 states, the land ordinance principle of using at least section sixteen for the support of schools gave rise to public schools. The states carried on the responsibility years later when costs outstripped revenues, but the federal government established a good policy of supporting "schools and the means of education." The federal government did not dictate curriculum or the extent of levels, but it built a floor of support beneath the young states.[1]

Alternatives to Tax-Supported Schools

There were, in addition, numerous attempts to foster greater access to schooling. These were in the form of charity or humanitarianism, but they all whetted an interest in tax-supported schools. Those who owned property, however, looked with a jaundiced eye at anything that might lead to free schools because they knew they would have to pay the majority of the costs for schooling. So every alternative was tried before the reality of tax-supported schools emerged in the mid-nineteenth century.

Sunday schools were one of the first alternatives that stimulated a public interest in education. An English idea, the Sunday school was an effect of the Industrial Revolution. Children left "idle" on Sunday after working in the factories were corralled on the Sabbath for some schooling, which included the study of catechism. The idea was popularly received in both England and America and, until about 1850, Sunday schools fulfilled a secular and sectarian function. They were inadequate, however, to meet the educational needs of children on such an expedient basis.

Monitorial instruction was another early nineteenth-century approach that helped to popularize education, although it was designed as much to save money as to educate children. Another English transplant, monitorial instruction was a method whereby one master teacher with the assistance of bright pupils handled hundreds of indigent children. Discipline obviously was the key to the approach. Records indicate that punishment was often severe. Pupil monitors had various duties ranging from taking attendance to hearing lessons, distributing learning materials, and maintaining order. The method of monitorial instruction was so inexpensive that it caught on well in big cities as an alternative to outright taxation for schooling. However, monitors could not provide what a trained teacher could accomplish. Hearing recitation was less of a challenge than teaching skills, interpreting content, and inspiring children. There was no substitute for the teacher. By the mid-nineteenth century the monitorial method was replaced by tax-supported schools. It helped, however, to fill a need when schools were not commonly available.

Rise of Common Schools

Tax-supported schools (common to all people) were not quick to develop in America. The Founding Fathers voiced a concern that the Republic would survive only if people could read and write. Americans who traveled abroad to study or to observe educational programs, especially in the German states or in France, awakened an interest among other Americans about the need for free schools. Furthermore, in the early 1800s, speakers usually from New England talked to settlers on the frontier as part of the Lyceum, which was a speakers' bureau whose individuals found among the pioneers a strong interest in tax-supported public education. Settlers wanted to hear more about the topic of education.

Horace Mann: Pioneer of the Common School Movement
(New York Public Library Picture Collection)

Embryonic trade unions in the 1820s also believed that their fortune was tied with educational opportunity. The members of these unions were always eager to query politicians about their educational stance. Strangely, these unions representing the lower classes joined hands with the humanitarians of the day, Horace Mann and Henry Barnard, for example, to found public schools in the 1840s and 1850s. An idea had arrived.

The most successful attempts during this period to provide free, open, secular schools were in Massachusetts, Connecticut, Rhode Island, Pennsylvania, and New York. The most celebrated educators of the first half of the nineteenth century were Horace Mann and Henry Barnard. They, of course, were only two of many who were zealous about free common schools, but their efforts were very commendable. Mann became the first secretary (superintendent) of the state board of education in Massachusetts in 1837. Barnard was elected to a similar post in 1838 in Connecticut. Both men were educational journalists, describing the educational scene at home and abroad for thousands of Americans. They wrote exemplary state superintendency reports; they established public teacher training institutions for elementary or common schools; and they traveled across numerous states preaching the word of free schools. Their impact was profound.

The young states initiated an interest among local communities to tax themselves for schools. The states generally offered aid if local school districts would exert tax effort themselves. Eventually, state legislatures exerted control, which in

Henry Barnard: A leader in the
Common School Movement

theory was theirs anyway as a result of the Tenth Amendment of the Bill of Rights, which gives all functions not assigned to Congress to the states or to the people. As a result, state superintendents forged a more centralized approach or system than had existed in colonial America. Authority for education since 1791 has been shared with local school districts because state authority is delegated partially to local school boards. Real control has always rested with state legislatures and their departments of education.

States in the nineteenth century began taxing themselves for common schools (eventually schools embodying eight grades), public normal schools, and public universities. Compulsory attendance began in Massachusetts in 1852 and was completed nationally in 1918; Mississippi was the last state to compel children to attend school. Now, most states require children to attend school from ages six until sixteen, although most stay until 18 years of age.

The Morrill Act

In 1862, an educational event occurred that proved to be a turning point in higher education. The Morrill Land Grant College Act was a congressional victory for people who desired a more practical curriculum than had existed for over 200 years in America. With this federal legislation, the study of agriculture, engineering, applied science, and liberal education would become common in many colleges and universities in subsequent decades. Skill in technology now was a legitimate academic pursuit and was eagerly sought.

Congress enticed states to participate in the legislation by offering 30,000 acres per representative and senator in each state if, within five years, that state would adapt its existing public university to the above program or build a new institution devoted to the substance of the act. An additional program was required of every state desiring to participate. The Reserve Officer Training Corps (ROTC) became part of every school that considered itself a land grant college.[2] Congress was concerned about getting better officers in the Union army so, partly to provide for the national defense, an education bill was passed. This Morrill Act proved to be a windfall for the nation. Applied science was given the green light to develop in higher education. In over 30 states the leading public institution eventually became the land grant college. Universities like Michigan State, Ohio State, University of Illinois, and Purdue are fine examples of land grant institutions. Their mission is diverse and practical.

Educational Progress: Civil War–World War II

The nineteenth century was marked by rapid educational progress. Educational opportunity was advanced with the ratification of the Fourteenth Amendment in 1868, which guaranteed equal protection before the law. Eventually, blacks and other minorities would be able to seek relief from discriminatory educational practices largely on the basis of this amendment. "Separate but equal" policies in almost all phases of national life characterized the treatment of nonwhites. Jim Crow was alive and well until the mid-twentieth century in some regions of the country, but the principle of the Fourteenth Amendment would prevail. Most of the litigation in racial desegregation occurring today flows from an interpretation of this concept of equal protection before the law. (More discussion of racial desegregation is presented in Chapter 9.)

Schools were well established by the end of the nineteenth century. High schools became very common after 1875 and capped off the common school. The high school was considered both a terminal school and a preparatory institution for college. Teacher training was taken more seriously than ever before in both universities and normal schools. States had firm control of public education. The pressures on public education would now become different.

Schools by World War I were extremely crystalized. Compulsory attendance extended to age 16 in almost all states by this time. Child labor legislation was complementing the states' interest in school attendance legislation. Immigrants, however, posed a new problem for the schools because the background of the immigrants was different from that of previous decades. At the turn of the century, southern and eastern Europeans immigrated at the rate of almost a million a year. They spoke little or no English and had different religious views and

Modern education is rooted in the past.
(*New York Public Library Picture Collection*)

lifestyles. Schools were reflections mainly of northern and western European views and nationalities and were instilled with Protestant attitudes. A clash was inevitable between those who controlled the schools and those who would attend.

The various settlement houses in the large cities of the midwestern and eastern regions of the country were doing more for the immigrants than the schools were. Settlement houses offered food, job skills, and rudimentary education to the immigrants. Schools, on the other hand, were offering chiefly the English language as their form of Americanization. Ghettos or enclaves mushroomed in number between 1880 and World War I, thereby putting pressure on schools to change.[3] Politicians, business people, farmers, and labor leaders criticized the public school for its inability to incorporate their particular interests. The school was an insulated institution for sure, but it could not become all things to all people.

Out of this need for change arose progressive education. John Dewey, professor of philosophy and educational theory at Teachers College, Columbia University, became the reluctant spokesman for progressivism in education. Writing prolifically, Dewey called for a new definition of democracy that was more participatory than representative. He placed the school in the vanguard of social change. The child should no longer, in theory at least, adapt to preconceived knowledge and experience. The curriculum should be tailored more to children, their abilities, their interests, and their future aspirations. The school should be the vehicle or tool for reshaping the academic, social, political, and economic world in which children would mature.

Progressivism in education became an influential movement in the 1920s and 1930s. Reform was popular, and much of what characterizes so-called modern education today was spawned during that era. The emphasis on individual learning, vocational or career education, early childhood education, audiovisual education, and social education blossomed under the care of progressive educators. Elementary schools incorporated the progressive tenets more effectively than secondary schools, probably more because of their ability to be less structured and content-oriented than for any other reason. Progressivism did work, however, in some secondary schools as indicated by the famous Eight Year Study (1933–41). This study showed that a required traditional high school curriculum did not ensure success in higher education. Graduates of so-called experimental high schools did just as well as their counterparts from traditional high schools.

Educational Progress: World War II–Present

Largely a result of World War II and a return to conservative views, progressivism lost its momentum and disciples. By the 1960s educators rarely called themselves progressive anymore. The movement became tainted in the public mind. Low academic standards, permissive discipline, and relative views on a variety of issues all characterized progressive education, even though the facts did not warrant such criticisms. Progressivism in education never dominated educational thought, yet it was seen as the culprit for most problems.

When the Russians launched Sputnik in 1957, Americans became uneasy about their schools. Consequently, in 1958 the National Defense Education Act (NDEA) was passed so that the better students would become competent in mathematics, the sciences, and foreign languages. To surpass the Russians in the space race would require gifted students capable of thinking in scientific and mathematical content. Progressive education was not seen as a philosophy appropriate for a space age. Sputnik sounded the death knell for progressive thinking, but its decline began much earlier.

The 1960s became the era of accelerated civil rights and federal influence in education. The Civil Rights Act (1964) generally forbade discrimination by any agency using federal funds. Since all public schools were utilizing federal money in some capacity, the tenets of civil rights legislation were relevant. The Department of Health, Education, and Welfare and the Justice Department encouraged or enforced compliance with judicial or legislative interpretations of equality before the law. The U.S. Supreme Court case of *Brown* v. *Board of Education*, Topeka, Kansas (1954), required that public schools dismantle racially dual facilities. School districts, however, complied in a medley of ways. The Civil Rights Act prompted faster compliance and thereby put more teeth into the spirit of the *Brown* decision. The Department of Health, Education, and Welfare worked mainly with school districts that were voluntarily desegregating, while the Justice Department initiated court action against school districts ineffectively complying with the mandate to dismantle racially dual facilities "with all deliberate speed."

Congress also passed an important legislative program in 1965 called the Elementary and Secondary Education Act (ESEA). This act helped to enhance educational opportunity, especially for children of low-income parents. The impact of the legislation was that academically behind, normal children, who were also from low-income families, were given supplemental academic assistance in order to succeed in school. Poverty was to be lessened through education, which was the goal of President Lyndon Baines Johnson.

In 1981, much of the ESEA was revamped and renamed the Education Consolidation and Improvement Act (ECIA). However, the lessening of poverty through education remained the goal of Chapter 1 of the 1981 act. Chapter 2 of the act embodied about 40 previously separate programs, which were repackaged into "block grants" with less federal control. In 1988 the ECIA was repealed, along with other federal programs, and placed into a revitalized ESEA. The authorization for this change was a congressional act known as the Hawkins-Stafford School Improvement Amendments. Chapter 1 remains basically the same, but it is funded more generously. It also now includes funding for a dropout prevention program as well as for disadvantaged preschoolers and their illiterate parents.

Chapter 1 continues to be the most potent and controversial authorization of federal educational funds. Programs targeted for normal, academically disadvantaged, and poor youth have been compensatory in nature and reach about 5 million students annually. Chapter 1 accounts for almost 20 percent of the total annual federal educational budget. Since 1988, Congress has instituted a "program improvement initiative" to ensure that youth in Chapter 1 programs meet minimum academic standards. If students generally do not, the school must enter a formal arrangement with the state to compose plans to help bring "targeted" students up to minimum achievement standards. The problem is that, thus far, only about 20 percent of the school districts with Chapter 1 programs have designed specific goals to raise minimum standards. The number of such districts has increased since 1990 but not rapidly enough.[4]

During the 1970s significant federal legislation intensely affected public schools. Three congressional acts left their indelible mark: Title IX, Education Amendments (1972); The Family Educational Rights and Privacy Act (1974); and the Education For All Handicapped Children Act (1975). The first, Title IX, forbids sex discrimination by any agency using federal funds. This certainly includes all public schools. The impact of such legislation touches not only athletics in terms of recruitment, funding, scheduling, and offerings, but also employment practices as well as the curriculum. Males and females have to be treated equally with few restrictions in reference to funding, access, and opportunities of all types.

Schools under the influence of Title IX have altered their approach to women especially. Pregnancies, for example, are considered "health problems" because maternity leave policies are determined more by the expectant mother and her doctor than by the board of education. Advancement within the system also has to be based primarily on credentials, not on stereotypes like "men make better principals." Curricular offerings which had been limited to one sex only now are available to both sexes.

One comment should be made in reference to Title IX. A U.S. Supreme Court case in February 1984, *Grove City College* v. *Bell,* changed Title IX somewhat in that the title was interpreted as legally enforceable in light of "programs only" rather than applicable to the "entire school." However, Congress through its 1988 civil rights legislation restored the effect of Title IX to the entire school. This fact becomes significant in that sexism is reduced more generally.

The Family Educational Rights and Privacy Act (1974) further altered public school policy in regard to official school records. Parents and guardians of children under 18 now have the right to inspect, copy, and challenge, if necessary, written comments or other data on so-called official school records. Permanent records, test data, counseling information, and health facts are examples of official records parents and guardians may inspect. These rights transfer to youth when they reach 18. Teachers and administrators are more accountable for written material because they must verify the accuracy of comments now more than ever before.

The Education For All Handicapped Children Act (1975), commonly called P.L. 94–142, was designed to enlarge the civil rights of special children and youth between ages three and 21. Categories of disabilities range from mental retardation to physical and emotional disabilities. The major principles of the act were as follows:

1. An appropriate education for special-needs children between ages 3 and 21
2. Nondiscriminatory evaluation
3. Individualized education program
4. Least restrictive environment
5. Due process for youth and parents
6. Parental participation in decision making and in formulation of policy
7. In-service education for teachers[5]

The act came to be associated with the term "mainstreaming," but most special educators prefer the use of the term "least restrictive environment." Mainstreaming implies that a special child will be grouped with non-special children, but that depends upon the severity of the child's disibility and the appropriate setting. Mainstreaming also implies it will benefit such children solely if they are mainstreamed. The value may be just the reverse because non-special children may learn or mature more, in many instances, by the integration. In other words, the act calls for a two-way street. The words "special" or "disabled" are now commonly used in place of "handicapped."

In recent years, federal legislation in special education has been significant. In 1990, Congress passed the Americans with Disabilities Act (ADA) as an enlargement of similar legislation passed in 1973. The ADA guarantees equal opportunity for individuals with disabilities in employment, public accommodation, and transportation. Also in 1990, Congress passed The Education of the Handicapped Act Amendments, which changed the name of P.L. 94–142 (the 1975 Act discussed above). This revised version, called the Individuals with Disabilities Education Act (IDEA), expands discretionary programs, mandates transition and assistive technology in a student's individualized education program, and adds autism and traumatic brain injury to the list of special education categories needing more attention. Emotional disturbance and attention deficit disorder are also cited as areas requiring greater support.

Since 1990, a new view of placement for children with disabilities has swept the nation, spurred largely by the parental advocacy movement. The concept is called "inclusion" (sometimes called "full inclusion") and places such children only in regular classrooms in their neighborhood schools with needed support services. The agenda is to integrate all students irrespective of disability. Obviously, severity of disability may prevent some students from immediate inclusion, but many believe that the local school district should assume more responsibility for the academic needs of all children. The state heretofore has been almost totally responsible for the education of profoundly disabled youth.

There are degrees of support, however, for the idea of inclusion. Some believe that the "least restrictive environment" has resulted in a segregative and ineffective atmosphere because of the partial "pull-out" process of students needing special services. Supporters of the "pull-out" view, however, believe that neighborhood schools and regular teachers will be hard-pressed to meet the needs of children with disabilities, even if human and material resources are available. Unfortunately, court action will probably decide many of the implied questions.[6]

In 1991, Congress also passed a Civil Rights Act, which forbids job discrimination on the basis of race, religion, sex, and national origin. As mentioned, it had in 1990 passed the Americans With Disabilities Act, which prohibited discrimination against persons with disabilities. Congress left open the definition of disability to ensure protection for such people as recovering drug abusers, alcoholics, individuals with human immunodeficiency virus (HIV) infection or AIDS or with other contagious diseases. Civil rights legislation has become much more comprehensive in recent years.

The 1970s also witnessed an event that may shape educational policy differently at the federal level; however, it will depend upon whether the Republicans or Democrats in future years control not only the White House but Congress as well. In 1979, President Jimmy Carter initiated a Department of Education with a new cabinet position, that of secretary of education. For the first time a person responsible for education at the federal level was officially close to the president. The National Education Association (NEA) had worked tirelessly to transfer education from a bureau to a cabinet level. For the first time in history the NEA succeeded with President Carter in 1979. Most recently education was linked with the Department of Health, Education, and Welfare; its secretary had cabinet status but had to speak for many interests, not education alone. Now education is a singular, vested interest at the federal level.

Another belief, however, is that a Republican administration normally holds the view that education constitutionally belongs more to the states, because of the Tenth Amendment, than it does to the federal government. Decentralization is a key concept to most Republicans. The more funding and control of education by state legislatures, the better education will be, according to most Republicans. President Ronald Reagan was no exception to this view. At one time, he preferred to reduce the Department of Education to a bureau and remove the secretary of education from his cabinet. However, the education bureaucracy and Congress did not let this happen. But the mere presence of a Republican president changes the scope of education at the federal level because educational funding is viewed differently in terms of the national budget.

President Bush's major educational involvement occurred as a result of a governors' conference in 1990, which culminated in a report called *America 2000: An Education Strategy.* Six national goals were articulated with reference to the public schools:

1. All children ready to learn when they begin school
2. High school graduation rate of at least 90 percent
3. Student competency in the core content of English, mathematics, science, history, and reasoning skills
4. First place ranking in international competition in mathematics and science

5. Adult literacy to succeed in a global economy
6. Schools free of drugs and violence[7]

In April 1991, President Bush formally introduced America 2000 with the announcement that there would be 535 "new American schools" created, at least one in each congressional district, to reflect excellence in teaching, learning, and educational technologies. New bonds are forged between federal and state levels in that governors' academies for in-service training, alternative certification, and a number of other state endeavors will be created to help reform public education. Funding, however, has been modest in the implementation of America 2000.

President Bill Clinton, as governor of Arkansas in 1990, helped to create these goals and, as president, has endorsed much of *America 2000* under the rubric of *Goals 2000*. President Clinton will be supportive of congressional legislation for public education and will encourage measures such as "choice" within the public sector rather than between public and private schools. It is expected that President Clinton will also endorse major goals of both the American Federation of Teachers and the National Education Association. He also is an advocate of national standards and testing to stimulate quality at the state and local levels.

The Department of Education has much work ahead if educational enterprises at the national level are to be consolidated. Presently, the department focuses primarily on elementary and secondary schools, the disabled, ethnic education, teacher centers (continuing education), and research. Many other interests, such as veterans' educational benefits and employment training programs, however, are centered elsewhere. The department's status will always depend, in part, on the political makeup in Washington, D.C.

The decade of the 1980s had been marked by dissatisfaction with public education. The reform movement, underway before *A Nation at Risk* (1983), was spurred on especially by this report. President Reagan and many of his conservative supporters enthusiastically endorsed this report, which cited that 13 percent of American seventeen-year-olds and about 40 percent of minority students were functionally illiterate. In addition, the report stated that on nineteen international academic tests, American students were last on seven tests and never first on any.

The National Commission on Excellence in Education, which penned the report, in essence called for several things:

1. High school requirements should be increased to include four years of English, three years of social studies, science, and math, one-half year of computer science, and at least two years of foreign language for college-bound students.
2. Standards and expectations should be reevaluated and improved to stress achievement, realistic grading, and periodic achievement testing. Textbooks need to be adopted with greater care so that scholarship and content appropriateness are guaranteed.
3. More and better use of time should be made to ensure quality. The school day should be lengthened to seven hours and the school year to 200 days plus.

Such things as increased homework for high school students, better discipline, promotion, and attendance policies also need to be developed and implemented.

4. Teachers' salaries need to reflect the market, performance, and an improved evaluation system. Professionalism depends on differentiating teachers in terms of effectiveness.[8]

From 1983 on, the educational establishment has pondered these recommendations and their implications. The reactions are mixed. Some critics claim that without federal money to improve schooling the recommendations are empty. Others feel that the single salary schedule, and tenure especially, are under attack. Such a revision, they believe, would introduce favoritism and reward the few at the expense of the many. Other critics feel, in reference to content and standards, that it is rather simplistic to believe that more subject matter in the liberal arts and higher test scores will make America less "at risk." The authors believe that this report says much about what should constitute the curriculum, but it does not say enough about what kind of student should emerge from school. Cognitive and affective competencies are as important as content.

The positive value of this report and others is that education is put on center stage, at least for a while. The public tends to demand better education when national attention is caught. Standardized tests have shown over the last few decades that students, by comparison with their predecessors, are reading and comprehending at a lower level, are expressing themselves less clearly in writing, are less competent in mathematical concepts, and are less effective in drawing inferences from written materials.[9] In perspective, however, schools have been faulted frequently before and have risen to the challenge. There is no reason to believe this will not happen again.

During the early progressive era of this century, the schools were blamed by the public for numerous social ills as well as for academic incompetency. In 1938 conservatives in education met nationally and created an essentialist manifesto or platform, which in many respects looks much like *A Nation at Risk*. During the 1950s, conservative critics wrote prolifically about curricular weaknesses and the distorted missions of public schools.

Numerous critics of the 1960s and 1970s were a different breed, in a sense, because they began to see the public school as beyond redemption. This trend to move away from public education because it is considered hopeless is not a passing fancy. Home education and private school enrollment are indeed on the upswing.

In regard to criticisms of public schools, two major sources of publications appeared from 1991 to 1993, the series by Gerald Bracey and the findings of the researchers in Sandia National Laboratories. Both sources suggest that much of the critical reports on public education were issued without careful collection and analysis of data. International comparisons, both believe, were tenuous and often out of context. Instead, they cite steady progress in American education although the performance of minority, urban, and immigrant youth needs drastic improvement. Strong leadership and a national consensus on educational goals are crucial factors in educational reform. Both the Bracey publications and Sandia Report are uplifting and in the spirit of the Harold Hodgkinson interpretations done a decade earlier and corroborated by him again in 1993. All underscore the productive work of the public school.[10]

Reformation of the curriculum, some believe, is no longer the solution to the educational ills of the nation. The new Right, for example, see the public school failing in a number of ways: values, content, discipline, as well as forced social and racial mixture. The far Left, on the other hand, see the school as a vehicle for too much social conformity, for perpetuating a caste system, as well as for limiting vertical mobility, particularly in racial and ethnic terms.

The public school is in the midst of ferment. This thesis-antithesis process, however, can be wholesome. The public school needs to improve and with greater attention should come support, morally and financially. History has shown that the public school has often been vulnerable and slow to react to social need; however, the record also indicates it can be a responsive institution.

The reform movement through the early 1990s continued unabatedly. Some 41 states had increased their high school graduation requirements, 33 states had required student competency tests, and 24 states had initiated teacher career ladders and salary revision. Despite these improvements, the dropout rate rose well over 20 percent, and of those who dropped out many were low-income minority students. Furthermore, in 1988 there were about 750,000 homeless school-age children nationwide, of whom only 43 percent attended school regularly. In 1987 the Stewart B. McKinney Homeless Assistance Act was passed by Congress to provide schooling for these children.

The McKinney Act has provided funds in recent years to facilitate integration of opportunities for homeless children, not only with the services of the school, but also with the efforts of community agencies such as churches, clothing dispensaries, health agencies, and so on. All barriers to a free, appropriate education are attacked under the auspices of the McKinney Act. It is estimated that, on any given day, 100,000 homeless children live in shelters, one-half of whom are under six years of age. This number does not estimate the thousands more who are "doubled up" with friends or acquaintances.

Physical exhaustion and cognitive, motor, social, and emotional deficiencies are acute problems. Parents (often single parents) suffer from fatigue and depression and commonly exhibit little interest in enhancing educational opportunities for their children.[11]

The dissatisfaction with public education, in general, even found expression in 1987 in best-sellers. Allan Bloom's *The Closing of the American Mind: How Higher Education Has Failed Democracy and Impoverished the Souls of Today's Students* and E. D. Hirsh, Jr.'s, *Cultural Literacy: What Every American Needs to Know* were both scathing attacks on higher education and the public schools. The authors believe respectively that a return to the liberal arts will again open the American mind and facilitate literacy. The content of the liberal curriculum is crucial to both men.

Educational Pioneers

Before moving to the next discussion on developing an educational viewpoint, it will be helpful to state briefly the major contributions of several representative individuals who influenced the direction of American elementary and secondary education. Much of what has occurred in educational history would probably have happened regardless of these representative educators; nevertheless, they either articulated or well synthesized the educational beliefs of their era, or they gave direction to fertile ideas that later became commonplace. Their imprint was indelible.

Jean Jacques Rousseau (1712–1778)

Rousseau, a Frenchman, could not be classified as a very practical or successful educator in his own time, but he was important because he emphasized fostering "affective" qualities in children which educators value today. In his chief work, *Emile,* Rousseau laid out an educational program designed for a tutor and student, but the scheme was highly impractical. The student, Emile, learns (with guidance) mainly by his experiences and their consequences. He tends to do the right things because his nature is inherently good. Feelings, compassion, sensitivity, and so on are naturally cultivated and books are almost nonexistent, but eventually basic vocational skill and social and civic concern are stressed. Emile ultimately enters willingly into a "social contract" with others to enable society to function, but it is the individual who is supreme. Social institutions tend to corrupt human nature; however, the right kind of education, Rousseau believed, could reform society.

Rousseau's impact on American education is felt primarily in a concern for the natural elements in education. Respect is given to the child as a child, not as a "little adult." Harmony exists in the curriculum because it is fitted to the child's needs and interests. Open education is an example of how this idea is valued. Cognitively speaking, Rousseau had little to offer; affectively speaking, however, he made a great contribution. He saw the child educated only when his feelings, emotions, and attitudes were developed in a positive manner. Childhood education was given a boost by Rousseau. Educators today subscribe to the theory that the child possesses the potential for goodness.

Johann Pestalozzi (1746–1827)

Pestalozzi, a Swiss educator, was well known for his efforts with orphan children as well as with the general area of elementary education. Like Rousseau, his personal life was filled with disappointments, but his tenacious attitude to reform society through education proved to be productive. He wrote several books, chief of which was *Leonard and Gertrude*. In this volume, the basic theme was social reform by means of proper education. Personal lives and social institutions were rejuvenated and became more moral as a result. Although this thesis was partly unrealistic, it nevertheless propelled the topic of education into the limelight when educational opportunity was very rare.

Pestalozzi is remembered for his concern for poor children and for his methodology of teaching, which stressed concrete experience before abstract bookishness. He established work-study programs on an agricultural basis for abandoned children. This combination of study and manual work is now the idea underlying distributive education and work-study programs often sponsored by federal funds in both secondary and higher education.

Pestalozzi's methodology was heavily centered around the use of objects to show children concepts such as number, color, weight, and size. The more a child actually worked with objects, the more he or she could later understand abstraction. Nature study also became important as a source of first-hand involvement with real things. In a powerful sense, this object training fostered cognitive and emotional readiness to learn. The use of objects was overplayed in the United States; the idea, however, eventually led to audiovisual education and nature study as respectable areas of the curriculum. Early childhood education capitalized well on the use of objects in learning activities.

Pestalozzi was widely heralded in the nineteenth century in Europe for his interest in improving society through education and in this country for his emphasis on the use of objects, especially in elementary education. Later educators, such as John Dewey, synthesized the philosophy of Pestalozzi with other theories and consequently gave direction to the modern elementary school.

Friedrich Froebel (1782–1852)

Froebel, a German, was the originator of the kindergarten, only he conceived it to be a place of learning for children from ages three to seven. He believed society could be reformed through the improvement of children—intellectually, socially, emotionally, spiritually, and physically. Froebel's efforts in Prussia during the 1840s were most productive. He designed the toys (which were almost nonexistent at the time) for the kindergarten. Toys to take apart for research or analysis and toys to put together for synthesis or wholeness were common in his kindergarten. Unity was a key concept to convey in the use of toys and activities. Circles were drawn on the floor to bring children together for group or social activities. In his *Education of Man* he stressed spiritual and social purposes for the kindergarten. He wrote abstrusely, but he implemented effectively.

The kindergarten under Froebel was a setting for intellectual stimulation and emotional security. Love and respect for children by the teacher were prerequisites for teaching at this level. Besides social education, other goals and activities constituted the kindergarten. Rhythmic activities, nature study, fantasy, creative drawing, free play, psychomotor skills, and the use of diverse toys all characterized this aspect of childhood. The kindergarten, as fashioned by Froebel, had a timeless ring to it.

Kindergarten blossomed in the United States after 1848. Private kindergartens conducted in German and English flourished for a couple of decades until William T. Harris, superintendent of schools in St. Louis City, and Susan E. Blow, a volunteer teacher and devotee of Froebel's views, initiated in September, 1873, the first continuous public school kindergarten in the United States. After 1873, the early childhood movement mushroomed nationally; the public school kindergarten was, of course, an integral part of this growth and has remained a vital rung in the educational ladder.

Johann Herbart (1776–1841)

Herbart, also a German educator, focused his efforts on secondary education. He became a philosopher and educational theorist at the university level. In his *Science of Education and Outlines of Educational Doctrine,* Herbart expressed his educational views. The aim of education to Herbart was morality: virtue, individual excellence, charity, and justice. The mind, he believed, was not a series of compartments of separate ideas but rather a mass of ideas emerging and submerging into one's consciousness and subconsciousness.

Because of this mixture of mental ideas, facts, and concepts, the school must connect and relate knowledge as often as possible. New knowledge must be related to previously learned information before generalizations and applications are made. Herbart believed that subject matter should be correlated, themes should be stressed as core ideas, and history and literature should be emphasized to show how culture has evolved. Herbart, in essence, helped to develop a new theory of educational psychology and methodology.

Herbart's other strong interest was to make education as scientific as possible. He established a "chair of pedagogy" and advocated a fusion of theory and practice, expressed in clinical experience. His disciples later crystallized his thinking by listing steps which could apply objectively to teaching any lesson. The steps are outlined as follows:

1. *Preparation* (clearness of purpose and readiness to learn and teach)
2. *Presentation* (concreteness and clearness of ideas)
3. *Association* (relatedness of new ideas and concepts with known information; internalized knowledge)
4. *Generalization* (universalizing ideas and concepts)
5. *Application* (drill, projects, or pertinent use of material)

The use of this Herbartian method became fashionable and has evolved into the emphasis on lesson planning commonly practiced in schools today. The "association" aspect of this system (number 3) was Herbart's applied psychology because it implied unity of thought and connectedness of content. Herbart, in conclusion, was a pioneer in the areas of educational psychology and teaching as a science.

John Dewey (1859–1952)

Dewey, the first American educator to be discussed here, is considered the best representative of the entire progressive movement in American education, which flourished roughly during the last quarter of the nineteenth century and first half of the twentieth. Other exemplary educators could be written about in this section. People such as Francis W. Parker, William James, or William H. Kilpatrick also could warrant close attention as influential American educators of this era; however, Dewey philosophically gave justification to the need for change in educational theory and practice.

Dewey, a professor of philosophy and education for almost all of his adult life, philosophically synthesized theories of earlier educators and gave a democratic meaning to them. In practically all of his voluminous writing (several hundred articles and some forty books), Dewey advocated a strong concern for the psychological and social aspects of the individual, the social needs of the group (of society), and the cultural content to be transmitted. Good education, in other words, gave attention to society, the child, and the subject matter. Dewey's most publicized and timeless work was his *Democracy and Education*, but his *Experience and Education* is extremely helpful in understanding more clearly his basic educational attitudes. These two volumes offer much insight into his thinking.

In his educational writings, Dewey concentrated on a number of crucial points. He redefined democracy to include the aspect of active participation. Students as citizens must at times be leaders as well as followers. Democracy is an active process. It is based upon majority rule, but the rights of the minority must be protected. Truth also is relative to time and place. Discipline in schools, therefore, must lean toward permissiveness in order to foster participatory democracy. Passive students, Dewey believed, do not magically become active citizens and learners.

Furthermore, Dewey believed, education is a lifelong process of which schooling is but a part, but schooling is not to be viewed as a preparation for some predetermined future. The child should be respected as a total organism with intellectual, social, physical, and emotional needs. The school must in good faith address them all. The child often determines much of the content as well as the approach to learning. Past knowledge is not sacred in itself but becomes pertinent to the needs and interests of the learner. Content should be organized on a problem or thematic basis, and the content itself is not selected by adults alone. Vocational skills and practical arts are valued as much as general education. The curriculum, in other words, becomes comprehensive; that is, a diversity of content is offered to meet the needs and interests of learners.

Dewey has been attacked by some modern critics of education, but the faults of progressive education probably lay more with his disciples. Yet he contributed to the extremism of "child-centered learning" because he wrote unclearly at times and failed, along with other so-called progressive educators, to articulate and promulgate a clear and practical meaning of progressive education. His impact upon education and schooling is still felt today. The seeds of many "new" ideas were sown by Dewey and his followers. The technology may be new today but the premise is old. Dewey's influence on many contemporary educational psychologists has also been evident in reference to their concern for the stages of childhood as well as for experiential and problem-oriented education.

William C. Bagley (1874–1946)

Bagley was a conservative educator and colleague of Dewey's at Teachers College, Columbia University. He is probably most remembered for his leadership in directing and articulating the conservative reaction to progressive education, which culminated in the famous "An Essentialist's Platform for the Advancement of American Education," written in 1938.

Today, Bagley would be a national spokesman for the conservative movement in education. Many of the comments in his platform are still relevant. The school, he believed, should focus primarily on the needs of society. Literacy in terms of time-tested knowledge is vital. Everything else is incidental to the goal of literacy. Adults select the content of the curriculum because immature children and youth cannot know their long-range needs. Social issues and problems are incidental to a mastery of content. Social promotions are absolutely wrong because they demean the intellectual purpose of education.

The "essentials of the essentialist" boil down chiefly to those exacting studies in the fields of mathematics, the sciences (especially the natural sciences), and the humanities. They are prerequisite to those abilities which allow the learner to make intelligent judgments individually and collectively. Students can become possessors of a "common core of ideas, meanings, understandings, and ideals representing the most precious elements of the human heritage." Obviously, this belief implies a structured curriculum, high standards of achievement, adult-imposed authority, much homework in terms of reading and writing, and the use of intellectually oriented reporting processes. The child's role is to adapt to a set curriculum and, as a result, he or she will gain greater academic self-reliance and inner freedom because of humane adult direction. The educational pendulum has swung more in this direction over the last several years.

Summary

American public education, especially below the college level, has evolved from colonial assumptions about educational opportunities. Little was done to overcome illiteracy during this period, but the seeds were sown throughout America. The free school, tax-supported and secularly controlled, emerged after 200 years of struggle. The American colonist generally valued education, but in a clannish manner. Religion, gender, wealth, and a classical curriculum greatly affected students' opportunities to improve their lot in life. This trend would not change much until the nineteenth century.

During the last century, the common school was designed at public expense. It became a feeder school for both the high school and university. The educational ladder became complete. State legislatures and their state departments of education assumed more control of formal schooling. Because of the Tenth Amendment of the U.S. Constitution, states by implication have inherited powerful control over public education. Consequently, states began to forge a uniform approach to the curriculum, textbooks, teacher certification, and standards.

In the twentieth century, critics from various sources attacked the public school for its indifference to racial, ethnic, and religious minorities and for its insensitivity to career goals for students. Cynically, one could view the school as an institution designed to keep children in their teens off the labor market and to instill in them an attitude of mass conformity conducive to control by industry.

In a more optimistic vein, however, the public school has served as a vehicle for social change and vertical mobility for millions who otherwise would have been relegated to inferior social status. All one has to do is look closely within one's family to see how schooling has been a key to a better life—materially, socially, and personally. Public education, however, is certainly in need of continued renewal as the periodic national reports on education have indicated. The public school has shown historically that it can adapt to social need, and it will adapt constructively again.

Implications for Future Teachers

Future teachers cannot function successfully if they do not become aware of such things as major federal legislation, particularly regarding children with disabilities. The student who begins a career devoid of an historical and theoretical educational base is at a disadvantage. As a new teacher undertakes his or her duties, it is hoped that in-service education (including graduate study) will build on the initial historical and political concepts the teacher has brought to the school district.

Discussion Questions

1. Discuss the rise of the common school in the nineteenth century. In your view what should its mission be today?
2. What does progressivism mean in a general sense? What brought it into existence during the twentieth century especially?
3. What is the relationship between the terms "equality of educational opportunity" and "quality in education"?

Notes

1. Ellwood P. Cubberley, *Public Education in the United States* (New York: Houghton Mifflin, 1934), 91–94.

2. H. G. Good, *A History of American Education* (New York: Macmillan Co., 1960), 290–95.

3. S. Alexander Rippa, *Education in a Free Society: An American History*, 7th ed. (New York: Longman Publishing, 1992), 142–46.

4. "Improvement Plan for Chapter 1 Seen Needing Overhaul," *Education Week*, XI (March 25, 1992), 1 and 32.

5. Ann Turnbull, Judith Leonard, and A. Rutherford Turnbull, *Educating Handicapped Children: Judicial and Legislative Influence*, (unpublished) 1979, 12.

6. "Selected Key Federal Statutes Affecting the Education and Civil Rights of Children and Youth With Disabilities" (Learning Disabilities Association), *LDA/Newsbriefs*, 26 (September/October 1992), 16–17.

7. *America 2000: An Education Strategy* (Washington, D.C.: U. S. Department of Education, 1991).

8. *A Nation at Risk: The Imperative for Educational Reform*, A Report to the Nation and the Secretary of Education, United States Department of Education, by the National Commission on Excellence in Education, April 1983.

9. *Ibid.*

10. *See* G. W. Bracey's three "Reports on the Condition of Public Education," *Phi Delta Kappan*, 72 (October 1991): 104–17; 73 (October 1992): 104–17; 75 (October 1993): 104–17; C. C. Carson, R. M. Huelskamp, and T. D. Woodall, "Perspectives on Education in America," Sandia National Laboratories, Albuquerque (April 1992); and H. Hodgkinson, "American Education: The Good, the Bad, and the Task," 74, *Phi Delta Kappan* (April 1993), 619–26.

11. S. Koblinsky, *et al.*, "Educating Homeless Young Children," *Day Care and Early Education*, 20 (Fall 1992), 24–29.

Recommended Readings

Bell, Terrel H. "Reflections One Decade After *A Nation At Risk*," *Phi Delta Kappan*, 74 (April 1993): 592–97.

Bracey, Gerald W. "Why Can't They Be Like We Were?" *Phi Delta Kappan*, 72 (October 1991): 104–17.

Bracey, Gerald W. "The Second Bracey Report on the Condition of Public Education," *Phi Delta Kappan*, 73 (October 1992): 104–17.

Bracey, Gerald W. "The Third Bracey Report on the Condition of Public Education," *Phi Delta Kappan*, 75 (October 1993): 104–17.

Carson, C. C., Huelskamp, R. M., and Woodall, T. D. "Perspectives on Education in America," Final Draft, Sandia National Laboratories, Albuquerque, N.M., April 1992.

Commager, Henry Steele, ed. Doc. no. 82, "The Northwest Ordinance of 1787," *Documents of American History*, Vol. 1 (to 1898). New York: Appleton-Century-Crofts, 1968: 123–24, 128–32.

Cremin, Lawrence. *The Transformation of the School: Progressivism in American Education, 1876–1957*. New York: Knopf, 1961.

Cremin, Lawrence. *American Education: The National Experience, 1783–1786.* New York: Harper & Row, 1980.

Cremin, Lawrence. *American Education: The Metropolitan Experience, 1876–1980.* New York: Harper & Row, 1988.

Dewey, John. *Democracy and Education.* Toronto: Macmillan Co., 1916.

Dewey, John. *Experience and Education.* Toronto: Macmillan Co., 1938.

Katzelson, Ira, and Margaret Weir. *Schooling for All: Class, Race, and the Decline of the Democratic Ideal.* New York: Basic Books, 1986.

Parker, Franklin. "Ideas That Shaped American Schools." *Phi Delta Kappan* 62 (January 1981): 314–9.

Plunkett, Virginia R. L. "From Title I to Chapter 1: The Evolution of Compensatory Education." *Phi Delta Kappan* 66 (April 1985): 533–8.

Pulliam, John D. *History of Education in America,* 6th ed. New York: Merrill, 1994.

Rippa, S. Alexander. *Education in a Free Society: An American History,* 7th ed. New York: Longman Publishing, 1992.

Spring, Joel. *The Sorting Machine Revisited: National Educational Policy Since 1945.* New York: Longman, 1988.

Spring, Joel. *The American School, 1642–1993.* 3rd ed. St. Louis: McGraw-Hill, Inc., 1994.

Spring, Joel. *American Education,* 6th ed. St. Louis: McGraw-Hill, Inc., 1994.

Ulich, Robert. *History of Educational Thought.* New York: American Book Co., 1950.

Chapter 4

Developing an Educational Viewpoint

Prospective teachers need to develop a consistent viewpoint about the purposes of schooling, about curriculum and organization, and about how pupils should be evaluated in terms of their progress. Expressing such constructive views about the school is no easy task, but it is a valuable experience.

This chapter contains material to help future teachers develop a more systematic view or attitude about formal education. Educational philosophers for centuries have concerned themselves with various purposes of education. Prospective teachers should be abreast of these classical educational philosophies and how they relate to the classroom. After an overview of the representative educational "isms," an attempt will be made to assist future teachers express an attitude about formal education.

Major Educational Philosophies

Essentialism

Essentialism as an educational philosophy is grounded in the oldest and most commonly accepted philosophy found in the public school. Its root word is "essential," implying that certain studies are more crucial than others. As a *formal* movement, it dates from 1938 when William C. Bagley of Teachers College, Columbia University, Michael J. Demiashkevich of George Peabody College for Teachers, and others met in Atlantic City to found an official movement advocating a return to a core of basics.[1] These academicians in general believed, even long before 1938, that progressive education encouraged academic mediocrity and excessive concern for student needs or interests. Actually, if one were to remove the date and names from the 1938 essentialist platform, one might be convinced it was written recently. It sounds much like the "return to the basics" movement of the last few years.

Nothing was radically new in the essentialist philosophy. For centuries, conservative educators have believed that the function of formal education is to transmit the accumulated knowledge of the past in order to make youth literate. An education steeped in the liberal arts is the ideal curriculum for everybody.

Essentialists, often called traditionalists or conservatives, believe literacy has a broad meaning. It involves first a skill in reading, but it also implies an enlargement of ideas and intelligent judgment concerning the preservation of a democratic society. The students begin with the specific study of reading, writing, and computing, and they then advance to a relative mastery of a "common core of ideas, meanings, understandings, and ideals" representing the human heritage. This implies study in foreign language, fine arts, history, and the natural and social sciences. The industrial arts and health education are not to be neglected. Essentials also include other ideas not necessarily classified as subject matter. Such things as mature adult guidance, humane discipline, and permanent values are all essentials for a democratic society. The public school is charged with the task of instilling these ideas and values.

Essentialism, as a formal movement, reached its peak in the 1980s. Its growth was steady after World War II, when disenchantment with progressive educational practices became widespread. Writers in the disciplines of history, English, and the sciences began publishing scathing articles and books about their views of progressive education and its connection with problems in public education. When Sputnik was launched by Russia in 1957, the American public began to see America's loss in the space race as a cause-effect relationship between formal education and second-class status. Progressive education was seen as too permissive, embodying low academic standards, and possessing no clear direction for student maturation. The essentialists offered an alternative: reformation of the curriculum with special attention given to the academically talented.

The 1960s stalled this essentialist alternative somewhat because progressive innovations and an anti-establishment sentiment emerged to force the schools into different directions. The rebellion of some youth in the 1960s really did not occur because of the schools but because of a larger political reaction—partly to the continuing Vietnam War and emerging civil rights. Ultimately, essentialism was the educational victor, in a sense, because the school was seen as the vehicle for social reform through higher standards and better classroom discipline. The 1970s were the transition years for a return to conservatism.

Human nature, it is believed, is basically the same everywhere—we all have the same needs, the same desires, and the same weaknesses. Consequently, the best education is a liberal education with emphasis on mathematics and language. Discretely organized content arranged in a sequential manner will enable the student, after 12 years of formal schooling, to function more effectively, personally and vocationally. The essentialists believe there is no better common denominator for a pluralistic society than a general or liberal education. Equality of educational opportunity is predicated on everyone receiving an equal chance to master the "essentials."

Progressivism

Although the so-called progressive viewpoint in education dates long before the twentieth century, as a *formal* movement in American education it is only about 70 years old. European educators such as Rousseau, Pestalozzi, Froebel, and Herbart had redirected educational thinking over a century and a half ago, but their ideas were not widely received until disciples popularized their "new" ideas in this century.

The public school has been strongly influenced by progressive theory and practice. Even though it is now formally a dead movement, its contributions live on because educators attempt to fit the curriculum to the perceived needs of children as well as to their immediate interests. This kind of philosophy is difficult to implement because the child is seen as a total organism (intellectually, socially, emotionally, physically, and spiritually) and each need must be addressed. It is a small wonder that progressive educators are vulnerable. Progressives often have broad social, political, and economic goals as well—the spectrum is diverse. One progressive educator may see the school's role as mainly curricular, whereas another may envision the school's function to effect political change. It is difficult to classify educators who espouse beliefs that relate to this philosophy of education. Some avoid the label because of stereotypes. Most "liberal" educators prefer more specific categories in terms of their beliefs.

The early American progressivists generally drew their sustenance from John Dewey. Dewey was a philosopher-educator at Teachers College, Columbia University, for most of his career. He saw education primarily in sociological and psychological terms: There is the society and there is the child. This is an ancient dualism, but no one fused the needs of both better than Dewey. He redefined democracy, the purposes of the school, and subject matter, and he clarified the needs of the child. He believed in both subject matter and student concerns, but some of his disciples overemphasized the latter and therein lay the problem.

Progressive education meant many things to educators and the public. The term almost escapes definition, but the movement became a formidable force despite its vagueness. It would have occurred even without John Dewey writing prolifically about the child, about democracy, about society, about experience, and so on. He provided the philosophical force, but someone else would have galvanized the movement if he had not. The wave of millions of immigrants, for example, from southern and eastern Europe after 1880 pressured the school to accommodate non-English-speaking children who were ethnically quite different from those children of northern and western European heritage.

About 1910, politicians, business leaders, journalists, union leaders, farmers, and settlement workers (social workers) all saw their particular cause potentially enhanced by the public school. The school, in a sense, could be a common denominator for social change or reform. The lay community was critical and insistent. However, in fairness to the educational bureaucracy, it was a difficult time. Teacher education was in its infancy; compulsory education brought new children to the schools, for example, minorities and exceptional children; resources were paltry; and paper work was voluminous. The school was under siege.

Lawrence A. Cremin, writing about progressive education as a movement from 1876 to 1955, defined it in the following manner. Progressive education meant

1. Enlarging the function of the school to incorporate concern for the quality of family and community life
2. Developing new techniques of teaching
3. Fitting the curriculum to the variety of children in the public school and
4. Diffusing culture among the populace without diminishing the value of that culture, specifically the sciences and the arts[2]

Progressive education is grounded in pragmatism, which is the belief that, if ideas have value, they must have a practical or "cash" value. The idea to be learned must be of personal use to the learner. Pragmatism is not a new view—it incorporates the concept of relativity of knowledge. Past facts or events are not "sacred" in themselves. Orthodox views and values are not accepted blindly. Experimental attitudes are valued in all areas of subject matter. Problem solving and objective or scientific methodology dominate in terms of approach.

In pragmatic terms, the student views the past only in relation to the present and future. He or she begins a particular topic of study wherever interest or need lies. This, of course, implies some teacher direction, but the student has a voice. Contemporary events may be a starting point for the student as the teacher tries to harness these events to relate past knowledge to the present, but there is to be no "forced feeding." The student must internalize or personalize what is learned if it is to be useful. The progressive educator is very much concerned about literacy, but the approach is different from that of the essentialist. Knowledge and methodology are repackaged to involve the learner to a greater degree.

Progressive education is best reflected by numerous theories and practices in both public and nonpublic schools. The list is significant:

1. The open classroom
2. Individualized instruction
3. Self-paced instructional materials
4. Grouping by needs and interests
5. Affective education
6. Problem-based curricula, such as themes focusing on the environment, social issues, and political questions
7. Vocational or career education
8. Counseling

9. Creative and social programs such as drama, school newspapers, and athletics
10. Special education

These representative innovations or theories are not solely the consequences of progressive thinking, but the emphasis on all facets of the child's welfare is the concern of the progressive educator. Intellectual growth should be viewed in context of social, emotional, and physical development; consequently, the school must address the "whole" child.

Minor Educational Philosophies

Perennialism

Perennialism is derived from the word "perennial" meaning "enduring, everlasting, or continuing." Educators who identify themselves as perennialists advocate a curriculum of timeless values and knowledge. They advocate a program of studies which is highly general, nonspecific in terms of specialization, and certainly nonvocational. These educators believe that, at least through grade twelve, and ideally through undergraduate school, the study of the liberal arts is the best vehicle to foster wisdom and morality, as Robert M. Hutchins advocated. Hutchins believed a thorough study of the liberal arts would enable a student to "get ready for anything." If he or she can read, write, and compute well and has had the formal opportunity to think about the great ideas of Western society, then life in all its manifestations will be enhanced. The student will be quite literate, will think about political, social, and economic issues, and will certainly possess the tools for vocational success. The student will be in complete possession of his or her talents and abilities.

Educational beliefs determine learning style.
(Ken Karp)

The "great books" of Western society constitute the curriculum because the student reads selected adult works arranged by epochs or eras. The works will be either abridged translations or original works whenever possible. There is much discussion of ideas and a great deal of written reaction to present themes and issues. Perennialists, like Hutchins and Mortimer Adler, have stressed that the great works of Western society were written for the common person, not for a chosen elite. Consequently, they believe that children need to be inducted into this Western heritage if they are to understand the world in which they live.

Perennialists are more educationally conservative than essentialists. Vocational skill and academic specialization are not the goals of formal study. Both strongly urge students to steep themselves in the liberal arts, but essentialists do not mind a major emphasis of study or even a broad selection of electives in general education. Essentialists will compromise on vocational education if the student shows no propensity for purely liberal study. Perennialists, however, believe that the student must be immersed in the "great conversation" with the past, which implies no specialization.

Although it is easy for a critic of such a philosophy to say that perennialism is inappropriate for public education, it cannot be easily swept away. Perennialism is a formidable point of view. When one looks at the education of the framers of the American Constitution, one sees a classical educational background. Not one of these Founding Fathers was educated in the "relevant" issues of his era. Each was immersed in Latin and Greek prose and poetry with a little science and mathematics to round off his secular curriculum. Catechism and Bible studies were also a major part of the student's formal schooling. When the Founding Fathers turned their rhetorical skills to the issues of their day, they were incisive. The esoteric debates and the *Federalist* papers are examples of how liberal studies can prepare people for democratic participation.

Perennialism is based in part on Aristotle's view that language and mathematics are the heart of formal education. Humans are by nature curious, and they are more alike than unlike in terms of needs and desires. Schooling should focus on those common needs and desires in order to make students more uniformly rational and moral.

Perennialism has been more characteristic of parochial and private education rather than public education. In a sense, it is related to the Thomistic philosophy of Thomas Aquinas (1225–1274), which undergirds Catholic education. Perennialism, as espoused by Hutchins and Adler, is a secular philosophy of education. The curriculum embodies absolute ideas and values, which help to develop both the character and the intellect. Truths are constant and must be discovered by the student.

Social Reconstructionism

As stated previously, perennialism is educationally more conservative than essentialism. Likewise, reconstructionism is more liberal than progressivism. On a continuum, perennialism and reconstructionism are drastically far apart. Social

reconstructionism originated in the fabric of progressive education, but its proponents envisioned the school as a lever for social, political, and economic reform
more than most progressives of the first half of this century. Since progressive
education meant many things in terms of theory and practice, social reconstructionism, as a result, also had legitimacy. It still has its adherents, such as Theodore
Brameld, but not as many as in the 1930s. Reconstructionists, such as George
Counts and Harold Rugg, saw the school truly as the lever for social reform. The
transmission of cultural heritage was not the major function of the school; rather
it was the reformation of society, specifically the reconstruction of American
society. These educational activists of the 1930s believed strongly that the age of
individualism was ending. An age marked by the integration of social life, collective planning, and control was beginning.[3]

Social reconstructionism emphasizes the connection between school and
community in facing problems that exist in the community. The school must work
to ameliorate the conditions of poverty, racism, and social injustices. The 60
prominent leaders of this movement in the 1930s were influenced by the Depression of that decade. They believed that very serious social and economic problems
existed which needed the prompt attention of educators. These problems, in part,
were as follows:

1. Science and technology were rapidly creating a sense of insecurity among the
   populace.
2. The drive for profit had over-shadowed the desire to engage in work for its
   own sake.
3. The quest for profit had distorted religious and moral teaching because personal gain was seen as an imperative in all endeavors.
4. Individualism reached a point whereby collective action seemed alien to the
   notion that material success should result in a social conscience.
5. Competition became so highly valued that social welfare was looked upon as
   an ideal based upon self-interest.
6. The capitalistic system tended to interfere with planning to control social
   conditions.
7. Political democracy was rapidly falling under the influence of industry; consequently, the majority view of the public was that those in control of industry
   should make the important decisions. Democracy became vulnerable to a
   growing cynicism.[4]

Naturally, not all progressives were this extreme in their view that the school
was the catalyst for social change. Those who espoused radical social reform,
however, believed enthusiastically in an activity-oriented curriculum. The school
was a miniature community wherein *real* issues were tackled whenever feasible.
Children were participants in life. Projects, problems, discussions, social criticism,
field trips, and so on, dominated the classrooms of those who wanted to instill in
children a critical or reconstructionist spirit. Naturally, this kind of radical educational philosophy kindled the wrath of the lay community who believed the

school's function was to reflect their will, not to change it. In other words, if society valued capitalism, competition, and so on, it certainly was not the professional's right to instill disdain for those beliefs. The American Legion, the National Association of Manufacturers, and the Daughters of the American Revolution, for example, became upset with the writing of many of the leading social reconstructionists of the 1930s.

In sum, not many educators today are practicing social reconstructionists even though some people believe public school teachers are either pawns in the hands of "social engineers" or "change agents" themselves. In a sense, most educators desire social change as a result of their teaching.

Existentialism

Existentialism is grounded in the belief that since each individual is responsible for his or her own fate, the student must develop to maximum potential in regard to ability and desires. This belief is different from other views that have roughly the same goal because individualism is stressed to a greater degree. The student selects much of the content to be studied and the manner in which skills are to be mastered. Individual projects and reflective thinking are crucial modes of learning.

Essentially, the curriculum is not structured or "laid out" by the teacher. A student's experiences form much of the direction for learning; however, the arts and the humanities usually become fertile fields for seeking self-fulfillment or expression.

The teacher and the student must develop an honest and open relationship, which is mutually reinforcing. Since the teacher does not impose adult authority or group values, there is a great deal of freedom, which is thought to develop self-discipline and direction. Not many public school teachers are practicing existentialists; however, school counselors and psychologists may lean strongly in this direction because they usually deal with personal and immediate needs or problems. Famous existentialists were Sören Kierkegaard (1813–1853) and Alexander Sutherland Neill (1883–1973).

Developing an Initial Educational Statement

Prospective teachers need to develop a systematic educational viewpoint. This viewpoint will change somewhat over the years. In other words, it will be a dynamic viewpoint, but the student's fundamental beliefs, the authors contend, will not substantially change. Experience will temper beliefs about grading or discipline, for example; however, the fundamental purpose of the school will probably remain the same in the mind of the prospective teacher for years. All teachers employ a philosophy of education. Some may "feel" their way along, reacting expediently to crises and tasks, while others will act more rationally and with direction. It is the hope of the authors in this chapter to stimulate more thought about educational purpose.

At this point, it will be beneficial to the prospective teacher to examine his or her beliefs. Students should now turn to Appendix A on page 369 and complete a self-scoring test on educational viewpoints before continuing.

The first major item a student should consider when thinking about any institution that calls itself a school (whether it be parochial, public, or private), is its societal purpose. The curriculum, discipline, classroom organization, and student performance all stem from the mission of the school. If prospective teachers consider this fact, then consistency in view is easier to develop.

The following outline may be helpful in composing a systematic attitude about formal education below the college level. The points embodied in this outline are cited by representative terms as *extreme* positions, with the conservative, traditional, or essentialist views mentioned first, and the experimental, pragmatic, or progressive views stated second. The student can more easily relate to the outline if two polarized positions are given because the student may find some value in one or the other viewpoint and, as a consequence, develop an eclectic position. Good schools, it is believed, embody philosophical diversity, so one's philosophy of education should be a genuine or personal one and not an attempt to please a school district or principal. A teacher's values will show, in time, by actions as well as by words. The outline follows:

I. School's purpose:
 1. "Intellectual" versus "socialization"
 2. "Transmission of the cultural heritage" versus "emphasis on societal problems and themes"
 3. "Transmission of permanent values" versus "focus on objective or scientific method"
II. Curriculum:
 1. Subjects—"liberal arts" versus "comprehensive curriculum"
 2. Organization of content—"prescribed" versus "needs" and "interests"
 3. Achievement—"3 R's" versus "experience"
 4. Individual differences—"group needs" versus "whole child"
 5. Transfer of training—"deferred value" versus "immediate value"
 6. Motivation—"adult stimulus" versus "child initiative"
 7. Classroom management—"adult rules" versus "rules by child and teacher collaboration"
III. Evaluation of student performance: "group norms" versus "individualized criteria"

Discussion of the preceding outline can provide context for the descriptive, representative terms included in each category. If the role or broad purpose of the school, be it public or non-public, is clear in the teacher's mind, most points will unfold naturally. Consistency of attitude is crucial.

If the school's purpose is mental growth, all other purposes are subordinated. The school's function is to make children as literate as possible by equipping them with academic skills to pursue further knowledge primarily in books. Accumulated knowledge must become part of each child's experiences through grade 12. Accompanying this literary heritage are time-tested values, such as a respect for free enterprise economic policy, law and order, truthfulness, honesty, and so on. What is strongly implied by this traditional or conservative view of the public school is that other facets of the child's life are delegated to the home, church, peer group, or other social institutions in the community. The school is only one institution, entrusted to impart knowledge. Any other purpose forces the school to exceed its mission.

The progressive practitioner, on the other hand, views his or her institution from the standpoint that the child is a total person, not a vessel into which information is poured. The child has social, intellectual, physical, emotional, and spiritual needs which the school must address. Socialization does not mean popularity with the peer group. It means self-reliance, respect for the rights of other people, and concern for the environment. In a sense, the well-socialized child may, at times, have to maintain an unpopular position. He or she will have to resist the peer group when the latter wants to exploit, to pollute, or to use alcohol or drugs. Self-reliance may mean temporary loneliness or unpopularity.

Teachers adhering to this more liberal view of the school seek to "round out" the student in order that all needs are addressed. Societal problems such as racism, sexism, pollution, crime, and so on, are issues that must be part of the curriculum if the school is to be a miniature society. These are typical issues that beset society at large; consequently, if children are to become problem solvers and participants, then the creative process must begin when they are young. Content is to be used, not stored for adulthood. The past must be relevant to the present. Problem solving implies using information from many sources to diagnose and remedy social ills.

Subject matter is reorganized so that a child sees the interrelatedness of home, community, and school. American history, for example, will include national shortcomings as well as successes. Science will embody social issues like environmental abuse. Literature will entail works on social criticism. Family life and sex education will permeate the curriculum; for example, topics such as death, divorce, child abuse, and sex education will be incorporated into English, physical education, biology, and social studies.

If a prospective teacher is progressive, then values must be viewed pragmatically. The only absolute value is the devotion to objective or scientific thinking. Orthodox anything is suspect. The past is not sacred. Social institutions and economic or political policies are analyzed, criticized, or supported by evidence. Social ritual is viewed anthropologically, not patriotically. Values become relative to time, location, and circumstance.

Naturally, one can see that progressive discipleship means rippling the waters at times. The community may be offended occasionally. The local school board must reflect lay interest and, when school philosophy clashes with vested interests in the community, conflict may occur. Parents or school patrons, for example, may not like the "humanistic" attitude of certain teachers or the stance of the school about creation science. School board philosophy and policy take precedence over a teacher's philosophy because, if the board determines that teachers cannot offer units on family life and sex education, then a teacher must live with that decision. There will still be enough freedom to influence children according to one's personal philosophy, but this does not mean the teacher has license to indoctrinate. Statutes, court decisions, and school board policies alter personal philosophy, but effective teachers integrate these forces into a consistent approach in the classroom. No one's philosophy should ever be completely modified by external forces. What happens in the classroom is profoundly influenced by the teacher's point of view.

Much attention has been given to the mission of the school. When a prospective teacher is clear about fundamental purposes, attitudes become cohesive. In considering the nature of the curriculum, the conservative position places emphasis upon the liberal arts. In the elementary grades, the fundamental processes of reading, writing, and computing are ingrained. The focus is on prerequisite skills. Books, workbooks, drill, memorization, and recitation are tools to learn the fundamentals well. Vocational skills and elective offerings are lower on the list of priorities than is traditional subject matter. Generally speaking, the liberal arts to the essentialist comprise the following specific subjects: English, history, mathematics, the sciences, and a foreign language. These subjects take priority. They are to be offered in specific form; that is, English is not "language arts," but composition and literature. Mathematics and the sciences are specific—for example, algebra, geometry, botany, physics, and so on. Mastery is viewed as in-depth study of nonvocational subject matter. Essentialists may accede to student or parental pressure concerning vocational or career education, but by no means will they say that vocational subjects are on a par with liberal studies.

The experimentalist or progressive educator articulates different views about the curriculum. The progressive teacher recommends a comprehensive curriculum. Liberal or general education is respected by the progressive teacher, but there is also concern for the practical arts and for career education. Equal respect is given to both liberal and vocational studies. If a student wants to take business courses, home economics, or electives, he or she is not dissuaded. General education is fused with student choices. Thus the school offers a buffet of subject matter and the student is given latitude to select. College preparatory and terminal needs are equally considered.

The essentialist states that students need to pursue skills in a step-by-step fashion. Prerequisite knowledge leads to more complex knowledge. Subject matter should be arranged chronologically and sequentially if understanding is to occur. Since children and adolescents do not fully know what their needs are, adults should lay out a prescribed curriculum that introduces students to the heritage in all its forms. Therefore, the curriculum is planned beforehand and the methodology is structured.

If a teacher is progressive, the organization of content is determined jointly with the student. The teacher remains aware of school district policies but allows more freedom in classroom activities. Questions, problems, issues, and themes in all subject areas are starting points. The teacher uses resources outside the classroom, as well as those within, to harness interest. The teacher attempts to diagnose student needs in order to lead students to higher academic and personal levels. For example, if a pupil seems interested only in automobiles, baseball, or rock music, the teacher tries to harness that specific interest through reading materials, science projects, art activities, and so on. In other words, there is very little in a child's life that does not have academic relevance. If the child sees connections between his or her immediate interests and those of the teacher, then learning has more meaning.

The concept of "achievement," the third point under the topic of Curriculum in our outline, is a complex one. To the essentialist or traditionalist, the meaning is clear. The use of textbooks, library materials, and teacher expertise will elevate students from the level of ignorance to awareness. Reading, especially, is a vicarious experience that enables students to become intellectually and emotionally involved with life. The child who can read well has a springboard to employment, to wise use of leisure, and to greater opportunity for social contact. The surest road to achievement is through relative mastery of reading, writing, and mathematical skills from kindergarten through grade 12. There is little time, the conservative educator believes, for deviation from a textbook approach to schooling or literacy. Projects, field trips, and so on may be enjoyable but, if overdone, can impede the process of education. Having fun does not necessarily mean getting an education.

The progressive educator, on the other hand, believes that the child must experience the ideas to be learned. Reading is surely a necessary skill, the progressive argues, but so are other activities. There are many avenues to the acquisition of knowledge and skills. The progressive places them all under the umbrella of "experience." Problem solving, field trips, projects, small-group work, media, conversations, and resource persons all provide opportunities for children to learn. Ideas, skills, and attitudes are obtained by a variety of methods. Reading, writing, and computing are certainly three ways to learn, but there are other approaches. The progressive teacher tries to integrate activities so that abstract ideas become internalized. Not all learning can be immediately personalized, but the more it is sought, the greater the benefit.

The next point in our preceding outline, "individual differences," has been a source of debate between conservative and liberal educators for a long time. Traditionalists have always maintained that humans are more alike than unlike and therefore should share common experiences. The school should offer a curriculum that enables everyone to share equally in appreciating our heritage as well as to have an equal chance in achieving material success. We live in a competitive world. Literate people have better opportunities for fuller and richer lives. If children are allowed to pursue mainly individual concerns, they may miss a chance to compete for a better life. Children are seldom aware of their long-range needs, so a liberal curriculum for all will best prepare each child for the future.

Because the progressive believes in curricular choices, the classroom approach will be different. The child is unique and has diverse needs—social, intellectual, physical, emotional, and spiritual. The curriculum must be adapted to the child. Each child will be at different levels of growth in every facet of life; consequently, group activities or instruction can be only a small part of the day's activities. Some group interaction is wholesome to acquire social skills, for example, but instruction is best carried out individually or in small flexible groups. The progressive teacher realizes that, in most schools, an elementary teacher is often in charge of over 20 children, and a secondary school teacher is in charge of one hundred or more students; consequently, it is impossible to totally individualize instruction. However, the goal to tailor instruction to individual needs is not scrapped by sheer numbers. The progressive teacher simply must work harder to garner instructional materials and human assistance to individualize instruction whenever possible. The needs of the "whole" child must be addressed on an individual basis.

The concept of transfer of training is also a controversial issue between conservative and liberal educators. The traditionalist educator believes that certain subject matter (the liberal arts) has inherent personal and vocational value to the learner, which will be valuable in the future. The student may not see immediately the value of certain studies but will at a later time. This is the idea of deferred value of knowledge. The teacher encourages the child to learn because the subject helps to prepare the student for life or for adulthood. An aspiring athlete, musician, or dancer, for example, may not understand why the coach or director requires drill, memorization, or selected skill exercises, but the "payoff" will come later when the student fits it all together. The teacher knows what is best because of experience.

Traditional teachers do not apologize for forcing children to memorize facts. Memorization will enable students to draw automatically upon information when the need arises to think about complex situations. If the student has to struggle with the multiplication tables, when the task at hand is reasoning about a "word" problem in arithmetic, then the student will be hampered. The child may be "pained" by drill and memorization, but appreciation will come later. Even Aristotle thought learning at times had to be painful.

The progressive, on the other hand, believes that subject matter has no automatic relationship or transfer value to life in general. Knowing, for example, a plethora of facts about the local, state, or federal government alone will not make one a good citizen. Studying mathematics extensively will not necessarily make one more reasonable. If the school wants people to be better citizens, or better managers of money, or simply more rational, then the teacher must plan realistic situations in which the student becomes a participant and makes judgments about concrete situations. Real problems in the student's life must be part of the curriculum. The more identical the variables within and outside school, the greater the transfer of knowledge.

The school, in other words, must utilize field trips, projects, discussion, and media to illustrate certain relationships. The student must see the meanings or principles of formal study before rote drill or memorization is undertaken. *Relevance* is a key word to the progressive educator because it shows the student the immediate value of any study. If relevance cannot be made obvious, the teacher must seek ways to make connections between the child's life and the purpose of the study. Naturally, this can be an awesome challenge for the teacher because some subject matter inherently has only long-range value. Association, however, between the child's world and the content to be learned should be a goal.

When a prospective teacher considers the idea of motivation as part of a philosophy of teaching, then certain variables emerge. The essentialist naturally believes the teacher should direct learning in terms of effort. This educator believes in general that "effort begets interest," not the reverse. Success breeds more success. In learning any subject, the reward is the mastery of the task at hand. There is no need for external payoffs such as candy, coupons, or free time because the goal of learning may become the acquisition of an external reward rather than the mastery of the content itself. Obviously, some privileges can accompany successful effort, but the student should not be imbued with the notion that learning has to have a tangible, external value. If learning is to be a lifelong process, then it must be pursued as an *end* in itself.

The "modern" or progressive teacher sees motivation differently from the traditionalist teacher. The progressive does not believe that learning must always be associated with external reward; however, learning must be useful if it is to be of value. Learning should be undertaken for its own sake *only* if the learner has the maturity to appreciate the practical use of the content. Many progressive educators recognize, however, that much required study at face value has little relationship to the child's experiences. Therefore, the pupil must be induced to study to reach a level of interest. Ideally, of course, interest will initiate effort in the learning process. Sadly, human nature frequently needs prodding. The more the teacher can motivate the student to accomplish an assignment, the more the student will get personally involved with the content. Any ethical means possible to motivate a student is permissible if the results are sustained effort and accomplishment. Rewards, privileges, and generous praise are basic methods to stimulate interest. Most teachers probably fall somewhere in the middle on this issue.

A teacher's view of classroom management and organization certainly reflects his or her philosophy of education. If the teacher subscribes to a conservative view of management, then rules are imposed upon children. The students adapt or conform to adult standards. Cooperation is rewarded and defiance is punished. This doesn't mean that the essentialist teacher is inhumane or indifferent to children's needs; rather, it implies that learning can take place only when there is order in the classroom. The essentialist believes it is easier to relax the enforcement of rules than to recapture teacher control because of neglect. Joint decision making between pupils and teachers has merit, but the teacher's authority takes precedence.

The progressive educator strongly endorses teacher-pupil consensus on this topic. If the school wants democratic participation, then classroom discipline must be somewhat permissive. Children involved with projects must at times be leaders or followers, and must have a voice in *how* learning is to be carried out. If everything flows from the teacher, then inevitably children remain passive. Students, the progressive believes, do not become creative upon reaching adulthood. They must be engaged in the learning process from an early age on. There should be no false division between work and play.

Enjoyment should accompany learning, so this may mean some noise and occasional "controlled chaos." Self-discipline is the ultimate goal of the progressive educator, who believes this is achieved chiefly by social interaction. The conservative educator believes, on the other hand, that inner freedom or control comes after the right habits and attitudes are imposed.

The classroom is limited by state laws and school district policies in terms of instructional time and subjects, but the day-to-day activities can still be influenced by the teacher. Students in progressive classrooms are given much latitude in directing their own learning. The teacher becomes more a facilitator of learning rather than an imparter of knowledge, skills, and attitudes.

Obviously, a progressive attitude requires support from the principal; planned freedom may mean occasional interference with the desires of other teachers or parents. It may appear to some that student involvement is equated with lowered standards. The teacher may seem to lack direction. Frankly, there is always a risk when teacher authority is withdrawn in order to encourage greater student self-discipline. This is why the teacher's philosophy must be understood and endorsed, especially by the principal. A board of education, as well, must also encourage instructional diversity if progressive views are to flourish.

The last major item on the preceding outline is the matter of evaluation of student performance. School board policy is crucial on this point, but there is some latitude for the teacher. If the teacher understands the mission of the school in which he or she instructs, then the idea of measuring student performance is clear. The conservative educational view stresses that since life is basically competitive, classroom activities should also be. People achieve social or personal worth largely by how well they compete with their peers on given tasks. The salesman, the doctor, the mechanic, and the musician all compete for their respective status. Performance is compared with the achievement of others.

The school is charged with making people literate; consequently, report cards must reflect academic growth predicated upon group norms. Conservative educators do not believe the "whole" child can be defined or identified, much less measured. What are the norms for emotional or social growth? The expertise of the teacher is academic, no more, no less! The teacher can competently reflect intellectual growth only in terms of how well one child performed comparatively with his or her peers. The report card, consequently, should embody letter marks, percentages, or numeral values. Comments are certainly appropriate. Anecdotal or incidental evaluations on citizenship, social skills, and so on, are necessary, but the heart of the report is the comparative, academic evaluation. Conferences are encouraged by the traditionalist teacher to clarify grades to both the student and parent, but conferences are never a good substitute for written reports of comparative progress.

The progressive educator must be consistent on the matter of reporting student progress if he or she is to be effective. If one believes the school serves as an agency for socialization, then reporting total progress is necessary. A teacher has to conform to the accepted school district or private school policy on reporting student progress if continued employment is desired, but there are ways to mitigate the severity of grades. Evaluation can be determined partly in terms of individual growth and potential. Comments and conferences can take on greater meaning and be more substantive relative to individual criteria. Growth is defined and measured in such areas as social and emotional development, even if it is by teacher and student judgment only. Intellectual achievement is judged in relation to the individual, not the group. Grades, therefore, become relative.

When possible, self-evaluation of achievement is encouraged. Pass or fail standards are instituted whenever school policy permits. The progressive does not want too much ritual to develop around grades. The subjective factors are more crucial. In the elementary school, substituting conferences for a report card at the second or third quarters of the school year is a good way to encourage parent-teacher contact. This implies ample time for discussion and planned comments. In other words, the progressive teacher attends to the child's many needs in a variety of ways.

Belief in the "whole" child means all his or her needs are on a continuum and, hence, deserve the attention of the school. It is only logical, then, to report progress or lack of progress to the student and to the parent. The progressive teacher stresses the importance of diagnosing and remediating the needs of the child. This often necessitates referral to other expert professionals, but teachers of the progressive mold are concerned with all facets of growth that influence intellectual development.

Consistency of educational view is clearly seen at the point of evaluating student performance. If a teacher articulates a progressive view of the school and then reflects only intellectual growth, inconsistency is evident. If subject matter mastery is seen as the top priority of the school, then competitively based report cards are the logical upshot of that view. The curriculum has to be designed to reflect the school's purpose.

Value of a Philosophy of Education

The authors have stressed in this chapter the value of a consistent attitude about several broad themes concerning schooling. This attitude will certainly be tempered by experience; that is, it will be dynamic, but fundamental positions will not be drastically modified. Prospective teachers, for example, may believe ardently that classroom management should be determined by a highly democratic process, but they may find, in the first few years of teaching, that strong authority is called for in certain situations. This does not imply that the teacher's view at the time is inconsistent with his or her attitude about the mission of the school. It simply says that experience partially modifies one's educational position.

A teacher also may change positions philosophically about methodology because a certain approach may not be effective with a particular child or group of children. Consequently, instruction must be modified. This is flexibility, not inconsistency. A philosophy of education, in other words, is a statement of attitude that offers general direction, not a mold for daily behavior. The authors believe, however, that a general position about the school's purpose will change little over the years. The value of consistent thinking about educational purpose gives the prospective teacher the chance to reflect upon the importance of one's subject area or grade level.

The authors recently surveyed over 40 public school districts in the St. Louis area about their employment applications for teachers. Of the approximately 40 districts, only a few required a written philosophy of education to accompany the application for employment. In those few, the candidates were asked to relate their philosophies to that of the districts, not necessarily to obtain agreement, but to indicate if the applicants had ever given serious thought to educational purpose.

Even though few school districts in this selected metropolitan area required written statements concerning a philosophy of education, perusal of the employment applications clearly indicated that philosophical questions were posed in an indirect manner. The following representative questions were asked on the respective employment applications:

1. What are the most important ways a teacher can help students?
2. What single factor do you consider most conducive to learning in the classroom?
3. If you could teach one thing to your students, what would that be?
4. If you were employed as a teacher in this district, what skills and personal qualities would you bring to your assignment to ensure a successful teaching experience?
5. Why do you wish to teach here?[5]

Personnel directors and principals are usually the individuals who do the hiring. Their interviews are often "loaded" with philosophical queries. Questions about mainstreaming the disabled, classroom discipline, the importance of teaching, grades, the educational role of parents and students, and so on are always on the agenda of open-ended questions in the interviews. Administrators are not seeking finished or polished responses from candidates; rather, they want to see if prospective teachers have ever given much thought to what education is about. They are also seeking compatibility of purpose between that of the school principal and faculty with whom the candidate will work. This does not imply that the principal seeks total conformity. It means that educational goals can hopefully be cooperatively pursued even though values may differ.

In many preservice teacher-education programs involving clinical experiences (especially student teaching), students are asked to express in writing their attitudes about a number of educational questions to facilitate clinical placement. If a student is direly opposed to an unstructured open classroom, such placement may be harmful to children as well as to the student teacher. Written position statements can also foster better communication between the clinical supervisor and the student teacher. Many directors of student teaching have expressed the view that written philosophies of education can help to synthesize preservice preparation for teaching. The philosophy of education should be written prior to student teaching and reexamined during and after the semester or quarter in which the clinical experience occurred.

Here are some practical suggestions based upon the authors' past experience about composing a philosophy of education. The following points may be helpful in formulating the statement:

1. Type your viewpoint in essay form, using the outline offered in this chapter as a mental guide only. The paper should be double-spaced and no more than two pages in length.
2. The first paragraph of your philosophy should embody comments about the purpose of the school in general. The remaining paragraphs can encompass comments about the curriculum you plan to teach.
3. Do not let the philosophy sound *too* formal. It must be personal and genuine.
4. Avoid terms that may be foreign to others, such as *progressivism*, *essentialism*, and *socialization*. Express your ideas with as little terminology as possible.
5. State your views in a positive way. It is better to say what you advocate and let the reader infer what you do not support.
6. Avoid sexist language, but do not overdo the use of "he" or "she." It is better to substitute synonyms such as "pupil," "person," and so on.
7. Let the draft of your paper "sit awhile." Proofread it for corrections and ask someone to do the same. Repeat this process as often as you need in order to perfect the statement. Make sure the paper is free of typing, spelling, and grammatical errors. Good quality typing paper is a must for the sake of appearance. This statement reflects much about you and your university.

A final point should be made about the practical value of possessing a systematic view of schooling. In almost every public and non-public high school, about every seven years, an accreditation process takes place. There are six regional accreditation associations that examine and validate programs in secondary schools, universities, and colleges across the country. The process for such accreditation usually occurs in the following manner: The high school faculty and administrators spend a year of introspection concerning their educational purpose and how that mission is met. They write rationales, collect and organize data, and compile both qualitative and quantitative information.

Following this year of introspection, the school then invites a team of educators representing the respective areas. The total group can sometimes number up to 50 people. The team is organized to represent all aspects of the school, from physical plant, to subject areas, to the administration, as well as to the students themselves. Some examination is undertaken of the school district at large, but it is the specific high school that is under scrutiny.

The field team usually examines the school's philosophy of education carefully on the first day of the three-day visit. The team wants to know if "what they say is what they do." There is no intent to make liberals, conservatives, or eclectics out of the faculty even though recommendations may ultimately push the school in certain philosophical directions. The team cites strengths, weaknesses, and concerns and formulates recommendations during the three days. This visit occurs after careful study of the compiled report of the one-year self-study. The visit validates what the report embodies. The school is studied literally in every facet, from basement to roof.

Philosophy has practical meaning as seen by our discussion of accreditation. Faculty and administrators develop their educational rationale. They examine their strengths and weaknesses and then ask disinterested experts to critique their views. Philosophy of education is the crucial part of the whole process. If future teachers learn to articulate their views early, then writing a philosophy of education will be no alien experience. The format of writing may vary, but the substance is basically similar in form.

Summary

This chapter presented information on essentialism, progressivism, perennialism, social reconstructionism, and existentialism. Since most schools have reflected essentialism and progressivism in educational theory and practice over the years, more attention was given to these two views. Actually, most teachers today are eclectic because they see value in parts of both extreme views. In order to be systematic, it is necessary to know something of other positions before a personal philosophy is developed.

Implications for Future Teachers

Teacher-educators strive to inculcate prospective teachers with a sense of purpose about their future work. This purpose is vital only if it includes a view about the mission of the school, the nature of the curriculum needed to fulfill that mission, and the ways in which achievement can be assessed, especially in regard to the learner. Prospective teachers cannot develop a realistic philosophy of education by reading and thinking alone. A philosophy must be "tested" by observation, simulation, and practice in field and clinical experiences. The university and the school district must share the responsibility for developing teachers who are imbued with purpose, who are morally responsible, and who are well-informed professionals.

Discussion Questions

1. Define the following terms: essentialism, progressivism, perennialism, existentialism, and social reconstructionism. Differentiate among these philosophies of education.
2. Summarize briefly the differences between educational essentialism and progressivism in terms of the following criteria: mission or purpose of the school, type of curriculum both at the elementary and secondary school levels, attitude about classroom organization and management, and attitude about reporting student progress.
3. Cite examples of how a philosophy of education can be useful in a teacher's career.
4. List several important practical points in writing a philosophy of education. Be sure to consider length of statement, appearance, and so on.

Notes

1. William C. Bagley, "An Essentialist's Platform for the Advancement of American Education," *Educational Administration and Supervision* 24 (April 1938): 241–56.
2. Lawrence A. Cremin, *The Transformation of the School* (New York: Vintage Books, 1961), viii–ix.
3. Harold Rugg, *Foundations for American Education* (New York: World Book Co., 1947), 580.
4. W. H. Kilpatrick, ed., *The Educational Frontier* (New York: The Century Co., 1933): 54–58.
5. Paul D. Travers, "An Analysis of Teacher Employment Applications," unpublished, 1991.

Recommended Readings

Bagley, William C. "An Essentialist's Platform for the Advancement of American Education." *Educational Administration and Supervision* 24 (April 1938): 241–56.

Buxton, Thomas H., ed. *The Many Faces of Teaching.* Lanham, Md.: University Press of America, 1987.

Carnegie Task Force on Teaching as a Profession. *A Nation Prepared: Teachers for the 21st Century.* New York: Carnegie Corporation, 1986.

Cooper, Jed Arthur. *Clifton L. Hall: Eloquent Essentialist.* Minneapolis, Minn.: Burgess International Group, Inc./Alpha Editions, 1988.

Cooper, Jed Arthur. *Exemplars in Educational Philosophy.* Minneapolis, Minn.: Burgess International Group, Inc./Alpha Editions, 1988.

Cremin, Lawrence A. *The Transformation of the School.* New York: Vintage Books, 1961.

Dewey, John. *Democracy and Education.* New York: Macmillan Co., 1916.

Dewey, John. *Experience and Education.* New York: Macmillan Co., 1938.

Holmes Group. *Tomorrow's Teachers: A Report of the Holmes Group.* East Lansing, Mich.: Holmes Group, 1986.

Morris, Van Cleve. "Progressive Education." *CBE Bulletin* V (November 1960): 6–8.

Chapter 5

School Organization and Curriculum

Curricular change in America since the colonial period has been reflected by a variety of educational agencies. A history of curriculum in this country is a history of education. Each generation builds upon and modifies the curriculum it inherits. In this chapter we will look chiefly at what is historically considered to be elementary and secondary education. It may be helpful (1) to survey several examples of national and state influences upon the curriculum, (2) to consider several historic events which helped to shape the curriculum below the college level, (3) to look at some "modern" ideas about the curriculum, and (4) to survey the impact of the computer upon elementary and secondary curricula.

Curriculum is defined in two major ways. It can be a program of studies, a collection of courses at a specific educational level; or it can be more broadly viewed as all the experiences a child or youth has in educational institutions. This last point would include not only required subjects of study but also the creative and informal experiences the student encounters. The authors feel that curriculum has greater meaning than just a list of subjects a school offers. Intramurals, counseling, and interest clubs, for example, are all integrally related to a child's well-being and, consequently, must be considered part of the curriculum.

As discussed in Chapter 4, a teacher's philosophy of education is played out in the implementation of the curriculum. Curricular activity is really philosophy in action. When patterns of curriculum are discussed shortly, it will be easy to detect points of view among the various advocates about the nature of the child, the purpose of study, and educational methods. The teacher implements his or her philosophy in selecting content within broad limits and decides how to transmit and measure that content. The teacher also works under the umbrella of other philosophies, most directly that of the principal and the board of education. There is still, however, much latitude for professional choice because if a teacher is educationally conservative, liberal, or eclectic, such views will be felt by the children in one way or another. Teachers, in other words, work within a legal framework shaped by state law and the local school board. That framework is further influenced chiefly by local administrators, parents, and teachers. Philosophies of education converge at various points along the way. The teacher's attitude, however, affects learning.

Some National Influences on the Curriculum

Public school curricula are established in context of social and political events at national, state, and local levels. For example, when vocational education became a national concern over 70 years ago, state legislatures enacted vocational programs to parallel those initiated by the federal government. High schools, in turn, reflected that interest by incorporating formal study in agricultural science and practical arts. Students who had no immediate interest in attending college could now learn salable skills before graduating from high school, or they could plan to pursue such practical endeavors in higher education. Subsequent federal legislation through the 1960s strengthened or spawned many opportunities: distributive education, cooperative education, and work-study programs. These, in turn, stimulated state supplementary legislation, which similarly prompted changes in high school curricula. Not only were programs of study modified, but the entire view of the schools was altered. Not all students participated, of course, in these programs, but the schools began to serve a broader number of students. Many schools, as a result, became more comprehensive.

Career education, another example, also has its roots in the progressive philosophy of the early twentieth century. It reached its zenith in the 1960s and 1970s, but it has strong ties with much of this early federal interest in vocational education. Career education embodies content which helps elementary school children develop a greater awareness of and respect for all types of occupational endeavors and which assists older youth to select careers in accordance with their abilities and interests. Obviously, career education is broader than learning technical skills for employment only. Fifteen occupational clusters undergird the meaning of career education. It may help an individual to see the need for higher education to decide upon a career, as well as to consider more immediate training or education for employment purposes. The vocational and career impetus in education developed at the national level stimulated change at the state and local levels. Both the program of studies and educational climate at the local level were modified drastically.

Examples are numerous of how curricula in elementary and secondary schools are modified greatly by national concerns. Consider how Sputnik, following its launch in 1957, stimulated the development of more intensive study in mathematics, the sciences, and foreign languages in most of America's schools. The United States at that time felt inferior to the Soviet Union in the space race. The remedy was perceived to be curricular reform. The 1960s witnessed great zeal in rewriting curriculum at all levels. It was the decade of curricular change and innovation.

Social studies, for example, felt the winds of curricular revision at the national level. Organized knowledge, analysis, inquiry, discovery, and so on, all became topics of research among social studies educators. Pupils and students were encouraged to think like social scientists. They were "doing social science" in the classroom. What spurred even more intense interest in social studies curricula during this period were events occurring outside the school, namely, the civil rights movement and the Vietnam War. Citizenship, or the making of a good citizen, was being rethought. The field of social studies was in ferment.

Other areas of the curriculum were also undergoing structural change in the 1960s. The National Science Foundation was instrumental in initiating reform in mathematics. Content was viewed in terms of its structure and was pushed downward into the grades. Consequently, some students may now be exposed to mathematical areas such as statistics, algebra, and calculus much earlier. Discovery, reasoning, and theory are commonplace themes in mathematics in schools below the college level.

The science curriculum has been changed considerably. Jerome Bruner, a leading psychologist, along with colleagues from several disciplines initiated an inquiry approach. The sciences were especially affected. Ecology, genetics, and evolution, for example, became prominent themes in biological study. The student acts as scientist in his or her inquiry. Science curricula were rewritten and what emerged received much fanfare. The Biological Science Curriculum Study (BSCS) became a very popular scientific program. The Physical Science Study Committee also gained acclaim.[1]

Other national groups were also advocating curricular change during this post-Sputnik period. The Association for Supervision and Curriculum Development has a record of constructive work in suggesting curriculum projects. Also, the Council for Basic Education has always been an advocate of improving standards and substance in all school curricula. The National Education Association has been another catalyst for realistic reform of the curriculum from preschool through grade 12. All of these groups represent a national effort to increase learning in the classroom.

While content was given greater priority among some curriculum planners on one end of the continuum, advocates at the other extreme emphasized concern for emotional factors, value development, and personal attributes in organized school experiences. Open education, a theory known to earlier American progressive educators, had taken root well in England and was given increased publicity in that country during the 1960s. As a result, "openness" became more characteristic of many American schools. Individualized curricula, with much attention given to non-gradedness, open space facilities, a deemphasis on grades, and flexibility in the acquisition of content, all began to permeate many schools below the college level during the 1960s. Some school districts even attempted to fit the curriculum to the child to a greater degree by building open space schools with movable walls to facilitate flexible grouping patterns, team teaching, and greater spontaneity in planning activities. Consequently, philosophical clashes occurred among all involved in curriculum construction over the next 20 years, resulting in the present swing of the educational pendulum back toward more structured content and activities. The pendulum has a tendency to swing periodically in educational philosophy. Open education will have a resurgence at some point in the future.

In this discussion of national influences upon the curriculum, one more item should be cited before the topic is concluded. The recent rash of national reports still has to be measured in terms of respective impacts. One report, however, has had its "trickle down" influence upon public education, although its thrust was primarily focused upon the high school. That report, of course, was the 1983 *A Nation at Risk* by the National Commission on Excellence in Education. Some of its recommendations have been politicized, for example, merit pay, but overall the report has triggered much genuine curricular change at the state and local levels. There is more discussion at all levels about the "new basics" (English, mathematics, the sciences, the social studies, foreign language, and computer instruction) than has taken place in over 25 years. There is much more concern for specifying objectives for learning, for mastery in learning and teaching, and for effective testing. A mastery of the English language is central to much of the reform movement in curriculum, whereas more homework is urged for all students.

Some recommendations may go unheeded, such as the length of the school day (to seven hours) and school year (to 200–220 days per year); however, the heart of the report has been taken seriously. It is safe to say that for the next few years, at least, numerous educational discussions, at some point, will include the recommendations of *A Nation at Risk*. It will rank as a significant historical benchmark. Furthermore, while not directly related to the curriculum as such, career ladders for teachers have been stimulated by the report because merit pay was endorsed. Presently, this concept is reflected in the growing number of statewide teacher career ladders. The nation was shaken out of its lethargy in 1983. It is good to witness greater public interest in education. Much of this public involvement will be productive. An annotated list of representative national studies and reports may be found in Appendix B.

Some State Influences on the Curriculum

The Tenth Amendment of the U.S. Constitution is the conduit by which the states take control of public education:

> *The powers not delegated to the United States by the Constitution, nor prohibited by it to the States, are reserved to the States respectively, or to the people.*

Since control of public education is decentralized, the various state legislatures through their state departments set curricula for the public schools. School districts add to the basic structure set by the legislature and state department, but they must adhere to the framework established for them. The local boards of education are the fingers of the state at the local level. Power is delegated to them by the state. It can be rescinded if necessary. Determining curriculum is one of those duties a local board must administer well to ensure equality of educational opportunity. Table 5-1 displays a common state program of studies for public schools from kindergarten through grade 12. It is assumed that the course offerings in this table are those of the best school districts in terms of a quality program. It should be noted further that computer science is not listed as available for formal credit as it is in some states; however, the computer as a tool for learning is being integrated with subject offerings throughout the curriculum from kindergarten through grade 12.

The examples of curriculum in Table 5-1 for the various levels do not reflect all that the school district is charged to undertake. Special education and pupil services, such as counseling and testing, are always available. In addition, cocurricular and creative activities provide intellectual, physical, and social well-roundedness in youth. It is hoped by providing this type of curriculum that not only basic academic skills will be ingrained, but also the student will develop a better sense of career direction and greater maturity.

State departments of education and local school districts publish manuals, usually called curriculum guides, to assist teachers in better understanding the philosophy and organization of the components of the curriculum. Every subject in the curriculum has an accompanying guide that usually embodies detailed information about the goals, objectives, competencies, and instructional activities for each grade or subject level. These curriculum guides are indispensable to the teacher and should be perused frequently by prospective teachers even prior to student teaching. These guides, of course, cannot substitute for textbooks, but they provide direction for the teacher. Theory and practice blend well in the better guides. Practitioners themselves are often the authors of these manuals. Because of the growing cost of facsimile reproduction, now there are companies that reproduce these guides on microfiche. Students and teachers can avail themselves of a broader range of material. Storage is becoming a problem for many libraries, so the use of microfiche is a good remedy.

In the present climate of curricular reform at the state level, teachers can expect a greater number of initiatives to improve formal learning experiences for children and youth. Most states are upgrading standards for graduation from high school; more English, mathematics, science, and social studies units will be required for graduation. Proficiency or competency tests also are becoming a fact of life from the primary grades on. There has been some controversy surrounding skills tests in terms of grade promotion and graduation; however, it seems that the use of these state-mandated tests will be tied more and more to receiving credit at least in the basic skills courses. In other words, if a student cannot pass the various parts of a state examination, then he or she may not be considered competent to receive credit for related courses or subjects. In fact, testing is going to have far-reaching effects upon the prestige of the district. Teachers especially will be judged by the instructional "output" of their students. While this may not

TABLE 5-1 Public School Curricula and Allotted Time[2]

Level	Minimum Allotted Time
Prekindergarten (parent education and screening)	
Kindergarten	174 days, 522 hours (one-half day receive 25 minutes daily in art, music and physical education)
Grades 1–6 (1–8 self-contained) (language arts, reading, writing, speaking, spelling, and listening) mathematics science social studies health (also drug, alcohol, and AIDS education) art music physical education	locally developed schedules adopted by local boards of education 50 minutes per week
Junior High/Middle Grades 5–9 language arts, mathematics, science and social studies physical education and health/safety OR physical education and health/safety combined OR physical education and health/safety visible in required courses OR integrated in block scheduling art and music four additional courses available (speech, agriculture, home economics, industrial technology, foreign language, computer literacy, and developmental reading)	900 minutes per week in the aggregate 2 periods per week 1 period per week 3 periods per week 2 periods per week adjusted time above 1500 minutes per year each class 1500 minutes per year
Grades 7 and above U.S. and Missouri Constitutions, history and institutions, includes instruction and examination	instruction and examination
High School (Grades 9–12) English/language arts/communication foreign language (must be 2 units of one language) social studies (American, world history, government, and geography) mathematics (algebra, geometry, trigonometry, calculus, and math analysis) science (biology, chemistry, and physics) fine arts (art and music)	40.5 units of credit offered* 6 units 2 units 5 units 4 units 4 units 2 units

TABLE 5-1 *Continued*

Level	Minimum Allotted Time
vocational education (at least four occupational programs)	12 units
physical education	1 unit
health (also drug, alcohol and AIDS education)	1/2 unit
practical arts (nonvocational education)	4 units

*A unit of time is usually 45–50 minutes per day, five days a week, for one school year. Students in every state must take 20–25 units to graduate.

seem entirely fair because of the numerous variables involved in successful learning, it is nevertheless going to be a widespread reality.

Historic Development of Curriculum

In the following section on curriculum below the college level, it may be helpful to survey the types of educational agencies that have characterized educational opportunity in America since the colonial period. In Table 5-2 there is a tabulation of the most representative institutions of the periods cited. The purpose for this listing of agencies is to show not only how curriculum changed, but how educational opportunity was also enlarged. Higher and adult education are included on the chart to show continuity from preschool through adulthood.

Curriculum in the colonial period was classical. Those boys from the upper socioeconomic levels who desired careers in law, medicine, theology, or commerce certainly had to be well grounded in Latin and have some knowledge of Greek. Higher education set the curriculum for its feeder level, namely, the Latin grammar school or the institution of private tutoring. Since Latin was the medium of instruction in all of higher education in colonial America, it became the language of instruction for younger boys who were destined for social prominence. Latin denoted elitism because regardless of how capable a poor boy might be, he had a slim chance to attend college. Girls had only the remote possibility of some academic tutoring by an enlightened parent.

The New England dame school (boys and girls, ages 3 through 7 years), in addition to instilling rudimentary English skills, also provided beginning Latin to wealthy boys or those of professional promise. Latin was also inherent in the curriculum of the seven- to eight-year Latin grammar school. Boys in the Southern Colonies received a parallel curriculum from tutors in order that they could attend William and Mary or study abroad at Oxford or Cambridge. Latin, in other words, was the key to curricular content. It shaped preschool through higher education in almost all of colonial America. The exception occurred in the parochial school of the Middle Colonies because there the ethnic language was the

TABLE 5–2 Major Educational Agencies (Period of Widespread Public Acceptance)

Colonial Period	Revolution to Civil War	Civil War to World War I***	World War I to Present
Home Education (0–21)* M, F**	District School (6–13 or 14) M, F	Kindergarten (5) M, F	Preschools, etc. (6 weeks–4) M, F
Dame School (3–7) M, F	Common School (7–13) M, F	Common School (7–13) M, F	Kindergarten (5) M, F
Apprenticeship (7–21) M, F	Home Education (0–21) M, F	Parochial School (6–13) M, F	Elementary School (5–10 or 13) M, F
Latin Grammar School (7–15) M	Tutoring (7–15) M	Junior High School (13–14) M, F	Middle School (9–14) M, F
Tutoring (7–15) M	Academy (7–15) M	High School (14–17) M, F	Junior High School (13–14 or 15) M, F
Parochial School (6–13) M, F	Parochial School (6–13) M, F	Junior College (18–19) M, F	Parochial School (6–13) M, F
College (16–19) M	College (16–19) M	College (18–21) M, F	High School (14–17) M, F
		Normal School (18–20) M, F	College (18–21) M, F
			Adult Education (21 on) M, F

*Approximate age of child, youth
**Sex of student
***Education for ages 6 to 16 becomes compulsory for both sexes

medium of instruction. College often was not desired by boys of those diverse religious sects found in the Middle Colonies.

Outside Pennsylvania, Delaware, and parts of New York, most people of lesser social rank in colonial America spoke English while in school or during vocational training. Reading the New Testament and related religious material in English was a practical and necessary activity in New England. Similarly, apprenticeship training for destitute children in the Middle and Southern Colonies carried with it the need to instill some skill in English in order for children to acquire craft or artisan status. Of course, in the Middle Colonies, the New Testament was the core of the content in the parochial school, but it was studied in French, German, Dutch, or Swedish, for example. Language diversity was greatest in such colonies as Pennsylvania, New Jersey, Delaware, and New York.

Materials for learning were scarce in most of colonial America. Children learned to read using adult books imported from Europe. It was definitely a period of children adapting to a set curriculum—they were viewed as little adults preparing for an adult world. Some reading materials, however, were made for children, especially in New England. *The New England Primer* was popular because it contained the alphabet, selected prayers, the catechism, and rhyming religious and secular couplets that conveyed moral messages. The hornbook, another useful tool for learning, was literally a transparent animal horn covering wood with printed prayers and the alphabet on it. These materials reflected the strong religious motivation in the early curriculum. The use of the Bible, catechism, and Psalter also reinforced this fact. Generally speaking, materials for children were not widespread until after the Revolution when spellers, arithmetic texts, geography books, readers, and history texts began to appear in larger numbers throughout the states.

At the secondary school level (a school using Latin as the spoken and written language) textbooks were usually the classics. Ezekiel Cheever's *Accidence*, however, was a popularly used textbook during the colonial period in learning Latin grammar. But textbooks for youth were as rare in the Latin grammar school as they were in other schools.

Readers became more common in the nineteenth century. Growing secularism, nationalism, and an increased interest in childhood itself, stimulated largely by such Europeans as Jean J. Rousseau, Johann Pestalozzi, and Robert Owen, helped to advance the cause of childhood directly and the use of better reading materials indirectly. One tends to think only of William H. McGuffey and his series of six eclectic readers when reading is thought of in the nineteenth century. The fact is, however, that there were other successful readers before and during the life of the McGuffey readers. Approximately 60 million youth learned to read (or tried to) using the McGuffey series between 1836 and 1920. This graded series was phonetic in approach, used abridged content from traditional literature, controlled new words, used diacritical marking, and embodied rules for reading. It truly helped to mold the common school into grades or levels.

Before McGuffey got a foothold on the market, however, other readers had appeared. Noah Webster's blue-backed *American Spelling Book* (1783) was both a speller and reader and replaced in many regions *The New England Primer*. Also his *The Little Reader's Assistant* (1790) was well received. Caleb Bingham's *American Preceptor* (1794) was a graded reader and considered an advanced reading book. Patriotic literature was in much of the reading material for children, which consequently helped to instill a nationalistic spirit. These texts were but a few of the materials available in reading during this period.

In arithmetic, Warren Colburn's *First Lessons in Arithmetic on the Plan of Pestalozzi* (1821) helped to place arithmetic in the curriculum. Mental arithmetic became highly fashionable subsequent to 1821. Geography also gained legitimacy by the use of such well-received texts as Jedediah Morse's *Geography* (1784) and his *Elements of Geography* (1795). Samuel Goodrich's *Peter Parley's Method of Telling about Geography* (1829) combined pictures, maps, and diagrams and became an instant best-seller. History, too, got a boost; both Goodrich's *A History of the United States* (1822) and Webster's *History of the United States* (1832) became widely used and even helped to stimulate the study of civics in the common schools.[3]

The common school curriculum was certainly influenced by materials of this kind. Content was organized by difficulty, which helped to classify children by age and ability. With so many texts now making their way into American life, the curriculum of the common school was crystallizing. Reading, spelling, arithmetic, geography, history (civics), and eventually nature study were to form a core of studies in the elementary school. Today, over forty major publishers produce materials for these core areas. As a result of this crystallization, grade levels would soon appear. The educational ladder began to extend upward to the high school, which mushroomed in growth during the last quarter of the nineteenth century. Compulsory education, however, did not become a reality until well after the Civil War.

The secondary school curriculum changed drastically in the nineteenth century because Latin and Greek lost their stranglehold on the curriculum. Reading, writing, geography, arithmetic, bookkeeping, history, English grammar, and the U.S. Constitution were an integral part of the curriculum before the Civil War. Of course, college preparatory studies were also included, for example, the classics, but their prominence was challenged by new studies. Toward the end of the nineteenth century, the high school was lengthened to include grade 12. It included more options and began to look like the modern comprehensive high school which today includes general and vocational programs. College preparatory and terminal curricula were reflected in the high schools by the end of the century. Laboratories and field work also became intertwined with specific programs in science, home economics, manual arts, and agricultural study.[4] In other words, the high school became less bookish and more pertinent to daily life, especially for those not pursuing a preparatory program for college.

Committees of the National Education Association (NEA) in the 1890s were instrumental in advancing the curricula of both the elementary and high schools. It is important to take a brief look at the results of their work because schools at both levels have been influenced profoundly. First, the NEA Committee of Fifteen (1893 to 1895), pertaining to elementary education, should be considered. The report dealt with teacher education, the program of studies, and the organization of urban schools. Teachers, it was assumed, were not born but made, which implied the need for a thorough grounding in academics, child growth and development, and methods of teaching. The curriculum, furthermore, should represent the major branches of knowledge, organized in such a way to fit the child's psychological, intellectual, and social levels. The curriculum would appear thus:

1. Language
2. Arithmetic
3. Geography
4. History
5. Natural sciences
6. Drawing
7. Vocal music
8. Physical culture
9. Physiology
10. Hygiene
11. Manual training for boys (upper grades)
12. Sewing and cooking for girls (intermediate and upper grades)[5]

Content was to be correlated as frequently as possible. This was consistent with the methodology of that period. Correlation of content was fashionable among followers of Johann Herbart, a German philosopher who had died about fifty years earlier. His theories were promulgated in the 1880s in the German universities. It is interesting to note the similarities between the subjects on the preceding list with those subjects cited in Table 5-1.

The NEA Committee of Ten on Secondary School Studies (1892 to 1893) was another committee of far-reaching influence and controversy. It originated in an era of mental discipline that grew out of the old notion of faculty psychology that the mind is composed of a series of compartments, each compartment capable of being trained by drill, memorization, and repetition. This prompted the belief that formal study should focus in depth on few subjects. A wave of criticism ensued. Some educators believed that the high school curriculum should be a buffet of offerings to help the student explore content.

The Committee of Ten ushered in an era of college dominance. Better articulation between college and high school had been needed. Secondary schools, it was expressed, should not exist to prepare youth for college alone, but those who desired to go should be encouraged. The more practical subjects of art, music, manual training, and commercial subjects, however, were slighted, because the assumption was that those subjects which prepare a student for college also prepare the individual best for the challenges of practical life. A classical or liberal curriculum, it was believed, would be good for everyone.

While recommending that admission requirements become more flexible to enter college, there still remained an inflexibility about the proposed curricula.

The committee outlined four courses of study, namely, classical, Latin-scientific, modern language, and English. As a result, Latin and Greek were dropped in most colleges and universities; one could gain access to higher education without skill in either language; however, the emphasis obviously was still on traditional subjects of study. The high schools literally became subservient to colleges and universities.[6]

Another report of widespread value also directly resulted from the effort of the NEA Committee of Ten. In 1895 a Committee on College Entrance Requirements was formed, commonly entitled the Committee of Thirteen, which actually was created to implement the proposals of the earlier Committee of Ten. In 1899, the recommendations of the Committee of Thirteen were published. In brief, the assumptions of the earlier Committee of Ten were supported, but what was now new was the idea of "constants" required for college entrance: four units in foreign languages, two units in mathematics, two in English, one in history, and one in science. A number of electives would complement these required units.[7]

The concept of a unit gained support in 1910 when the Carnegie Foundation defined high school as an institution requiring sixteen units of study; each unit of credit was given for a class meeting five periods per week for 120 clock hours per year. The Carnegie unit has since become standardized with some variation on the amount of time required for credit. Obviously, the unit idea is still inherent in the organization of the high school and the recommendations of the Committee of Thirteen also have a familiar look to them in context of the 1983 *A Nation at Risk*.

Another NEA commission, created in 1913, had a lasting impact upon the way in which the curriculum has evolved over the years. The Commission on the Reorganization of Secondary Education labored diligently between 1913 and 1921, publishing thirteen reports on a variety of traditional content areas including moral values and guidance. In 1918 the commission's *Cardinal Principles of Secondary Education* appeared and marked the beginning of a new era. Society at this time was changing rapidly. World War I was bringing the United States into interdependence with other nations; technology was creating new knowledge; immigration, especially from southern and eastern Europe, became a difficult matter for schools; and formal education at all levels was becoming widespread. The public school needed a unifying set of purposes; this was provided in part by the commission's proclamation of its seven cardinal principles (words in parentheses are paraphrased from this report):

1. *Health* (health instruction, health habits, and physical activities)
2. *Command of fundamental processes* (proficiency in reading, writing, arithmetical computation, and the elements of oral and written expression)
3. *Worthy home membership* (includes boys and girls)
4. *Vocation* (secure livelihood for oneself and one's dependents)
5. *Civic education* (development of qualities that enhance participation in the activities of the neighborhood, town, city, state, and nation, as well as a better understanding of international problems)

6. *Worthy use of leisure* (to obtain from leisure the "re-creation of body, mind, and spirit")
7. *Ethical character* (given high priority)[8]

Public education took on a new view and, in a sense, has never been the same. The seven principles are inherent in practically all of the philosophy one reads about public education. They are compelling ideas and are capable of being redefined every generation. Certainly, conditions have changed in regard to world politics, social problems, and natural resources, but the elastic nature of these seven principles makes them timeless. Those who have experienced secondary public education realize that probably few schools anywhere live up to the challenges of these cardinal principles, but the attempt usually results in better schools.

When further considering the impact of national commissions and the formulation of educational objectives, attention must be given to the 1938 Educational Policies Commission of the National Education Association. Hundreds of educators met over a period of time and developed a list of four interdependent major objectives with numerous, specific behaviors associated with each major objective. The major objectives were as follows:

1. Objectives of self-realization
2. Objectives of human relationship
3. Objectives of economic efficiency
4. Objectives of civic responsibility[9]

Each major area was then subdivided into specific subsets to give greater meaning to each of the four major categories. These interrelated and broad objectives assisted school districts in planning curricula and communicating purposes of education.

The public school curriculum had also been influenced after World War II by an official movement called "life adjustment" education. This technically lasted over a decade, but it seems to have ever since remained a straw man for those who want to blame most national ills on the public school. In 1945 the U.S. Office of Education sponsored a conference on vocational education, at which time the term "life adjustment" was first coined. The idea was to improve the school experiences of some 60 percent of secondary school youth who had little interest in either a vocational-technical program or a college preparatory curriculum. Approximately 60 percent, in other words, were potential dropouts, so the desire was to adapt the curriculum more effectively to their needs. The term "life adjustment" was never defined and resulted in a medley of curricular reaction to make the curriculum more comprehensive. Anything that seemed experimental or even different in approach was given publicity in order to make school more meaningful. The roots of life adjustment obviously extended back a few decades.

As a consequence of this imprecision of definition, life adjustment education became vulnerable. It was equated with undue or extreme interest in the needs and desires of students. Immediate needs dominated over content to be studied or standards to be applied. When in 1957 Sputnik dramatically put the United States behind Russia in space programs, life adjustment education became the culprit. Life adjustment became in the decade following World War II broader in scope to the point that the concept seemed to apply to all students, not just those original potential dropouts who first constituted the concern. Its focus became too large.

Life adjustment seemed to apply to the perpetuation of the status quo rather than to the improvement of the cultural environment. The advocates of life adjustment, however, did believe in change. Their views were similar to those principles embodied in the seven cardinal principles of 1918. Home membership, life experiences, work, and recreation were all important themes to these educators. Similar to progressive education, its lack of a consistent guiding philosophy signaled its demise. It has been loosely equated with progressive education. Life adjustment education was more an effect of progressive education, rather than an integral part. The sad feature of the life adjustment movement was that its noble purpose to help those students with no particular purpose in secondary education went unfulfilled. It became too general in purpose during a period when society was growing very skeptical of progressive education. If progressive education had continued after World War II with strong public support, no doubt life adjustment would have experienced longer life, too, as a formal movement. Its goals were worthy, but in practice they were difficult to implement.

The public school curriculum today has evolved to look typically like that cited in Table 5-1. The program of studies has been shaped by many forces, some of which are cited in this chapter. National teacher organizations, curriculum associations, governmental agencies, and local citizens all play a strong role in influencing the curriculum at the local level. The school's program is affected directly by legal requirements and school policymakers, and indirectly by such forces as technology, textbook publishers, commercial test makers, Alec Gallup and Lou Harris polls, as well as by political events. In other words, even when requirements are set by legislatures and state departments of education, the political mood in the community, the state, or the nation can swing the educational pendulum. Witness the way in which the numerous national reports in the 1980s have reshaped the schools' offerings in terms of the "new basics." Consider also how the computer has rapidly forced a rethinking of curriculum, particularly in how content is conveyed to students. The computer has taken the nation by storm.

The curriculum must be viewed as the product of a dynamic process of thinking, which blends or synthesizes content from many sources. Even if the school deliberately tried to keep the content of the curriculum constant, it could not. The textbook industry, with its some 40 or so major publishers, is continually offering new views and approaches. These new ideas can eventually alter the curriculum considerably. Commercial test makers are also a powerful influence on the school, especially in an enthusiastic age of measuring the performance of both students and teachers. Standardized achievement tests and criterion-referenced tests in the local school district stress certain content more in the instructional process, particularly as accountability becomes a growing public issue. Even the findings of the major pollsters on educational topics play a role in shaping educational policy. The more national publicity is given to major educational questions, the more, it seems, that state and local officials try to respond or adjust the curriculum to reflect the will of the public. Often this is a very wholesome process because it stimulates communities to think about their schools. The Gallup polls, for example, for the past 20 years have surveyed public opinion about curriculum, students, teachers, and the administration of schools. School districts and politicians are sensitive to this kind of educational information. Consequently, the curriculum can be affected. Consider how long the basic skills have been bandied about as a topic of discussion.

Compulsory Education

The educational ladder in the United States was made complete in this century; state legislation now compels children to attend school either to or through age 16. No nation prior to this had so successfully linked educational levels, except for Prussia in the nineteenth century. Educational theorists for centuries had advocated an educational "ladder," but their respective societies were not ready to act upon the idea. Martin Luther and Jon Comenius, for example, in the sixteenth and seventeenth centuries respectively, had urged their contemporaries to organize schools based upon age from elementary through higher education but to no avail. Prussia implemented the ladder very effectively; however, not all youth had the opportunity for formal education beyond the *volksschule* (elementary school). England was America's major source of educational thought; this is ironic because the dominant belief in England was that schools did not have to be provided for all children. The initiative for schooling was primarily left to the family.

Compulsory education began in earnest in the United States in Massachusetts in 1852, with the passage of a school attendance law. This law required all children between the ages of eight and 14 years to attend school for 12 weeks each year, six weeks on a consecutive basis.[10] States followed the initiative of Massachusetts so that by 1918, compulsory attendance was common throughout the nation. Most states employed the model used in Massachusetts to the degree that boys and girls were required to attend school for a number of consecutive weeks within a framework of 12 to 20 weeks overall. As child-labor legislation became more common, the age and number of required weeks for attendance also increased. Today, the pattern is generally that a child is required to attend school from age six to 16 years, for a consecutive period of about 180 school days yearly.

Compulsory attendance (and child-labor legislation) modified the curriculum. No longer could parents keep a child home. The salutary effect of getting children and youth out of the factories certainly returned childhood and health to their lives. This legislation also improved the labor market because cheap labor was drastically reduced and jobs became more plentiful for adults. Society was becoming more technical and industrial and labor organizations were becoming more visible. It was good for organized labor to keep youth in school.

Educationally, the curriculum would become taxed to the degree that now *all* children were expected to be in school. Exceptional children, offspring of non-English-speaking European immigrants, and unruly teenagers were now required to attend school. The curriculum during the early part of this century was strained. Teachers were not educated to cope with this new population, nor was the curriculum geared to meet all needs. Americanization meant learning a little English and "special education" meant isolating some children (on the basis of crude standards) from so-called typical children. Frankly, the settlement houses of this early period had more realistic curricula for preschoolers, youth, and adults. In a sense, the public school failed to serve well the nonwhite, the immigrant, the poor, and the exceptional child. But slowly the public school responded over the ensuing decades to become more egalitarian and responsive. There are obstacles still to overcome today, but no institution has more potential to enhance avenues of vertical mobility for *all* people than the public school with its comprehensive curriculum.

All is not well concerning compulsory attendance legislation. The model for compulsory attendance was set in an agrarian age and later revised upward in terms of age to keep youth out of the labor market. Some educators believe that it would be much more profitable to lower the upper age to 15 years instead of retaining it at 16. The belief is that many teenagers would benefit by early employment with the option to obtain formal schooling when desired. Forcing some youth to remain in school defeats the hope of initiative to learn.

Alternatives for youth choosing to leave school are these:

1. Make schools more voluntary by increasing the number of alternatives. By reducing the number of required classes, schools can become less custodial.
2. Stimulate businesses to help prepare youth for gainful employment by means of intense supervision in and out of school. This implies an "on the job" approach to training and education.[11]

Because of the recognized success of Headstart programs for preschool children, some people would like to lower the entrance age for compulsory attendance to age four years. Content is being pushed downward into the elementary grades. Research indicates that children can learn effectively at a young age. One-parent households are accelerating the push for preschools. Children need to be supervised when parents work. The growing number of latch-key children is increasing to a point that public schools, Y.M.C.A.s, and so on are supervising children before and after school. Custodial care may become part of the reason to require a younger admission criterion. Also, Montessori education has shown that children, even as young as 30 months, can enjoy formal learning experiences.

Society is changing and so may compulsory attendance laws. This will not occur easily, however, because many educators believe that learning is not necessarily enhanced by a formal setting too soon in those early years. Given the present conservative political mood, the upper leaving age probably will be kept at 16 for some time. The lower entrance age might be reconsidered first, however, because success in later school years is facilitated by early exposure to basic academic and social skills.

Compulsory attendance laws are also controversial because of the emergence of the popularity of home instruction. Of course, this mode of instruction has been significant since the colonial period when it was dominant. Today, however, it has become popular again among some parents for a different reason; for example, dissatisfaction with the public school. Spurred on by the U.S. Supreme Court decision *Wisconsin* v. *Yoder* (1972), in which parents from the Amish church were granted the right to remove their children from school after the eighth grade (age 14), some parents now believe they can more effectively challenge state compulsory attendance laws. Although the *Yoder* case was based upon religious grounds and certainly is no precedent for any group to flout attendance laws, it nevertheless has stimulated hope among those dissatisfied with the public school to attempt to obtain legal permission to educate children at home. Believing that the public school has become either too humanistic in its philosophy or too lax in its intellectual climate, some parents consequently desire to teach their children at home.

According to current data, compulsory education laws in thirty-eight states and territories allow home instruction. The remaining states have no legal provisions for such instruction. Only a few of those states that allow this type of education require home teachers to be certified or children to demonstrate progress through regular testing. What is more common, however, among those states that include statutory provision for home instruction is the concept of "comparability" or "equivalency," which means that home and school subjects must be similar. Enforcement of this comparability or equivalency requirement is complex. Approval of home programs is varied. In some states, the department of education must approve the curriculum. In others, approval is obtained either by the court or by the local school board and its administrative staff. Because legal provision at the state level grants the right for home instruction by no means automatically gives this right to parents. It might be easy to teach some subjects at home, but offering an adequate curriculum with accompanying social skills and values is another matter.

The number of school-aged children educated at home in the school year 1990–1991 varied between 248,500 and 353,500. This represents less than 1 percent of the nation's school-aged youth and less than 10 percent of those educated in private schools. Home schooling is increasing, however, among parents who hold strong religious or ideological beliefs, either strongly conservative or highly liberal. Data on such schooling are difficult to obtain but usually are derived from state departments of education, curricular suppliers, and home school leaders.[12]

Curriculum Theory and Practice

In this section various types of curricular organization will be surveyed. Curriculum is philosophy in action, which is often easy to detect. Figure 5-1 on common school patterns shows the context in which various kinds of curricula will be viewed. There are age and grade variations on these two school patterns in Figure 5-1, but they represent the most typical school organization or structure in the country.

Within the context of these two fundamental ladders, the typical pattern of organization within each elementary school is a *self-contained* classroom; this means that one teacher is assigned to a definite number of children for most of

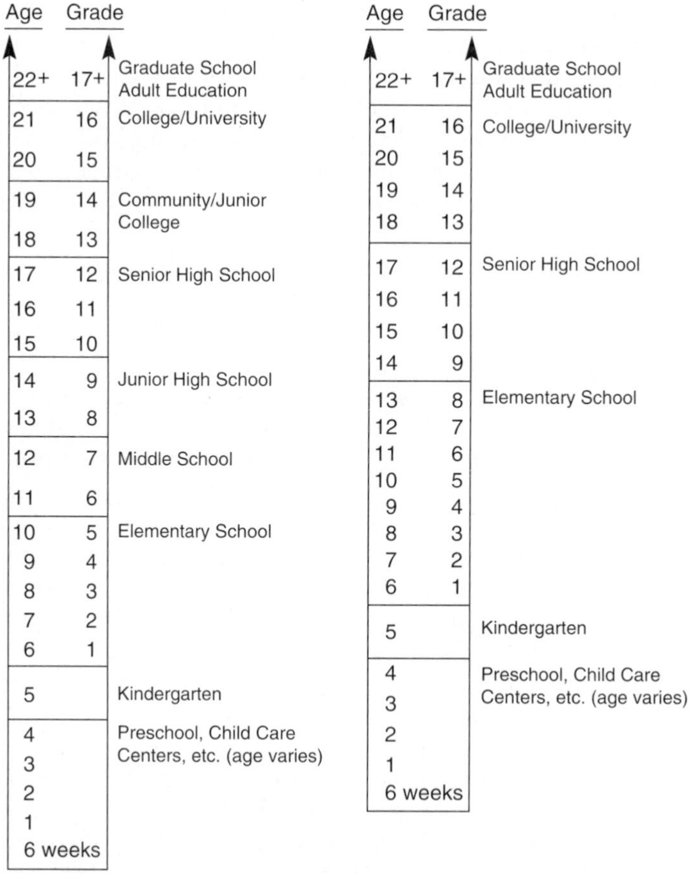

K - 12 grades may be ungraded (by levels).
Middle and junior high schools may vary by grade in some school districts.

FIGURE 5-1   Common School Patterns

the day. Of course, instruction in physical education and music may be under the direction of a specialist, but the remaining subject areas are the responsibilities of one teacher. There may be some exchanging of classes by teachers of self-contained classrooms according to their talents or interests, for example, in art and science, so that children obtain better instruction. This process is called *departmentalization.* Teachers may also arrange *team teaching* situations, which means that at least two teachers plan, coordinate, present, and evaluate pupil performance *together.* They work continually as a team, not individually.

At the secondary school level, the most common arrangement is for one teacher in each subject area to be assigned to five classes per day; each class lasts approximately 45 to 50 minutes. The remaining time may be used for planning. Team teaching also may be implemented at the secondary level; at least two teachers in a given area or related fields, such as the humanities and the social sciences, work together in every facet of planning and instructing. Generally speaking, subject matter classification is by content, which implies that one teacher instructs solely in that area.

The more content is viewed in terms of student interests and needs, the more the school patterns of organization move toward *multi-age* grouping or *ungraded* structure. In the elementary school, organization may be by levels which encompass two or three chronological ages and grades, for example, primary, intermediate levels, and so on. Children learn together irrespective of age because content is not viewed in discrete packages. Secondary education also may be organized in this manner. *Modular scheduling,* for example, utilizes the concept of modules (blocks of time) to fit individual and instructional needs. On some days, a teacher may use a high number of modules for a special project and return the extra modules to another teacher at a later time. Flexibility is inherent in this kind of organization because a student's schedule is individualized by the computer.

All flexible arrangements, such as modular scheduling, take place usually within the framework of a six-hour day, five-day week, and nine-month year. The calendar, however, can be arranged on a varied basis in that school cycles operate for twelve months a year. Only about 4 or 5 percent of all school districts in the nation operate all year. A *cycle* implies that a pupil attends school for so many consecutive school days, say forty-five, then is on vacation for the next 15 consecutive school days. The total number of school days per year remains the same, but the days are planned to extend over a calendar year. One of the major arguments for this cyclical arrangement is that children can retain knowledge better because there is no 10-week summer vacation; however, one of its chief liabilities is that family lifestyles may be interrupted sharply if children in the family in the same school district are on different school cycles. Vacations, athletics, and other school activities may be so varied that families have difficulty adjusting to year-round school programs.

Many educators organize learning experiences to highlight intellectual connections. They want youth to see the relatedness of what is studied in school to life in general. Educators desire that academic content, whenever possible, reflect a thread of continuity throughout the curriculum. This is thought of as *integration* in the curriculum. Terms such as "correlation," "fusion," and "core" are often used in elementary and secondary schools to express this principle of integration.

"Correlation" is a term which implies that teachers instruct as usual in their respective subjects in the elementary or secondary school but jointly agree upon a number of themes throughout the year which connect much of their respective subject matter. Teachers of art, science, music, and social studies, for example, might agree upon a theme such as the "human need for creative expression" and, consequently, relate content among those subject areas. It is thus hoped that students infer that a particular body of knowledge is not an isolated structure, but usually interwoven with other content.

"Fusion" is another important concept in curriculum planning. This term implies that at least two subject areas can blend around a common framework. An "American studies" class at the secondary level is a combination of American history and literature. It may be quite easy in this case to show a connection between the literature of a period with the historical events of that same era. There are, however, other ways to make connections between these two subjects. "Strands of intellectual thought" as a theme can be examined in an historical and literary context. Content within the sciences, another example, can merge or cluster around a theme dealing with the physical environment.

"Core" curriculum is the most dramatic means of making connections throughout the curriculum. Large blocks of time, usually at the secondary level, are periodically merged around a common theme or problem designed to harness the interests of students. A diversity of knowledge is brought into the study. Themes can vary from sexism, racism, war, pollution, to earning a living. Core curriculum enables a student to see the relevance of knowledge to his or her personal and social experiences. Obviously, the role of the teachers involved in the core approach is to direct learning.

In the elementary school, this core concept is best implemented by a "no grade" approach. Teachers, however, at this level have long taught core curriculum when presenting units, such as "life in colonial America" or "customs of the American Indians," both of which encompass a significant part of the school day and embrace a variety of content. The core concept can cut across all subject matter.

Individualized instruction is also an approach to relate the interests of the student to the content of the school. Unstructured, ungraded schools lend themselves easily to student projects, to problem solving, and to the idea of using knowledge as needed in lieu of learning for some future, but yet unknown, purpose. The use of the computer will be discussed later in this chapter; no medium for learning has had an impact upon society like that of the computer! While still in its infancy in the schools, the computer's potential for learning is profound. Individualized instruction will become more common by means of computer use in drill, remediation, and enrichment. The computer will not replace the instructor, but the role of the teacher will change. Learning will always take place best in context of human interaction and values, but as an aid to learning the computer is nonpareil. Furthermore, the computer will have a dramatic effect because modular scheduling will be refined to fit individual abilities and interests. In other words, the computer will assist the child personally, and it will help organize learning experiences for all children.

Naturally, a teacher's philosophy or that of the school district will dictate the structure of learning. The more conservative approach means the classroom is organized by blocks of content. A self-contained classroom (one teacher per group of pupils) or a secondary school classroom organized by set blocks of time need not be conservative in its approach to learning, but such an approach normally is found in that context. An "open" classroom, on the other hand, can certainly flourish in a self-contained classroom if time does not constantly dictate learning experiences. The idea of openness focuses on a student-centered approach in organizing learning activities. It runs counter to an authoritative or arbitrary approach in the selection of content or learning activities.

Conservative educators, conversely, are not unanimous in their views about the most appropriate pattern of curricular organization. Some have subscribed strongly to curriculum projects which are highly organized in reference to common ideas or principles and methods of intellectual inquiry, for example, the student as physical scientist or the student as a creative writer. Others are more inclined to support a curriculum of separate subjects with as much mastery of organized content as possible. When the student "does" science or literature, educators emphasize generalizations across "broad fields." Language arts, the natural and social sciences, the humanities, and mathematics become the framework of the curriculum. Unified study takes place within each of these broad areas with the focus on common ideas and principles. Broad fields actually emerged decades ago when educators saw the need for content reclassification of isolated subject matter into "families." Language arts, for example, is now a family of reading, spelling, grammar, speaking, listening, and writing skills rather than fragmented blocks of knowledge taught separately. The area of social studies, another example of a broad field, comprises history (sometimes a part of the humanities), political science, sociology, anthropology, economics, and geography. Other broad fields are composed of their respective disciplines in a similar manner. Instead of students delving deeply into one discipline, for example, they learn principles derived from all the respective disciplines in that family.

At the high school level, the idea of "comprehensive curriculum" is well accepted because not all youth will be going on to higher education. The term comprehensive means all-encompassing because the high school curriculum offers a wide variety of courses and activities which appeals to students planning for college or seeking gainful employment upon graduation. A comprehensive curriculum implies that effective counseling is available to help students become aware of the school's offerings. Vocational education and general education, in other words, are of equal value. A student's career choice will dictate the electives taken and the amount of general education pursued. Of course, the number of credits for high school graduation is being increased, but much latitude is given to the student to select courses. Without adequate funding by the community, which allows the school to offer a realistic technical and general program and effective counseling to direct students to find their appropriate careers, the concept of a comprehensive curriculum cannot exist. Poor, small school districts usually do not implement a comprehensive curriculum effectively.

Curricular theory and practice are influenced by "objectives." Throughout most of educational history, these ideas have been written in general and vague terms. In recent times, however, more specific objectives are written at all educational levels which have a measurable meaning.

Teachers at all grade levels are now being asked to write statements that specify what students will be able to do after completing a specific amount of academic work. Writing such behavioral objectives enables the teacher to select materials, activities, and procedures prior to the learning experience. Clear objectives allow the teacher to determine where problems may emanate as well as to appraise the total effectiveness of the teaching and learning involved in the unit.

A behavioral objective consists of three parts:

1. The *condition* is the context in which the student is expected to perform a particular requirement or behavior. The condition specifically pertains to the situation in which the student will demonstrate skill or mastery after the student has been taught. The more detailed the requirements for performance, the better.
2. The *action* is the response the student will demonstrate to display mastery. Action implies a process that is measurable by or observable to the teacher.
3. The *criterion* is the exact amount of knowledge, the quality of the student's response, and the rate of response acceptable for success in mastering the concept or knowledge to be learned.[13]

"Competency-based instruction" focuses more on what kind of student should emerge from a school rather than solely on what content should go into the curriculum. In other words, skills are more important than units of credit or length of class period or years of schooling. There are essentially five characteristics of competency-based instruction:

1. It is a learner-centered philosophy because each role of the learner as wage earner, individual, citizen, family member, and consumer is valued. "Living" skills are crucial and become measurable competencies.
2. A system of goals and outcomes becomes obvious to everyone. The system becomes public.
3. It exhibits a real-life orientation. The concerns of the individual and of society become more integrated with existing curricula.
4. It reflects an attitude of flexibility about the use of time. Mastery is a personal matter and may take much time.
5. It displays an honesty about what is expected to happen in school. There is no hidden agenda. Accountability is consequently enhanced. What is learned must be demonstrable to the learner, teacher, and parents.[14]

Another important aspect of curriculum theory is the use of various levels of "taxonomies" in planning content and activities. A taxonomy is a system of classification. Experts in educational evaluation studied the idea of defining objectives systematically. They developed a taxonomy, or classification system, of educational objectives. The teacher's task is to try continually to move children to higher levels within domains once basic steps are mastered. There are three domains:

1. *Cognitive* (memory and reasoning)
    a. *knowledge*—remembering or recognizing without necessarily understanding the concept
    b. *comprehension*—understanding material without necessarily relating it to anything
    c. *application*—using a general concept to solve a problem
    d. *analysis*—breaking an idea into its parts
    e. *synthesis*—creating something new by combining ideas
    f. *evaluation*—judging the value of materials as they might be applied
2. *Affective* (emotional)
    a. *receiving*—being aware of something in the environment
    b. *responding*—showing some new behavior as a result of experience
    c. *valuing*—showing definite commitment or involvement
    d. *organization*—integrating a new value into one's general values
    e. *characterization by value*—acting consistently with the new value
3. *Psychomotor* (physical ability)
    a. *reflex movements*—involuntary response to stimulus (blinking)
    b. *basic movements*—combination of reflex movements (walking)
    c. *perceptual abilities*—translation of stimuli received through the senses into appropriate movements (jumping rope)
    d. *physical abilities*—basic movements prerequisite to higher skills (weight lifting)
    e. *skilled movements*—complex movements embodying efficiency (dance)
    f. *nondiscursive communication*—ability to communicate through body movement (facial expressions, gestures)[15]

Because of societal and world conditions generally, some curricular themes are beginning to receive serious attention. These themes are not necessarily new ideas, but the concern for them has become much more significant. "Global education" is one of these current themes, approaches, or movements which is dependent not entirely upon specific knowledge obtained in a course or subject but also upon an attitude or point of view developed throughout formal study about the following broad areas:

1. Human values and cultures
2. Global systems (economic, political, technological, and so on)

3. Global problems and issues (hunger, environment, war, and so on)
4. Global history (Western and non-Western cultures)[16]

Global education will help to prepare youth for an interdependent world. Obviously, most of the content in the elementary and secondary schools would lend itself to an "international" viewpoint in the sense that little we do as a society is autonomous in nature. National problems and priorities have international effects. Social studies, fine arts, foreign languages, literature, and the sciences, for example, can be adapted to heighten student sensitivity to other cultures and issues. The authors see teachers with a global concern encouraging youth to study about other peoples, to learn other languages, to discuss international current events, to seek acquaintances and friends of other cultures, to respect and improve the environment, and to become concerned about the quest for peace and human rights. These ideas cut across the curriculum and have been employed by effective teachers for a long time, but the difference now is the movement needs to be more systematic and general in order to prepare youth for citizenship in the twenty-first century.

Another significant contemporary theme in the curriculum is "multi-cultural education." Historically, the "melting pot" was an accepted concept, theoretically at least, in reference to the school as immigrants came to the United States. The process did not work well, however, because ethnic diversity and language were demeaned while English and middle-class Protestant values were promulgated. Today, multicultural education stresses greater tolerance, respect, and cooperation among racial and ethnic groups. The overall goal of educators concerning multicultural diversity is to foster commonality, such as learning standard English and common values, by working through the ethnic language and culture. Individual learning, field experiences, and bilingual teaching are strategies to facilitate respect for ethnic lifestyles and values. The major problem seems to be when and how standard English and common culture are emphasized.

Multicultural education in a broader sense is sometimes thought of as that type of education which enables one to interact positively in a variety of cultural settings, which extend beyond even race or ethnicity. Religious and gender differences and values, for example, require a perspective that can be obtained only through planned instruction. A sense of cultural pluralism is acquired when the climate of the school and curricular activities foster a respect for cultural diversity.

Specific curricular strategies are also gaining attention. "Cooperative learning" is popular in that small groups of students of varying abilities work together on assignments, fulfilling academic and social purposes. "Critical thinking" is also fashionable in regard to teaching thinking skills and problem solving to children. Learning how to analyze is learning how to think in all subject matter.

"Mastery learning" will continue to be dominant in many schools. This approach implies success in learning as a goal. By defining specific objectives, teaching, assessing, correcting, and retesting those objectives, successful learning becomes more attainable. Some controversy surrounds mastery learning concerning the number of children who can be accommodated at one time by this style of instruction; however, when implemented well, successful completion of lessons or units is the motivating force for each student. Learning sequences are tied to objectives. Progress is assessed by testing. If a student fails a test after instruction, different material and approaches are used, while those who passed are given choices: enrichment, the next assignment, or perhaps are asked to help those who failed the test. Individualizing instruction and heavy reliance on diverse materials and strategies are crucial to help all students master concepts. Content and teaching strategies in all grades can be adapted to this viewpoint.

"Whole language" is a "new" concept in curriculum that reflects a unification of reading, writing, and speaking throughout the instructional program. In basal readers, for example, skills are supplanted by a "holistic" view of the child in that he or she brings experiences to school and, while there, the teachers strive to capitalize on those experiences and enrich them. This view implies a focus on meaning rather than a dissection of paragraphs. Phonics are developed in the context of a story, rather than by matching symbols and sounds in isolation. The teacher may read (assisted reading) while students follow along silently and at intervals react, create, or predict subsequent content or meaning. The shift toward whole language implies a child-centered, experimental view of instruction, using varied activities and a plethora of materials.

"Accelerated learning" is another curricular innovation that focuses on helping children "at risk," students who traditionally had to work faster than their peers to catch up, despite the fact that they were usually far behind and were seldom expected to excel. The ideal underlying accelerated education is the mainstreaming of at-risk youth prior to secondary school. Devotees of such learning strive to provide instruction that is "enriched, engaging, active, and inter-disciplinary." Accelerated schools have a focused approach, a site-based independence regarding instructional matters, and a strong bond with parents. Activities to clarify and strengthen skills and understanding are strongly encouraged.

"Outcome-based education" is a form of curricular restructuring that affects the entire educational establishment. Almost 60 percent of the states already have or are developing goals that will stimulate much change in what and how the curriculum is organized. "Outcomes" are often euphemistically called "performance standards" to minimize controversy; however, the major viewpoint underlying outcome-based education is grounded in experiential learning resulting in *applied* knowledge, skills, and understanding. Assessment is predicated upon products in lieu of grades *per se*. Collaborative learning in teams, for example, to perform tasks or to complete projects, or reliance upon portfolios, essays, journals, or other creative applications can substitute for traditional grading and reporting.

Outcome-based education is rooted in progressive education, particularly the embodiment of concepts such as cooperative learning, mastery learning, the use of students' experiences, and holistic assessment. The teacher is a director or facilitator of learning or, as some say, a "coach." Learning is not clock-driven. Time is used more flexibly. Presidents Bush and Clinton have stimulated implementation of this approach first by means of *America 2000,* which advocates curricular experimentation and improved student performance. The controversy stems from layperson or parental fears that schools might, at worst, be agents of social and moral change or, at best, be unable to define and report substantive content.

In sum, the curriculum is undergoing dramatic revision.

The Computer and the Curriculum

Technology is generally thought of as the use of the discoveries of science as well as the application of the technical advances of industry, manufacturing, commerce, and the arts. In context of schooling, the particular technologies are mainly electronic: radio, commercial and cable television, audio tapes, audiovisual tapes, discs, computer, computer conferencing, microwave and satellite transmissions, and computer-based education.[17] Currently available CD-ROM disks can hold huge amounts of text and pictures along with sound. Students can browse through a textbook on screen. It is generally believed that schools have lagged far behind industry in the use of these technologies, even though their application offers the possibility of reaching more learners, with significant results at relatively low costs.

There has existed for several years a rampant fear among educators that the computer, one of the most pervasive technologies, will render teachers obsolete. That fear, however, is unlikely to occur. Likewise, the computer will never be a panacea for educational ills. It will, however, be a powerful aid in the classroom as well as provide an impetus for change in the teacher's role and methods of instruction. A closer look at one of the most powerful technologies, the computer, in formal education below the college level may be helpful in understanding the impact of technology upon the curriculum.

Computers are electronic mechanisms designed to process information at speeds almost equal to that of light. A computer embodies five essential ingredients: (1) input, (2) the central processing unit containing arithmetic/logic circuits, (3) memory or storage, (4) control, and (5) output. The basic means of communication are alphabetic symbols, which are combined to form words. These words are then combined in a syntactical way to form sentences, which comprise complex thoughts. The essential elements of the computer are the binary symbols 0 and 1, which are often called binary digits or "bits." The computer differentiates these bits by electricity and magnetism. These bits are then combined to form words which can specify a quantity, or instruction, or a name. Words represented electronically then link the person with the computer.

There are three categories of computer: mainframes, minicomputers, and microcomputers. The primary distinction among these categories refers to the amount of "memory" each has or the amount of information that can be stored. Other aspects refer to how information is entered, processed, and accessed. For our purposes, it is unnecessary to present a detailed explanation of each type of computer. For the most part, mainframes and minicomputers are used primarily for administrative purposes such as scheduling students. The microcomputer has emerged as the most practical type of computer for instructional classroom use.

Communication between the learner and the computer takes place by means of a program, which contains statements representing sentences in English and arithmetic expressions. In brief, once the program is submitted to the computer, the statements and expressions are translated into machine language, which results eventually in electronic components that enable the machine to calculate, sort information, compare data, make decisions, and so on.[18]

Computer language has become so widespread that people knowledgeable about computers assume almost everyone can converse with them in the lingo of this technology. There is an abundance of such languages in existence. Several of the many computer languages are the following:

1. FORTRAN (Formula Translator)
2. ALGOL (Algorithmic Language)
3. COBOL (Common Business Oriented Language)
4. PL/1 (Programming Language 1)
5. BASIC (Beginner's All Purpose Symbolic Instruction Code)
6. APL (A Programming Language)
7. QUICKTRAN (adaption of FORTRAN)
8. SNOBOL (symbol manipulation language)
9. LISP (List Processor)
10. SIMSCRIPT (event oriented language)
11. GRAIL (Graphic Input Language)[19]

Computers can be extremely useful to educators both in regard to school administration and individual instruction. Administratively, computers are excellent record keepers to store data about students, faculty, and staff personnel. Retrieval programs can call forth such data as needed. Scheduling, grading, and attendance data also are categorized very efficiently to facilitate school programs. Financial information is also organized in a more efficient manner that results in better decisions about personnel, plant, and instructional needs. Libraries, as well, are converting to retrieval information systems and management procedures in regard to card catalogs and library cards. The computer seems to have almost limitless uses in the administration of schools.

It is difficult to generalize about the computer and its various curricular applications. It is even more difficult to set forth a curricular syllabus that would summarize how teachers are teaching the computer; however, the following discussion is an attempt to at least outline some instructional related uses of the computer. As was indicated, the microcomputer is the most practical type of computer that can be used for instruction. A single station would consist of a central processing unit, a monitor, a keyboard, a disc drive, and a printer. The data are stored in floppy discs. Data may also now be stored in hard disc, which is an integral part of the disc drive unit.

There are two things a teacher can do with a computer: teach by using the computer and teach about the computer. Teaching with a computer depends on the available software. Software is the computer program that tells the computer what to do: for example, what information to display on the screen, and what type of response to make upon command. A great deal of software is currently available and, of course, more is on the way. This software can be placed into three categories: drill and practice, tutorial, and simulation.

Thus, computers can do a number of things for the learner. They can involve the learner in an active manner, something which he or she may be seldom accustomed to in an intellectual sense. The aspect of immediate feedback provides a motivation not always available in a class setting where one teacher tries to meet the needs of perhaps 30 pupils.

Computers also are interactive because the learner and computer can engage in the learning process. The student becomes intellectually involved and has the opportunity to grow without a great deal of teacher stimulation. In a definite sense, this interaction becomes a personal experience. In addition, computers have the capacity to be physically coupled with anything that produces or responds to an electronic signal. In other words, the computer is versatile in regard to videotape players, electronic musical equipment, physical education monitoring equipment, and so on. It becomes an invaluable teaching tool on both a personal and collective scale.

The tailored learning experiences that the computer promises also can be crucial to improved learning. The computer, unlike other media, can create lessons instantly, can diagnose instructional problems on the spot, or can capitalize on a learner's strength, if necessary, in order to encourage more intellectual growth. A corollary of this instant formal instruction is that computers can stimulate a learner to pursue a subject in depth without much human guidance.

Finally, the computer has excellent potential for abstract thinking because pupils can compose relationships in reference to computer games, as well as to concepts involving such academic areas as biology, economics, or physics. By creating models utilizing logic, the pupil puts to use thoughts which might have remained inert if they were only read but not applied.[20]

Teaching about the computer involves the development of a sequential curriculum in two areas: computer literacy and computer programming. There are usually three instructional objectives for computer literacy: (1) understanding what the computer can and cannot do, (2) understanding how to operate the computer, and (3) the role of the computer in society.

This first area of a computer curriculum should emphasize the "hands on" approach. Students should be encouraged to explore the computer's capabilities and not be concerned about errors. This area is best suited to the elementary school grades but may be extended into the middle school or junior high school depending on the needs of the students and community.

The second area, computer programming, might begin in the middle school or junior high school grades and extend into senior high school. Programming is coupled with using the computer as a tool. Thus, courses should be offered in computer language such as BASIC, FORTRAN, COBOL, or PASCAL.™ These languages have a direct transference to a practical application in other subject areas. For example, a student with FORTRAN language skills can use these skills in solving problems presented in science and mathematics courses. A student proficient in BASIC can use his or her skills in business-related courses such as accounting.

This does not mean that computer usage will occur without obstacles. Experts in this form of technology see some major problems regarding its implementation. Experts do not see the computer adapted well to some curricular areas such as the humanities and fine arts because the computer depends on a systematic body of rules and procedures. Such correlation in these subject areas is not yet possible and may never be. Academic fields depending heavily on creativity, intuition, judgment, and so on, do not lend themselves easily to formal rules, the basis for computer programming. The computer, in addition, cannot solve fundamental questions regarding public education such as finance, equality of educational opportunity, or for that matter, public confidence in the schools. Furthermore, the mature judgment needed to select and integrate appropriate software is a rare commodity among educators. The computer can be too easily seen as a panacea for instructional problems.

There is, however, a more important caution that teachers and administrators must be aware of in the use and future development of computer technology in schools. Certainly, children and young people must be exposed to the computer in a sequential program that begins with computer awareness, then using the machine as an instructional aid, and finally learning how to program computers. Leadership will be required of educational administrators to develop strategies for preparing teachers, staff members, students, and parents to utilize this new technology and understand other future advances.

On the other hand, in order to balance involvement in the new technology, teachers and administrators must become more humanistic in their outlook. Technological advances tend to isolate individuals from one another and emphasize solitary activities. What happens, in essence, is that information collection, storage, and use increase while human interaction decreases. In the final analysis, one may know more but understand less. This can also lead to a decrease in human relations skills.

Therefore, teachers and administrators must see the necessity of developing innovative ways to interact among themselves and with students and parents. Educators need to recognize that the technological society of the future will require people to have a deeper appreciation of the fine arts. Art, music, drama, and so on, demonstrate and communicate feelings, attitudes, and beliefs which will become increasingly more important with each new advance in technology.

Teachers and educational administrators of the immediate future must understand and make use of technology as well as appreciate the necessity of creating ways to improve human interaction.[21]

The most exciting phenomenon since the arrival of the stand-alone computer is telecomputing, also known as "on-line telecommunications." Satellites beam signals to towers worldwide; these then transmit information to networks that send the information through optic fibers or copper wire to computer users belonging to a particular network. "Access" is the objective of telecomputing, which in most cases requires a computer, telephone line, telephone modem, and the software that allows the computer to interpret the signal carried by the telephone wires. In some locations, cable wires or optic fibers may link the computers directly into a network's station where a tower receives the satellite signals.

There are many on-line commercial services, which, for a fee, provide educational programs and information in addition to electronic bulletin boards and electronic mail (E-mail). Through bulletin boards, teachers and students can access regularly the information they need. If teachers and students want to participate in discussions with other teachers and students, they can do so through electronic mail. Through E-mail, for example, students can learn about pollution levels or temperature changes by comparing data with other students worldwide. Further, on-line research can be conducted by accessing information from hundreds of libraries without leaving the computer terminal. Internet is a system that links most on-line networks worldwide. To access Internet, a school district must have an account with a network. Eventually, the National Research and Education Network (NREN) will engulf Internet. The U.S. Congress authorized $2.9 billion for the development of NREN by passage of the High Performance Computing Communications Act In 1991. The NREN will be a faster and more spacious superhighway of information available to researchers, universities, schools, and other agencies.

Summary

Curriculum has traditionally meant an array of academic courses or subjects for youth arranged by adults in a prescribed manner over a period of time. In recent decades, however, the idea of curriculum has been enlarged to include all of the school-sponsored formal and informal experiences a youth encounters in thirteen years of schooling. In a technical sense, one can use the term *curriculum* to denote a specific list of required and elective offerings in the school or school district; however, it can have a more general meaning.

A teacher's philosophy of education in context with other viewpoints about education, for example, national concerns or state and community interests, has much to do with the direction of the curriculum. A program of courses and activities has no meaning until the teacher puts life into it. Curricular patterns are shaped by social and political forces. The educational ladder, ranging from preschool through adult or higher education, is compulsory in most states from age six to sixteen. Within the framework of this educational ladder, schools vary a great deal due to the prevalent philosophy of education in that particular school district, school, and classroom.

Formal education has been affected by a number of events over the decades. Early educational materials appeared in great numbers during the nineteenth century, more than had existed throughout the colonial period. Readers, arithmetic texts, spellers, geographies, history texts, and so on, began to crystallize the program first in the common school and later in the high school. The use of textbooks (and standardized tests) has had a profound effect in classifying students and giving form to the educational ladder.

Committees of the National Education Association (NEA) also have played a major part in shaping formal education through grade twelve. The Committee of Fifteen (1893–1895), for example, did much to set in motion the curriculum and philosophy of elementary education. Likewise, the Committee of Ten (1892–1893) rendered an extremely important report on secondary school studies which, in turn, was followed by a related report of the Committee of Thirteen (1895–1899). This last committee helped to standardize the secondary school curriculum and coordinate it with higher education. Another result of these two committees on secondary education was the unit of credit. In 1910 the unit was given greater meaning when it became known as the Carnegie unit, defined by the Carnegie Foundation. At that time the unit of credit was awarded for a class meeting of five periods a week for a total of 120 clock-hours per school year. The unit of credit is not much different today. While administratively logical, adherence to units of credit restricts other arrangements, such as competency-based instruction.

A final word on another NEA commission is relevant to this discussion on curriculum. The Commission on the Reorganization of Secondary Education, begun in 1913 and concluded in 1921, issued thirteen reports on the curriculum, one of which was its 1918 *Cardinal Principles of Secondary Education.* These principles have been pertinent to secondary education since their inception, namely, concern for health, the acquisition of basic skills, wholesome home membership, vocational skills, good citizenship, worthy use of leisure, and character development. These aims have been integrated with goals for secondary education in countless instances at national, state, and local levels.

Curricular theory has been a controversial theme over the years. Educators have struggled with the purposes of elementary education, goals for secondary schooling, and how to integrate content at all levels to better fit children's needs and interests. Curricular themes, such as the comprehensive school, correlation and fusion of content, broad fields, core curriculum, and so on, are all ways to better serve the needs of students through high school. The philosophy of education of the school district and classroom teacher is reflected in the organization of the classroom itself. Much of this organization can be seen as a continuum, ranging from conventional subject matter classification in a fixed framework of time to integrated subject matter in a more flexible framework of time and age groupings.

The trend toward competency-based instruction also is continuing unabatedly in public education. Competencies which stress results in student behavior and performance are being formulated at state and local levels. Educators and the public are concerned about "outcomes" of formal education, even though much of the interest in education at the national level focuses more on the "input," the content of schooling. Defining specific, measurable educational goals and activities is no easy task, but truly worthwhile. It can also help to win greater public confidence.

The computer is the best example of how the technological revolution has influenced almost all human endeavors, including formal education. Its place in school activities, administratively and instructionally, is assured, but refinement is needed. Such issues as better preparation of teachers in using the computer and the selection of appropriate software to enhance the curriculum are crucial. Computer awareness among educators implies skill in the operation of the computer and good judgment about its use in strengthening academic skills and attitudes about learning.

Implications for Future Teachers

No bond is stronger between a university and a public school district than that concerning curriculum. Teacher-educators and public school teachers and administrators continue to discuss the following curricular issues:

1. Who decides content?
2. To what extent do state and national standards "drive" the curriculum?
3. What role should local educators play in reference to decision-making?
4. How much should the curriculum focus on experiential learning?

Obviously, neither a school of education nor a school district is an island in this matter. Each needs the other to forge a curriculum in the context of state and national requirements and standards.

Discussion Questions

1. How do the authors define curriculum? Do you think this definition has changed since colonial times? Explain.
2. Identify and discuss several representative national, state, and local influences upon the curriculum of a school district.
3. How has the educational ladder been modified since the colonial period? What changes do you think still need to be made in regard to age and grade level?
4. Define the following curricular terms: comprehensive curriculum, core curriculum, correlation of content, fusion, broad field, behavioral objective, competency, taxonomy, and mastery learning.
5. Define briefly multicultural education, global education, whole language, and accelerated education. How do these curricular innovations in part help to meet the needs of a greater number of students?

6. What is "open" education? Is it compatible in the context of a self-contained class-room?

7. How can the computer aid in the quest to individualize education? What are some cautions to consider in the implementation of the computer in the classroom?

Notes

1. Jerome S. Bruner, *The Process of Education* (New York: Vintage Books, 1963), p. X.

2. Classification standards of The Missouri School Improvement Program are being phased in through 1996. See *Standards and Indicators Manual (1993–94)*, Jefferson City, MO: Missouri Department of Elementary and Secondary Education, 1993), 1–4.

3. For more specific information about textbooks and the nature of the schools during the period, *see* Clifton Johnson, *Old Time Schools and Schoolbooks* (New York: Dover Publications, 1963), chaps. 10, 11, 13: see also Ellwood P. Cubberley, *Public Education in the United States*. (New York: The Riverside Press, 1919), chapter 8.

4. Cubberley. Ibid., 408–10.

5. "Report of the Committee of Fifteen," *Journal of Proceedings and Addresses, 1895,* National Education Association (St. Paul, MN: 1895): 232–8; also, Edgar B. Wesley, *NEA: The First Hundred Years* (New York: Harper and Brothers, 1957), 296–7.

6. "Review of the Report of the Committee of Ten," *Journal of Proceedings and Addresses, 1894*, National Education Association (St. Paul, MN: 1895): 645–69.

7. "Report of the Committee on College Entrance Requirements," *Journal of Proceedings and Addresses, 1899*, National Education Association (Chicago: University of Chicago Press, 1899): 632–78.

8. *Cardinal Principles of Secondary Education: A Report of the Commission on the Reorganization of Secondary Education* (Washington, D.C.: U.S. Bureau of Education Bulletin, no. 35, 1918, 32.

9. *The Purposes of Education in American Democracy* (Washington, D.C.: National Education Association, Educational Policies Commission, 1938), 47–125.

10. Cubberley, *Public Education in the United States*, 379.

11. Howard M. Johnson, "Are Compulsory Attendance Laws Outdated?" *Phi Delta Kappan 55* (December 1973): 231.

12. "State Home-Instruction Laws as of August, 1984," *Education Week* IV (January 30, 1985): 14; also, Howard Richman and Susan Richman, "Legalization of Home Schools Should Proceed," *Education Week* VIII (September 14, 1988): 32; also Patricia M. Lines, "Estimating the Home Schooled Population," Working Paper, October 1991 (Washington, D.C.: Office of Educational Research and Improvement, U.S. Department of Education), 1–4.

13. Robert G. Packard, *Education and Teaching*, (Columbus, Ohio: Charles E. Merrill, 1974), 139–44.

14. Dale Parnell, *The Case for Competency-Based Education*, Fastback 118 (Bloomington, Ind.: Phi Delta Kappa Educational Foundation, 1978), 18–27.

15. B.S. Bloom *et. al., Taxonomy of Educational Objectives, Handbook I: Cognitive Domain* (New York: David McKay, 1956); D. R. Kratwohl et al., *Taxonomy of Educational Objectives, Handbook II: Affective Domain* (New York: David McKay, 1956); and A. J. Harrow, *A Taxonomy of the Psychomotor Domain: A Guide for Developing Behavioral Objectives* (New York: David McKay, 1972).

16. W. K. Kniep, "Development Education: Essential to a Global Perspective," in *The International Development Crisis and American Education,* C. Joy and W. K. Kniep, eds. (New York: Global Perspectives, 1987), 145–58; also Kenneth A. Tye, ed., *Global Education: From Thought to Action, The 1991 ASCD Yearbook,* (Alexandria, VA: Association for Supervision and Curriculum Development, 1991), 14–7.

17. William C. Norris, "Via Technology to a New Era in Education," *Phi Delta Kappan* 58 (February 1977): 451.

18. Justine Baker, *Computers in the Curriculum,* Fastback 82 (Bloomington, Ind.: Phi Delta Kappa Educational Foundation, 1976), 9–12.

19. Justine Baker, *The Computer in the School,* Fastback 58 (Bloomington, Ind.: Phi Delta Kappa Educational Foundation, 1975), 33.

20. Decker F. Walker, "Reflection on the Educational Potential and Limitations of Microcomputers," *Phi Delta Kappan* 64 (October 1983): 103–5.

21. Ronald W. Rebore, *Educational Administration: A Management Approach* (Englewood Cliffs, NJ: Prentice-Hall, 1985), 278–9.

Recommended Readings

ASCD Curriculum Update. Quarterly publication of the Association for Supervision and Curriculum Development, Alexandria, VA, current year.

Bloom, Benjamin S., ed. *Taxonomy of Educational Objectives. Handbook I: Cognitive Domain.* New York: David McKay Co., 1956.

Bruner, Jerome S. *The Process of Education.* Cambridge: Harvard University Press, 1960.

Cawelti, Gordon, ed., *Challenges and Achievements of American Education, The 1993 ASCD Yearbook,* Alexandria, VA: *Association for Supervision and Curriculum Development;* 1993.

Commission on the Reorganization of Secondary Education of the National Education Association. *Cardinal Principles of Secondary Education.* Washington, D.C.: Department of the Interior, Bureau of Education, Bulletin no. 35, 1918.

Conant, James B. *The American High School Today.* New York: McGraw-Hill, 1959.

Cremin, Lawrence. *The Transformation of the School: Progressivism in American Education, 1876–1957.* New York: Alfred A. Knopf, 1961.

Dewey, John. *Democracy and Education.* New York: Macmillan Co., 1916.

Dewey, John. *Experience and Education.* New York: Collier Books, 1963. (First published in 1938.)

Goodlad, John I. and Associates. *Curriculum Inquiry: The Study of Curriculum Practice.* New York: McGraw-Hill, 1985.

Goodlad, John I. *The Dynamics of Educational Change.* New York: McGraw-Hill, 1975.

Kepner, Jr., Henry S., ed. *Computers in the Classroom.* Washington, D.C.: The National Education Association, 1986.

Knowles, J. Gary, Stacey E. Marlow, James A. Muchmore. "From Pedagogy to Ideology: Origins and Phases of Home Education in the United States, 1970–1990," *American Journal of Education,* 100 (February 1992), 195–236.

McNeil, J. D. *Curriculum: A Comprehensive Introduction.* Boston: Little, Brown, 1977.

J. C. Culbertson and L. L. Cunningham, eds. "Microcomputers and Education." *Eighty-fifth Yearbook of the National Society for the Study of Education; Part I.* Chicago: NSSE, 1986.

National School Boards Association, *Electronic School*. Alexandria, VA: The Association, 1993.

Shane, Harold G. *Teaching and Learning in a Micro-electronic Age*. Bloomington, Ind. Phi Delta Kappa, 1987.

Taba, Hilda. *Curriculum Development: Theory and Practice*. New York: Harcourt, Brace and World, 1962.

Tye, Kenneth A. *Global Education: From Thought to Action, The 1991 ASCD Yearbook*. Alexandria, VA: Association for Supervision and Curriculum Development, 1991.

Chapter 6

Teacher Activism

The National Education Association and the American Federation of Teachers, AFL-CIO

Two major teacher organizations are competing enthusiastically for new members. One, the National Education Association (NEA), is strong essentially in suburban America, whereas the other, the American Federation of Teachers (AFT) (AFL-CIO), has its basic strength in older urban city school districts. The NEA outnumbers the AFT by almost three to one, leading observers to wonder how such a ratio could permit so intense a competition; however, the AFT's concentrated hold on many large urban school districts and its historic success with labor tactics have assured its significance. Both groups are attempting to make inroads into each other's "territory," especially now that unionization among white-collar workers in suburban communities is much more acceptable than it was thirty to forty years ago. Neither group, however, is that successful in reference to organizing teachers in rural school districts.

The reason for the lack of success of both groups in rural America is the control exerted upon teachers by boards of education and their administrative staff. Boards often see organized teacher strength as a powerful pressure upon their right to determine policies affecting salaries, working conditions, and fringe benefits. These powers have been traditionally and legally vested in boards of education. Despite legal changes in most states to allow collective bargaining, there is still friction in sharing decision-making affecting the welfare of teachers.

Both organizations speak for most of the nation's classroom teachers. There are approximately 2.5 million public school teachers in the United States, instructing almost 43 million youth enrolled from kindergarten through grade 12.[1] The membership of the NEA is approximately 2.2 million educators, of whom 1.9 million are classroom teachers (K–12).[2] The AFT, on the other hand, enrolls about

800,000 members, of whom the majority are classroom teachers (K through 12).[3] Obviously, some teachers do not care to join either the NEA or AFT for a variety of reasons, ranging from philosophical differences with the respective policies of both organizations to an unwillingness to pay dues to any teacher organization. It is safe to say, however, that both the NEA and AFT represent well over 80 percent of the teacher force (K through 12) in the United States.

Even though members rarely speak with a unanimous voice on any issue, the consensus view in each group has considerable impact upon the nation's schools. Policies affecting such national concerns as racial desegregation, curricular reform, academic freedom, and even the economy are promulgated vigorously; however, each group derives its strength from the "grassroots." Local involvement in school district or community activities is the prerogative of members in either the NEA or AFT. In other words, there is no dictatorial policy emanating from the national headquarters of either group. Policies are largely the outgrowth of local and state concerns and voted upon by the respective membership at the annual national meetings. Figures 6-1 and 6-2 illustrate the organizational structure of the NEA and the AFT.

Background of the National Education Association

The original name of the National Education Association was the National Teachers Association (NTA). This association was founded in 1857 as a result of the interest of ten state associations who thought the time had come to form a national organization. Representatives met in Philadelphia that year and heard an impressive appeal to make the calling of teaching a profession, as well as to promote the cause of public education. In this address, the members were challenged to initiate, when feasible, standards for upgrading the field of teaching. The NTA, it was urged, should obtain the legal right to admit and reject candidates for teaching. Licensure was to be vested in teachers themselves. Competency testing was recommended as a way to improve the profession. As a result of this improved professional behavior, teachers would make better salaries and the public would have more confidence in the quality of its teachers. Members left the meeting with great zeal, but the direction of the NTA for decades took another route, mainly that of curricular reform.

The NTA underwent structural change within 13 years. Its scope had become broader than promoting the welfare of only the classroom teacher. Three NTA departments technically were not teacher departments: The American Normal School Association, the National Association of School Superintendents, and the Department of Higher Education were connected with education but represented roles different from those performed by classroom teachers. As a result, in 1870 the name of the NTA was changed to the National Educational Association (NEA) to better reflect the diverse interests of the association. When the NEA obtained its charter from Congress in 1906, the name was changed again to the National Education Association, which has remained intact since that incorporation. From

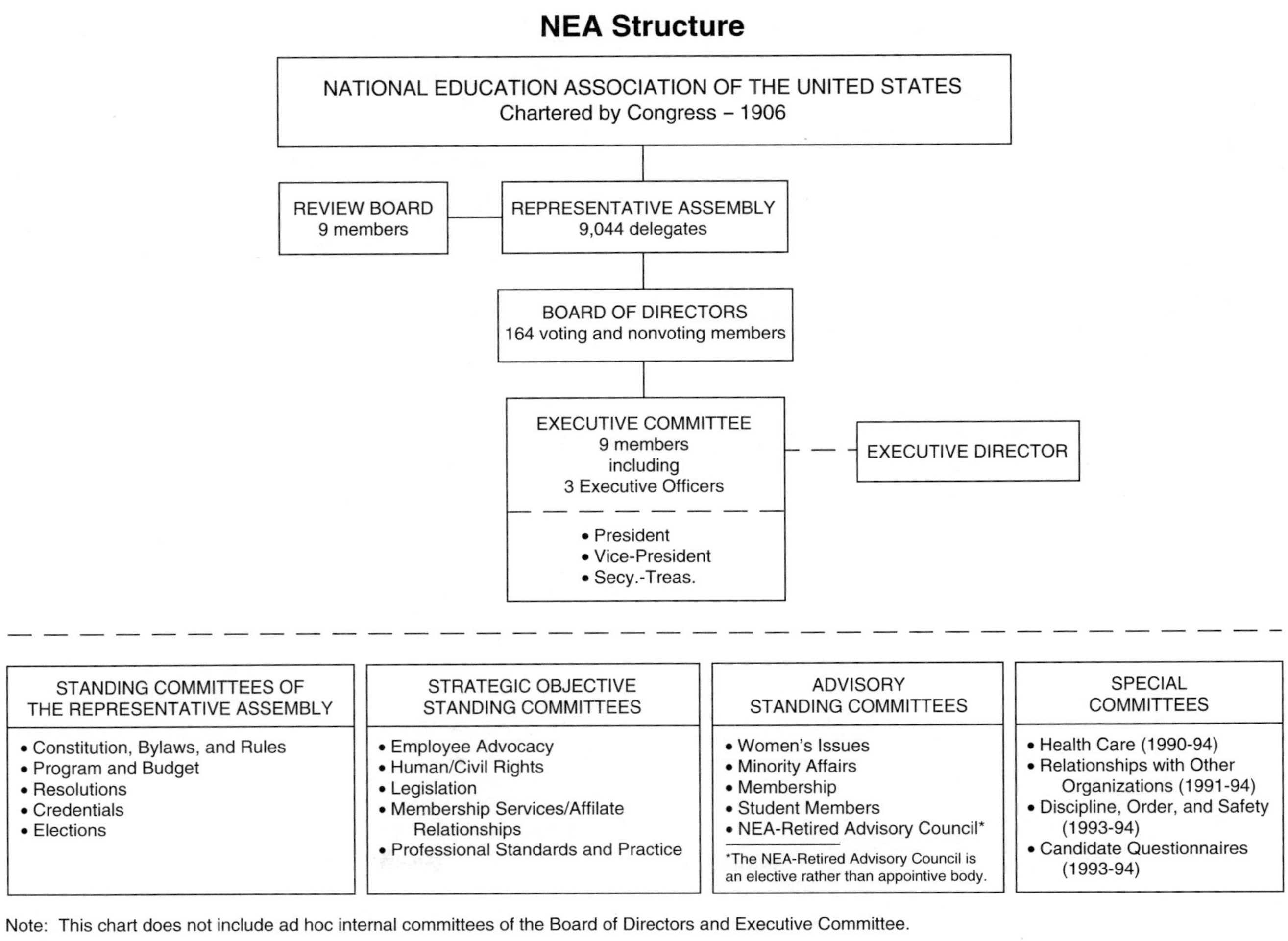

NEA Structure

NATIONAL EDUCATION ASSOCIATION OF THE UNITED STATES
Chartered by Congress – 1906

REVIEW BOARD
9 members

REPRESENTATIVE ASSEMBLY
9,044 delegates

BOARD OF DIRECTORS
164 voting and nonvoting members

EXECUTIVE COMMITTEE
9 members
including
3 Executive Officers

- President
- Vice-President
- Secy.-Treas.

EXECUTIVE DIRECTOR

STANDING COMMITTEES OF
THE REPRESENTATIVE ASSEMBLY

- Constitution, Bylaws, and Rules
- Program and Budget
- Resolutions
- Credentials
- Elections

STRATEGIC OBJECTIVE
STANDING COMMITTEES

- Employee Advocacy
- Human/Civil Rights
- Legislation
- Membership Services/Affilate Relationships
- Professional Standards and Practice

ADVISORY
STANDING COMMITTEES

- Women's Issues
- Minority Affairs
- Membership
- Student Members
- NEA-Retired Advisory Council*

*The NEA-Retired Advisory Council is an elective rather than appointive body.

SPECIAL
COMMITTEES

- Health Care (1990-94)
- Relationships with Other Organizations (1991-94)
- Discipline, Order, and Safety (1993-94)
- Candidate Questionnaires (1993-94)

Note: This chart does not include ad hoc internal committees of the Board of Directors and Executive Committee.

FIGURE 6-1 NEA Structure 1993–94

Source: NEA Handbook, 1993–94, Washington, D.C.: National Education Association, 1993, p. 12. Used with permission.

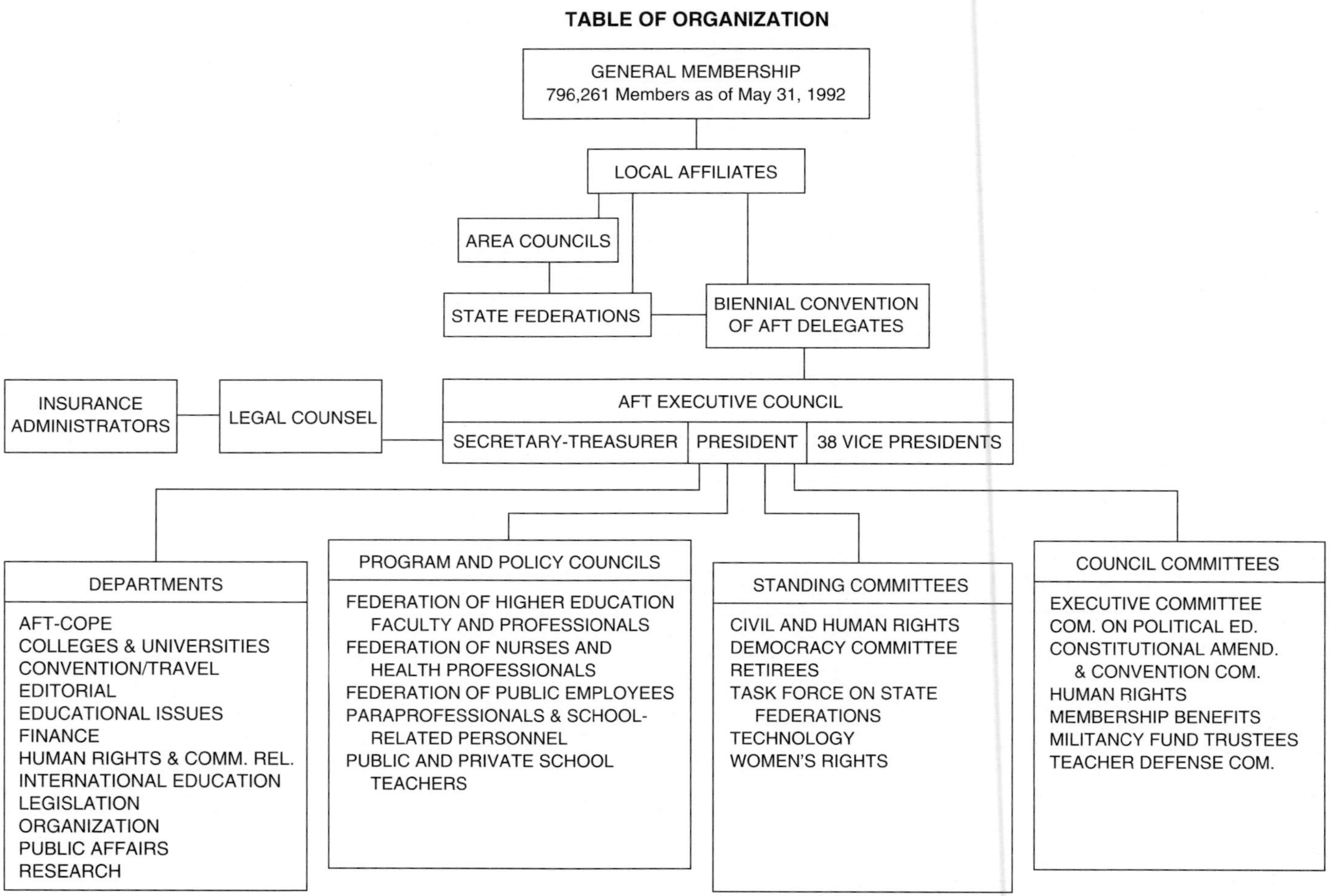

TABLE OF ORGANIZATION

FIGURE 6-2 American Federation of Teachers—AFL-CIO

Source: Constitution of the American Federation of Teachers (AFL-CIO), 1992, Washington, D.C. American Federation of Teachers, AFL-CIO, 1992, p. 24. Used with permission.

a theoretical viewpoint, this comprehensive approach to education may make sense, but historically one could argue that it served to divert collective effort away from local issues which could have improved teacher welfare more rapidly. Today, the NEA is vitally concerned about the economic well-being of its members; however, many believe this was not always the case. By including such diverse administrative and collegial interests early on in the NEA, the association tended to keep its priorities more at the national level rather than in the classroom at the local level.

The NEA, nevertheless, has had a profound impact upon American education. It helped to set national priorities for education even though education constitutionally is a state matter. It helped to shape public opinion in regard to the nation's educational ladder—preschool through the university—and it has stimulated change in regard to teacher education. Its historic record of creating prestigious national committees is a story of American education in itself.[4] For example, the Committee of Fifteen on Elementary Education (1893–1895) gave the elementary school much of its present curricular form. The Committee of Ten on Secondary School Studies (1892–1893) was another example of how the NEA provided direction for American education, although not without criticism by today's standards. The Committee of Ten reinforced a very conservative attitude about education. The theme of the report was subject centered and preparatory in terms of traditional college and university curricula. "Practical" courses, such as manual training and consumer subjects, were neglected. The value of academic discipline, in other words, was paramount and this helped to shape the high school for years to come. One can say that the findings of this Committee of Ten have a modern ring when compared with the recommendations of *A Nation at Risk* (1983).

These two examples of prestigious NEA committees are but a brief glimpse of far-reaching influence. Other diverse themes were also intensively investigated by committees: higher education, teacher education, state and city school systems, rural education, school hygiene, and so on. American education was profoundly influenced by these esoteric studies. The NEA has played a role in every major educational movement over the last century.

The NEA, in recent times, experienced a significant change in its approach to teacher activism. Until 1960, the NEA was opposed to such things as collective bargaining, striking, mediation, or anything pertinent to labor tactics. Professionalism traditionally was associated more with the performance of one's duties than with any economic benefits related to that employment. This attitude changed in the early 1960s. Teachers were growing more restless about low salaries and poor fringe benefits. It was also a period of burgeoning student enrollment, thereby causing financial difficulty for school boards in terms of overcrowding. Teachers wanted better working conditions. They wanted to participate to a greater degree in policy decisions that directly affected their welfare.

What precipitated change in the governance of the NEA was chiefly the success the AFT had in mobilizing the teachers of New York City in 1960 and 1962, despite the fact that more teachers in that district were members of the NEA than of the AFT.[5] This signaled alarm to the NEA because many believed that the association was not responsive enough to issues at the local level, whereas the AFT was. The stereotype was that the NEA was administratively dominated; consequently, change was in order. At that time, the NEA nationally out-numbered the AFT by almost ten to one; however, the aggressive stance of the AFT and its foothold in big cities really helped the AFT to compensate for its fewer numbers.

The NEA, after 1963, restructured itself to increase the voice of the classroom teacher in every aspect of NEA deliberations, from the national to the local levels. Committee membership was a key point. The requirement now in force is that all committees shall be comprised of at least 75 percent classroom teachers with a minimum of 20 percent ethnic-minority teachers on each committee. With this proportion of teachers represented on committees, the control by administrators in the association has lessened dramatically. The NEA has become a strong advocate of the classroom teacher. Teachers can now outvote administrators on key policy decisions. This point, however, is becoming moot as more and more administrators are leaving the ranks of the NEA.

As a result of this changing philosophy of teacher activism within the NEA dating from the mid-1960s on, the NEA's tactics have become similar to those of the AFT. It traditionally abhorred strikes and advocated only sanctions or negotiations. Presently, it sees strikes as sometimes necessary as a last resort. The NEA is no longer defensive about advocating such labor tactics as collective bargaining, for example. It does not feel apologetic, as stated earlier, that it is now considered both a union and an association. Through its committee structure, liaison is maintained not only with labor organizations and coalitions but also with political parties.

In 1966, an historic event further strengthened the influence of the NEA. It merged with the approximately 75,000-member American Teachers Association (ATA), a black association dating from 1904. Originally, the ATA was named National Association of Teachers in Colored Schools, founded by J.R.E. Lee of Tuskegee Institute. It evolved into the ATA and eventually enrolled both black and white educators. By 1966, sentiment developed to merge both the NEA and ATA. The significance of this merger beyond the sheer increase of NEA membership was the advancement of civil and human rights of all educators and children. Racism, as an issue, now can be more effectively attacked at the national, state, and local levels.

The NEA, over the last two decades, has become a formidable power in furthering the cause of public education as well as the economic welfare of teachers. Its Bill of Rights, adopted in 1991, reflects well much of the modern philosophy that propels the association. A careful reading of this document (*see* Box 6-1) indicates that teachers desire full first-class citizenship both as individuals and public employees.

After looking briefly at the background of the AFT, the authors will cite some comparisons between the NEA and AFT.

BOX 6-1   *Bill of Rights for Educational Employees*
Adopted by the 1991 NEA Representative Assembly

Bill of Rights for Educational Employees

Preamble

We, the educational employees of the United States of America, aware that a free society is dependent upon the education afforded its citizens, affirm the right freely to pursue truth and knowledge.

As an individual, the educational employee is entitled to such fundamental rights as dignity, privacy, and respect.

As a citizen, the educational employee is entitled to such basic constitutional rights as freedom of religion, speech, assembly, association, and political action and equal protection of the law.

In order to develop and preserve respect for the worth and dignity of humankind, to provide a climate in which actions develop as a consequence of rational thought, and to ensure intellectual freedom, we further affirm that educational employees must be free to contribute fully to an educational environment that secures the freedom to teach and the freedom to learn.

Believing that certain rights of educational employees derived from these fundamental freedoms must be universally recognized and respected, we proclaim this Bill of Rights for Educational Employees.

Article I—Rights as Members of the Education Community

a. As members of the education community, individual educational employees have the right—

Section 1. To maintain and improve their job-related skills.

Section 2. To influence effectively the formulation of policies and procedures that affect the nature and quality of the services that they perform.

Section 3. To safeguard information obtained in the course of their employment.

Section 4. To work in an atmosphere conducive to learning, including the use of reasonable means to preserve the learning environment and to protect the health and safety of students, themselves, and others.

Section 5. To express publicly views on matters affecting education.

Section 6. To attend meetings of and address the relevant governing body and be afforded access to its minutes when official action may affect the nature and quality of the services that they perform.

b. As members of the teaching profession, teachers have the right—

Section 1. To be licensed under professional and ethical standards established, maintained, and enforced by the profession.

Section 2. To maintain and improve their professional competence.

Section 3. To exercise professional judgment in presenting, interpreting, and criticizing information and ideas, including controversial issues.

Section 4. To influence effectively the formulation of policies and procedures that affect their professional services, including curriculum, teaching materials, methods of instruction, and school-community relations.

Section 5. To exercise professional judgment in the use of teaching methods and materials appropriate to the needs, interests, capacities, and the linguistic and cultural background of each student.

Article II—Rights as an Employee

As employees, educational employees have the right—

Section 1. To seek and be fairly considered for any position commensurate with their qualifications.

Section 2. To retain employment in the absence of a showing of just cause for dismissal or nonrenewal through fair and impartial proceedings.

Section 3. To be fully informed, in writing, of rules, regulations, terms, and conditions affecting their employment.

Continued

BOX 6-1   *Continued*

Section 4. To have conditions of employment in which health, security, and property are adequately protected.

Section 5. To influence effectively the development and application of evaluation procedures.

Section 6. To have access to written evaluations, to have documents placed in their personnel files to rebut derogatory information, and to have removed false or unfair material through a clearly defined process.

Section 7. To be free from arbitrary, capricious, or discriminatory actions affecting the terms and conditions of their employment.

Section 8. To be advised promptly in writing of the specific reasons for any actions which might affect their employment.

Section 9. To be afforded due process through the fair and impartial hearing of grievances, including binding arbitration, as a means of resolving disputes.

Section 10. To form, join, or assist employee organizations, to negotiate collectively through representatives of their own choosing, and to engage in other concerted activities for the purpose of negotiations or other mutual aid or protection.

Section 11. To withdraw services collectively when reasonable procedures to resolve impasse have been exhausted.

Article III—Rights in an Organization

As members of an employee organization, educational employees have the right—

Section 1. To acquire membership in employee organizations based upon reasonable standards equally applied.

Section 2. To have equal opportunity to participate freely in the affairs and governance of the organization.

Section 3. To have freedom of expression, both within and outside the organization.

Section 4. To vote for organization officers, either directly or through delegate bodies, in fair elections.

Section 5. To stand for and hold office subject only to fair qualifications uniformly applied.

Section 6. To be fairly represented by the organization in all matters.

Section 7. To be provided periodic reports of the affairs and conduct of business of the organization.

Section 8. To be provided detailed and accurate financial records, audited and reported at least annually.

Section 9. To be free from arbitrary disciplinary action or threat of such action by the organization.

Section 10. To be afforded due process by the organization in a disciplinary action.

Source: NEA Handbook, 1993–94, Washington, D.C.: National Education Association, 1993, pp. 372–74. Used with permission.

Background of the American Federation of Teachers

The American Federation of Teachers (AFT) (American Federation of Labor-Congress of Industrial Organizations) originated during the ferment of progressivism in American history at the turn of the century. The AFT is a unique organization because it is the only teacher association affiliated with organized labor, specifically the AFL-CIO. The inception of this union affiliation had two roots: one in San Antonio in 1902; the other in Chicago in the same year. The difference between the two developments was basically that, in the case of San Antonio, affiliation took place with the national labor federation, the AFL; whereas in the situation in Chicago, affiliation was enacted with the local federation of labor. Because of these two developments, heated discussion has continued to this day in regard to the relationship of organized labor with public education.

From 1901 until 1916, twenty locals in ten different states affiliated with organized labor, but not on a national basis. Consequently, many of the locals died under pressure of organized resistance, mainly from local school boards. The occurrence that seemed to swing the tide toward national affiliation of many locals with the AFL was the addition of two more Chicago locals in 1912–1913, which independently affiliated with local labor federations. This combination of Chicago locals laid the foundation for national ties three years later. Chicago played a crucial role in this entire process. The Chicago Federation of Teachers was founded first in 1897 (affiliated with local labor, 1902) while in 1912 and 1913 respectively, the Chicago Federation of Men Teachers and the Chicago Women High School Teachers took the same step. The nucleus was formed; a national organization was on the horizon. In 1916 eight charter locals, with an initial membership of just under 3,000 individuals, formed the American Federation of Teachers (AFT). The AFT was given a charter by the American Federation of Labor on May 9, 1916. It has remained ever since within the umbrella of labor affiliation.[6] When the American Federation of Labor joined with the Congress of Industrial Organizations in 1955, the AFT relationship was then with this combined force.

Much of the initial momentum for affiliation on the part of teacher organizations with organized labor was a strong desire among teachers to reform public education, especially in big cities. The union movement in education was part of the progressive phenomenon in American history. It was a reaction movement to corrupt school board politics; however, public opinion never has been overwhelmingly in support of teacher unionization. The growth of the AFT has been steady but unsystematic. During the 1920s and 1930s, organized resistance to unionization was intense.

Frankly, the real growth of the AFT did not occur until after its success in New York City in 1962 when it was elected as the bargaining agent for the city's teachers. Its militant stance even mobilized teachers who were members of the rival NEA local in that city; consequently, it has been in the national limelight ever since. Its gadfly role has provided an impetus for change within the NEA because the NEA has been forced to concern itself with more grassroots issues like salaries, class size, working conditions, and fringe benefits. The rewriting of the NEA constitution in the early 1970s to increase teacher participation within the Association was partly a consequence of the growing success of the AFT in urban school districts. The AFT has been a competitive organization despite its comparatively small numbers. Its strength is in urban areas but, as unionization among public employees has become more palatable nationally, growth has increased. Suburban school districts are fertile areas for potential members. Both the NEA and AFT compete to attract and retain members.

Benefits of Membership

National Education Association

Educators join organizations like the NEA and AFT for both idealistic and practical reasons. No organization could last long if it served only to be a source of fringe benefits; however, personal dividends must be an inherent part of an organization's efforts to seek and retain members. Ideally, individuals join the NEA and AFT to promote public education at all three governmental levels and to enhance educational opportunity for all social classes, races, and minorities, but they also desire special privileges as a result of their membership. In this section, an overview will be made of the more immediate dividends of participation in the NEA and AFT.

As a function of membership, the NEA offers a variety of publications. Members receive: for example, a newspaper entitled *NEA Today* and a special bulletin embracing issues pertinent to professional and personal matters. Furthermore, the state associations publish tabloids as well.

For years the NEA also has had an excellent reputation in regard to its research studies. The NEA research division investigates a multitude of themes related to school curricula, to civil rights, and to other germane social and political issues influencing public education. Research findings are available for a nominal cost to members and are held in high regard by most educators. Much of this research is unavailable elsewhere.

Since the preservation of teacher rights, especially academic freedom, is critical to public school teachers, the Kate Frank/Du Shane Unified Legal Services Program is invaluable to members. Another service is the Educators Employment Liability Program, which provides coverage up to $1 million for litigation arising out of accidents occurring to students while members are legally responsible for their instruction or supervision. The Attorney Referral Program also benefits members because they can receive, from participating lawyers, free consultation and discounts for personal legal matters.

Other special services available to NEA members provide a considerable financial saving and opportunity. Such plans as life insurance, accidental death and dismemberment, supplemental in-hospital and homeowners' insurance are available at group prices. These by no means cover all of the programs related to professional and personal benefits, but they illustrate the broad variety of services the NEA provides it members.[7]

American Federation of Teachers

The national headquarters in Washington, D.C., publishes materials for members of the various segments of the AFT. The *American Educator* is a quarterly professional journal of high quality for all members, as is the *American Teacher,* a monthly newspaper. *On Campus* is published for members of higher education. Finally, the *Reporter* is a quarterly newsletter for paraprofessionals and other school-related personnel.[8]

The AFT is a union of professionals. As a result, its national office supports a diversified policy to meet the needs of its members. In recent years, the AFT, on a national level, has conducted a number of workshops and surveys and disseminated a wealth of materials to enlighten members about such topics as school finance, teacher education, educational standards, and classroom management. The results of these activities are available to all members.

The AFT operates a defense fund to protect the rights of its members, particularly those members in jeopardy of losing job security. The legal costs related to collective bargaining come from the AFT's defense fund. The AFT's militancy fund is also a direct benefit for members. If a strike lasts five days, for example, the AFT will pay interest on a loan secured by the striking member. In addition, the AFT will pay legal fees in regard to strikes and, if necessary, will help in mitigating the burden of fines assessed for striking.[9]

Like the NEA, the AFT also provides its dues-paying members with a variety of insurance coverages, such as professional liability insurance and accidental death benefits. Special group rates on supplemental insurance programs are available on a competitive basis.[10] With approximately 800,000 members, the AFT can also offer its members a diversified number of benefits, ranging from expert consultation on educational matters to individualized insurance programs.

The following discussion is offered to contrast the NEA and AFT.

Comparisons: NEA and AFT (AFL-CIO)

Increasingly, it is difficult to contrast these two national organizations, the NEA and the AFT (AFL-CIO). Decades ago, the task would have been easier; however, they not only have become more complex but there are "gray" areas of differences. Similarities seem to be growing to the point that a merger someday may even be a possibility. Serious negotiation, however, would have to take place between the two groups to resolve the issues of the role of the AFL-CIO and members within the NEA who are administrators. Presently, there is a moratorium declared on mergers at any level. In one sense, a merger may mean more efficiency and direction for a large comprehensive organization. On the other hand, the gadfly role the AFT has played over the years has stimulated the NEA to play a more proactive role concerning teacher welfare, especially at the local level. There has been consideration in the 1990s about the merger of both organizations; however, it is still an embryonic idea. Merger is to be considered as an issue in future annual meetings of both organizations.

Membership

Both the NEA and AFT believe in unified membership. If one joins either organization, dues must be paid to all levels of that organization. Both groups believe that teacher advocacy must be on three fronts—national, state, and local. Educational lobbyists, for example, believe they must work to enlighten Congress about desirable legislation while, at the state level, teacher representatives try to influence legislators to support similar causes. Politically, visibility is costly for teacher organizations. Dues are the primary means of support for political activities for both organizations. It is usually easier to see how dues are expended for local concerns, but it is believed that for teacher activism to be effective it should permeate political and educational activity on all three levels of decision making.

The NEA membership policy concerning administrators within the organization is a controversial one. Members see a conflict of interest in many ways if principals and supervisors are active in policy making. These individuals represent management; they evaluate the performance of teachers. Administrators have been leaving the NEA in large numbers simply because they no longer see the organization as their advocate. Some administrators, however, feel rooted to the NEA because they were once teachers and realize that whatever educational or economic gain for teachers is achieved in a district usually means economic advantage for themselves.

The NEA policy about administrators as members is left largely to the discretion of the local affiliates. They can include or exclude administrators as local members and, hence, as state and national members as well. In some places, administrators, because of the inherent possibility of conflict of interests, are excluded from local affiliation only.

Both the NEA and AFT have broadened their views about nonteachers belonging to each group. The AFT first sought other public employees, including support personnel such as school nurses and secretaries, to join their ranks. Principals have been shunned because of their managerial/evaluation functions; however, many principals have aligned themselves independently with the AFL-CIO. This broader view of membership is basically why the AFT ranks have increased to roughly 800,000 members. The NEA has taken a somewhat similar view because custodians and school nurses, for example, are free to join. The premise is that those in an educationally supportive capacity are now needed in the organization as long as they are not in an evaluative role concerning teachers.

The AFT is much more sensitive about its ranks being "teacher pure." The AFT, in fact, maintains the position that no one holding a nonteaching position of principal or higher can join. Teachers holding supervisory authority can be admitted if the local allows it. Those educators excluded from the AFT can, however, form their own locals and affiliate with labor. AFT policy has long held that teaching embodies an employer-employee relationship. Consequently, any formal ties within the AFT between administrator and teacher may constitute acute conflicts of interest. Many members, it is believed, could even be stifled in terms of organizational participation if their principal or supervisor is present at meetings. Even though the NEA is a comprehensive organization, it is becoming more like the AFT in this regard. When certain members of a group have the right to hire, fire, or discipline others, some NEA members believe that rapport may be damaged.

Since both the NEA and AFT have taken strong positions against fringe benefits to non-public schools such as tax credits and possibly vouchers, it is clear that nonpublic school teachers generally will have little in common with either group. The NEA in fact, believes tax credits and voucher plans would constitute bad educational policy, bad economic policy, and bad public policy, so it will continue to assist groups in support of the public school.[11] The AFT president, Albert Shanker, has gone on record over the years attacking vouchers as a possible means of school support. It should be noted, however, that the AFT will charter locals in private schools below the college level on the same basis as it will for those in the public sector.

Both groups are interested in mobilizing faculty in higher education. The issue of church and state in education is a more crucial one below the college level because of the factors of compulsory education and tax support. The NEA and AFT believe that public schools below the college level should be the primary recipients of tax support. Private schools, they believe, certainly have the right to exist, but at their own expense—except for a few benefits, such as the federal surplus commodities program or fire and police protection. Enrolling such faculty on a separate basis, the NEA and AFT advocate, is not incongruent with their stance about tax support for public schools only.

Both groups see a good potential in higher education for new members. If there is only a moderate increase in K-through-12 enrollment over the next several years, the need for new members will continue to force both groups to be fiercely competitive. Potential members outside the traditional markets will surely be exploited. New markets, in combination with the need to replace teachers leaving the profession for retirement or different careers, will keep both the NEA and AFT very active.

Organized Labor

The NEA and AFT differ sharply on this point. The attitude of the NEA concerning organized labor embodies the view that it is an organization different from those groups affiliated under the umbrella of the AFL-CIO. The NEA simply prefers to be a teacher advocate on an independent basis. Through its committee structure, the NEA maintains close ties with organized labor, but this is different from AFL-CIO affiliation. Educational concerns may sometimes conflict with labor views on planned state legislation or tax proposals; consequently, the NEA prefers to make independent judgments on these matters. Vested interests, the NEA believes, can be kept more in balance if an organization of teachers remains basically autonomous. The NEA believes that cooperation with organized labor on common concerns is extremely desirable.

The NEA, furthermore, employs the tactics of organized labor without apology. It supports collective bargaining laws for public employees, undertakes strikes, and supports related activism such as mediation and arbitration. The NEA, according to many individuals, is looking more like a union all the time. As stated earlier, the Department of Labor has classified the NEA as a union; however, the NEA thinks of itself as both a union and an association. Regardless of its category, the NEA desires to remain structurally independent. This point has been a serious issue in any discussion on merger with the AFT.

The AFT, on the other hand, sees nothing but advantages in relation to its affiliation with organized labor. It views teaching inherently as an employer-employee relationship.[12] Both sides will have common and uncommon goals. The employer cannot always support the concerns of the employee. Hence, educational personnel need to collaborate with other affiliates to further those costly but necessary goals such as higher salaries, smaller classes, more support services, greater academic freedom, and increased insurance benefits. Although these dividends might be obtained on an independent, collective basis, they can be attained more expeditiously by close cooperation with organized labor.

The AFT believes organized labor in the United States has always been supportive of public education. The embryonic trade unions in the early nineteenth century clamored for free, tax-supported schools. Later, the American Federation of Labor, under the leadership of Samuel Gompers, crusaded for educational reform. Certainly today, the AFT believes the AFL-CIO is a confederation of working people who hold public education in high regard and who offer political support when necessary. In other words, the tradition of organized labor in the United States is tied symbiotically with public education. Affiliation with labor implies no obligation on the part of the AFT to support only those causes of organized labor. The relationship is not a dictatorial one.

There are, according to the AFT, some palpable benefits of affiliation with the AFL-CIO. First, there is the benefit of political support for educational causes. Lobbying for desired social or educational legislation cannot be done by educators alone. Federal legislation, for example, is crucial to the welfare of children and teachers at the local level. Because the various state legislatures are so powerful in regard to education at the local level, teacher representatives and their allies must lobby legislators continually. Most states now have laws allowing public school teachers to bargain collectively. If it were not for the support of organized labor, legislatures would have passed little school legislation. The same argument can be said of educational concerns in Congress. Educational bills for the disabled, for the economically disadvantaged, and so on, have the backing of organized labor. It takes a collaborative effort to strengthen public education.

A second palpable benefit of affiliation with organized labor, the AFT argues, is "sympathy" support during a confrontation with a board of education. Legal experts and strike organizers can come from other geographic regions to offer their expertise in helping to resolve the local dilemma. Low-interest loans can be provided by locals to AFT strikers. Members of other AFL-CIO affiliated locals who may serve the school district in some capacity may withhold their services. They may also refuse to cross the teachers' picket line during a strike. The teachers involved in a strike may advertise their concerns in the various labor newspapers at little or no cost. Most of these job actions are almost impossible to undertake without the moral and financial support of other AFL-CIO union locals.

A third direct benefit of such union affiliation is the support of other unions in a variety of ways. Since there are approximately 15 million members of international unions, whose workers reside in the United States, it is hoped that these members and their families will be in favor of public education in basic ways:

1. Supporting school tax elections
2. Voting for appropriate people for political and school board positions
3. Enlightening fellow citizens about the cause of public education

Collective Bargaining and Negotiations

The change within the NEA over the last 20 years concerning collective bargaining or negotiations for public employees has been a radical one considering its history. Traditionally, the NEA has viewed labor tactics as unprofessional. During the early decades of the AFT, the NEA was opposed strongly to AFT affiliation with organized labor basically on the grounds that the public school serves all social classes, not just a single social segment. Labor affiliation meant collective bargaining, which was viewed by the NEA as an antithetical process to becoming a profession. Through the 1960s, the NEA's approach in dealing with boards of education to win concessions for teachers was essentially through negotiations and sanctions. The former process meant discussion with teacher representatives and consultants of the NEA, but no written agreements or obligations on either side were common. Sanctions often implied public censure by the NEA usually upon a board of education; however, little activism by teachers ever occurred beyond rendering negative publicity.

As the AFT gained greater national visibility in the 1960s, the NEA became more competitive in regard to teacher welfare at the local level. Professional or collective negotiations became an NEA euphemism for collective bargaining. The NEA thought negotiations for teachers might become a sound legal goal at the state level, but the AFT took the position of collective bargaining for all public employees (including teachers) as a more palatable position.

Presently, both the NEA and AFT are somewhat consistent in their view about the process of collective bargaining for all public employees and both support implementation at the state level. The NEA ironically now has a liberal view about labor cooperation. Collective negotiations, or bargaining has radically changed American education over the last two decades. Today, over half of the states have enacted collective negotiations laws affecting teachers. The underlying consideration in collective negotiations is participation in the decision-making process, which is a natural extension of our democratic heritage. Teachers do not want boards of education to make decisions about their salaries, fringe benefits, and working conditions without direct input from their representatives.

"Collective negotiations" is the process by which representatives of the school board meet with representatives of the school district employees to make proposals and counterproposals for the purpose of agreeing on salaries, fringe benefits, and working conditions for a specific period of time. To implement this process, it is necessary for the board of education to adopt a policy that will give the administration the authority to implement negotiations.

Collective actions by employees have a long history in the private sector going back as far as the medieval guilds. These actions have always been influenced by the economic, political, and social conditions of the times. Four major congressional acts provide legal guidelines for collective bargaining in the private sector: The Norris-LaGuardia Act of 1932, the National Labor Relations Act of 1935, the Labor-Management Relations Act of 1947, and the Labor-Management Reporting and Disclosure Act of 1959. Collective negotiations in the federal government have been affirmed by Executive Orders 10988 and 11491. Thereby, federal employees have the right to organize and bargain collectively but cannot strike.

Public school teachers are state employees working in a local unit, the school district. Therefore, they are not covered by federal legislation but rather by the acts of state legislatures. There are substantial differences in the state statutes granting collective negotiations rights to teachers.

There are five aspects to the collective negotiations process: recognition and bargaining unit determination, the scope of negotiations, the bargaining process, impasse procedures, and master agreement administration.

The recognition and bargaining unit determination process answers the question, "Who represents whom?" Recognition is the acceptance by an employer of a bargaining agent as the authorized representative of a bargaining unit. There are two types of recognition, multiple and exclusive. Experience dictates that exclusive recognition is the most effective. The three most commonly used recognition procedures are membership lists, authorization cards, and elections. In an election, a third party, such as the Federal Mediation and Conciliation Service, should be engaged to handle the mechanics of the election process.

The bargaining unit is composed of all the employees covered by the negotiated master agreement. The criteria for deciding who belongs to the unit are the following: a community of interest among employees, effective bargaining power, and effective school administration.

The scope of negotiations usually includes salaries, fringe benefits, and working conditions. A major problem in defining "scope" is the fine line between educational policy, which is the prerogative of the school board, and a condition of employment, which is negotiable.

The "at the table" negotiations process must begin with the formation of negotiating teams. The teams are responsible for developing strategies, formulating goals, setting the ground rules, preparing proposals, and participating in at-the-table sessions. When an agreement is reached by the negotiating teams, ratification by the respective governing bodies (teachers, school board) is the final step in the process.

If there is persistent disagreement that cannot be resolved through the at-the-table process, an impasse has been reached. The three usual procedures for resolving an impasse are mediation, fact-finding, and, where permitted by law, arbitration. Mediation is a voluntary procedure by which a third party intervenes for the purpose of ending the disagreement. Fact-finding is a procedure by which an individual or panel holds hearings for the purpose of reviewing evidence and making a recommendation for settling the dispute. Arbitration occurs when both sides submit the dispute to an impartial third person who makes a decision that the parties are required to accept.

There is nothing more disruptive to a school district than a strike, which is sometimes used by unions when negotiations reach an impasse. Although strikes by teachers are illegal in most states, a large number of strikes occur each year.

The process of collective negotiations is usually ineffective unless the negotiated agreement is put into writing. This formalizes the provisions that will govern the parties for the term of the agreement. It is the responsibility of the administration to implement the master agreement. Furthermore, the administration is limited only by the specifics of the agreement, which is commonly referred to as "management prerogative." In the day-to-day interpretation of the master agreement, it is certainly possible for violations to occur. Most written agreements, therefore, provide for a grievance procedure by which individuals, the union, or the administration may allege that the agreement is being violated.

"Collaborative bargaining" appeared in the mid 1980s as an alternative to the traditional bargaining model in an attempt to defuse the hostility that can accompany collective negotiations. Here, a single team is composed of teachers, board members, and administrators. The team's mission is problem solving rather than engaging in bargaining. All team members must be involved in extensive staff development for this model to be successful. Time will reveal if this is an acceptable alternative to collective negotiation.

Merit Pay

The subject of paying teachers in a differential manner based upon the perceived quality of their performance has, for a long time, conjured up much emotion by teachers and the public alike. While there has seldom been much disagreement about the fact that some teachers are better than others and should be rewarded for the quality of their performance, just how to reward them fairly becomes another matter. Almost everyone agrees that to pay good teachers well will help retain them in the classroom. This may also attract other aspiring, potentially superlative teachers. Many people, in addition, stress the point that until good teachers are paid competitively with other professionals, they will end up in school administration, industry, or another profession. Few people will argue with any of these foregoing assumptions.

The problem, however, becomes more a question of how to evaluate teachers objectively in order to financially reward them accordingly and yet, at the same time, maintain morale and cooperation among all teachers. Teachers see themselves as unique because their roles usually differ sharply one from another. Students, academically and emotionally, also vary from class to class, giving rise to different expectations and satisfactions. Measuring chiefly academic achievement as a criterion of merit does not truly reflect the total effort and success of every teacher. Creativity in the classroom is difficult to standardize. The problem of evaluation is compounded by the problem that differences among teachers are often more subtle than obvious. It is not so much a problem of good versus bad teaching, but rather good versus slightly less than good teaching. What objective criteria differentiate these more subtle differences? Too often, the differences between good and bad teaching may be unduly related to the evaluator's philosophy.

Merit pay schedules exist in numerous school districts, although most teachers are paid on the basis of a single salary schedule reflecting formal education and years of successful teaching. Merit salary considerations, however, are becoming more politically appealing as conservative forces are felt more strongly in public education. The Gallup polls have traditionally held that the public favors merit pay while teachers oppose it. Most of the public surveyed also believes that academic achievement, or improved academic performance as measured by standardized tests, should be a significant criterion in determining merit pay for teachers. The fact that the issue is becoming politically more popular indicates that legislatures and state departments will continue to develop merit plans in the context of "career incentives" for teachers.

Merit pay for teachers in theory is sound. It stimulates teachers to think of themselves as key elements in the students' progress, thereby enlarging the concept of accountability. The teacher, it is believed by those advocates of merit pay, should be responsible for a product of some kind, and student achievement is the logical product for which the teacher should be held accountable. Simply because it is difficult to evaluate teacher success in this regard is no reason, some believe, to avoid trying to differentiate good from mediocre teachers. Advocates of merit pay believe that, since human beings by nature are competitive, merit pay can capitalize on that competitiveness and, consequently, the school benefits in terms of improved quality of instruction.

Merit pay, furthermore, tends to lessen mediocrity in the sense that all teachers will have the opportunity to receive greater recognition if they pursue excellence. Greater prestige and financial reward will accompany that recognition of excellence by both colleagues and the public alike. There will be a greater sense of professionalism if teachers are differentiated by achievement and rewarded appropriately. The result may tend to keep teachers in the classroom. Presently, a teacher aspiring to a higher standard of living will often leave the classroom and become, for example, an administrator simply because of the opportunity to earn more money. It is, however, axiomatic in the education industry that a good teacher does not necessarily make a good administrator. The skills are different for each role. Therefore, if one has become a good teacher, why not help that person stay in the classroom by means of a superlative salary?

The NEA and AFT believe that, once all teachers make adequate salaries, then perhaps criteria can be established to differentiate teachers according to their annual performance. Teachers advocate that they also should be judges of excellent teaching. Committees of teachers, it is believed, constitute a sound means of recognizing differences among their peers. Teachers should play a strong role in establishing the criteria to determine meritorious performance. The NEA and AFT realistically see such accountability legally coming as a requirement of employment, so they want to play a crucial part in its planning and execution. Otherwise, they believe, administrators alone will be the judges of good teaching and only a few teachers will make good salaries. Until recently, both the NEA and AFT had opposed differentiated pay and supported only the single salary concept because of subjective factors in the evaluation process. Greater fairness could be achieved, they believed, by implementation of the criteria of formal education and successful experience alone (usually years of teaching) as the basis for salary increases.

As mentioned earlier, the public will continue to expect greater accountability in terms of educational performance by both students and teachers. As a result, what is emerging in some states is the concept of "career ladders" or performance incentives for teachers. These embody frequent evaluation, greater responsibility and recognition for stellar performance, and higher salaries for that achievement. "Career ladder" is a relative term for a plan whereby teachers are differentiated by teaching experience, added responsibility, and evaluation of performance. As teachers move through the system in regard to successful years of teaching, they achieve higher status, both in light of recognition and salary. Responsibility, leadership, and frequent evaluations all become characteristics of career ladder plans. Both the NEA and AFT are taking supportive stances on such career ladders. Both organizations desire that these ladders will be based upon competitive salaries for all teachers before "career" options become available to those seeking additional responsibility with commensurate reward. A number of serious questions face legislatures and state departments in designing performance incentives (including career ladders) for teachers. If these career ladders or incentives are intended to enhance excellence in teaching, then each of the following representative questions must be addressed in the local districts where the ladders or incentives will be implemented:

1. Where does the responsibility lie for the control of career ladders? Does it lie with the state or with the local school district?
2. What should the criteria be to establish meritorious recognition for teachers?
3. How should the evaluations of teachers in the various categories be undertaken? Should administrators also be evaluated?

4. What significance should written examinations play in the advancement of teachers on the career ladder?[13]

Both the NEA and AFT will strive to play a larger role in the planning and execution of the various performance incentives as they develop. If teachers do not become involved closely with their formation, they will have little voice in what will have profound consequences upon their welfare. The AFT, NEA, and others are seeking to establish a national professional teacher board, which would become involved with testing prospective teachers and maintaining standards of competence.

Ethics

Both the NEA and AFT are concerned about ethical behavior in the classroom on the part of all teachers and administrators. State laws vary on what constitutes ethical practice for teachers, especially in their dealings with children, but most states want teachers to be moral and humane and to fulfill their contractual duties. Ethical standards are seldom determined by teachers, but rather by legislators. In a sense, this demeans the notion that professionals determine their own ethical code of behavior. In public education, noneducators determine what is appropriate professional behavior.

The AFT has traditionally not concerned itself with developing a specific code of ethics, probably because it feared that boards of education might use such codes against teachers if their activism becomes excessive. If codes, in other words, were open to interpretation, teachers might suffer. The AFT prefers to promulgate statements of teacher rights in regard to first-class citizenship and academic freedom (*see* Box 6-2). The lack of a code does not necessarily mean that the AFT has little regard for personal ethical standards. It means that enforcement of the tenets of an AFT code of ethics is not believed to be feasible. The AFT recently, however, is supporting an ethical code as part of a national teacher board, so its position may be changing on this point.

The NEA, on the other hand, has supported a code of ethics since 1929. It has been revised six times since; its last revision took place in 1975 (*see* Box 6-3). Interest in the code has waxed and waned over the decades, with the greatest interest expressed during the 1960s. The courts have declared, in recent years, that the code is applicable to NEA members only, thus weakening its enforcement. Tenets of the code which pertained to contractual obligations of the teachers were excluded. This did not weaken its intent but did reduce the content of earlier codes. For example, the code over the last 20 years has been reduced from four principles to two.

One of the serious problems that the NEA has experienced over the life of the codes has been enforcement. Today, the state and local NEA associations deal mainly with rendering their own ethical opinions, although the review board at the national level is empowered to deal with ethical cases. Statistics have not been

BOX 6-2   *American Federation of Teachers Bill of Rights*

The teacher is entitled to a life of dignity equal to the high standard of service that is justly demanded of that profession. Therefore, we hold these truths to be self-evident.

I. Teachers have the right to think freely and to express themselves openly and without fear. This includes the right to hold views contrary to the majority.

II. They shall be entitled to the free exercise of their religion. No restraint shall be put upon them in the manner, time, or place of their worship.

III. They shall have the right to take part in social, civil, and political affairs. They shall have the right, outside the classroom, to participate in political campaigns and to hold office. They may assemble peaceably and may petition any government agency, including their employers, for a redress of grievances. They shall have the same freedom in all things as other citizens.

IV. The right of teachers to live in places of their own choosing, to be free from restraint in their mode of living, and the use of their leisure time shall not be abridged.

V. Teaching is a profession, the right to practice which is not subject to the surrender of other human rights. No one shall be deprived of professional status, or the right to practice it, or the practice thereof in any particular position, without due process of law.

VI. The right of teachers to be secure in their jobs, free from political influence or public clamor, shall be established by law. The right to teach after qualification in the manner prescribed by law is a property right, based upon the inalienable rights to life, liberty, and the pursuit of happiness.

VII. In all cases affecting the teacher's employment or professional status, a full hearing by an impartial tribunal shall be afforded with the right of full judicial review. No teacher shall be deprived of employment or professional status but for specific causes established by law having a clear relation to the competence or qualification to teach, proved by the weight of evidence. In all such cases, the teacher shall enjoy the right to a speedy and public trial, to be informed of the nature and cause of the accusation, to be confronted with the accusing witnesses, to subpoena witnesses and papers, and to the assistance of counsel. No teacher shall be called upon to answer any charge affecting his employment or professional status but upon probable cause, supported by oath or affirmation.

VIII. It shall be the duty of the employer to provide culturally adequate salaries, security in illness and adequate retirement income. The teacher has the right to such a salary as will: (a) afford a family standard of living comparable to that enjoyed by other professional people in the community; (b) make possible freely chosen professional study; (c) afford the opportunity for leisure and recreation common to our heritage.

IX. No teacher shall be required under penalty of reduction of salary to pursue studies beyond those required to obtain professional status. After serving a reasonable probationary period, a teacher shall be entitled to permanent tenure terminable only for just cause. They shall be free as in other professions in the use of their own time. They shall not be required to perform extracurricular work against their will or without added compensation.

X. To equip people for modern life requires the most advanced educational meth-

Continued

BOX 6-2 *Continued*

ods. Therefore, the teacher is entitled to good classrooms, adequate teaching materials, teachable class size, and administrative protection and assistance in maintaining discipline.

XI. These rights are based upon the proposition that the culture of a people can rise only as its teachers improve. A teaching force accorded the highest possible professional dignity is the surest guarantee that blessings of liberty will be preserved. Therefore, the possession of these rights imposes the challenge to be worthy of their enjoyment.

XII. Since teachers must be free in order to teach freedom, the right to be members of organizations of their own choosing must be guaranteed. In all matters pertaining to their salaries and working conditions, they shall be entitled to bargain collectively through representatives of their own choosing. They are entitled to have the schools administered by superintendents, boards, or committees which function in a democratic manner.

Source: American Federation of Teachers, Washington, D.C. Used with permission.

publicized in recent years concerning code violations, hearings, and recommendations, so it is somewhat unclear about what status or priority the code has. The tenets of the code, however, have applicability to every member of the NEA. Given the overwhelming number of teachers in the NEA, its potential is great.

No state, in the authors' opinion, has yet to tie certification requirements with the NEA Code of Ethics. From the viewpoint of the NEA, nonmembers might then flout ethical standards, particularly if state law is weak in outlining positive or high standards of professional behavior. The NEA prefers that a code of ethical standards be developed by teachers for teachers. In this manner, public confidence can be increased and greater professional stature can be achieved. The NEA can control its own destiny to a greater extent by setting standards for admission, retention, and expulsion. For any occupation to be truly considered a profession, it must reflect a code of ethics. Teaching still has a way to go before a consensus is reached among all practitioners about a clear, enforceable code of ethics. As stated earlier, if the AFT and others are successful in implementing a national teacher board, issues such as ethics, incompetence, and assessment will become themes teachers will consider. Hence, greater professionalism will result.

Some Critics of NEA and AFT Activism

Neither the NEA nor the AFT is without its organized critics. School administrators and boards of education have long constituted the bulk of the opposition to teacher activism such as collective bargaining or striking. Because teachers are public employees, it is believed by many that teachers should not exhibit the kind of labor tactics seen in the private sector. Over the years, however, school boards

BOX 6-3 *Code of Ethics of the Education Profession*
   Adopted by the 1975 NEA Representative Assembly

Preamble

The educator, believing in the worth and dignity of each human being, recognizes the supreme importance of the pursuit of truth, devotion to excellence, and the nurture of democratic principles. Essential to these goals is the protection of freedom to learn and to teach and the guarantee of equal educational opportunity for all. The educator accepts the responsibility to adhere to the highest ethical standards.

The educator recognizes the magnitude of the responsibility inherent in the teaching process. The desire for the respect and confidence of one's colleagues, of students, of parents, and of the members of the community provides the incentive to attain and maintain the highest possible degree of ethical conduct. The Code of Ethics of the Education Profession indicates the aspiration of all educators and provides standards by which to judge conduct.

The remedies specified by the NEA and/or its affiliates for the violation of any provision of this Code shall be exclusive and no such provision shall be enforceable in any form other than one specifically designated by the NEA or its affiliates.

Principle I—Commitment to the Student

The educator strives to help each student realize his or her potential as a worthy and effective member of society. The educator therefore works to stimulate the spirit of inquiry, the acquisition of knowledge and understanding, and the thoughtful formulation of worthy goals.

In fulfillment of the obligation to the student, the educator—

1. Shall not unreasonably restrain the student from independent action in the pursuit of learning.
2. Shall not unreasonably deny the student access to varying points of view.
3. Shall not deliberately suppress or distort subject matter relevant to the student's progress.
4. Shall make reasonable effort to protect the student from conditions harmful to learning or to health and safety.
5. Shall not intentionally expose the student to embarrassment or disparagement.
6. Shall not on the basis of race, color, creed, sex, national origin, marital status, political or religious beliefs, family, social or cultural background, or sexual orientation, unfairly:
   a. Exclude any student from participation in any program;
   b. Deny benefits to any student;
   c. Grant any advantage to any student.
7. Shall not use professional relationships with students for private advantage.
8. Shall not disclose information about students obtained in the course of professional service, unless disclosure serves a compelling professional purpose or is required by law.

Principle II—Commitment to the Profession

The education profession is vested by the public with a trust and responsibility requiring the highest ideals of professional service:

In the belief that the quality of the services of the education profession directly influences the nation and its citizens, the educator shall exert every effort to raise professional standards, to promote a climate that encourages the exercise of professional judgment, to achieve conditions which attract persons worthy of the trust to careers in education, and to assist in preventing the practice of the profession by unqualified persons.

In fulfillment of the obligation to the profession, the educator—

1. Shall not in an application for a professional position deliberately make a false statement or fail to disclose a material fact related to competency and qualifications.

Continued

BOX 6-3   *Continued*

2. Shall not misrepresent his/her professional qualifications.
3. Shall not assist entry into the profession of a person known to be unqualified in respect to character, education, or other relevant attribute.
4. Shall not knowingly make a false statement concerning the qualifications of a candidate for a professional position.
5. Shall not assist a noneducator in the unauthorized practice of teaching.
6. Shall not disclose information about colleagues obtained in the course of professional service unless disclosure serves a compelling professional purpose or is required by law.
7. Shall not knowingly make false or malicious statements about a colleague.
8. Shall not accept any gratuity, gift, or favor that might impair or appear to influence professional decisions or actions.

Source: NEA Handbook, 1993–94, Washington, D.C.: National Education Association, 1993, pp. 376–77. Used with permission.

and administrators have learned to negotiate their differences with NEA and AFT groups.

A new phenomenon seems to be emerging in the sense that some teachers find membership in either the NEA or AFT in conflict with their political or economic philosophy. One group of 20,000 members called the Concerned Educators Against Forced Unionism (CEAFU) is the educational wing of the National Right to Work Committee. Its mission is to oppose such principles as "exclusive representation," "agency shop," and "maintenance of membership" agreements. In the case of exclusive representation, a group of teachers seeking to be the bargaining agent for all teachers in the school district actually can turn out to represent only a *minority* of the teachers in that school district. The majority of teachers then would have little to say about their welfare. Selection predicated on the belief that the group with the most members represents all teachers irrespective of their membership or beliefs is unfair.

Agency shops are repugnant to members of CEAFU because nonmembers must pay a fee to the representative bargaining agent or possibly be fired. The assumption is, because all teachers benefit from any settlement with the board of education, then all should bear the cost of negotiations. It is the bargaining agent's way of getting "freeloaders" (in its view) to share the burden. Some states have accepted legally the concept of agency shop in regard to teachers. Another issue abhorrent to members of CEAFU is the maintenance of membership agreements. This concept means that once a contract between the teachers' elected or appointed bargaining agent and board of education is ratified, then resignation from membership in that association or local becomes more difficult. With both agency shop and maintenance of membership agreements, greater control is exerted by the union. People supporting the "right to work" principle oppose such growing unionism.[14]

The John Birch Society is an organized lay group of approximately 100,000 conservative citizens who ardently oppose much of the activism of both the AFT and NEA. This society, dating from 1958, has been committed to the mission of fighting communism (considered an international conspiracy) and promoting a free enterprise economic policy with as much local, political control as possible. In terms of education, the society encourages increased parental and citizen control, especially as expressed through boards of education. Teachers are viewed as public employees with very restricted rights in terms of collective bargaining or striking.

The public school, in the Birch view, is in need of drastic reformation in that its mission needs to be narrowed to the transmission of intellectual skills only. The less the school serves as a "change agent" in regard to traditional values, the better. Obviously, teachers advocating militant positions in either the NEA or AFT are not going to win community support from local Birch members.

In conclusion, it should be pointed out, just because one does not agree with either the philosophy or tactics within the NEA or AFT does not mean that one endorses the principles of CEAFU or the John Birch Society. Some teachers are forming independent local associations because they disagree with the directions of the two dominant organizations. Other teachers join no professional groups, which is, in the authors' view, the least desirable option of all. Teachers who participate in professional activities will have more opportunities to influence their careers.

Summary

The National Education Association (NEA) and the American Federation of Teachers (AFL-CIO) are the two dominant teacher organizations in public education below the college level. The NEA, founded in 1857, has grown to 2 million members, with its strength rooted in suburban school districts. Its direction over the years has moved drastically from that of seeking cooperation among all vested interests in public education to that of teacher advocacy in terms of improved salary, fringe benefits, and working conditions. It has become more of a union in recent years, but it thinks of itself as both a union and an association. Its scope, of course, is much greater than the pursuit of economic advantage only.

The AFT is the only organization for teachers affiliated with organized labor on a national basis. It was founded in 1916 after years of effort by local affiliates to cure abuses of school boards in several big cities. Affiliation with labor was seen as politically advantageous, although its growth since has been irregular. Early decades brought fierce resistance to the unionization of public school teachers. The AFT's strength has traditionally been in the big cities. Presently, its membership consists of approximately 800,000 members. Membership has increased because of new categories of support personnel in education, such as school secretaries, bus drivers, and nurses. The NEA has taken a similar attitude about the membership of nonsupervisory school personnel in its ranks.

The NEA and AFT are growing similar in some respects but different in others. Both have become such energetic teacher advocates that almost all activity is teacher directed. Their respective positions about collective bargaining and merit pay are similar, although it remains to be seen how each specific group will continue to react to mandated career ladders for teachers in the various states. It is logical, of course, to assume that both organizations will strive to be instrumental in the planning and prosecution of these state proposals.

Differences between the two groups lie particularly in the arena of labor affiliation. The AFT finds theoretical and practical reasons for affiliation with organized labor under the aegis of the AFL-CIO. This relationship is advantageous. The NEA, on the other hand, sees more advantage to independent activism, without the possibility of becoming too interdependent with organized labor; however, it does seek close cooperation. This difference will be a major point of negotiation if the two groups ever reach the point of merger.

Another major difference is the stance on a written code of ethics. For over sixty years, the NEA has promulgated a written code to foster a greater sense of professionalism. Its efforts have been somewhat unsystematic, but increased implementation of a clear enforceable code is still a hope. The AFT stance on this matter is indifference. Rather, it believes that greater concern about economic and political issues will foster increased teacher stature and a sense of professionalism. It should be noted, however, that although the AFT is not presently implementing a code of ethics, it is attempting to upgrade the profession by supporting the call for a national entry examination for all teachers, local school board specialty examinations, and one- to three-year internships for all beginning teachers. In this manner, the AFT believes, beginning teachers will be of higher quality. If its national teacher board becomes a reality, greater professionalism will result.

Both the NEA and AFT have their share of critics, from administrative groups and dissident teachers to politically ultra-conservative lay organizations. The more adamant and political both groups become in behalf of teacher welfare, the more reaction they will generate.

Implications for Future Teachers

New teachers (especially in public school districts) are eagerly sought by representatives of professional teacher organizations. These organizations are concerned with vital teacher issues such as: salaries, working conditions, fringe benefits, and curricular matters. It is believed by these authors that the sooner prospective teachers learn about these major organizations, the more informed choice they can make as new teachers. University and school districts complement each other in the process of making an informed choice.

Discussion Questions

1. Discuss the advantages and disadvantages of an AFT-NEA merger. How would one large organization be more advantageous in terms of improved educational standards and teacher welfare? Explain.

2. Cite several differences and similarities between the NEA and AFT.
3. Why is a written, enforceable code of ethics important to teaching in the public school?
4. What growing conflicts do you envision between a conservative public and its schools?
5. Should an agency shop for teachers exist in all states? Why or why not?

Notes

1. Debra Gerald and William Hussar, *Projections of Education Statistics to 2002.* (Washington, D.C.: National Center for Education Statistics, 1991), 9.
2. "NEA Membership, July 30, 1993," *NEA Handbook, 1993–94* (Washington, D.C.: National Education Association of the United States, 1993), 164.
3. *Constitution of the American Federation of Teachers, AFL-CIO, August 1992* (Washington, D.C.: American Federation of Teachers, AFL-CIO 1992), 24.
4. Edgar B. Wesley, *NEA: The First Hundred Years* (New York: Harper and Brothers, 1957), 55.
5. Fred M. Hechinger, "The Story Behind the Strike," *Saturday Review* 45 (May 19, 1962), 54.
6. Aileen W. Robinson, *A Critical Evaluation of the American Federation of Teachers* (Chicago: American Federation of Teachers, 1934), 3–5.
7. *National Education Association Handbook, 1993–94*, 162–3.
8. *Introduction to the American Federation of Teachers, AFL-CIO* (Washington, D.C.: American Federation of Teachers, 1988), 23.
9. *Constitution of the American Federation of Teachers (AFL-CIO), 1992*, 13.
10. *In Search of Excellence*, pamphlet no. 15, American Federation of Teachers (Washington, D.C., n.d.), 13.
11. *National Education Association Handbook, 1993–94*, 246–7.
12. Jack Barbash, *Union Philosophy and the Professional*, pamphlet no. 22 (Washington, D.C.: American Federation of Teachers, n.d.), 1–4.
13. Lynn Cornett, *Career Ladder Plans: Questions Faced by States*, pamphlet, Southern Regional Education Board (Atlanta, 1984), pp. 1–6. For a good analysis of performance incentives, see also *Career Ladder Clearinghouse*, Atlanta, GA.: Southern Regional Education Board, (April 1994), 1–10.
14. *Compulsory Unionism in Education*, brochure, Concerned Educators Against Forced Unionism: A Division of the National Right to Work Committee (Springfield, VA., n.d.), 1–3.

Recommended Readings

Concerned Educators Against Forced Unionism. Pamphlet. Springfield, Va.: The National Right to Work Committee, n.d. Publication lists are available, 8001 Braddock Rd., Springfield, VA 22160.

Constitution of the American Federation of Teachers, AFL-CIO. Washington, D.C.: American Federation of Teachers. Annual Edition.

Eaton, William Edward. *The American Federation of Teachers, 1916–1961*. Carbondale Ill.: Southern Illinois University Press, 1982.

Eberts, Randall W., and Joe A. Stone. *Unions and Public Schools*. Lexington, Mass.: D.C. Heath and Company, 1984.

Lieberman, Myron. *Education as a Profession*. Englewood Cliffs, N.J.: Prentice-Hall, 1956.

National Education Association Handbook. Washington, D.C.: National Education Association. Annual Edition.

Payne, Stephen L., and Bruce H. Charnov. *Ethical Dilemmas for Academic Professionals*. Springfield, Ill.: Charles C. Thomas, Publisher, 1987.

Ruben, David. *The Rights of Teachers*. Washington, D.C.: National Education Association, 1983.

Wesley, Edgar B. *NEA: The First Hundred Years: The Building of the Teaching Profession*. New York: Harper and Brothers, 1957.

West, Allan M. *The National Education Association: The Power Base for Education*. New York: The Free Press, 1980.

Chapter 7

Academic Freedom and the Public School

In this chapter on academic freedom in context of the public school, we provide an overview to help the future teacher better understand the sensitive balance between the public school and the local community it serves. Parents and other lay citizens can play an extremely important role in influencing the content and methodology of the school through grade twelve. By means of advisory groups, PTOs or PTAs, school board membership, parent-teacher conferences, nonschool vested-interest groups, and even by formal and informal protests, parents and other citizens can cause the school to accommodate their needs or concerns. In the ensuing discussion, the topics of censorship, creation science, family life and sex education, and growing student rights will be considered to show increased lay involvement.

Taxpayers have the legitimate right to hold the school accountable for what it purports to accomplish. Beyond this point, however, the task of the school is to ascertain how representative and valid citizen concerns are before reacting in a serious manner. In other words, individuals may believe their concerns are crucial, but they may be educationally unsound. The school, although sensitive to its patrons, has to focus first on the long- and short-term needs of its clientele, the students. The rule of thumb among educators has long been that the citizens of the school district should help determine the philosophy and goals of the district and then hold the district accountable to those purposes, but the means of accomplishing or fulfilling those expressed aims should be left to the professionals—the teachers and administrators. In practice, this theory is difficult to implement; however, it is the approach most educators desire.

Academic freedom is usually thought of in reference to two criteria: (1) the freedom to teach and (2) the freedom to learn. A third factor is now pertinent because students in public institutions are legally becoming first-class citizens. As such, their right to learn is enlarging and consequently broadening the concept of academic freedom. They can participate as first-class citizens in the educational process, except when they restrict the right of another to learn or interfere with the governance of the school.

Academic freedom as a concept has been historically rare in Western education. The German universities beginning in the eighteenth century gave legitimacy to the idea of academic freedom, but this freedom rarely extended to political life outside the institutions themselves. American educators of the nineteenth century traveling abroad occasionally remarked about this paradox or inconsistency between school and society in terms of free speech, for example, in the German states. Even in the United States during the nineteenth century, educators in the common school and later in the high school were expected to be as politically neutral as possible in terms of their teaching and personal life. It was assumed by prominent educational leaders of that period that schools should be bastions of security for children. The political controversies of society at large, in other words, had no place in the curricula of the public schools of the nineteenth century.

The progressive educators of the first half of this century were the first to link issues and themes between school and home. John Dewey, for example, saw the school as an embryonic community. Educators, he believed, should begin with the experiences of children. Critical thinking was advocated from childhood on in the sense that children were urged to identify problems, gather data, set hypotheses, test theories, and apply the results.

If critical thinking was to be effective, then it had to apply to the entire curriculum, not to isolated subjects such as to the physical sciences. The upshot of this educational goal was a greater sense of relativity about knowledge. Leading pragmatists of that era believed knowledge had to "earn its keep." Knowledge had to be useful. Cherished views were consequently challenged and traditional curricula revised. The result was that educators and the public alike took sides on educational philosophy, goals, and methodology. Even conservative critics today blame many of the present educational ills on those early progressive educators, especially on John Dewey. Progressive educators are viewed by some as being too relative, especially about values. This kind of an educational attitude can obviously upset many people in the community, causing possible repercussions against the school. The school has to be prepared for such responses.

Book Censorship

Censorship in this context is the process of examining written materials in order to suppress them, partly or totally, especially if morally or politically objectionable or offensive. Censorship is often initially thought of as a negative process carried out by some ultraconservative individuals who fear divergent views. In fact, however, everyone at some point acts as a censor, particularly when dealing with young people. The mere selection of content to be included in the school at the exclusion of other educational material can imply censorship of sorts.

Parents, teachers, school administrators, and school board members, especially, must act as censors at times. It is a misconception that censorship is only the interest of individuals with ultraconservative views. Those espousing a politically liberal viewpoint are often very much concerned about either making their view publicly clear or suppressing viewpoints antithetical to their own. Censorship is a form of intellectual discrimination, and although it is necessary at times, when carried to extremes for a prolonged period it can distort facts and reality. A representative list is offered to cite a few major nongovernmental conservative and liberal pressure groups interested in public school textbooks and related curriculum material:

A. *Conservative Groups*
   1. *Liberty Alliance* is extremely sensitive to public school materials which erode traditional Christian and family values. Materials highlighting values analysis, values clarification, situation ethics, death education, sex education, environmental education, and global education are all highly suspect by members of this organization. The Reverend Jerry Falwell is the inspirational leader of this group. Humanism and collectivism are abhorrent themes to members. Political and economic issues are also part of the Alliance agenda.
   2. *Stop Textbook Censorship Committee* and *Stop Library Book Banning Committee* are two nongovernmental groups under the guiding force of Phyllis Schlafly. Her belief is that secular humanists play a dominant role in censoring textbooks and library books, so they must be stopped from further censorship. The first group attacks certain textbooks and curricula in the public school, while the second group pressures librarians to buy only books which are conservative, supportive of family, patriotism, and free enterprise.
   3. *Educational Research Analysts* is an extremely influential, small Texas agency headed by Mel and Norma Gabler. Its reviews of textbooks as well as presentations by the Gablers have received wide visibility. The views of Liberty Alliance are consistent with those of the Gablers. The relativism espoused by John Dewey and his progressive educational followers is continually under attack.
   4. *Citizens for Excellence in Education* was founded in 1983 by Robert Simonds to purge atheist views from the public schools mainly by assisting conservative Christians to get elected to school boards. About 1,000 chapters exist across the nation.
B. *Liberal Groups*
   1. *National Organization for Women* has been very active in the crusade for the equal treatment of males and females in textbooks. This organization is very sensitive about how effectively the theme of gender is reflected in a nonstereotypic manner in published materials.

2. *National Association for the Advancement of Colored People* is fundamentally concerned with the equal treatment of ethnic groups in textbooks as well as with a nonstereotypic presentation of their roles in daily life.

3. *People for the American Way* was founded by television producer Norman Lear to combat the censorship by conservative groups. One of the group's special projects is its Schools and Library Project to counteract the indoctrination of moral majoritarians. The group is dedicated to the preservation of freedom in academic and literary matters.

4. *Council for Democratic and Secular Humanism* is an organization devoted to combating the beliefs of the Liberty Alliance, as well as to promulgating the tenets of secular humanism. Its journal *Free Inquiry* contains ideas which advocate full discussion of diverse ideas.

5. *The American Civil Liberties Union* is in theory neutral in conservative versus liberal confrontations; however, it frequently is found in defense of liberal causes. One of the great concerns of this organization is the preservation of the separation of church and state in educational matters.

In recent years the most turbulent example of textbook, library, and supplemental book censorship occurred in Kanawha County, West Virginia. The basic issue underlying the strife there in the summer of 1974 and school year of 1974–1975 was a matter of who controlled the public schools—the educational professionals or the parents?

Kanawha County in 1974 was made up of over 200,000 citizens, two-thirds of whom were relatively urban and affluent. The remaining one-third were rural poor, many earning their livelihood in the Appalachia coal mines. Generally speaking, this lower one third had been economically and politically exploited for decades by lumber and coal-mining companies. Educational opportunity and an adequate standard of living were far beyond their grasp. Some of these Appalachia poor would become directly involved in an educational conflict having social and economic roots. Although other educational issues were involved, it was ironic that textbooks would catapult Kanawha county into the national limelight.

The basic process of selecting textbooks in the school district of Kanawha County involved two committees, one for elementary and one for secondary education. After receiving state-approved textbook lists (not all states use such lists), the two teacher committees made their selections, wrote their evaluations, and recommended 325 textbooks and supplemental books to the school board for adoption. Parents played no role in the recommendation of these texts, but they would shortly become very much involved. The books heavily represented the areas of reading, literature, and language to meet the diverse academic needs and abilities of the students. The book collection was placed both in the public library and school board reading room for public review, but it received scant attention. The board voted unanimously to adopt the books, but they delayed purchase until further examination was made. Explosions, literally and figuratively, followed in rapid succession.

Before the winter of 1975 ended, many of the recommended textbooks and supplemental books were labeled "dirty, anti-Christian, and anti-American." Local ministers were divided on the question of support for the texts. Diverse groups also got involved before the issue was resolved: The Kanawha County Council of Parents and Teachers, the National Association for the Advancement of Colored People, the National Education Association, the American Library Association, the John Birch Society, and even the Ku Klux Klan are examples of those who had a role in the controversy. The flames were also fanned by the comments of the U.S. commissioner of education, who seemingly took the side of the parents in stressing the need for traditional values in textbooks.

In short, the result of this textbook controversy was a school board compromise: Banned from school use were texts and supplemental books which contained themes of (1) an invasion of a child's privacy related to home life; (2) racial strife or hatred; (3) a debasement of religious, ethnic, or racial groups; (4) an encouragement of sedition; (5) a demeaning of patriotism; and (6) the support of an alien form of government to the detriment of the United States. Using God's name in vain and offensive language were also board reasons for censorship. Parents, in addition, were to play a significant part in the screening of proposed texts by means of committee membership.

It became obvious in the aftermath of the textbook controversy that books triggered the protests, but they were really only part of the problem. Parents had for years felt excluded from policy making in Kanawha County. The school district had grown unresponsive to its patrons and become insular in attitude in that professionals decided almost everything. In 1975 there were larger economic and social issues in terms of lay protest; however, had the school board and staff been more cognizant of parental values and solicited broad participation, perhaps the book protests would not have happened. The lessons of Kanawha County, West Virginia, have application everywhere.[1]

In a situation parallel to the controversy in West Virginia, in 1983 a number of Christian fundamentalists in Tennessee protested a reading series used in grades one through eight. They contended that it advocated secular humanism as a religion, initiated chiefly by John Dewey. These parents basically believed that the required use of the reading series violated their right of free exercise and their constitutional right to rear their children as they believed.

The upshot in 1986, after much litigation, was that the children of these parents were entitled to an exemption from the required reading series which offended their religious beliefs. No separate reading program was required for these children; instead, the affected children were to be legally excused from school during the reading session. They also were required to take the state prescribed reading tests to demonstrate achievement after their reading instruction at home.

In 1988, however, the Sixth U.S. Circuit Court of Appeals held unanimously that simply reading the texts did not interfere with the children's right of free exercise of religion. The U.S. Supreme Court then refused to hear the parents' appeal, so the Circuit Court's ruling stands.

Although this national test was a setback for some Christian fundamentalists, the battle over secular humanism will continue. For some parents perceive that when cultural and practical interests rather than theological interests are the focus of education, children will lose all sense of morality.

To indicate how widespread the phenomenon of conservative lay involvement is becoming in curricular matters, Box 7-1 is offered to reflect one aspect of that growth. Phyllis Schlafly gives suggestions to parents on evaluating textbooks. These questions by Schlafly remain consistent with those often asked by members of *Eagle Forum*, in which she is a guiding force.

During the 1990s, conservative Christian candidates have been winning hundreds of elections in a nationwide push for power at the local and state levels, establishing themselves as a grass roots political force within the Republican Party. The fundamentalist Christian Coalition, associated with television evangelist Pat Robertson, regularly advocates conservative programs opposing abortion and laws that guarantee the rights of women and homosexuals. The Coalition endorses candidates who seek the following: removal of certain books from school libraries; approval of school prayer; teaching of abstinence in sex education classes; and teaching creationism. A liberal political organization called People for the American Way continually monitors election results and other activities of the religious right as it affects public education. The influence of conservative and liberal political forces is especially focused on public school textbooks.

School Policy on Censorship

It is imperative in this decade that public school districts develop policies concerning the selection of *all* educational materials used in the schools. Such policies enable school officials to express or reflect what they represent to the community.

BOX 7-1   Parents Should Scrutinize Their Children's Schoolbooks

Many parents have been taking a look at their children's school materials. They are finding that far more is wrong with schoolbooks than the limited vocabulary, the choppy and childish sentences, and the boring stories.

Here's a checklist of what parents can look for if they take a long, hard look at elementary school materials. The "it" in these questions can be a textbook, a teacher's manual, a workbook or mimeographed papers used in class.

Is it anti-parent? Does it lead the child to believe that parents are ignorant, old-fash-

ioned or out of touch with the modern world? Does it suggest that the child not tell his parent what he is taught in class?

Does it instruct the child not to take home the textbook or questionnaire or other school materials? Does it encourage the child to seek advice from organizations or adults other than his parents?

Does it present information which depresses the child, leads him to a negative view of himself, his family, his country or his future? Does it produce fear and

BOX 7-1 *Continued*

despair in the child, instead of faith in his family and country and hope in the future?

Is it preoccupied with death and tragedy? Does it encourage the child to dwell on unhappy or tragic events, or to foster and retain bad feelings such as hate, anger and revenge? Does it require the child to write morbid exercises, such as his own epitaph or a description of the last person who died in the child's family?

Is it anti-parent and anti-religion by leading the child to reject the moral standards and values he has been taught in the home and church? Does it lead the child to believe that there are no absolute moral standards, no eternal verities, but that the morality of an act depends on the situation?

Does it present courses about sex, alcohol or illegal drugs in such a way as to encourage experimentation? Does it accustom the child to the use of gutter language?

Is it anti-religion? Does it lead the child to believe that religion is unimportant or out-of-date? Does it censor out all knowledge of the importance and influence of religion in American history?

Does it force the child to make choices in hypothetical situations which require him to decide that it is all right to lie, cheat, steal, kill, have sex outside of marriage, have an abortion or commit suicide? Does it force the child to confront adult problems too complex and unsuitable for his tender years, such as nuclear war?

Does it force the child to answer questionnaires or surveys that probe into the child's or his family's attitudes, feelings, behavior, customs or political preferences, all of which invade the family's privacy and are none of the school's business?

Does it force the child to write journals, diaries or compositions about such things? Does it require classroom discussion of personal and private matters which embarrass the child in front of his peers?

Does it spend precious class time on lessons, exercises and questions about feelings and attitudes, rather than teaching knowledge, facts and basic skills? Does it force the child to play psychological games in class or to engage in role-playing of unhappy personal problems caused by divorce, premarital sex, pregnancy or VD?

Does it blur traditional concepts of gender identity and force the child to accept the radical feminist notion of a gender-free society in which there are no differences in attitudes and occupations between men and women? Does it induce role reversals by showing women in hard physical labor jobs and men as house husbands?

Does it debunk or censor out our nation's heroes such as George Washington and Abraham Lincoln, but spend much time and space studying controversial contemporary figures? Does it lead the child to believe that some kind of global or world government would be preferable to the American constitutional Republic?

Does it lead the child to believe that government spending programs are the formula for economic prosperity, instead of hard work and perseverance? Does it lead the child to believe that disarmament rather than defense can prevent a future war?

Are you shocked by these questions? If you would read the testimony presented by hundreds of parents and teachers at the seven Department of Education hearings held in March, you would know that they describe what's really wrong with education.

Source: Phyllis Schlafly, "Parents Should Scrutinize Their Children's Schoolbooks," *St. Louis Globe-Democrat*, August 20, 1984, p. 2E. Used with permission.

There are several points to consider in the formation of a selection policy on educational materials:

1. A written philosophy of education for the school district should undergird the specific objectives of selection for all educational materials.
2. Specific goals widely circulated in regard to the use of the textbooks and other materials for each subject can enhance better understanding by everyone about why a particular text, film, and so on, is used. The goals do not have to be lengthy, but they should be pertinent to the instructional program.
3. The selection policy should also designate those specific individuals responsible for selecting all instructional materials. A chart of people involved facilitates better communication for anyone seeking information.
4. Selection procedures should be in writing.
5. The policy of instructional selection must also apply to the issue of how educators should deal with such items as gifts from publishers, free and inexpensive materials, lost materials, and so on.
6. A statement must be included on how controversial materials are viewed in terms of intellectual freedom.
7. It is recommended that intellectual freedom grounded in the First Amendment of the U.S. Constitution be underscored in any discussion of reconsideration. The selection policy should include the following points:

   a. A complaint form should exist for any material that is criticized.
   b. A review committee of school personnel should examine the educational material in question.
   c. The school board should study the report of the review committee before action is taken.[2]

Creationism and the Theory of Evolution

Legislatures and the courts have begun to take an active role these past few years in deciding how evolution should be addressed in public school classrooms. Proponents of scientific creationism have been pressing for equal or balanced instructional time with evolution in both textbooks and classrooms, despite the fact that most people believe that creationism is religion and evolution is science.

Supporters of evolutionary theory maintain that the universe is approximately 15 to 18 billion years old, while the earth is probably about four and one-half to five billion years of age. Presumably, life on earth (molecule-to-man theory) originated with basic marine forms about 3 billion years ago. The human species is at the pinnacle of this evolutionary process. Evolution occurs by genetic mutation and natural selection. There is disagreement among evolutionists, however, in regard to the speed of evolution. Is it a gradual process or does it occur in rapid spurts?

Advocates of creationism, on the other hand, are usually fundamentalist Christians who believe literally the creation account in the Bible. They state that both the earth and universe are about 7,000 to 10,000 years old. Plant and animal species were created by God in their basic present forms; that is, a distinct ancestry exists for both. Fossils are explained in relation to the great flood in Noah's era: Both plants and animals were buried and consequently preserved. Furthermore, creationists believe that radioactive dating techniques are fallacious.

Creationists are of one mind when it comes to the teaching of evolution in the public school. They believe that it is antithetical to the teachings of the Bible, that it destroys the religious faith of children, and that it becomes a "religion of no religion." Knowing that they cannot totally expunge evolution from the public school, creationists insist on an equal or balanced instructional opportunity as well as a fair treatment of creationism in science textbooks. In this manner, they believe, students will recognize that evolution is only a theory, not an absolute set of truths, which seems to be the inference when only evolution is reflected in the curriculum.

Much of the modern controversy about evolution and creationism began in California. In San Diego in 1979, the Creation-Science Research Center (CSRC) protested the use of a document entitled "Science Framework for California Public Schools." In brief, the center resented the document on the grounds that evolution emerges as the only credible theory of the origin of life. Furthermore, the center believed that the guidelines in the document were inherently imbalanced because creationism was also based upon scientific principles; consequently, it was as legitimate as the theory of evolution. Evolution, it was argued, is repugnant to those who believe in creationism, so California actually was violating the religious freedom of all those who believed in creation science. The center, frankly, believed that because of this document California was actually indoctrinating students in secular humanism, a religion in itself. The present judicial view, however, is that evolution is not a secular religion.

The protest was litigated (*Segraves* v. *State of California*, 1981), but the CSRC reduced its accusations to request that fundamentalist children should have a right to their religious beliefs and that the state should not teach evolution dogmatically. The court, however, did not believe the "Science Framework" document was a dogmatic statement, but it did insist that evolution be taught more as theory and not as indisputable fact. The center saw this as somewhat of a victory, but its real success came with the national publicity generated by the case.[3]

In 1981 Arkansas and Louisiana passed "balanced" time laws; however, the Arkansas legislation was soon challenged by the American Civil Liberties Union and in 1982 was declared unconstitutional on the premise that creation science has no scientific or educational merit. Creationism was considered religion, thereby creating an entangling situation. In the same year Louisiana's statute also was struck down by a federal court and again in the U.S. Supreme Court, *Edwards* v. *Aguillard* (1987). Nevertheless, creationists saw attendant national publicity as genuinely advancing the cause of creation science. Since creationists also realize that constitutionally evolution cannot be banned from the school, they take the position that balanced time is an alternative. Presently the courts are not sympathetic, but public opinion, in some quarters, is aroused. The cause of religious fundamentalism is advanced despite court setbacks.

The creation/evolution debate continues heatedly into this decade, especially in California. However, there is some recent modification of creationist belief. As stated, evolution, (also known as "descent with modification") offers no underlying reason for evolving descent. Creationism, on the other hand, assumes a divine origin of life. Within this context, some creationists subscribe to the idea of a possible "micro-evolution" for nonhuman species, and some even go so far as to accept evolution as a divine plan. Creationists also discuss the "intelligent design" theory, which assumes an overall framework undergirding life, but evolutionists reject this idea, seeing no evidence of a "supernatural architect."

A new theory, also consistent with creationist belief, called "abrupt appearance," claims that life appeared suddenly and develops rapidly in brief periods of geological time, rather than at a steady rate. Evolutionists have debated a theory of "punctuated equilibrium," but this is not consistent with the idea of "abrupt appearance." Creationists do seek to inject a variety of scientific theories about the origins of life into classroom instruction. The Institute for Creation Research near Vista, California, coordinates this effort.[4]

In a powerful sense, creationists can be considered successful technically even if not in the courts. This success, however, will continue to be gauged by how well the science textbooks and related instructional materials in the public school will incorporate scientific creationism. Over 66 science textbooks (grades one through twelve) have been printed by a number of commercial publishers. These texts supposedly meet the criteria set by creationists for appropriate instruction in the subject, which means that evolution is not overemphasized, that creation science is given "some prominence" in the textbooks, and that the two models are presented with equal emphasis.[5]

In addition to commercial publishers, the Accelerated Christian Education, Inc., is producing materials for kindergarten through the sophomore year of college, all based upon tenets of creation science. Approximately 4,000 Christian fundamentalist schools are implementing these materials at a rapid pace. Textbooks, workbooks, curriculum manuals, and tests, based upon the meanings found in Genesis, are published by this religious corporation located in Texas.[6]

Family Life and Sex Education

Since 1964, one of the most controversial topics of the curriculum in many school districts has been that of family life and sex education. It is not only sex education in itself that has occasionally caused difficulty, but the other components of family life instruction; for example, marriage, divorce, death, and dying have elicited negative reactions from some parents. In this discussion, however, only sex education will be considered because its controversial place in the curriculum is similar to the other themes of family life instruction.

When the U.S. Supreme Court handed down its opinion in the *Engel, Schempp,* and *Murray* cases in 1962 and 1963, many citizens reacted hastily by declaring that the schools would become godless as a result of removing the rituals of nondenominational prayer, Bible reading, and the Lord's Prayer from the school day. Moral education, however, got a boost because educators strove to fill the void left by the removal of these religious practices.

The American Association of School Administrators, for example, in 1964 called for value instruction as part of its famous publication *Religion in the Public Schools.* This call helped to renew interest in the entire area of moral education. One of the many nonschool groups that thought the time was ripe to assist school districts in this regard was called Sex Information and Education Council of the United States (SIECUS). For years, sex education had floundered as a possible theme in the curriculum, but the 1960s brought a resurgence. Sex education, of course, has religious and moral overtones which arouse public interest.

The organization SIECUS since 1964 has been made up of a variety of volunteers from the fields of medicine, counseling, education, and religion. The task as a council was simply to serve as a clearinghouse for pertinent research in sex education and to recommend programs to interested school districts. There was no compulsion, coercion, or legal relationship with any school district. The makeup of the council, however, was controversial because some members were heavily associated with planned parenthood programs and sex research, for example. This tended to cast the image in some minds that SIECUS was a change agent from traditional to liberal values. It was thought that the council was trying to use the schools as pawns for its particular causes. The council is now called the Sexuality and Information Council of the United States.

The first major publicity given to the theme of sex education took place in 1964, in Anaheim, California, when the school board implemented a family-life and sex-education program. Four years later two opponents to sex education were elected to the school board, signaling the demise of the program. That began an era of successful protest, especially by the John Birch Society, founded in 1958 as a conservative organization to fight communism. Sex education helped to catapult the Birch Society into the national limelight because members saw school-sponsored sex education as a tool of social engineers to undermine traditional sexual mores and parental authority.

Proponents of sex education concede that the topic is ideally handled by the home and church because of the delicacy of values and privacy; however, many also believe that neither institution can meet the challenge without the school. Actually, the peer group (despite its misconceptions about sexuality) also can be an effective source of sex information and values for many students. The school, with its increased social burdens over the last few decades, has become one of the primary vehicles for the acquisition of sex information. The public school, in fact, since 1970 has played an increasing role as a sex educator. In almost 200 school districts in large U.S. cities, it was reported recently that about three-fourths of those districts with junior and senior high schools offered some sex education. Corroborative research indicates this to be a fact. Sex education in the school has become more prevalent during the last decade.

Although sex education has become more common in public schools (17 states require and 23 states encourage sex education), instructional requirements for courses on health and the human immunodeficiency virus (HIV) drop after tenth grade. Ironically, older students are at greater risk. Another problem is that most schools offer pertinent information only in health classes rather than in appropriate content.[7]

The fact that schools are offering more sex education does not necessarily mean quality instruction. Sex education is not a cure-all for sexual problems, nor does it replace family instruction when good communication occurs. Sex education, however, has become by necessity another charge of the school.

Sex education is a relative term; in one school district it can mean merely an elective course at the secondary school level, and in another, a comprehensive, integrative theme throughout the grades. Proponents prefer not a course in sex education but a 12-year fragmented curriculum associated with pertinent subject matter, for example, health, biology, literature, home economics, social studies, and physical education. Ideally, every teacher can become a sex educator in the sense that the teacher communicates with students as a caring and sympathetic adult, refers students to specialists such as a counselor when needed, or recommends appropriate reading or graphic materials in the context of professional expertise. Of course, these approaches are always employed within the framework of school district policy. Every teacher involved with instruction in sex education needs to function under the aegis of a board of education policy. The support of school administrators is also necessary.

To illustrate what sex education can mean at one school level, the following outline of possible objectives and goals for kindergarten and grade one shows that sex education is not a subject per se, particularly in the elementary school. The subject does become more formal as children get older, but content is still parceled out to pertinent subject areas whenever possible. The objectives and goals for kindergarten and grade one are as follows:

  I. Respecting the privacy and rights of others
    A. Privacy in separate bathrooms for boys and girls; for example, partitioned stalls.
    B. Hygienic habits in use of toilet, cafeteria, playground, and so on.
    C. Sense of privacy as inherent right of every person.
    D. Development of self-esteem.
 II. Childhood safety
    A. Promptness in arriving to and departing from school.
    B. Caution in speaking to strangers and resistance to offers of rides without permission of parents or guardians.
    C. Awareness of abusive behavior by older students or adults.

III. Attitudes toward family life
  A. Opportunities to communicate (orally, written, dramatically, artistically, physically) those joys, anxieties, sorrows, and rivalries experienced especially at home.
  B. Awareness of a child's social rights and responsibilities about courtesy, teamwork, tolerance, patience, maturity, truthfulness, honesty, fairness, and privacy.
IV. Animals in classroom
  A. Judicious use of live-bearing pets to learn about reproduction as a normal, joyful experience.
  B. Opportunity to develop responsible attitude about the rights of animals and their care.
  C. Mature attitude about human reproduction and accompanying terminology.
V. Group and individual discussions
  A. Experiences on playground, cafeteria, and so on, which have educational and social implications.
  B. Experiences with other children, family members, or adults which are gratifying or create confusion, and so on.
  C. Experiences that involve field trips to broaden perspectives about other people.

The suggested objectives and goals obviously are best implemented *incidentally* throughout the year when the opportunities for meaningful activity or discussion are possible. When the teacher sees exploitation on the playground, for example, constructive use of the experience might be made. Responsibility toward classroom animals, as another example, is an ongoing activity which lends itself to self-discipline, sensitivity, and teamwork. Sex education, in sum, is the development of a wholesome attitude about life in all its manifestations.

Many of the above objectives are amplified as the child moves through the grades and additional concepts on sexuality are added to fit appropriate levels of age and maturity. The philosophy of the curriculum on sex education, however, remains constant throughout the grades.

Nothing threatens human life like the acquired immunodeficiency syndrome (AIDS). The Center for Disease Control states that in the United States, cases are doubling every fourteen months, estimating that in 1992 about 1 million people were infected with HIV. The World Health Organization also indicates that in 1992 HIV was increasingly transmitted by heterosexual intercourse. By the year 2000, it is estimated that from 40 to 110 million people will be infected.[8]

It has become common knowledge that AIDS is contracted basically by oral, anal, or vaginal sexual contact with an infected person, or by sharing an infected person's drug needles or syringe. The infection is also transmitted from a mother to her baby before or during birth. Additionally, some persons with hemophilia have contracted AIDS by receiving infected blood during transfusions. The AIDS virus is not caught like a cold or flu. Casual, nonsexual contact will not transmit AIDS. Experts state that "safe behavior" in regard to AIDS involves (1) not having sex, (2) having sex only with a mutually faithful, uninfected partner, and (3) not shooting drugs. If one chooses to have multiple sexual partners, however, condoms are the best preventive measure against AIDS.

What can the schools do to stem the tide of this epidemic? Parents and educators need to work together to enlist the support of medical, religious, social, and legal agencies. Health education needs to start early. In context of parental and community standards, children need to get the facts about AIDS. They need to be taught values, responsibility, and the courage to resist peer pressure. Sexual abstinence, restraint, and responsibility must characterize all instruction in sex education. Discussion of mechanical prevention, condoms, for example, must take place eventually in sex education courses or discussion, but with parental permission in a moral context. In a recent nationwide poll on education, 88 percent of those polled indicated that sex education should be in the curriculum, and 57 percent stated that condoms should be available in high schools to combat AIDS. How these ideas or desires are implemented remains a source of controversy.[9]

Children with AIDS are admitted to public schools on a case basis if they are medically diagnosed as children who (1) do not bite, (2) do not kick, (3) can control bodily secretions, (4) have no open wounds, and (5) are toilet trained. This "apparent nonexistent" risk to other children then justifies school enrollment. These children are legally considered as children with disabilities covered by Section 504 of the Rehabilitation Act of 1973 and Americans with Disabilities Act of 1990. They must also be given the opportunity to receive a free, appropriate education as guaranteed by Public Law 94-142 (now called Individuals with Disabilities Education Act). If these youth are absent, home tutors must be made available. Obviously, such placement of children requires continual review medically and educationally. Constant communication between the school board and superintendent with the school patrons is vital to reducing fear and instilling confidence.[10]

The following common arguments for and against family life and sex education are those which the authors have read and heard for some years. Though briefly cited, these arguments can stimulate more thought about the place of the topic in the public school curriculum.

For

1. The school is charged with the responsibility of dealing with all phases of human relationships; human sexuality is but one area of these relationships. Ideal family life and sex education are not subjects but rather attitudes toward human growth and development that permeate social studies, science, physical education, health, and the humanities. Values and physiology are interwoven wherever they logically connect. In the ideal sense, practically every teacher is a sex educator.

2. It is documented that many adolescents learn sexual information from their peers, not their parents. Hence the school must strive to provide correct information about sexual development: physical, emotional, and social.
3. Because school-age youth spend so much time watching television, the school must attempt to offset the harm done through the portrayal of commercialized and exploitative sexuality.
4. Because more adolescents are participating in sexual activity, they need better information about contraception and sexual responsibility.
5. The best way to fight venereal disease, and especially HIV, is to provide correct information in the school.

Against

1. Because religious or value indoctrination is not a function of the school, the teacher must provide sexual information *devoid* of values. Hence, it is impossible to satisfy parents about an appropriate context for sex information.
2. The child undergoes latency stages of growth; for example, 6 to 11 years of age. This is a period when imposed sexual information may cause emotional harm.
3. Sex education is often imparted in the context of relativism, which focuses too much on student desires.
4. There is too little school time for the academic "basics," much less for sex education. Thus we should let the home and church (and even the peer group) perform the function of sex education.
5. Venereal disease, sexual experimentation, and permissiveness are partly a result of school-sponsored sex education.
6. Teachers are ill prepared to deal with such complex areas as family life and sex education. Their training generally has not been adequate to teach appropriate psychological, social, physical, and religious concepts.
7. If sex education is to be given, it should be for parents only. In this manner, the school and home can supplement each other.

Hatch Amendment

In 1978 a U.S. senator from Utah, Orrin Hatch, successfully proposed in Congress an amendment to the General Education Provisions, which has since been known as the Hatch Act or Amendment and is popularly called the "child privacy act." The Hatch Act has two major components which apply to activities funded directly by federal money.

1. Parents and guardians can inspect all instructional material including teacher's manuals, films, tapes, and other supplementary material used for their children who are involved in any research, experimentation program, or

project. These terms apply to any attempt "to explore or develop new or unproven teaching methods or techniques."

2. Students cannot be required to submit to psychological or psychiatric examination, testing, or treatment if the major purpose is to obtain information about

   a. political affiliations
   b. mental and psychological problems possibly embarrassing to the students or family
   c. sexual behavior and attitude
   d. illegal, antisocial, self-incriminating, and demeaning behavior
   e. critical appraisals of persons closely related to students
   f. privileged relationships, such as with lawyers or doctors
   g. income beyond that required by law unless permission is granted by parent, guardian, or the student is of age.[11]

To complement the Hatch Amendment, the U.S. Department of Education in 1984 established new regulations in order to handle complaints filed under the Hatch Amendment. These regulations basically give parents the right to limit their children's involvement in some types of federally funded school programs, particularly testing of a personal nature. The 1984 regulations define psychiatric or psychological examination to be a process of getting information (including a group activity) that is not basically related to academic instruction but designed more to extract information about attitudes, habits, traits, feelings, opinions, and beliefs. If the treatment is designed primarily to affect behavioral, emotional, or attitudinal characteristics of the individual or group, then the treatment as well is subject to the 1984 regulations.

The federal regulations offer parents the opportunity to file complaints about such psychological or psychiatric testing or treatment. Local school systems therefore must provide a procedure to hear and act upon these parental complaints. The state is involved as well if the complaint is more pertinent to that level. The Department of Education also has enforcement capability over these regulations even to the extent of terminating federal funds.[12] In this regard, funds apply only to those programs and activities supported by the U.S. Department of Education. Specifically, a cutoff of federal money pertinent to the Hatch Amendment would mean the funds of Chapters 1 and 2, special-needs education, bilingual education, impact aid, vocational education, and adult education. Obviously, such a cutoff would be nearly disastrous to a local school district.

There has been much confusion about the implementation of the Hatch Amendment (1978) and the Department of Education regulations (1984). Senator Hatch claims the amendment and regulations apply only to programs that receive federal funds. He also believes that courses not supported by federal funds are exempted. For example, sex education courses paid for with state and local money even though the school district may be receiving some federal funds on a formula basis, such as through Chapter 1, should not be applicable to the amendment or regulations. The point is that a direct relationship must exist between federal funds and those items listed in the Hatch Amendment.

Some conservative groups, however, view these federal restrictions as applying more broadly than to only those federally funded activities listed in the regulations. Phyllis Schlafly, for example, president of Eagle Forum, believes that parents under these federal regulations have the right to inspect and react to *all* the educational materials used in their children's classrooms. Letters from several conservative groups have been widely circulated to assist parents who are seeking the help of the U.S. Department of Education in regard to investigating complaints based upon the tenets of the Hatch Amendment and supplemented by Department of Education regulations.

Conversely, a liberal group called People for the American Way has been circulating information packets nationwide to apprise educators of the federal regulations surrounding the Hatch Amendment. The National Education Association also has been very active in lobbying Congress to preserve academic freedom by overturning the possible effects of the Hatch Amendment. Recently, in addition, thirty-one educational associations have joined forces under the title of the Hatch Amendment Coalition to criticize the role of the U.S. Department of Education in implementing the 1978 amendment. One of the chief tasks of the coalition has been to disseminate guidelines for local school districts in coping with these federal regulations.

Students as First-Class Citizens

At the beginning of this chapter, the authors defined academic freedom as encompassing three criteria: the freedom to teach, the freedom to learn, and the viewing of students as first-class citizens. The reason the last criterion is included in this definition is basically that if society considers students as "full" citizens, then, for example, they have the right to free speech and free assembly. They possess, in addition, the right to privacy and should receive no cruel or unusual punishment.

Of course, there are restrictions upon these constitutional rights, but, in general, opportunities to learn increase as students legally become full citizens. The right to hear unpopular ideas, to discuss or read controversial material, to print sensitive ideas in a school newspaper, to be free from physical retaliation or from unwarranted invasion of privacy, all enhance the student's opportunity to learn. The student can become more of a participant in the acquisition of subject matter, skills, and attitudes. Naturally, these rights are contingent upon the degree to which a student might interfere with someone else's right to learn or with the operation of a school's program.

In context of this position about the status of the learner in the public school classroom, one U.S. Supreme Court case has served as a watershed decision in terms of the student quest for first-class, legal status in public education. In a strict sense, it dealt with one issue only, but in spirit it opened the floodgate for subsequent issues involving such things as corporal punishment, suspension, and search and seizure. Student rights have increased dramatically since this famous decision, in 1969, entitled *Tinker* v. *Des Moines Independent Community School District*. It was one of the most important educational decisions ever rendered by the U.S. Supreme Court because of the precedent set for students to challenge school boards on other kinds of issues related to student rights.

The case had its roots in an anti-Vietnam War protest in 1965, when a group of people from Des Moines, Iowa, went to Washington, D.C., to publicly oppose continuance of the war. On returning to Des Moines, several students decided that wearing black armbands to school might be helpful to make the public more aware of the evils of further American military involvement in Vietnam. An editorial in the high school newspaper by one member of the group stated the intentions of several students to wear black armbands. The students desired to wear the armbands from December 16 through New Year's Day; however, upon learning of the plan, principals of the five schools in Des Moines met and decided that no black armbands to protest the Vietnam War were to be worn to school. (Other political symbols, however, were not singled out for prohibition.) The administrators' fear was that other student factions might clash with these students and cause serious disruption in the operation of the schools. The case involved a confrontation of First Amendment rights versus school regulations.

Although this situation initially involved over a dozen students, the *Tinker* case specifically involved two high school students, John Tinker and Christopher Eckhardt, and John's sister Mary Beth, a student in the junior high school. Only five students were suspended and told to return when they removed the black armbands. They refused and returned to school as planned after New Year's Day.

Three students solicited the support of the Iowa Civil Liberties Union and filed suit but lost in the U.S. District Court on the grounds that school officials who fear disruption can act to prevent it. The case was then appealed to the U.S. Court of Appeals, Eighth Circuit; however, a split decision by this appellate court affirmed the decision of the district court.

On appeal to the U.S. Supreme Court in 1968 the three students still maintained that the wearing of a black armband was constitutionally protected by the First Amendment as a form of free speech. The students saw their protest as symbolizing free speech. The U.S. Supreme Court in 1969 overturned previous rulings by agreeing with the plaintiffs.

In a landmark decision, the Court stated that students and teachers do not shed their constitutional rights to freedom of speech or expression in the school. The Court realized that school officials have to maintain order, but it saw in this situation no action that interfered with the educational process. The Court went on to say that public schools are not centers of "totalitarianism." Such schools do not possess complete control over their students, who, in other words, are "persons" under the Constitution.

The Court, in sum, saw no facts in *Tinker* that could have led school officials to foresee trouble from the wearing of black armbands. No violence or disturbance occurred, no interference with school activities took place, and no individual's right to learn was impeded. The Court on the basis of the First Amendment, consequently, ruled in favor of the students in reference to the wearing of black armbands as a form of free speech.

The implications of this *Tinker* decision were profound. School administrators temporarily felt helpless; they generally believed that violence almost had to erupt before they could act. In this sense, *Tinker* did not help school officials ward off potential trouble between opposing factions of students by establishing specific guidelines for school administrators. *Tinker* was also extremely significant in another manner by its effect upon student dress codes. Before 1969 most high schools had dress codes, but after *Tinker* most were dropped or changed to statements of "rights and responsibilities," which usually included statements about school and political symbols, appropriate dress, and hair length. Although dress codes and hair length are distinct issues from the *Tinker* case, school boards legally began to look at students differently. Consequently, students were allowed to express their personalities in a more adult manner.

In a related sense, the doctrine of *in loco parentis* (in place of the parent) was reevaluated by school officials. In 1969 school officials were told by the U.S. Supreme Court that public schools do not possess "absolute authority" over students. Teachers and administrators, in other words, during the compulsory school day do not act completely as substitute parents. School officials cannot deny students their constitutional privileges except when school activities are disrupted or when another individual's right to learn is thwarted. The doctrine of *in loco parentis* is still an educational responsibility, but the U.S. Supreme Court has to decide issue by issue where the line is drawn between school regulations and the constitutional rights of students.

In subsequent cases in the U.S. Supreme Court during the 1970s, the impact of the *Tinker* case became more apparent by a changing legal attitude about the status of students in public education. To survey representative issues to portray this point, the following Supreme Court cases are offered: In *Goss* v. *Lopez* (1975) the Court reaffirmed that a school may suspend or expel a student, but due process must be a key concept in handling the suspension. A student, even if suspended for fewer than 10 days, at least has the right to know why he or she is suspended and to offer a rebuttal. In view of suspension beyond ten days, however, formality increases. The student must receive a written statement of the reasons for suspension, and a hearing must be provided with the chance for the student to confront witnesses. In a sense, this formal hearing operates in a quasi-judicial manner. The student may remain silent, may bring witnesses or a lawyer, and may appeal the school's decision. It is genuinely a different suspension process from earlier years. The Fourteenth Amendment was the basis for *Goss* in terms of due process.

In a second issue of educational significance involving the Eighth Amendment, the Supreme Court surprised many people by upholding corporal punishment in the schools. In *Baker* v. *Owen* (1975) the Court laid down guidelines for the administration of corporal punishment, such as the proper use of formal hearings, warnings, and witnesses. Due process was a principle the Court tried to formalize in this decision. On the heels of the *Baker* case, however, the Court in *Ingraham* v. *Wright* (1977) relaxed some of the requirements set down in 1975, particularly in reference to uses of formal hearings, witnesses, and so on. The Court, though, still requires that reasonableness prevail in the administration of corporal punishment. Reasonableness in this situation entails the consideration of such factors as age, sex, health, and size of the student. Obviously, the type of instrument used also is crucial because injury is more likely if a potentially dangerous device is applied. Such punishment must always fit the offense and never be used out of malice.

In many states corporal punishment is permissible; however, it is imperative that prospective teachers soon learn upon employment the pertinent state law, the school board policy, as well as the view of the building principal concerning the application of corporal punishment. Reasonableness and common sense are always terms used in connection with this issue.

The American Civil Liberties Union and the National Education Association are two good examples of organizations opposed to the application of corporal punishment. Probably the use of physical force to modify student behavior someday will be banned because a growing number of people believe that by the use of force in the schools, the schools consequently convey the message to students that misbehavior can be corrected by force, that violence is socially appropriate. Many educators see this attitude as abhorrent. Some school practitioners believe, however, that it is desirable to keep the ultimate threat of paddling as a deterrent to misbehavior simply because the school is very rapidly losing authority over the child. Usually the child cannot be detained after school or compelled to arrive early. Very few measures can be applied to "encourage" appropriate behavior. The pupil eventually realizes how little control can be exerted and therefore behaves with impunity.

Numerous other school-related issues have been recently challenged or litigated, though not necessarily reaching the U.S. Supreme Court. Dress codes, as mentioned earlier, are being incorporated into statements of rights and responsibilities in numerous high schools, but technically dress codes are legal and common especially in junior high schools. Hair length of males has been a litigated theme dozens of times with little legal precedent to follow in public education. Search and seizure policies also have been challenged by students on the basis of the Fourth Amendment in reference to school lockers. The general judicial policy, however, is that the school owns the locker. As stated by the New York Court of Appeals in *People* v. *Overton* (1969) the administrator is responsible for the governance and maintenance of physical facilities. Consequently, inspecting a locker falls within the purview of school officials, especially if there is reasonable suspicion that illegal objects or materials are present in the locker. However, the due process of students is still a factor to consider. Reasonableness and common sense must be inherent in the administrator's behavior.

Two U.S. Supreme Court cases have given school officials a degree of legal authority over students. In *New Jersey* v. *T.L.O.* (1985), the Court found that under typical circumstances a search of a student by a school official is justified when there are "reasonable grounds" that a search will reveal evidence that a student has violated the law or rules of the school. Furthermore, in *Bethel School District No. 403* v. *Fraser* (1986), the Court ruled that school officials can prohibit the use of vulgar and offensive terms in school-sponsored activities. In the Court's view, this prohibition does not violate the First Amendment.

In *Honig* v. *Doe* (1988), the U.S. Supreme Court rendered an opinion profoundly affecting youth with disabilities, as well as their school officials. The Court said that school personnel must obtain parental consent before removing a disruptive student with a disability from his or her educational placement before complaint proceedings are completed. These students are expected to learn with non-special students to the greatest extent possible, and, when disruption occurs, consensus between parents and school officials must be reached before any action is taken. In other words, these students cannot be removed if behavior is a result of their disability, something difficult to determine. This case is very significant to all educators.

In the case of *Honig* v. *Doe,* two emotionally disturbed children in California were given a five-day suspension for allegedly destroying school property, perpetrating an assault, and making sexually explicit remarks to other students. After the five-day suspension, the students were suspended indefinitely while waiting for expulsion proceedings.

The students sued the school district in a U.S. district court, contending the indefinite suspensions violated the "stay put" provision of the Education for All Handicapped Children Act (EAHCA). This provision ensures that a student is kept in his or her current educational placement during any proceedings that may result in a placement change.

This case is significant because the district court's injunction prevented the expulsion of a special student for behavior arising from the student's disability. The school district appealed the decision to the U.S. Court of Appeals, which determined the indefinite suspension was, in fact, a change in placement under the "stay put" provisions of EAHCA.

The Court also stated that no "dangerousness" exception existed in the EAHCA law, although the indefinite suspension and expulsion of students for behavior that arose out of their disabilities was a violation of EAHCA. Finally, the Court also ruled that suspensions up to thirty days did not constitute a change of placement.

Regarding the same case, the California Superintendent of Public Instruction filed for a Supreme Court review of the dangerous exception issue, asking also if the state was required to provide services directly to students when individual school districts did not. The U.S. Supreme Court found no emergency exception for dangerous students was included in EAHCA. The Court stated, however, if a special student poses an immediate threat to the safety of others, school officials could suspend that student up to 10 school days.

The Supreme Court thus upheld the decision of the U.S. Court of Appeals, but modified that Court's decision on fixed suspensions by stating that a student could be suspended for up to 10 days rather than 30 without violating the change in placement provision. The Supreme Court also upheld the Appeals Court's decision that the state could be required to provide services directly to students if local school districts failed to do so.

A recent U.S. Supreme Court case has probably been the most significant since *Tinker* in regard to student rights and the First Amendment. In the 1988 case *Hazelwood School District* v. *Kuhlmeier,* the justices ruled that a high school principal did not violate the First Amendment by excising two pages from a student newspaper. The ruling broadly affects "publications, theatrical productions, and other expressive activities" which may be perceived to be school-sponsored activities. Editorial control is now possible if pedagogical concerns are involved. School-sponsored publications, plays, and so on, are now a part of the curriculum.

The case was initiated when the principal of Hazelwood East High School in suburban St. Louis removed two pages from the May 13, 1983, edition of the school newspaper. The principal objected to two articles, one dealing with teen pregnancy in the school, the other with divorce. He argued that the privacy of some students might be invaded. He also argued the article on pregnancy was inappropriate for younger students. The principal believed that comments in the article dealing with divorce were too personal in that a parent could be identified and should have been notified as to consent and response. Students on the newspaper's staff appealed but ultimately lost.

This decision differs from *Tinker*. In *Tinker,* students can express personal views on school premises unless there is reasonable belief that disruption will occur. However, in *Hazelwood* the expressive or published forms of student speech can be censored if deemed inappropriate for the level of student maturity, or if there is the possibility that the public will infer school sponsorship of individual views or comments. Although this decision is controversial, the authors do not believe this case is totally a setback regarding student rights. Expressive activities are truly a part of the curriculum and should be reasonably controlled by pedagogical concerns, but these concerns should always prevail only in context of the First Amendment. Some states are defining legal limits of control to ensure student rights affected by *Hazelwood.*

Since this case four states (Colorado, Massachusetts, Iowa, and Kansas) have enacted legislation to ensure student press freedoms except for obscene, libelous, and disruptive expression. Statutes also absolve school officials of any civil or criminal liability for articles appearing in school publications. Overall, it is believed that the *Hazelwood* case has had a chilling effect upon student freedom.[13]

In sum, these representative judicial views indicate the changing legal status of students in public education. Much of this change was initiated by the landmark *Tinker* case handed down by the U.S. Supreme Court in 1969. As the legal rights of students increase, it is believed their academic freedom grows as well. Their rights to hear diverse information and to pursue new avenues of inquiry and independence enhance opportunities for learning.

Positions on Academic Freedom

Academic freedom in the public school below the college level is really an open-ended issue. How much freedom a teacher has depends greatly on one's philosophy of education. There are several major liberal and conservative arguments concerning the degree of academic freedom in the public school, but these authors see one major argument on each side of the issue. In regard to a literal interpretation of academic freedom, the authors believe the principal thesis is that a forum for open discussion of ideas commensurate with the age and maturity of youth allows truth to sweep away superstition. The effect of such a forum avoids the "forbidden fruit" that students desire if ideas are suppressed. An open forum enhances critical thinking because ideas are weighed on the basis of their own merit, not by personal bias, persuasion, or passion. Truth is the object. Community restraints, naturally, can be formidable if educators subscribe to a forum of open discussion, but students eventually learn that the school has no hidden agenda of knowledge to be revealed only upon adulthood.

On the other side of the coin, the authors believe the most defensible position among those arguments to restrict academic freedom in general education below the college level is the view that most children and youth really do not possess the maturity and knowledge to distinguish truth from error. Their experience is insufficient to make judgments about *complex* issues involving race, sex, economics, or politics, for example. Literacy and maturity must precede such judgments. This is why communities for decades have expected teachers to accept the conservative restrictions placed upon them in terms of teaching about controversial material. The assumption is that a teacher should reflect the will of the community in daily classroom activities.

Summary

Academic freedom is generally defined as the freedom to teach and the freedom to learn. A third factor appearing particularly in recent years greatly affects both freedoms: the pursuit by public school students of greater legal status as citizens. As students achieve the right, for example, to speak openly on sensitive political issues, or to assemble peacefully to protest a particular regulation or social issue, they may become more effective participants in the learning process. In a sense, their academic freedom is enlarged. Their horizons of knowledge can be widened. First-class citizenship should mean a better education. Statements of rights and responsibilities at the secondary school level are beginning to reflect this higher status.

Naturally, there are restrictions on the degree of academic freedom a teacher or student possesses. If a student interferes with the governance of the school by boisterous behavior or unbridled speech or interferes with another student's right to learn, then constitutional rights can be limited. Students cannot interfere with the educational program of the school.

The freedom to teach and the freedom to learn are contingent upon the degree of community pressure the school receives from both conservative and liberal lay groups. On a continuum of representative pressures ranging from conservative to liberal interests, one can see such views as "too much secular humanism in published school materials," or "too little emphasis on free enterprise economic theory advocated in social studies," to "too little attention given to the contribution of women or racial and ethnic minorities in published materials and classroom activities." In other words, community pressure on the public school can emanate from varied sources.

Community reactions in this regard reached their peak in one school district in Kanawha County, West Virginia, in 1974–1975. Lay interest in schools in that region had lain dormant for years, but it erupted in violence in a very short time. The issues were, at least at surface level, resolved by bringing parents and other citizens more effectively into the decision-making process of the school district. By no means, however, has national interest subsided on the part of some pressure groups about who controls the schools—the parents or the educational professionals? The conservative versus liberal confrontations in educational matters will be frequent throughout the next several years.

Certainly the rights to teach and learn are related to professional qualification and competency as well as to the age and maturity of the learner. It is not difficult to make professional judgments about the place of some sensitive material, especially in the elementary school, but when does exposure to "dangerous" ideas begin? If critical thinking is a desirable educational goal, then subject matter is not easily packaged by grade level. Students cannot be passive for eight or ten school years and then be expected to emerge from high school as thinking young adults. Not only is professional judgment crucial in this regard, but community participation is vital in reference to what the schools should accomplish. Without this participation, academic freedom will be limited.

Implications for Future Teachers

Prospective teachers, during their preservice academic preparation, engage in intellectual inquiry that ideally is scholarly, frank, open, and tactful. Unpopular views are often analyzed along with cherished beliefs. If, upon employment, these new teachers are not aware of the historic and ongoing struggle to keep schools committed to the idea of academic freedom, they will be unprepared to cope with the powerful lay and professional forces attempting to influence them in their particular causes.

Teachers must strive to keep the schools free and open. The sooner new teachers learn the social and political context of their employment, the more effective they will be. To move from the somewhat insulated confines of a university to the front lines of the classroom without knowledge, courage, and tact concerning controversial educational issues, could be professional catastrophe.

Discussion Questions

1. What is the definition of academic freedom? How does the growing legal status of students in the public school affect the academic freedom of teachers and learners? What are the reservations placed upon the constitutional rights of students in the public school?
2. Discuss changes which could occur in the public school curriculum as a result of community pressure from either the left or right side of the political spectrum.
3. Explain the Hatch Amendment. Why is it controversial?
4. What is a major argument to restrict academic freedom in the public school? Conversely, what is a major argument to allow greater academic freedom below the college level? What are other arguments on each side of the issue?
5. Why is it critical for the school to communicate effectively with its patrons about the AIDS epidemic in regard to curriculum and children with AIDS?

Notes

1. Franklin Parker, *The Battle of the Books: Kanawha County*, Fastback 63 (Bloomington, IN: Phi Delta Kappa Educational Foundation, 1975), 34 pp.

2. "Preventing and Surviving Censorship: Combatting the New Right," Participant's Manual. A training program developed by Western States Regional Office, National Education Association, n.d., 41–3.

3. Harvey Siegel, "Creationism, Evolution, and Education: The California Fiasco," *Phi Delta Kappan* 64 (October 1981): 95–101.

4. Peter West, "New Tactic Used to Push Teaching Creation Theory," *Education Week*, XIII (September 8, 1993): 1 & 26–7.

5. Ben Brodinsky, "The New Right: The Movement and Its Impact," *Phi Delta Kappan* (October 1982): 93–4.

6. *Ibid.*, 94.

7. Asta M. Kenney and Margaret Terry Orr, "Sex Education: An Overview of Current Programs, Policies, and Research," *Phi Delta Kappan* 65 (March 1984): 493; see also Jessica Portner, "AIDS Education Found Less Likely for Older Students" *Education Week.* XII (November 25, 1992): 1 & 14; also Ellen Fox, "Study Finds Fast Growth in Sex Education . . . ," *Education Week.* VIII (May 10, 1989): 1 & 19.

8. Warner C. Greene, "AIDS and the Immune System," *Scientific American.* 269 (September 1993): 99.

9. Mark Clements, "What's Wrong with Our Schools," *Parade Magazine* (May 16, 1993): 4–5.

10. Sally Reed, "Children with AIDS," Kappan Special Report, *Phi Delta Kappan* 69 (January 1988): K1–K12; and David L. Kirp and Steven Epstein, "AIDS in America's Schoolhouses: Learning the Hard Lessons," *Phi Delta Kappan* 70 (April 1989): 584–93.

11. U.S. Congress, *Protection of Pupil Rights* (Amendment to General Education Provisions), P.L. 95–561, 92nd Cong., 1978, 452.

12. *Student Rights in Research, Experimental Activities, and Testing: Final Rules with Invitation to Comment,* vol. 49, no. 174, Federal Register 35321–2, 1984.

13. Michael Simpson, "Legal Times," *NEA Today,* 11 (November 1992): 25.

Recommended Readings

Bennett, William J. *AIDS and the Education of Our Children: A Guide for Parents and Teachers.* Washington, D.C.: U.S. Department of Education, 1988.

Greene, Warner C. "AIDS and the Immune System," *Scientific American,* 269 (September 1993): 98–106.

Hefley, James C. *Are Textbooks Harming Your Children?* Milford, MI: Mott Media, 1979.

LaHaye, Tim. *The Battle for the Public Schools.* Old Tappan, NJ: Revel, 1983.

Parker, Franklin. *The Battle of the Books: Kanawha County.* Fastback 63. Bloomington, IN: Phi Delta Kappa Educational Foundation, 1975.

Parker, Franklin, and Betty Parker. "Behind Textbook Censorship," *National Forum,* LXIII (Fall 1988): 35–7.

Reed, Sally. "Children with AIDS: Kappan Special Report," *Phi Delta Kappan* 69 (January 1988): K1–K12.

Rippa, S. Alexander, "The Impact of the Business Creed," *Education in a Free Society: An American History,* 7th ed. NY: Longman, 1992, Chapter 10, pp 247–67.

Robbins, Jan C. *Student Press and the Hazelwood Decision,* Fastbook 274. Bloomington, IN: Phi Delta Kappa Educational Foundation, 1988.

Yarber, W. L. *AIDS Education: Curriculum and Health Policy.* Fastbook 265, Bloomington, IN: Phi Delta Kappa Educational Foundation, 1987.

Selected U.S. Supreme Court Cases:

Tinker v. Des Moines Independent Community School District, (1969) 393 U.S. 503.

Goss v. Lopez (1975) 419 U.S. 565

Baker v. Owen (1975) 423 U.S. 907

Ingraham v. Wright (1977) 430 U.S. 651

New Jersey v. T.L.O. (1985) 105 S. Ct. 733

Bethel School District No. 403 v. Fraser (1986) 106 S. Ct. 3159

Edwards v. Aguillard (1987) 107 S. Ct. 2573

Hazelwood School District v. Kuhlmeier (1988) 108 S. Ct. 562

Honig v. Doe (1988) 108 S. Ct. 592 and 484 U.S. 305

Chapter 8

Church and State
in Public Education

Curriculum

In this chapter, an overview will show the relationship between organized religion and public education in two major ways: (1) the curriculum in the public school and (2) publicly funded fringe benefits to nonpublic schools. The best means of indicating this interaction between religion and public education is to cite several representative U.S. Supreme Court decisions, which have had a profound impact upon both the public and private educational sectors over the last several decades.

The topic is an important one, especially in terms of the curriculum, because the religious heritage is a legitimate part of the curriculum and must be dealt with academically and objectively. Fringe benefits to nonpublic schools are continually being considered because many non-public school educators and parents believe they constitutionally deserve such benefits. On the other hand, many public school advocates believe that increased public aid to nonpublic schools is unconstitutional. Such aid will also financially hurt the public school because of a potential loss of students and tax dollars.

Religion is a difficult term to define to anyone's satisfaction, but a number of characteristics give clarity. It involves: (1) a belief about the meaning of life; (2) a commitment by the individual and the group to this belief; (3) a system of moral practices resulting from a commitment to this belief; and (4) a recognition by the proponents of this belief that it is supreme or absolute.[1] In terms of the public school curriculum, any instruction which deals with an organized system of beliefs, with pertinent ritual, with accompanying values, and with desired behavior will be considered instruction about religion.

The role of the church in a generic sense has always been sensitive in relation to secular matters, especially to public education. In the colonial period the schools were usually the handmaiden of a church-state relationship. There was little question in most localities about ties between the dominant church and the government which served its purposes. Schools were created in part to perpetuate the theistic goals of that particular relationship. Tolerance for minority views was practically absent in colonial America. Secondary schools and colonial colleges served as examples of how denominational preference helped to determine educational opportunity.

What the Founding Fathers had in mind when the First Amendment was written was not so much a fear of European threats to their religious liberty as it was apprehension of the settlers themselves, who became as intolerant as the Europeans from whom they had fled. Examples were rife in colonial America of independent thinkers who had met with dire hardships at the hands of colonists in control who held different religious beliefs. For instance, in Massachusetts Colony only members of the Puritan Church could hold office or vote, and in Virginia colonists had to pay fines if they missed Anglican Church services on Sunday morning or afternoon. Even in Pennsylvania, mistrust and intolerance were rampant because the various parochial schools were organized by different languages and religious views. Each ethnic sect was suspicious of the other, fearing loss of religious integrity if anyone thought of such a topic as tax support for schools.

By the late eighteenth century, three fourths of the young states still had established ties between church and state. This frequently meant loss of individual religious freedom and forced taxation to a church which often did not represent the religious views of the person paying the tax. This undemocratic process led Thomas Jefferson to submit in 1779 in Virginia a bill establishing religious freedom, which he had hoped when passed would serve as a precedent for other soon-to-be states.

The bill was debated heatedly for six years before it became law in Virginia in 1785. The law in essence guaranteed that no man "shall be compelled to frequent or support any religious worship, place, or ministry whatsoever, nor shall be enforced, restrained, molested . . . on account of his religious opinions."[2] This law served as an excellent example for other states to follow and also served as a model for the framers of the Constitution. It is said that Jefferson valued his Bill for Establishing Religious Freedom second only to his Declaration of Independence.

Jefferson and James Madison were the principal architects of the First Amendment of the U.S. Constitution, which reads in part that

Congress shall make no law respecting an establishment of religion, or prohibiting the free exercise thereof. (1791)

It is easy to see the connection between the theme of this first clause of the First Amendment and that of Jefferson's Bill for Establishing Religious Freedom in Virginia a few years earlier. The difficulty in terms of universalizing this concept was, however, that the thinking of the First Amendment applied to the Congress, not to the states. In other words, the U.S. Congress could not establish a national church and extract taxes from citizens to maintain it, nor could it compel people to attend church services of any kind. The states were left to continue as they wished in church-state matters, especially concerning education. In fact, Massachusetts and Connecticut continued such a church-state relationship until the 1830s.

Jefferson himself thought that the first clause of the First Amendment created a "wall of separation" between church and state; however, it would take a long time to decide what that term meant in context of U.S. Supreme Court decisions, and certainly in many ways the wall of separation is still not clear. Additionally, the Fourteenth Amendment, ratified in 1868, was necessary to bring down to the state level all the privileges, guarantees, and immunities of the U.S. Constitution. Theoretically, no state could establish a church or require church attendance or restrict religious freedom. Supreme Court decisions would clarify the intent of the Constitution in relation to specific issues. In all the court cases of recent years, the First and Fourteenth Amendments are discussed in context of their purposes.

Between the ratification of the First Amendment (1791) and the Fourteenth Amendment (1868), educators were almost at a loss to cope with the challenge of the separation of church and state in educational matters. Horace Mann, first state secretary of education in Massachusetts (1837), found quite a dilemma in this area. Mann was opposed to sectarian indoctrination in the public school partly because it served to divide or polarize people, yet he did not want the pendulum to swing to the other extreme of secularism. He fought hard, consequently, to keep Bible-reading exercises in the public school. The problem, though, was aggravated because the Protestants subscribed to the King James version of the Bible and the Catholics supported the Douay version. Unfortunately, there was no Annotated Revised Standard version yet on the market (as there is today), which would have been acceptable to both Catholics and Protestants. Also, had the Bible been more a tool to study about religion rather than a source for devotional exercises, the conflict may not have been so intense.

Simultaneous with Mann's insistence on the use of the King James version of the Bible in the public schools, there occurred a flood of Irish-Catholic immigration to American shores. This Irish emigration to America reached its peak between 1845 and 1850, when over one million predominantly Irish Catholics left their homeland to seek opportunity in the United States. With such numbers from Ireland alone, American Catholic officials were worried about how the spiritual needs of Catholic children would be met in public schools. Even earlier, in 1840 in Baltimore, for example, the Provincial Council of the Roman Catholic Church urged its priests to keep Catholic children Catholic by the avoidance of public school devotionals based on the King James Bible. The Church was adamantly opposed to Protestant devotional exercises in public schools.[3]

Mann's attitude about the use of the Bible in public education was a thoughtful one, but it caused problems because there was no consensus about the use of the King James version. Mann wrote in his *Twelfth Annual Report* to the Massachu-setts Board of Education (1848):

> *This Bible is in our Common Schools, by common consent. Twelve years ago, it was not in all the schools. Contrary to the genius of our government, if not contrary to the express letter of the law, it had been used for sectarian purposes—to prove one sect to be right, and others to be wrong. Hence, it had been excluded from the schools of some towns, by an express vote. But since the law, and the reasons on which it is founded, have been more fully explained and better understood; and since sectarian instruction has, to a great extent, ceased to be given, the Bible has been restored.*[4]

In addition to the problem of lack of consensus concerning the use of the King James version of the Bible, the school during this era commonly used Scripture for devotional exercises, which tended to alienate non-Protestants. An anti-Catho-lic sentiment likewise erupted in many places across the country, due in part to the heavy influx of Irish Catholics in the 1840s. "Native American" groups for many reasons openly opposed the "foreign elements" in American society. Street riots, church burnings, and verbal abuse were all too common during this period. In New York, Archbishop John Hughes concluded that part of the remedy might be to enlarge the parochial school system to include all school-age Catholic children. A definite schism was developing between public and parochial schools, partly because the climate of the public school did not embrace minority views. A respect for religious diversity was not the attitude of the public schools in most places.

The U.S. Supreme Court is still grappling with the same problems; it believes that religious heritage must be a part of general education, but not as devotional exercises. Although many people want such exercises, the Court nevertheless has banned them thus far. Consequently, many believe that this kind of judicial neutrality has created a "religion of no religion," which in essence is a form of humanism. The issue has never been settled.

Representative Supreme Court Decisions Affecting the Curriculum

The Constitution has meaning when the U.S. Supreme Court interprets it issue by issue. Several significant cases have been handed down by the Court in this century which closely touch the curriculum of the public school. This process of interpretation is continual. Certainly the last decade has proven to be an active one for both the Court and the schools in regard to such things as Bible reading and prayer. In this section, an overview of representative cases is offered about what the public school can and cannot do to instill in youth a knowledge of and respect for their religious heritage. The citation for each case used in this chapter appears in the recommended readings.

Released Time for Religious Instruction

After World War I especially, cooperation between public schools and representative churches was common to the extent that a designated amount of time per week was allotted for religious instruction. This went unchallenged because most parents desired to have their children instructed periodically in the religious tenets of their choice. By parental permission, children attended religious instruction during the school day, within the school building, taught by members of the clergy or religious order. The only cooperation the public school offered in addition to releasing children was the use of a room during the school day for a designated time per week, usually about an hour. Released time was a popular program.

This kind of religious program was challenged after World War II in Champaign County, Illinois, on the grounds that such a program established religion and was in violation of the First and Fourteenth Amendments. A Champaign Council on Religious Education was formed on a voluntary basis to handle all of the administrative and instructional details to circumvent the hazard of involving the public school in an unconstitutional manner; however, the problem was not avoided.

In *McCollum* v. *Board of Education* (1948), the U.S. Supreme Court decided it was clear that the use of the buildings for religious instruction during the school day violated the First and Fourteenth Amendments. A tax-supported public school system was used to help religious groups indoctrinate children. McCollum wanted her son to receive only a secular education (nonreligious education) during the compulsory school day. Released time during this compulsory period for religious instruction, in her view, was sectarian (religious) indoctrination and consequently unconstitutional. The Court concurred.

The upshot of this case was a shock to many school boards and parents. What had been traditional was now banned during the school day. An alternative approach was attempted in the New York City School District whereby children could receive religious instruction during the school day, but *off the premises*. The school board offered a program so that parents interested in sending their school-age children to churches of their choice for religious instruction during a designated time each week could do so by returning a permission slip to their respective schools. The children, in turn, were transported at parental expense to nearby churches, which then sent back to the home school an attendance report. Children not interested in religious instruction would remain in school for a study or library period. There was no coercion from the school to get children to participate in religious instruction.

The U.S. Supreme Court in *Zorach* v. *Clauson* (1952) believed that this alternative approach to what was banned in *McCollum* met the constitutional test because no establishment of religion took place. In fact, the majority opinion held that when the state "cooperates with religious authorities by adjusting the schedule of public events to sectarian needs, it follows the best of our traditions." The difference between the *McCollum* and *Zorach* cases lay in the phrases "within the building" and "off the premises." In *Zorach*, the children participated constitutionally in religious instruction off the premises. It should be noted that states can participate in the kind of religious program advocated by the Court in 1952 only if their respective constitutions allow such cooperation.

The *Zorach* decision has met with considerable controversy. Some critics have argued that the language in the majority opinion, such as that previously cited, can set a dangerous precedent because such cooperation may have no limit. The wall of separation could crumble. On the other hand, some proponents of nonpublic aid believe that if states cooperate in this manner, parents might be more satisfied with the public school. Sectarian instruction can be given off the property one hour a week, or one school day a month, or by some mutually arranged time during the compulsory school period. Also, religious instruction could be coordinated with social service to make it even more attractive to parents and students.

Parental interest in released-time programs over the years has lessened as a result of an exodus of families to suburban communities. Sidewalks are rare and churches are farther apart. Hence, transporting children to churches or centers, often at private expense, becomes more difficult. Coupled with this problem is a diminished zeal on the part of many parents to send their children to church or to religious instruction at all, no matter how convenient. But, if a state constitution allows released-time programs to exist, school districts may cooperate with churches in this regard on a voluntary basis.

Prayer and Bible Reading

The next few cases cited in this section have elicited more reaction in the two decades following their appearance than most cases have on any topic. Parents, school boards, and politicians have taken sides on the emotional issues which emanated from these decisions. The Supreme Court has been involved with religious issues that have a direct lineage to those of over 30 years ago.

The first case that had a powerful impact upon the public school curriculum, and that is still referred to quite often, is *Engel* v. *Vitale* (1962). The case developed as a result of a supposedly harmless prayer composed by the New York State Board of Regents and recommended to school districts across the state. It read thus:

> *Almighty God, we acknowledge our dependence upon Thee, and we beg Thy blessings upon us, our parents, our teachers, and our country.*

In the Union Free School District No. 9, New Hyde Park, New York, each class recited this prayer in the presence of the teacher at the beginning of every school day. The view of the New York Board of Regents was that all people of good will could subscribe to the views in the above prayer. Parents of 10 pupils, however, believed a school-sponsored prayer like that composed by the board violated the First and Fourteenth Amendments. They believed it was religious activity. The

Court agreed and prohibited a secular agency such as the Board of Regents, a state department, or a school board from composing a prayer, no matter how "brief or general" it might be.

What this case did not answer was the question about student-initiated prayer, or even the question about "meditation," which has since been a Court issue. The idea of *school sponsorship* of religious activities is what infringes upon the doctrine of separation. This brings in the establishment principle. The case elicited much animosity toward the Court on the part of citizens who thought it had rendered the schools godless. This case was to be the first of three controversial decisions.

In the following year, companion cases aroused public opinion and literally sent schools on a new academic path concerning the place of religion in the public school. In the first case, *Abington School District* v. *Schempp* (1963), the Court outlawed the use of the Holy Bible in the manner used throughout Pennsylvania. The Pennsylvania legislature in 1959 passed a law that "at least ten verses from the Holy Bible shall be read, without comment, at the opening of each public school on each school day." Parental written request could excuse children from these exercises.

The Schempp parents were Unitarian and did not care to have their two children exposed to a literal reading of the Bible, which ran counter to their religious beliefs. Readings were normally made without comment from the King James, the Douay, and the Revised Standard versions of the Bible. Jewish Holy Scriptures were also used periodically. The Schempp children did not want to excuse themselves from the brief readings because of possible social ridicule.

The Court believed that although the various versions of the Bible and Scriptures had excellent literary, historical, and moral value, Biblical use in the Abington School District was in violation of the First and Fourteenth Amendments. The Court's objection, in other words, was not the Holy Bible itself, but the role assigned to it by the Pennsylvania legislature for the public schools. In fact, the Court has always taken the position that religious heritage is important and children need to be exposed in an academic manner to that heritage. As a religious activity, however, the Court bans Bible reading even if it is "without comment."

In the second case, the Supreme Court considered a related issue that originated in Baltimore, Maryland. In *Murray* v. *Curlett* (1963) the Court struck down a ruling composed by the Baltimore Board of School Commissioners which read, in part, that a "reading without comment, of a chapter in the Holy Bible and/or the use of the Lord's Prayer" should be utilized as opening day exercises in the schools. Madalyn Murray and her son contested the regulation on the grounds that their religious liberty was in jeopardy. Belief in God was pitted against nonbelief, the Murrays argued, and belief in God as the source of all moral values was the message the school conveyed by the reading of the Holy Bible or the reciting of the Lord's Prayer.

The Court agreed with the Murrays and struck down these religious practices. The Court contended that the purpose and primary effect of the regulation by the Baltimore Board of School Commissioners advanced the cause of religion.

To meet the constitutional test, the regulation should have had a secular legisla-tive purpose and a primary effect that neither advanced nor inhibited religion. Conversely, the Court had to be careful not to inhibit religion by creating a "religion of no religion" by banning the religious practices of Bible reading and the recitation of the Lord's Prayer. The Court, in this case, believed it did not create such a secular view.

In the majority view of both the *Schempp* and *Murray* cases, the Supreme Court enunciated a positive position concerning the place of the Bible in the public school. It felt strongly that the Bible is "worthy of study for its literary and historic qualities." And in an often-quoted sentence, the Court stated that "one's education is not complete without a study of comparative religion or the history of religion and its relationship to the advancement of civilization." These two cases obviously were controversial, and in combination with the *Engel* decision, they created a medley of public and educational reaction.

Probably the most positive immediate result of these three judicial decisions of the early 1960s was a publication by the American Association of School Administrators (AASA) entitled *Religion in the Public Schools* (1964). Before the publication of this popular volume, public schools really had no clear direction concerning the role of religion in the curriculum. An eight-member commission, composed primarily of professors and school superintendents, eloquently ex-pressed the role of the public school in its relation to religion. The commission provided a set of guidelines to assist boards of education in setting policy and to help administrators and teachers implement that policy. The volume embraced positive methods to enhance religious pluralism by such means as school calen-dar, graduation exercises, observation of religious holidays, and so on. In sum, it portrayed a view that teaching about religion, exposing students to a religious heritage but asking no commitment from them, is the role of the school. The book was well received. It was brief, readable, and substantive. It was revised and republished in 1986.

Another effect of these court cases was the concerted action to amend the U.S. Constitution to allow voluntary prayer. Led in the 1960s by the late Senator Everett M. Dirksen (Illinois), the movement resulted in an inundation of letters to Congress to initiate an amendment. This movement, however, never garnered enough support to obtain ratification. The energy to amend the Constitution to allow voluntary prayer is still at a high level. Throughout the 1980s this issue was before the public.

The supposed religious void left by these three court cases helped to spawn an interest in moral education in many public schools. "Family life and sex education" was a point of interest and controversy first in Anaheim, California, and then in many localities across the country. Value clarification became more fashionable in dealing with hypothetical dilemmas to develop moral reasoning, which became a process that was greatly written about for the next 20 years. Also publishers have made available a host of materials on teaching about religion and religion-related themes.

One educational attitude that has resulted from these three cases on religion in the school is reflected in Box 8-1, "A Teacher's Code." This code implies a need for administrative support concerning a school district's policy on teaching about religion, but it certainly suggests that teachers need not be indifferent toward religious content. The authors highly recommend this code to prospective teachers. It does mean extra academic effort and some specialization on the part of all teachers involved, but the benefit is worth the effort. To expose public school students to their religious heritage in context of social studies and the humanities is educationally sound.

The issue of voluntary prayer continues to be very controversial. School districts in some localities have flouted previous judicial decisions on prayer and Bible reading in favor of devotions and sectarian observances. Twenty-five states, opposed to the removal of voluntary prayer from the schools, have implemented alternative practices. One was considered by the U.S. Supreme Court in 1985. Its roots can be traced to the *Engel* decision of 1962. The Supreme Court's opinion in

---

BOX 8-1   A Teacher's Code

1. Because of the potential explosiveness of the subject of religion, the teacher should make a particularly concerted effort to be informed on the subject.

2. Religion should never be discussed out of context. (In historically oriented courses, this is easily controllable; in problem or sociologically oriented courses, the task admittedly becomes increasingly difficult.)

3. The teacher should have sensitivity for the divergent religious views represented by the students in his classroom, not to accord such views favored treatment but to prevent embarrassment to any student when less favorable aspects of his religion are discussed.

4. A teacher should never permit himself to be led or drawn into a debate on a doctrinal point with an individual student.

5. A teacher does not serve the needs of his students most effectively by appearing as a neutral on crucial issues, but when personal preference of conviction is called for,

it should be duly labeled but never stated dogmatically.

6. Religion is not a sterile topic consisting of descriptions and statistics of various religious groups and leaders; if the subject is not carried to the point of explaining causation, the teacher has not adequately identified the fundamental basis for its inclusion.

7. The teacher must present a balanced account. This does not mean that the same number of shortcomings or attributes for the various religions under discussion should be listed; instead balance means that religious implications will be assigned their appropriate position in the hierarchy of causal factors in explaining an event or movement.

8. Shortcomings and failures of religious organizations and leaders are as significant as successes, and every teacher has an obligation to utilize such evidence in his presentations.

Source: Lawrence L. Little, ed., "A Teacher's Code," *Religion in the Social Studies.* (New York: The Religious Freedom and Public Affairs Project of the National Conference of Christians and Jews, 1966), pp. 91–93. Used with permission.

1985 struck down a 1981 Alabama statute; however, it did not proscribe similar legislation in the other 24 states.

In the Alabama decision, *Wallace* v. *Jaffree* (1985), the U.S. Supreme Court for the first time dealt with legislation providing for a "moment of silence" in public schools. An Alabama law in 1981 authorized teachers to "announce that a period of silence not to exceed one minute shall be observed for meditation or voluntary prayer, and during any such period no other activities shall be engaged in."

Ishmael Jaffree of Mobile contested the law in 1982 because he believed his three children were being led unconstitutionally in prayer. A majority of the Supreme Court agreed because the practice of voluntary prayer "indicates that the state intended to characterize prayer as a favored practice. Such an endorsement is not consistent with the established principle that the government must pursue a course of complete neutrality toward religion." The Court believed the intent of this 1981 legislation was religious in nature and failed to meet the necessary secular test for constitutionality. It concluded that the Alabama law "violates the First Amendment." Consequently, the Alabama moment of silence legislation was killed.

Voluntary prayer, as stated earlier, has been a point of contention between those who want some form of devotion or prayer in the public school and those who believe that religion has a place only as an academic study if it is to be school-sponsored. This latter group believes that every student presently has the legal right to meditate or pray silently anyway. The school, in their view, should not get involved. The Reagan administration, incidentally, had filed briefs supporting the Alabama law. The fate of "silence for meditation or voluntary prayer" in the other states will be decided eventually.

In recent years, the U.S. Supreme Court has been active in the area of prayer. In *Lee* v. *Weisman* (1992), the Court "settled" an issue that arose over prayers offered by a rabbi during a grade promotion ceremony in a Rhode Island middle school in 1989. The majority opinion stated that school-sponsored prayers at graduation exercises "coerce" students to participate, thus violating the establishment clause of the First Amendment. By implication, such prayer cannot be conducted at other school functions such as athletic events or honors banquets.

In the wake of this controversial decision, however, attempts are being made to circumvent the Court's ruling; that is, students determine whether there should be a graduation prayer, and, if so, select or compose a prayer and choose a peer to deliver it. In late 1992, the U.S. Supreme Court refused to hear an appeal of the Fifth Circuit Court in Texas, which allowed a non-denominational graduation prayer initiated by students. In effect, in only those states accountable to the Fifth Circuit Court is student-initiated and directed prayer not considered coercion in the manner discussed by the *Lee* case. The issue regarding the constitutionality of student involvement in prayer at school functions remains to be resolved at the national level. The evidence of school sponsorship is an important factor.

In 1988 a significant document was published for widespread circulation among professional and lay groups regarding the need for teaching about religion in the public school. The pamphlet, entitled "Religion in the Public School Curriculum: Questions and Answers," was timely and important because for the first time major religious bodies and educational associations jointly developed a consensus position concerning teaching about religion. Previously, professional groups had developed positions without the support of organized religion. Now, however, given the consensus position it appears the movement to teach about religious heritage has a chance to succeed for the first time.

Eight questions were cited in the pamphlet, and the responses to those questions were endorsed by 14 major organizations, which included the National Education Association, the American Federation of Teachers, the National Association of Evangelicals, and the Baptist Joint Committee on Public Affairs. The questions dealt with the constitutionality of teaching about religion, what "teaching about religion" means, where the subject belongs, and why it should be included.[5] Politically, this consensus pamphlet reflects a strong societal interest in incorporating the topic in the public school curriculum.

Before moving on to the topic of fringe benefits for non-public schools, it is important to mention a related legislative event that occurred in 1984; Congress passed the Equal Access Act. This act requires public secondary schools receiving federal financial assistance and maintaining a policy of a limited open forum to allow students to conduct meetings of their choosing in regard to religious, political, or philosophical themes. A limited open forum exists when a school offers an opportunity to any group classified as a non-curriculum–related group to meet on school property during noninstructional time. In other words, if a number of students want to study and discuss the Bible, for example, before or after their school day, they may.

This act requires that school officials must be careful not to sponsor such meetings, for example, promoting, leading, or participating in the activities; however, these officials can maintain order or discipline. Non-school individuals are prohibited from directing or regularly attending the activities of these student meetings.

School officials must also refrain from dictating the content of a meeting in such aspects as prayer or ritual. The idea of voluntary participation and student direction is a key concept of the Equal Access Act. Although many questions will emerge in ensuing years, the spirit of the law seems to have been accepted. One chief worry of educators may materialize because groups embracing unpopular views will be allowed to conduct meetings. Extremist groups will be controlled on constitutional grounds. Students cannot be denied participation on the basis of race, religion, sex, or ethnic origin, so if an extremist group denies admittance to any student on these bases, school officials can then become directly involved.

The Equal Access Act has changed public secondary schools dramatically. When free time before or after the school day is utilized by students in the manner prescribed by this act, something very different has taken place in public education. Religion can now be discussed by students in a sectarian context on a voluntary basis during noninstructional time in those secondary schools maintaining a limited open forum policy.

Recently, the U.S. Supreme Court considered a challenge to the Equal Access Act. In the *Board of Education of Westside Community Schools* v. *Mergens* (1990), the Court held that the Act, which allowed schools to create a limited open forum, must be implemented in an equitable manner. That is, if non-curriculum-related student groups meet during non-instructional time, equal access must also be provided for student religious groups. Such voluntary access does not violate the Establishment Clause of the First Amendment. The Court upheld the Act that, in essence, guarantees the right of students to hold religious group meetings in the school building within the context of a limited open forum.

In *Lamb's Chapel* v. *Center Moriches Union Free School District* (1993), the U.S. Supreme Court decreed that, if public schools are generally open to community groups after school, church groups also should be allowed to use the facilities after school. An evangelical Christian church wanted to show publicly a Christian film series on family life at the Center Moriches High School (NY) but was refused by the school board on the basis that the facilities cannot be used for religious purposes. The Court ruled, however, that no entanglement, government endorsement, or religious benefit would result from such use.

Aid to Nonpublic Schools

In part two of this chapter, we will provide an overview to help the prospective teacher better understand the delicate relationship between church and state in relation to so-called fringe benefits to nonpublic schools. Benefits, such as secular textbooks and transportation assistance, are of vital concern to some religious groups. Representative forms of such aid will be discussed by reviewing what the U.S. Supreme Court has approved over the last several decades.

The term "non-public or private schools" covers a number of religious and independent institutions. In terms of the number of students in such institutions, the enrollment as of 1993 reached 5.4 million students. Private school, in this context, means that it is an institution embracing levels through grade twelve and is not a "home" school. It must meet at least four hours or more per day, 160 days a year. Preschools without a first grade are not considered in this enrollment.

Private education is an important component of schooling below the college level. Students in Catholic schools represent the largest segment of the private enrollment, numbering about 2.6 million, prekindergarten through grade 12. During the 1992–1993 school year the Catholic enrollment increased by almost 1 percent, the largest single-year increase in the last 30 years. Since 1988, Catholic enrollment has been fairly stable. Enrollment in other private schools has continued to increase, growing in 1993 to approximately 2.5 million students. Of the total enrollment in religious schools, however, Catholic students represent about 63 percent.[6]

To indicate the variety of affiliated nonpublic schools, the following list of major denominational schools is offered (not all of the following are advocates of public aid):

1. Roman Catholic
2. Lutheran
3. Baptist
4. Hebrew Day Schools
5. Episcopal
6. Seventh-Day Adventist
7. Calvinist (Christian Reformed)
8. Friends
9. Presbyterian
10. Methodist
11. Eastern Orthodox
12. Christian Schools International

Right of Choice

The U.S. Supreme Court in 1925 rendered an opinion that has since been a judicial cornerstone for private education. In 1647 the Puritans assumed that parents had a choice in the type of school they desired for their offspring as long as certain competencies were attained. That belief continues to this day; however, at times it has been challenged.

In Oregon shortly after the close of World War I, a Compulsory Education Act was adopted by the voters; in essence it compelled children between ages eight and 16 to attend public schools only. Exceptions to this law were made for special children, for children already finished with the eighth grade, for children geographically distant from a public school, and for the children already exempted by the Court because of special permits.

The act would have destroyed private education in Oregon by abrogating the parents' right to choose the school they desired for their offspring. The Court found the intent of this act very harmful. Consequently, parents in Oregon, as a result of this 1925 Supreme Court decision, *Pierce* v. *Society of the Sisters of the Holy Names of Jesus and Mary* and *Pierce* v. *Hill Military Academy,* could continue to select nonpublic schools for their children.

Secular Texts

Following this famous 1925 Supreme Court decision, fringe benefit issues began to wend their way to the high Court. It now became even more acceptable to some people that if parents have the constitutional right to choose their child's school, then perhaps it is the state's duty to help them exercise that choice by means of selected secular benefits. The first celebrated case in this area was *Cochran* v. *Louisiana State of Board of Education* (1930). Louisiana believed that assisting any child in a private, parochial, or public elementary or secondary school was the prerogative of the state if that assistance meant support to the student to obtain a secular education during those years of compulsory education. Louisiana believed that providing secular textbooks met the constitutional test of neutrality. Textbooks could be evaluated in terms of sectarian influence or bias.

Cochran believed this state attitude violated the First and Fourteenth Amendments because nonpublic schools exist by choice and should be supported only by those who attend them. It was unreasonable, in his view, to use tax money to help those students, even if for secular purposes.

The Supreme Court disagreed, however. It believed the child benefited rather than the institution, an attitude which became known as the "child benefit theory." This assumption later undergirded veteran educational benefits in that the individual can pursue educational activities in private or public institutions. The assistance is to the person, not to the school. The "child benefit theory" still stands and has blossomed in many states in terms of selected fringe benefits, especially secular textbook assistance. The state must allow such aid by authority of its constitution, and then there must be a willingness by the state legislature or department to assist students in all schools below the college level.

Transportation

In a major case decided in 1947, the U.S. Supreme Court advanced the cause of assistance to nonpublic schools. In *Everson* v. *Board of Education*, the issue of transportation aid emerged in New Jersey. In Ewing Township there were no public or private high schools. It was agreed upon by state officials and parents that high school youths would utilize public transportation to and from Trenton, New Jersey, to attend the high schools of their choice. Parents, consequently, would be reimbursed with state funds for transportation costs only.

Everson contested the fact that parents of children in parochial schools were reimbursed for their transportation costs. According to Everson, this was an unreasonable use of public money. He believed only parents of students attending public schools should be eligible. The high Court disagreed, however, on the grounds that providing for the "general well-being" of a student has a constitutional basis irrespective of the school attended. To transport students, in other words, at state expense is promoting an element of safety during those years of compulsory schooling. This case allowed the states the choice to assist nonpublic students if their respective constitutions permitted such transportation assistance. The First and Fourteenth Amendments, the Court believed, were not violated in this particular context.

Federal Programs

A Supreme Court case decided in 1968 involved a federal program in public and private schools. In *Board of Education* v. *Allen*, the issue of lending (from public to non-public schools) secular textbooks purchased with federal funds under the sponsorship of the then Title II Elementary and Secondary Education Act was contested because parochial schools were involved. Both the First and Fourteenth Amendments were in question because of the establishment principle. This case was important because had the lending of secular textbooks been voided by the Court, one of the most important federal educational programs of all time would have been greatly diluted.

The Court decreed that it could not see any violation of the establishment principle in the matter of lending secular textbooks. The law did not interfere with religious instruction in the parochial school. The Court further stated that it could not accept the argument that secular textbooks would become instruments to teach religion in the parochial schools. It believed that sectarian schools also have a secular purpose, which they have demonstrated for a long time. Consequently, the use of these textbooks would further only a secular mission.

A related federal program was before the Supreme Court in 1985. Chapter 1, dealing with aid to low-income, academically behind, normal children in both public and nonpublic schools, became the object of a judicial challenge. The former Titles of the Elementary and Secondary Education Act (ESEA) were restructured by the Education Consolidation and Improvement Act (1981); however, Chapter 1 (formerly Title I, the heart of the ESEA) remained basically the same; however, in 1988 the Education Consolidation and Improvement Act was repealed and placed under a new Elementary and Secondary Education Act, but Chapter 1 remains intact. This recent Supreme Court opinion was extremely significant in terms of federal assistance to public and nonpublic schools below the college level.

In *Aguilar* v. *Felton* (1985) the U.S. Supreme Court considered issues that originated in New York City. This case involved a program for Chapter 1 students which entailed the practice of sending public school teachers to parochial schools to assist in remedial education. The rooms were stripped of religious materials, but critics still thought the program was unconstitutional.

Proponents of this annual, $20 million Chapter 1 program in New York City believed it was constitutional because the school board hired and supervised all the teachers in the program. No entanglement existed with parochial schools in its eighteen-year history. They further believed that by the very fact that few abuses were ever reported, the practice constituted a wholesome relationship between church and state.

The U.S. Supreme Court, however, held that even though this federal Chapter 1 program promoted worthy goals, the use of public school teachers in parochial schools raised the image of government involvement with religion. The majority opinion was based partly on a precedent set in the *Meek* decision (1975), which found that secular aid to nonpublic schools violates the Constitution if the aid benefits the school and its activities. In the New York case, such constitutional violation existed; consequently, the practice of sending public school teachers into parochial schools was struck down.

In the case of *Zobrest* v. *Catalina Foothills School District* (1993), the U.S. Supreme Court ruled that it is permissible for school districts to provide sign-language interpreters for hearing-impaired students in private religious schools. The Court's view was that such a program "distributes benefits neutrally to any child qualifying" under the tenets of the Individuals with Disabilities Education

Act. The student in question, James Zobrest, eventually transferred from a public middle school in Tucson, Arizona, to a Catholic high school and was denied the services of an interpreter for lip-reading and sign language. The Court, however, believed the interpreter was authorized to be available in the sectarian school.

In another important case involving the matter of the separation of church and state in public education, the U.S. Supreme Court upheld its so-called wall of separation. In *Kiryas Joel Village School District Board of Education* v. *Grumet* (1994), the Court decided that the state of New York had violated the requirement of government neutrality by "extending the benefit of a special franchise" to Hasidic Jews of the Satmar sect in Kiryas Joel, New York.

In 1989, the state had established a special school district for children with disabilities living in this orthodox community of 1200 residents. The constitutional question quickly became, however, whether or not the state can accommodate the religion and culture of a religious community by the creation of a public school district classified as special. A separate district was established to preserve the cultural integrity of the sect and still meet the needs of children with disabilities.

Even though such separation since 1989 helped to foster social cohesion within the Jewish community and also educationally serve those children with disabilities, the Court decided in this case that constitutional neutrality had been breached.

Secular Services

In two issues before the Supreme Court (1971) concerning support of non-public schools in Pennsylvania and Rhode Island, the Court disappointed advocates of parochial schools. In *Lemon* v. *Kurtzman* and *Earley* v. *DiCenso,* the establishment and free-exercise clauses of the First Amendment and the due process clause of the Fourteenth Amendment were germane. The cases embodied one statutory program each in Pennsylvania and Rhode Island, both of which provided state aid to church-related elementary and secondary schools.

The Rhode Island question (*Earley*) involved a salary supplement program which authorized the state to supplement the salaries of lay teachers of secular subjects in nonpublic elementary schools. Their duties had to be purely secular and the materials used had to be those utilized in the public schools. Also, supplement could not exceed 15 percent of the teacher's annual salary.

In the Pennsylvania issue (*Lemon*), secular educational services were purchased from nonpublic schools. Under "contracts" the state directly reimbursed nonpublic schools for their costs for salaries, textbooks, and instructional materials. Certain restrictions were imposed by the Pennsylvania legislature on these contracts. Reimbursement could pertain only to courses in mathematics, modern foreign languages, physical science, and physical education. The textbooks and materials had to be approved by the state superintendent. A secular purpose was supposed to permeate all subject matter affected by the legislation.

What emerged in both of the judicial analyses was the term "excessive entanglement." The Court saw too much overlapping of the missions of both the public and parochial sectors. In order to effect an objective program, it would have necessitated monitoring the programs in the parochial school by public officials. "Surveillance and control" would have become characteristic of the relationship between public and parochial schools. And in the case of Pennsylvania, the Court believed the so-called reimbursements were *de facto* grants to parochial schools. Both statutory programs, consequently, were declared unconstitutional. Legislation of this nature has to be secular in purpose, neutral in effect, and unentangling between church and state. The term "excessive entanglement" was commonly quoted in similar subsequent cases in the next decade. Advocates of aid to nonpublic schools were naturally discouraged by these two decisions, but that feeling was not to last the entire decade.

Related Educational Services

The concept "excessive entanglement" lingered on in the interpretation of another issue emanating in Pennsylvania and decided in the U.S. Supreme Court in 1975. In the *Meek* v. *Pittenger* case, the Pennsylvania legislature had attempted to aid its parochial schools by means of three basic programs: (1) auxiliary services such as counseling, psychological, speech, and hearing services; (2) materials and equipment of an instructional nature loaned to nonpublic schools; and (3) secular textbooks loaned to nonpublic schools.

The Court again employed the rationale of "excessive entanglement" to strike down the use of the auxiliary services, materials, and equipment, but it approved the textbook provision. Excessive monitoring of the programs, it was thought, would blur the missions of both the public and private schools. Again, proponents for increased aid to nonpublic schools saw their zeal dampened because the Court interpreted this aid to be an infringement upon the First and Fourteenth Amendments.

In a case shortly after *Meek*, proponents for increased aid were buoyed up as a result of *Wolman* v. *Walter* (1977). The Ohio legislature passed a multimillion dollar package to do the following for nonpublic schools: (1) administer and score standardized tests; (2) provide secular textbooks; (3) conduct diagnostic or therapeutic services; (4) provide funds for field trips; and (5) make available instructional materials. The Court approved all but the last two [(4) and (5)]. "Excessive entanglement" again appeared because monitoring and surveillance would have had to be undertaken to ensure conformity by the non-public schools to constitutional restrictions.

The Court stressed in the *Wolman* decision that in any such legislative program to nonpublic schools the intent must be secular, unentangling, and the primary effect of the legislation must neither aid nor inhibit religion. The legislation to assist nonpublic schools, in other words, must be neutral in effect. In the *Wolman* case, the Court saw less entanglement than in the *Meek* decision. In

Wolman, there was minimal educational contact and no influence of private on public schools (or vice versa) in the administration of services. The therapeutic services were in part conducted on a neutral site. The integrity of mission in both institutions remained intact.

The Ohio case uplifted the morale of many sectarian school advocates because the secular aspects of their parochial schools seemed to be, at long last, valued more highly. What had been discouragement now became hope.

Tax Deductions

In a case of a different nature, but nevertheless very significant in terms of the survival of many parochial and private schools, the U.S. Supreme Court in 1983 in *Mueller* v. *Allen* considered a crucial question. Minnesota granted state income tax deductions of up to $1,000 for each child's expenses in a public, private, or parochial school. The benefit was primarily to parochial parents who paid tuition. Public school parents simply had fewer expenses to deduct. This case had powerful implications for the nation in regard to deductions because interested states that are constitutionally permitted to assist non-public schools can now initiate similar tax deduction programs.

In the *Mueller* decision, the Court assumed no constitutional conflict existed because the state tax deduction "neutrally provides state assistance to a broad spectrum of citizens." Although tuition was the chief benefit to parochial and private school parents, other dividends would accrue in the categories of transportation and textbook expenses. As stated, public school students are included, too, but their expenses would not be as great as their counterparts in nonpublic schools, especially in parochial schools.

The Court believed this Minnesota law was constitutional because it had a secular purpose of ensuring an educated citizenry, it did not have the primary effect of advancing religion; and it did not excessively entangle church and state in granting state income tax deductions. The Court, in its majority opinion, believed that "there is a strong public interest in assuring the continued financial health of private schools, both sectarian and nonsectarian."

Shared Time

Another far-reaching case which the U.S. Supreme Court decided in its 1984–1985 session was *School District of the City of Grand Rapids* v. *Ball* (1985). The issue of shared time was the key to this case; public school teachers were teaching remedial and community education classes in private schools even though the program was funded by state and local money. These two programs of remedial and community education involved classroom instruction mainly by public school teachers on the premises of forty parochial schools. The state of Michigan in defense of shared time believed that the local board of education in Grand Rapids was simply trying to provide total education for the community. The classes, Michigan believed, were not part of a core program or curriculum, but rather special supplemental courses. Michigan did not believe that the concept of shared time as employed in Grand Rapids reflected excessive entanglement between church and state in education.

The U.S. Supreme Court in 1985 decided the issues in the *Grand Rapids* case in the following manner. The Court struck down both the remedial and community education programs as they existed. The remedial shared time program breached the constitutional line between appropriate governmental accommodation of religion and direct financial assistance. The majority view held that "the symbolic union of church and state inherent in the provision of secular, state-provided instruction in the religious school buildings threatens to convey a message of state support for religion to students and to the general public." The Court added that such shared time "poses a substantial risk of state-sponsored indoctrination. No attempt is made to monitor the shared time courses for religious content."

In regard to the community education program in Grand Rapids, the Court also declared that the program was unconstitutional because "of a substantial risk that overtly or subtly the religious message . . . during the regular school day will infuse the supposedly secular classes . . . after school."

What Can Be Done to Assist Nonpublic Schools?

What can be done to assist non-public schools depends upon what the U.S. Supreme Court has said is permissible, the respective state constitutions, the zeal of the churches for public support, and the desires of the various legislatures. The following points are believed to be fairly representative of ongoing and potential assistance.

Transportation Assistance   The following 27 states provide some form of bus service to nonpublic schools: Arkansas, California, Connecticut, Delaware, Illinois, Indiana, Iowa, Kentucky, Louisiana, Maine, Maryland, Massachusetts, Michigan, Minnesota, Montana, Nebraska, Nevada, New Hampshire, New Jersey, New York, North Dakota, Ohio, Oregon, Pennsylvania, Rhode Island, West Virginia, and Wisconsin.

Textbook Loans or Grants of Textbooks   The following 18 states assist non-public schools regarding textbooks: California, Colorado, Connecticut, Iowa, Louisiana, Maine, Massachusetts, Minnesota, Mississippi, New Hampshire, New Jersey, New Mexico, New York, Ohio, Pennsylvania, Rhode Island, South Dakota, and West Virginia.

Health and Auxiliary Services   The following 16 states provide some assistance to non-public schools in regard to health and auxiliary services: Arizona, Connecticut, Hawaii, Iowa, Kansas, Maine, Maryland, Massachusetts, Michigan, Minnesota, Mississippi, New Hampshire, New Jersey, New York, Ohio, and Pennsylvania.

Lunch Assistance   The following 12 states provide lunch assistance to public and nonpublic schools: Arkansas, California, Connecticut, Illinois, Iowa, Louisiana, Nevada, New Hampshire, New Jersey, Oregon, Pennsylvania, and Rhode Island.

Driver Education   The following 20 states provide assistance for a driver education curriculum: California, Connecticut, Delaware, Florida, Hawaii, Illinois, Indiana, Iowa, Louisiana, Michigan, Minnesota, Mississippi, New Hampshire, Ohio, Oregon, Pennsylvania, South Dakota, Utah, Vermont, and Wisconsin.

Shared Time Programs   The following nine states provide the possibility of shared or dual enrollment in their public and non-public schools: Colorado, Illinois, Iowa, Kentucky, Minnesota, New Hampshire, Pennsylvania, Rhode Island, and Washington.[7]

Dual enrollment and shared time are synonymous terms, but they have no connection with released time programs, which refer to religious instruction during the school day off the public school premises. Shared time implies a cooperation between non-public schools, especially parochial, and public schools in those content areas designated as secular only. Such programs in the public schools as driver education, home economics, special education, and business education lend themselves easily to shared time or dual enrollment.

The federal government has done a great deal to stimulate cooperation between church and state in education. State constitutions, however, can restrict these programs to before or after school. Most of the successful shared time programs have taken place in Pennsylvania, Illinois, Michigan, Wisconsin, and Ohio. In other words, shared time is not a common practice around the country.

Proponents for shared time programs believe that non-public school parents can at least derive partial benefits from their public school taxes, and conversely, public schools can elicit greater community support for their efforts when it really counts—at the time of tax elections. Educationally, these programs help to break down psychological walls of division between private and public school students, while at the same time enhancing the educational opportunities of nonpublic school students.

The chief drawback to these programs of shared time may be linked to the mission of the nonpublic school. In a parochial school a parent may desire a religious atmosphere to saturate all content and activities. If this is the case, then shared time or dual enrollment may encroach upon religious education. The missions of the non-public and public schools may become somewhat blurred by excessive entanglement if the spirit of the First and Fourteenth Amendments is forgotten or ignored. The future of shared time as a mutual benefit to public and non-public schools is unknown. It is, however, always an appealing topic of discussion because it seems to reflect compromise and afford all children greater educational opportunity.

Auxiliary Services   The U.S. Supreme Court in the *Wolman* decision (1977) approved speech, hearing, and psychological services that had been stricken in the

Meek case (1975). Standardized testing also was approved. The major difference was the manner in which the services were to be provided. In *Wolman*, the Court saw greater objectivity and neutrality. In *Wolman* the legislation in question did not violate the First and Fourteenth Amendments. It did not assist or hinder religion nor did it create excessive entanglement. The auxiliary services approved by the U.S. Supreme Court are those that a state can offer if its constitution permits.

Eastern states seem to have the lead in such services, and the best example of how these services can be offered may continue to be that of Ohio. Special education is always a fertile area for cooperation while Chapter 1 again has prompted collaboration, especially in compensatory education. Auxiliary services usually will be linked to these two areas of schooling.

Tax Deductions In the *Mueller* decision (1983) the U.S. Supreme Court allowed deductions for certain expenses on state income taxes in Minnesota for parents of youth in private, parochial, and public schools below the college level. The Supreme Court believed that the Minnesota model neutrally assisted a "broad spectrum of citizens." Obviously, parents of children in parochial schools will benefit the most. If state constitutions permit, this type of assistance may become more commonplace.

Vouchers The most visionary of all forms of aid to non-public schools has to be mentioned even though it is almost nonexistent below the college level. The idea of a voucher dates to the turn of the century, but it received greatest attention in the United States during the 1960s, but is again in the spotlight. A voucher means that a parent receives a redeemable cash coupon for educational services at an approved private, public, or parochial school for a partial or full day of school. Funding for education focuses more in this method on parents and less on public school boards of education. The voucher can be a tool to assist low-income parents to seek better educational opportunity as well as to allow parochial school parents to exercise educational choices.

Vouchers are naturally unpopular with public school advocates because they see a potential racial, academic, and social "elitism" resulting from a public acceptance of vouchers as a form of assistance to parents. The public school, it is feared, will be left with the very poor children whose parents could not afford costly private or parochial schools. In a sense, vouchers could permit unbridled free enterprise in education.

Proponents for the use of vouchers, however, see this method as the best means of allowing parents to fulfill their educational obligation. If the U.S. Supreme Court in its *Pierce* decision (1925) enabled parents to select the *kind* of school for their child, why then, proponents argue, cannot public money be provided to help parents secure the secular aspects of formal education? Advocates for vouchers see this method of finance as a just way of obtaining educational services. They also cite European examples, such as the Netherlands and France, where vouchers have given parents greater educational choice. Free enterprise in education, it is believed, can stimulate more school competition, greater accountability on the part of educators to parents, and more curricular development.

Vouchers have been discussed often in light of future funding of formal education, but they have been rarely implemented, primarily because of the church-state question. In a few locations such as New Hampshire, Indiana, and California, vouchers were tried experimentally but discontinued. Minnesota and Colorado have recently experimented with them at the secondary school level. Vouchers, to be sure, will continue to generate political heat, as was recently the case in California.

Tax Credits Congress in the last half of this decade may reconsider a tax credit for nonpublic school tuition against income tax owed the federal government. The Reagan administration had been advocating since 1981 the implementation of tax credit against the federal income tax as a realistic way of helping parents of nonpublic school children below the college level. The tuition tax credit proposal for parochial and other private schools had been voted upon but was killed on its last congressional attempt.

The public school lobby has been vehemently opposed to any kind of tax credit proposal and will challenge in the courts any bill that passes. Even though the U.S. Supreme Court in 1983 approved the Minnesota state tax deduction legislation, it presently has not stimulated passage of a federal tax credit plan for nonpublic school parents. Tax credits must at the moment be considered only a potential method of assistance.

Major Arguments for and Against Aid to Nonpublic Schools

The following major arguments are offered to indicate the division of belief and feeling concerning public support of nonpublic schools below the college level. Earlier discussion concentrated on selected U.S. Supreme Court decisions because they help to form a basis for developing a reasonable viewpoint in regard to assistance of non-public schools. The arguments for support are these:

1. Congress and the states have the constitutional obligation to promote the general welfare. To assist non-public school parents by supplying books, transportation, or auxiliary services, such as speech or hearing remediation, is actually promoting the general welfare of the nation. Assisting the child to obtain a secular education is in the interest of the child, not the parochial school or the church.

2. In 1925 the U.S. Supreme Court (*Pierce* v. *Society of Sisters*) reinforced the American tradition of allowing parents to select the *kind* of school they desired for their children, be it public or non-public. If this has been a traditional

view, why then cannot taxes be used to help parents exercise that right, especially in terms of secular education during the compulsory school years? Why should not all children be eligible for an equal portion of the educational tax dollar?

3. The public school traditionally has favored selected Protestant viewpoints. This bias resulted partially in the formation of the various parochial school systems. Catholics especially in the nineteenth century generally felt alienated in the public school. The prejudice against Catholics in society at large was reflected within the public school.

   Today, this Protestant bias has been largely eradicated; however, what has evolved is now a form of "secular humanism," a religion of no religion, which is a hostile view in the minds of many Catholics and Protestants. The public school is unacceptable if it does not reinforce the spiritual or moral desires of parents. The parochial school can complement the home better than the public school.

4. The public school cannot compete with the non-public school (even though the former is usually better funded) in terms of student discipline, intellectual standards, class size, and moral climate. When a student attends a school by choice, enrollment often is seen by that student as a privilege, not a right. If the student fails to meet expectations, which are always in the best interests of the student, then he or she can leave to make room for another student.

   Society, consequently, should financially support the notion of educational diversity in order to prevent a state educational monopoly which could result in educational stagnation.

A few major arguments against public support of non-public schools are these:

1. Parents have the right of choice in regard to private, parochial, or public education. If, however, they choose a non-public school, the financial burden should be totally theirs. If these parents want a free education for their children, they can send them to the public school.

2. Advocates of nonpublic schools who feel they pay a "double tax," public school tax and private school tuition, are misled. The two are discrete items because one is paid by choice. Their public school tax benefits the community in economic and cultural terms even if nonpublic parents do not directly avail themselves of the services of the public school. Other citizens do not benefit directly from public school taxes, such as single individuals or married couples without children, but they usually pay school taxes without asking for relief. Society at large also supports a prison system without seeking direct benefit from it.

3. No social agency has historically provided avenues of vertical mobility to all social classes like that of the public school. Despite the claims of some revisionist historians that the public school traditionally has effectively served

only a white, Protestant, middle-class clientele, many citizens can give testimony to the multitude of personal and career opportunities provided them by the public school. It deserves the support of the total community.

4. In a pluralistic society, the best agency to perpetuate a democratic philosophy is the public school. The multicultural climate of the public school is the best context in which youth can learn to live together as equals.

5. The U.S. Supreme Court for the past 25 years has been warning the nation about the "excessive entanglement" that may blur the distinct missions of both the public and nonpublic schools if they engage in sharing educational materials, services, and personnel. It is better to keep the support of each institution as separate as possible. One exists by private choice, the other by public taxes. There should be no overlapping of purpose. Such overlapping is clearly unconstitutional and tends to weaken the "wall of separation" between church and state in education.

Summary

Religion in relation to public education has two components: One deals with the theme of religious content in the curriculum and the other concerns fringe benefits to non-public schools. The U.S. Supreme Court in its several decisions concerning religious content in the public school curriculum has taken a positive stance. The Court has struck down ritualized, religious activity in the school such as Bible reading, the recitation of the Lord's Prayer, and school-sponsored nondenominational prayer.

However, the Court has urged public schools to teach about religion in an academic context. The religious heritage is important, the Court believes. No student's education, in fact, is complete without an understanding of the religious heritage. Such subjects as comparative world religions, the Old Testament as literature, and the Psalms as literature are examples of how religious content can be incorporated into the public school.

A medley of reaction occurred to these controversial Supreme Court cases in the early 1960s. On the one hand, many school districts began to implement religious content in an academic manner as appropriate religious materials became more plentiful. And, on the other hand, many citizens urged that Congress initiate the amendment process to allow voluntary prayer in the public school. This idea is still pertinent.

The second component concerning religion and public education deals with fringe benefits to non-public schools. The Supreme Court has been extremely active in this regard over the last several decades. Based upon the First and Fourteenth Amendments, the Court has upheld such fringe benefits to nonpublic schools as secular textbooks, transportation assistance, objectively administered auxiliary services, and state tax deductions for certain expenses in private, parochial, and public schools. These benefits are contingent upon approval by the respective state constitutions.

A term that seems to have emerged in recent cases is "excessive entanglement," which implies an unconstitutional overlapping of school missions between the public and private sectors. Legislation to aid non-public schools to survive judicial examination must be secular in intent and effect; it must neither aid nor hinder religion; nor can it be entangling. As a result of this acid test, many programs, especially during the 1970s, were ruled unconstitutional.

Given the present political mood of the nation, religion in relation to public education will continue to be a topic of interest.

Implications for Future Teachers

In the United States, the separation of church and state is keenly felt in formal education, prekindergarten through grade 12. Teachers must be especially sensitive to their students' religious diversity. Teachers must respect student pluralism and teach them about religion in context of their academic specialties. Teachers must know the difference between the secular and sectarian concepts in both theory and practice. They must observe practices in public schools that are both desirable and deplorable relative to religion and vow to foster greater awareness of and sensitivity to religious diversity. Simultaneously, they must fight sectarian ignorance, indoctrination, and discrimination.

Discussion Questions

1. What is the meaning of the first clause of the First Amendment, "Congress shall make no law respecting an establishment of religion"? What is the relationship between the First and Fourteenth Amendments in regard to religion and public education?
2. What has been thus far the U.S. Supreme Court's position about religious content in the public school curriculum?
3. What representative fringe benefits to nonpublic schools has the U.S. Supreme Court approved? What representative state programs for or benefits to non-public schools have been ruled unconstitutional thus far by the Court?
4. Which of the arguments cited in the text on both sides of the issue concerning assistance to nonpublic schools seem most defensible? What other arguments exist in support of, or in opposition to, public aid to independent schools?
5. Not all religious or private schools desire public financial assistance. What are their reasons for not wanting governmental support?

Notes

1. Arval A. Morris, *The Constitution and American Education* (St. Paul, MN: West Publishing Co., 1974), 374.

2. Edgar W. Knight and Clifton L. Hall, eds., *Readings in American Educational History* (New York: Appleton-Century-Crofts, 1951), 109.

3. Leo Pfeffer, *Church, State and Freedom* (Boston: The Beacon Press, 1953), 287.

4. Lawrence A. Cremin, *The Republic and the School: Horace Mann* (New York: Teachers College, Columbia University, 1957), 105.

5. American Academy of Religion, *et al.*, "Religion in the Public-School Curriculum: Questions and Answers," pamphlet, 1988.

6. "Private Elementary and Secondary Enrollment," *Statistical Abstract of The United States, 1992,* Washington, D.C.: Bureau of the Census, 158; "Catholic Enrollment," *Education Week* XII (April 21, 1993): 1; and "School Enrollments," *Education Week,* XII (January 27, 1993): 3.

7. Joseph Bryson and Samuel Houston, *The Supreme Court and Public Funds for Religious Schools* (Jefferson, NC: McFarland and Company, 1990), 63. Ellen Chatterton, Communications Research, Americans United for the Separation of Church and State, assisted in directing authors to the source cited above (1-13-94); also Brother John McGovern, Public Policy Research Associate, National Catholic Education Association, provided advice on obtaining data on public assistance (2-16-94).

Recommended Readings

American Association of School Administrators. *Religion in the Public schools.* A Report by the Commission on Religion in the Public Schools. New York: Harper & Row, 1964. Revised and republished in 1986 by Greenwood Press.

Bjorklun, Eugene C. "Secular Humanism: Implications of Court Decisions." *The Educational Forum* 52 (Spring 1988): 211–21.

"Character Education," *Educational Leadership* 51 (November 1993): 5–97. Issue devoted to this theme.

Haynes, Charles C. *Religion in American History: What to Teach and How.* Alexandria, VA: Association for Supervision and Curriculum Development, 1990.

McCarthy, Martha M. "Much Ado Over Graduation Prayer," *Phi Delta Kappan,* 75 (October 1993): 123–25; also, Barber, Larry W., "Prayer at Public School Graduation: A Survey," *Phi Delta Kappan* 75 (October 1993): 125.

Pitts, Mark Ellett. "Evangelical Christians and Schools," *Educational Forum* 51 (Fall 1986): 57–64.

Schools and Jehovah's Witnesses. Brooklyn, NY: Watchtower Bible and Tract Society of New York, 1983.

Wicks, Robert S. *Morality and the Schools.* Occasional Papers 32. Washington, D.C.: Council for Basic Education, 1981.

Selected U.S. Supreme Court cases:

Pierce v. *Society of Sisters* (1925) 268, U.S. 510.

Cochran v. *Louisiana State Board of Education* (1930) 281 U.S. 370.

Everson v. *Board of Education* (1947) 330 U.S. 1.

McCollum v. *Board of Education* (1948) 333 U.S. 203.

Zorach v. *Clauson* (1952) 343 U.S. 306.

Engel v. *Vitale* (1962) 370 U.S. 421.

Abington Township School District v. *Schempp; Murray* v. *Curlett* (1963) 374 U.S. 203.

Board of Education v. *Allen* (1968) 392 U.S. 236.

Lemon v. *Kurtzman; Earley* v. *DiCenso* (1971) 403 U.S. 602.

Meek v. *Pittenger* (1975) 421 U.S. 349.

Wolman v. *Walter* (1977) 433 U.S. 229.

Muller v. Allen (1983) 103 U.S. 3062.

School District of the City of Grand Rapids v. *Ball* (1985) 103 S. Ct., 31.

Aguilar v. *Felton* (1985) 105 S. Ct., 241, 3232.

Wallace v. *Jaffree* (1985) 105 S. Ct., 2479.

Edwards v. *Aguillard* (1987) 107 S. Ct., 2573.

Board of Education of Westside Community Schools v. *Mergens* (1990) 110 S. Ct., 2356.

Lee v. *Weisman* (1992) 112 S. Ct., 2649.

Zobrest v. *Catalina Foothills School District* (1992) 113 U.S. 2141.

Lamb's Chapel v. *Center Moriches Union Free School District* (1993) 124, L. ED., 2nd ed., 352.

Kiryas Joel Village School District Board of Education v. Grumet (1994), (Docket Number 93-517).

Chapter 9

Selected Social
Forces and
Public Education

Formal education below the college level is affected profoundly by social forces that originate outside the school. In this chapter, an overview of a few of these social phenomena will be offered to display the impact they have on the organization and curriculum of the school. These forces are noncurricular in nature, but their influence often has curricular implications as the school tries to adapt. The school by itself, obviously, cannot ameliorate the conditions which gave rise to each of these forces, but, in conjunction with other social institutions, it can improve the quality of life of its students. Students spend well over 13,000 hours of their lives in formal education through grade twelve; therefore, school plays a significant social role. The difficulty, however, is that its competition is formidable. The power of television and the peer group, for example, can at times give the impression that the school is impotent in improving the quality of student life. But in partnership with the family, with the church, and with business, the school can do much to eventually forge a better existence for those who spend many years under its supervision. Social reformation through education is a realistic aim of the public school.

The selected social phenomena included in this discussion are: (1) school racial desegregation as a process to increase educational opportunity for all students; (2) youth suicide as an alarming social problem; (3) alcohol use as one example of chemical abuse among adolescents; and (4) child abuse and violence in relation to a growing social awareness of their pernicious effects. In each instance, the role of the school will be cited.

Racial Desegregation in Public Education

Blacks in America had little opportunity for systematic schooling before the Civil War. There are on record early sporadic attempts to provide formal education for black youth, but, in general, these attempts never had any positive effect on public opinion. Slave codes in the South after 1830 were dominant in that in many southern states individuals caught educating blacks could be fined and imprisoned. There was a fear among some southern leaders that education and political power were intertwined. Slavery as an institution could exist more effectively if those in bondage remained illiterate. All this began to change after 1865. It should be noted, however, that educational opportunity for some four million freed blacks at that time did not instantly emerge. Decades of litigation and an enlightened public opinion would have to occur before blacks would be given the formal opportunity to learn and compete with whites.

With the creation of the federal Freedmen's Bureau in 1865, the first real formal educational opportunities for blacks occurred. The bureau's purpose was varied. It was established to manage abandoned lands in the southern states, as well as to control all subjects classified as refugees and freedmen. In the case of the latter, this meant about four million former slaves. The Freedmen's Bureau was, in essence, a network of religious, educational, and philanthropic agencies from the local through the national levels. Freedmen's schools were established in the South just after the Civil War and were staffed primarily by teachers from northern states who responded to a call from the National Teachers Association, later renamed the National Education Association. The educational impact of the bureau was short-lived, however, because southerners deeply resented northern intrusion into their daily lives. Reconstructionism, begun in 1867, also created much hostility throughout the South. It was becoming apparent, though, that education was going to be provided for blacks even if many might resist its coming.

The doctrine of "separate but equal" education was entrenched by the educational efforts of these freedmen's schools. It was assumed that segregation was constitutionally acceptable as long as supposed equal treatment was maintained. This doctrine had already been tested educationally in a state court before the Civil War and found acceptable, but it was to be examined again in a different context at the end of the century, only this time in the U.S. Supreme Court. The Fourteenth Amendment, ratified in 1868, would prove to be particularly germane in the diagnosis of this policy of "separate but equal" facilities.

In a sense, the federal government, which has had a very impressive record historically in regard to enhancing educational opportunity, played a key role in perpetuating the concept of segregation during the latter part of the nineteenth century. Racial segregation culturally was an acceptable belief, particularly in terms of educational opportunity. One wonders, however, had the U.S. Congress in the last quarter of the century approved the several attempts either to create a national system of education or to sharply increase federal aid to all states, especially to the very destitute states, if educational opportunity for all would not have become a reality much sooner? The various Blair Bills, for example, sponsored by Senator Henry W. Blair (New Hampshire) came close to passing Congress, but they failed every time to pass the House. Federal aid would have significantly assisted those states with the greatest need to combat illiteracy. The nation, however, was committed educationally to state and local control, even if that concept meant poor educational quality for almost everybody. Federal involvement in education was suspect because of the implied control. This fear is still held by many who support as much local independence as possible in educational matters.

Another kind of congressional action of this post-Civil War period that did little to enhance educational opportunity at the time but proved much later to be significant in this regard, was the Civil Rights Act of 1866. The act basically conferred citizenship upon blacks and helped to lessen the severity of black codes which had emerged. The act was vetoed by President Andrew Johnson, but it was passed again over his veto. There was some concern about whether the Civil Rights Act could withstand a constitutional test, so Congress incorporated most of its substance into the Fourteenth Amendment, ratified in 1868.[1]

One of the tenets of the act has had recent pertinence in the stipulation that all citizens have the right to "make and enforce contracts." Blacks in modern times have been allowed to enroll in private white schools (founded for racial reasons) even though these schools have avoided the use of any public funds in order to be racially separate. The courts have held that such schools cannot deny an attempt by blacks to enroll because this denies citizens the right to enter into a contract for education.[2] Very few blacks, however, have pursued this right; but it has democratic potential. Several years ago, the courts had also referred to this Civil Rights Act in context of the momentum for open housing. The right of all citizens to "purchase, lease, sell, hold, and convey real and personal property" was upheld.[3] Equal protection before the law became the backbone of the Civil Rights Act of 1866 and the Fourteenth Amendment.

This federal act, while not allocating funds for direct school support, nevertheless fostered greater equality of educational opportunity in a tangible way. If members of minorities have the right to greater economic security, then educational opportunity is also facilitated. The sad fact about this very auspicious beginning to provide greater equality was that the U.S. Supreme Court in 1896 approved "separate but equal" facilities in transportation; therefore, by *implication* school facilities also became legally segregated by race. This policy was not reversed until 1954.

Before surveying the educational impact of several major representative U.S. Supreme Court cases upon race and the schools, it is important to consider some points about educational opportunity. It is a term of many dimensions. One can think, for example, of opportunity in context of equal (or unequal) expenditure of tax dollars per student. It can mean, in another setting, providing a comprehensive curriculum to accommodate both the terminal and college-bound student. In another sense, it can mean preferential treatment in a qualitative manner regarding counseling, school-home rapport, economic assistance, and so on. In higher education, it can mean open or flexible admission standards with accompanying support to retain students. In other words, there are many ways to define educational opportunity. It is a term relative to the historic period and to the society that defines it. For the purpose of this chapter, educational opportunity is defined as legal and judicial effort to provide access to formal education at all levels irrespective of race or ethnic origin.

In the late nineteenth century, educational opportunity was seen as separate but equal education. It is this concept which led to the court decisions for the next several decades on *de jure* segregation (legal or intentional segregation). The first national test of this policy came before the U.S. Supreme Court, triggered by a Louisiana statute in 1890 requiring separate but equal transportation facilities. The issue was litigated nationally in *Plessy* v. *Ferguson* (1896). Homer Plessy, who was seven eighths white, declared publicly that he was going to ride in the section reserved for whites on the train from New Orleans to Covington. He was forcibly removed and fined, but he appealed the case to the U.S. Supreme Court. He contended the Thirteenth Amendment, which freed blacks, and the Fourteenth Amendment, which guaranteed equal protection before the law, were germane to his appeal. The Court believed only the Fourteenth Amendment was pertinent to his case and analyzed the situation on that basis and in context of the intent of the Louisiana statute.

The viewpoint of the majority on the Court was that all that could be done for Plessy was to ensure his civil or political equality before the law. If Plessy perceived the intent of the Louisiana statute to foster social inequality, the justices contended, that had to be considered outside the realm of the Court. Its prevailing view was "if the civil and political rights of both races be equal one can not be inferior to the other civilly or politically." Consequently, Plessy was denied relief because, in the Court's view, the intent of the 1890 statute was to ensure such equality.

The lone dissent in this case sounded much like the majority viewpoint in *Brown* 58 years later. Justice Harlan stated that to decide civil rights on the basis of color was wrong. "Our Constitution is colorblind," he asserted. He agreed with Plessy that a denial of the right to use the white facilities stamped a "badge of servitude" on him. This was wrong, Harlan believed, according to the Fourteenth Amendment. His dissent, however, was not heeded until it became the dominant position of the high Court decades later.

The only reference to education in *Plessy* was made concerning the schools of Washington, D.C. It was implied that since separate but equal facilities existed there, why was it not also appropriate in relation to transportation conveyances in Louisiana? Jim Crow was given judicial support on a national level, and by *implication* the precedent of separate but equal facilities was now established for education as well. From *Plessy* (1896) to *Brown* (1954) six Supreme Court educational decisions were made without overturning the policy of racially separate but equal facilities. This viewpoint also evolved into one which discriminated against non-whites, not just blacks. *Plessy* therefore had set a powerful precedent in regard to educational opportunity.

A second major representative case in relation to separate but equal educational opportunity was reflected in *Gaines* v. *Canada* (1938). In the mid-1930s Lloyd Gaines, a black alumnus of Lincoln University, Jefferson City, Missouri, applied to enter the University of Missouri law program but was turned down by the registrar Canada on the grounds that blacks could not constitutionally enroll. This issue had national import because sixteen other states were doing little or nothing to comply with *Plessy's* injunction of providing equal facilities if they were to be segregated.

Missouri and other border states tried to comply by offering out-of-state scholarships to universities which would accept black students; however, Gaines wanted to attend only the University of Missouri. After appeal to the U.S. Supreme Court, the Missouri legislature and the university received three options: (1) Deny law education to all students, black and white; (2) admit Gaines as an eligible student; or (3) provide a separate but equal law program *within* the state. The legislature chose option three and immediately established a program for blacks at Lincoln University. Gaines won only a partial victory because blacks did not have to continue their higher education in another state, but they still had to study formally on a segregated basis.

In a subsequent case, *Sweatt* v. *Painter* (1950), a similar decision was rendered that considerably weakened the policy of separate but equal. Hemann Sweatt, like Gaines, wanted to attend the law program in his state at the University of Texas at Austin. Texas and other southern states were doing nothing to provide even segregated opportunities in law education for blacks despite the imperatives laid down by *Plessy* and *Gaines*. Sweatt in 1946 was denied admittance on the same grounds as Gaines.

On appeal to the U.S. Supreme Court, Sweatt first won the concession that a separate program of law had to be founded within the state. Second, the Court told Texas that it would analyze the newly established law program in six months regarding its comparable value with that of Austin. At the end of the period the Court found unequal factors; the library holdings, the faculty, and the prestige itself were quite different between the two institutions. The new law program was inferior in quality, so Sweatt was admitted by the Court to the law program at the University of Texas. Sweatt's problems, however, continued. After two legal appeals about discriminatory behavior, Sweatt was finally accepted as a student in full standing.

The significance of the *Sweatt* decision was profound. Never before had the policy of separate but equal been tested to see if equal meant exactly that. In addition, a number of states still had not provided facilities of any kind for blacks, so *Sweatt* was a strong impetus for change.

Some states thought that it was possible to circumvent the litigation that would ensue if a black student were denied admission simply by admitting the student under a segregated policy; however, the Court rejected that approach in *McLaurin* v. *Oklahoma State Regents* (University of Oklahoma, 1950). George McLaurin, a black student desirous of a doctorate in education from the University of Oklahoma, applied for admission and was admitted, but on a segregated basis only. Study carrels, dormitory rooms, and so on, were available on a racially separate basis. After appeal by McLaurin to the U.S. Supreme Court, the University dropped its segregated policy and allowed McLaurin to continue as a student in full standing.

In theory, higher education was substantially opened up to minority students by 1950. Private colleges and universities also opened their doors at this time. The National Association for the Advancement of Colored People, which had been the main sponsor of *Gaines*, *Sweatt*, and *McLaurin*, believed the time had now come to deal with the more amorphous area of public education through grade twelve. The culmination of this interest was the famous U.S. Supreme Court decision, *Brown* v. *Board of Education* (1954). Without a doubt, this case has been one of the most important decisions ever made in the Court's history. It was the last major decision striking down state-mandated *de jure* segregation, that is, segregation caused by state law.

After the *Brown* decision *de facto* segregation emerged, which is segregation caused by residential change, custom, or behavior. It is more subtle because community leaders and school officials may in good faith pursue a racial desegregation policy but, if people move away and residentially create racial isolation, the school becomes less effective in overcoming segregated patterns within the district. The school board still has to try to desegregate facilities in an affirmative manner even if the district is rapidly becoming racially imbalanced. However, the district may be the victim of housing and employment patterns beyond its control. What does a school district do if there are not enough blacks or whites left to racially balance each school? Obviously, it is a difficult question, but compliance with judicial and legislative mandates is expected in terms of goodfaith effort.

The issue leading to the *Brown* decision began in Topeka, Kansas, when the Rev. Oliver Brown contested the fact that his daughter had to be bussed to an all-black school across town. By Kansas law, Topeka was allowed to maintain separate but equal education. On appeal to the U.S. Supreme Court, the Topeka case was selected as representative of other cases coming from South Carolina, Virginia, and Delaware. The major issue before the Court focused on the separate but equal doctrine approved by *Plessy* in 1896.

The justices found that the school districts had in good faith attempted to provide equal opportunity in regard to so-called tangible factors, such as buildings, curricula, teacher qualifications, and salaries. Had the Court taken a conservative position, it would have denied relief to the various plaintiffs because of the progress made in equalizing facilities, and so on. Instead, however, the justices unanimously believed that they had to go beyond the "issue of equal treatment" within a segregated context. They stated that they "must look instead to the effect of segregation itself in public education."

In dramatic prose the Court stated that "education is perhaps the most important function of state and local governments." The Court believed education to be "the very foundation of good citizenship." Education helps to awaken "the child to cultural values" and to prepare the child for "later professional training."

The pivotal question in this case dealt with whether minority children were still deprived of equal educational opportunities even though the so-called tangible factors mentioned above were equal. The Court unanimously believed they were. The view in *Brown* was that "separate but equal" no longer was an acceptable doctrine in public education. "Separate educational facilities are inherently unequal," the Court asserted. The due process clause of the Fourteenth Amendment was violated. The minority children in separate but equal facilities were denied equal protection of the laws as guaranteed by the Fourteenth Amendment.

What played a big part in the Court's opinion was research from the fields of psychology and sociology on the pernicious effects of segregation. Self-esteem and personality development, for example, were directly affected by the process of segregation. The Court believed that, if the *Plessy* jurists had had access to these psychological and sociological data, perhaps their conclusion would have been different. The social sciences, however, were in their infancy in 1896, so they could not be utilized very effectively. The *Brown* decision, consequently, overturned the thinking employed in *Plessy*.

In 1955 the Supreme Court, in responding to a request that separate but equal facilities be undone immediately across the nation, issued an opinion which has since been called *Brown* II. Not really a distinct opinion, it is remembered basically because of the judicial view that immediate dismantling was not realistic. The Court remanded the cases it had decided in 1954 to the District Courts to work out policies consistent with local conditions. The Court, however, wanted children admitted to the public schools "on a racially nondiscriminatory basis with all deliberate speed." The problem that evolved with this view, though, was that state and school district reaction was extremely mixed. Compliance differed. Some districts became national showcases within two years, while a few states even went to the extent of dropping all laws requiring compulsory education. The Courts had to remedy such slow compliance as promptly as possible to ensure "good faith implementation."

As stated earlier, the *Brown* decision of 1954 ushered in the more subtle form of *de facto* segregation when it ended state-mandated *de jure* segregation. This case has fostered a continual controversy in regard to its meaning. Some critics have viewed *Brown* as too much social engineering by liberal jurists. Others have understood the case to allow bussing, school district reorganization, and the like. In fact, *Brown* intended only to dismantle racially separate facilities and to make them unitary. *Brown* did not command bussing as a means of racial desegregation; rather, it decreed that racially segregated dual facilities were to be dismantled with all deliberate speed. The Court realized this process, in part, depended upon local conditions.

Subsequent Supreme Court cases have put more meaning into the spirit of *Brown*. For example, in *Green* v. *County School Board* (1968) the Court stated that so-called "freedom of choice" plans, whereby students select their own schools within a district and transport themselves at personal expense, do not constitute appropriate compliance. Such plans in themselves do not effect a unitary system.

Few blacks or whites leave their neighborhood schools to attend other schools voluntarily even though they are all in one school district. "Freedom of choice" or "open enrollment" (as it is sometimes called) is legitimate only in context of other approaches to bring about a unitary school system.

Brown received more judicial support as a result of *Alexander* v. *Holmes County Board of Education* (1969). In this case, the U.S. Supreme Court grew impatient with the slow implementation of "all deliberate speed" in Mississippi and decreed that additional time to desegregate was "no longer constitutionally permissible." It held that the school district in question had to "terminate dual school systems at once and to operate now and hereafter only unitary schools." This case signalled to the nation that "deliberate speed" was significant.

In another celebrated Supreme Court decision in 1971, the spirit of *Brown* was given greater form. In *Swann* v. *Charlotte-Mecklenburg Board of Education,* the Court in essence legitimatized bussing as a tool to desegregate schools. The Court believed that if school districts can bus to segregate, they can bus to desegregate. It held that "desegregation plans cannot be limited to the walk-in school." However, the reservations placed on bussing revolved around the problem of time or distance of travel, which could impair the health of students or interfere with the educational program. Age, of course, was an important factor in such bussing.

In *Swann,* the Court contended that "remedial adjustments" may cause inconvenience during the period of desegregation; however, this inconvenience should not outweigh the need to pair and group noncontiguous school attendance zones when necessary. The Court stated, though, that desegregation does not mean that "every school in every community must always reflect the racial composition of the school system as a whole." In general, however, the Court wanted to see more affirmative action taken to dismantle racially segregated schools.

In a case that is interesting primarily because it was the first major decision of the U.S. Supreme Court outside the South on the matter of racial desegregation, the Court looked at the difference between *de jure* and *de facto* segregation. In *Keyes* v. *School District No. 1* (1973), the problem of racial isolation was considered in several schools of the Park Hill area of Denver. School board policy fostered structuring attendance zones, organizing clusters of so-called feeder schools for racial purposes, and building new schools geographically to perpetuate segregation. The Court believed the Denver School District was entrenching a dual school system within its boundaries. The District, furthermore, perpetuated such a system by its policies on transportation, faculty and staff assignments, and student transfers, as well as by its use of mobile classrooms. The Court believed that all these educational actions contributed to racial isolation.

The justices struggled in *Keyes* with the problem of *de jure* and *de facto* segregation. The Denver School District believed that it had not intended to practice segregative educational policy. The causes, the district believed, were largely the result of socioeconomic differences and residence. Furthermore, Colorado as a state had never constitutionally or legislatively created *de jure* school segregation. Nor had it ever racially segregated by means of zoning or housing codes.

The Court's point, however, was that the differences between *de jure* and *de facto* segregation had become moot. The effects are the same in both cases. In essence, the Court redefined or extended *de jure* segregation to mean intention or purpose. Even if no law or constitutional provision to segregate exists, a school district must still take affirmative action to provide equality of educational opportunity. *De facto* segregation has the force of government behind it because it takes school board action to bus students, construct buildings, and so on. In a sense, this is intentional segregative policy when isolation continues. The authority of the equal protection clause of the Fourteenth Amendment, consequently, becomes pertinent. The Denver School District, as a result, had to take affirmative measures to correct the segregative policies in such practices as clustering schools, faculty and staff assignments, and attendance zones.

Keyes awakened the nation to the fact that segregation was as much a problem outside as it was inside the South. In fact, largely as a result of Court action after 1954, desegregated schools were more common in the South during this period than they were elsewhere. The North and West were now to experience their turn in desegregation litigation.

The struggle to ensure greater equality of educational opportunity in view of the Fourteenth Amendment will be an ongoing crusade. The U.S. Supreme Court has historically confined the matter of segregation to the schools themselves. Employment and housing opportunities formally have not been linked to increased educational opportunity in any major decision thus far; however, the social context is obvious to all who consider the issue of school desegregation. Additionally, the U.S. Supreme Court has refused in recent years to approve a massive school district reorganization plan involving the city and suburbs of Detroit, as well as those of Richmond, Virginia. Even metropolitanwide remedies involving school districts only are not yet successful in the courts. In the Detroit case involving the city and its suburbs, *Milliken* v. *Bradley* (1974), the Supreme Court rejected a remedy that would have merged Detroit with 53 suburban school districts. The Court believed all would have to be culpable if they were to be merged, but the Court found constitutional evidence of segregation only in the Detroit School District.

Again in *Milliken* v. *Bradley* (1977), (*Milliken II*), the Court ruled that Michigan should assume responsibility for half the costs of remedial programs, inservice training, guidance and counseling services, and community relations programs in the Detroit school district because the state had helped to create the segregation in the first place. This decision broadened the view that only facilities are to be considered in desegregation. Qualitative factors, such as counseling and remedial programs, also must be addressed if the effects of segregation are to be mitigated. In similar cases in other northern cities, the Court has maintained the view that racially neutral actions are not adequate; rather, the school districts must display evidence of affirmative action to enhance greater educational opportunity in unitary schools.

Despite friction in the desegregation plans attempted in recent years in Pontiac and Boston (which have since been resolved), such plans generally have been successful and met with little violence. In hundreds of school districts across the nation, schools have been racially desegregated. However, the future is unclear, particularly as priorities compete in regard to funding such programs that encourage greater academic and professional reform versus those programs which are designed to stimulate greater equality of educational opportunity. These two points are not mutually exclusive, but state and federal emphasis on specific areas such as Headstart, work-study programs, vocational education, education for children with disabilities, and bilingual education is crucial.

The following ideas are employed in part by some school districts to comply with court or statutory mandates to desegregate racially. They are offered to give an idea of what might be done to facilitate greater educational opportunity. Some ideas are more visionary than others:

1. Two or more schools can be treated as one. In one neighborhood, the school can offer the primary grades (1–3), and in the other area, the school can enroll children in the intermediate grades (4–6). This is sometimes referred to as the "Princeton plan" or the "pairing plan."
2. Several schools can be built on one campus. This is something like a village community, which can attract students from the entire district. "Campus park" is the term usually denoting the idea of a comprehensive program on one site.
3. A policy of "open enrollment" or "freedom of choice" allows students to attend any school within the district. This approach was singularly struck down by the courts between 1954 and 1970 unless it was employed in context of other good faith measures. Open enrollment is now being revitalized, however; and in approximately twenty states since 1980, local districts are offering choices among public schools. The choices can entail meeting the curricular needs of one student or offering a smorgasbord of public schools from which to choose. Minnesota has led the way in that students will eventually be able to choose a public school *within the state.* This policy (unlike that establishing "magnet school," explained in number 7 following) can involve *all* public schools.
4. Large school districts can be "decentralized." Instead of one huge district with one school board, the district can be divided into several subsystems with separate boards of education controlling the respective districts. The overall district boundary does not change, only the internal structure is changed.
5. Programs of "compensatory education" can be intensified to improve learning in low-income neighborhoods without changing the administrative organization. Approaches entailing smaller classes, longer school years, more diagnostic testing, more tutorial instruction, and so on, can improve the quality of the curriculum for minority groups. While not changing the racial makeup of the school district, this concept enhances quality education.
6. "Vouchers" from the public treasury someday may be given to needy students to attend schools of their choice. Schools enrolling a greater number of

low-income students would have more revenue. A sense of competition might develop among schools within a district to enroll needy students on a full or part-time basis. This idea is very controversial and largely untested in the United States. Support for vouchers, however, is getting more political attention on a national scale, especially in regard to Chapter 1 programs.

7. The "magnet school" idea implies that designated schools within a district will specialize in a given area like science, performing arts, and so on. The school is attended voluntarily, but the students must reflect a racial or ethnic mix.

8. "Metropolitan school district reorganization" can be a tool for desegregation. Compulsory bussing is used to transport students within a reorganized district.

9. "Teacher rotation" can be implemented to balance faculties by race, sex, and experience. This balance lends stability to the school.

10. "Centers" are sometimes employed in a district. The idea is to use one school (or schools) as one grade, thereby drawing students from a larger attendance area within a school district.

The Civil Rights Act of 1964 through its Title VI and VII has helped to encourage school districts to act upon some of the above approaches in order to bring about greater racial desegregation. School districts might seek technical assistance in facilitating desegregation or, in the case of obdurate resistance to compliance, might be sued on the basis of racial discrimination. The Justice Department is often involved in these kinds of suits.

Multiethnic Education

Multiethnic education is a general term which implies a total approach to making schools more pluralistic. This means that schools should reflect a racial and ethnic diversity in the composition of their faculty and staff, as well as a pluralistic attitude concerning curricula, textbooks, testing procedures, and counseling programs. Greater respect is given to racial and ethnic diversity in all aspects of the school's philosophy. Multiethnic education can be implemented in any school district, irrespective of its geographic locality.

Historically, American schools have been charged with the mission of assimilation: to create a melting pot of the diverse racial and ethnic groups that characterized America. This approach was particularly valued when approximately ten million immigrants came from eastern and southern European nations between 1880 and World War I. In 1911, it was estimated that in 37 of the most populous cities in the United States, one half of the youth in public schools were children of foreign-born parents.[4] This meant that the English language was seldom spoken or read at home. The schools, consequently, had an awesome task in trying to assimilate youth into American culture. Ironically, the various settlement houses in the big cities did a better job than did the public schools. In the schools at that time, cultural assimilation basically meant exposure to the English language and an acceptance of Anglo-Saxon values. According to the 1990 Census, the Philippines, Puerto Rico, El Salvador, and Vietnam were the major sources of immigrants between 1980 and 1990, a testament to increasing diversity in the United States. Despite heavy racial or ethnic concentrations in certain locations, the following racial or ethnic percentages reflect the demographic composition of the nation's 43 million public school attendees: Anglo-American (69 percent), African American (15 percent), Hispanic American (12 percent), Asian American (3 percent), and Native-American (1 percent).[5]

The public schools today no longer maintain the view that youth should be molded by the values of one race, class, or religion. In fact, some educators are even calling for a new educational philosophy that is predicated upon an "institutional pluralism," which holds that the public schools should be viewed as only one of many appropriate educational agencies. The rationale for this view stems from the belief that almost everyone maintains diverse roles in regard to school, vocation, ethnic group, church, and family. In planned ways, consequently, all these institutions might better fulfill certain educational functions without being divisive or counterproductive.[6] This rationale implies that schooling is only a part of education. Institutional pluralism could eventually lead to increased cultural pluralism because a greater number of diverse ethnic, racial, and religious groups would participate in the educational process. The public school, in the meantime, must employ strategies to recognize and value more highly the diverse clientele it already serves.

The following assumptions are considered significant by the authors when the theme of multiethnic education is fused with the curriculum:

1. A higher level of ethnicity (one aspect of pluralism) can be promoted in school by selecting textbooks that balance themes in regard to white and non-white groups. Stereotypes should never be part of the content; ethnic groups should be viewed in a variety of roles and settings.

2. Classroom projects should be encouraged to reflect the ethnic diversity of students or the community. Even if the school population or community is somewhat homogeneous, multiethnic programs are still beneficial to all students. Guest speakers, field trips, and discussions are excellent means to highlight differences and similarities among groups.

3. Bilingual educational programs need to be given greater national and state support, especially for Mexican-American and other Hispanic school-age youth. By giving legitimacy to the Spanish language and culture, for example, a stepping stone is created to a better use of English. Intensive English-as-a-second-language is also an important strategy to help non-English-speaking students succeed. If students leave school with a degree of literacy in two languages, then their chance of economic and academic success is increased.

   Counseling, testing, and so-called ability grouping also need to be reexamined in context of a multiethnic mentality. These assumptions are pertinent to every racial and ethnic minority in the United States.

4. Multiethnic education should incorporate curricular materials on the American Indian, whose well-being has been largely ignored for decades. It is estimated that 307 recognized Indian "entities" exist in the continental United States, in addition to 200 tribal entities in Alaska. The term "Indian entities" refers to tribes, bands, villages, groups, pueblos, Eskimos, and Aleuts. Approximately 200 languages characterize these entities in 34 states. The 1990 Census estimated that the Indian population to be 1,959,000; however, this figure is debatable because at least 300,000 American Indians are not in so-called entities.[7]

   Of this population it is estimated that slightly under 300,000 Indian and Alaskan native students are enrolled in one of three kinds of schools: public, federal, or tribal. Generally, the public schools enroll more mixed bloods and have over four times the enrollment of the latter two.[8] The quality of Indian education is still appallingly low. At least, however, the problem now is being addressed more realistically through the native culture rather than by imposition of white values.

5. Multiethnic education in a sense is a paradox because, on the one hand, it should be an inherent part of every public school, but, on the other hand, it should embody a high degree of voluntary student involvement. Since the term is relative, no student should be forced, for example, to be labeled as German-American, Mexican-American, or Afro-American. Students may be from families who "root" themselves differently from race or ethnic origin. Politics, class, religion, or economics may be a stronger base of cohesion. In other words, let the students initiate preferences after exposure to a broad range of knowledge.

6. Students should be encouraged to study a second language, at least in a minimal way, to develop an appreciation of another culture. Today, there are fewer so-called "national" problems because one nation's problems soon become another's. Technology, for example, has created commonality among nations. Proficiency in a foreign language can help to reduce an ethnocentric attitude.

In the remaining part of this chapter, other social forces (non-curricular forces) will be considered which have a strong impact upon the school. These forces are included in this chapter because the school can play a part in assisting both the students and the home in either eliminating the causes of these conditions or in mitigating their consequences.

Youth Suicide

A social phenomenon that deeply affects the well-being of the public school is youth suicide. In 1989 about 13 young people in the United States committed suicide each day. Mental health experts also estimated that each day approximately 50 to 100 more attempted it. In fact, suicide is now the third leading cause of death among Americans from 15 to 24 years of age, behind accidents and murder.[9] Statistics concerning suicide are unreliable, however, partly because of the stigma associated with the act, which is why it has been labeled the "last taboo."

Researchers have been somewhat reluctant to investigate causes, partly because of their fear that such publicity will stimulate multiple suicides among young people. Because it has become a national problem, however, there can no longer be any avoidance of its presence. The school itself will have to take a definite stance in helping to detect warning signs and consulting with other agencies on the matter. The sooner research indicates a profile of a high-risk young person, the more effective the school will be in identifying and referring such a person for assistance. Presently, it is known that the rate of young male suicides has increased sharply, but that of young females has increased only slightly. Ninety percent of all young male suicides are white, whereas among females there is little statistical difference among the races. It is also assumed by researchers that many more females attempt suicide than males, but males often choose more violent means and, consequently, do not survive.[10]

Research also indicates that one reason for suicidal behavior stems from environmental stresses which the young person perceives to be overwhelming. Suicidal fantasies might include escape from an intolerable situation; the desire to influence or penalize parents; the wish to obtain relief from painful feelings; or a desire to reduce the feeling of loneliness by reuniting with a deceased or absent relative or friend.[11] Parental and family deficiencies seem to play significant roles in contributing to a young person's suicidal tendencies. Evidence also indicates that the more disorganized the nuclear family is, the greater the risk of suicide. The presence of depression and suicide in the family's background also contributes to a high incidence of suicide among adolescents. The transmission of self-destructive behaviors and ineffective coping mechanisms from parents to children also seems to contribute to a higher risk of suicide in young people.[12]

Experts recommend that both parents and teachers can assist youth by detecting some major suicide warning signals in adolescents. These warning signals are the following:

1. Change in eating or sleeping routines
2. Increased isolation from family and friends
3. Increased activity and aggression
4. Drop in academic achievement
5. Unnatural generosity in regard to valued belongings
6. Increased interest in getting one's "life in order"
7. Frequent mention of suicide
8. Sudden interest in religious beliefs and afterlife
9. Recent personal loss as a result of death, divorce, or change of residence[13]

These warning signs may at times characterize many teenagers who have never entertained suicidal thoughts. The degree of intensity, however, of each warning sign, or the combination of signs, might help adults detect a serious problem in an adolescent. Some of these warning signs might even indicate another related condition, such as alcohol abuse. Teachers, particularly, who seek to interact frequently with young people, especially on an informal basis, can be key adults in observing and referring this problem to specialists. However, since 90 percent of all suicidal adolescents will talk *only* to their friends about their suicidal feelings,[14] the school possibly can utilize peer "counselors" in addition to an effective reporting system. Open communication is the key to assist those in need of immediate help. Young suicide victims are usually not mentally ill, although they have a record of impulsive and/or aggressive behavior. Substance abuse often aggravates the condition. Experts recommend a coordinated program of suicide prevention among health, social service, juvenile justice, and school officials.

Alcohol and Young People

A social problem that has also had deleterious effects on youth and society in general is the adolescent use of alcohol. Alcohol is a drug, a mind-altering substance. Its use has the greatest potential for abuse. Alcohol intake, along with other drug use, contributes to more than half of the teenage deaths in this country. It is estimated that approximately 3.3 million teenagers in the United States drink often and heavily. Of this number, one third frequently get into alcohol-related trouble. An estimated 8,000 young people are killed annually in drunk-driving accidents, while some 40,000 are injured. It is clearly documented that young people today are drinking at a younger age, drinking more frequently, drinking to get drunk, and drinking in combination with other drugs.

Young people, additionally, have a lower physical tolerance for alcohol than do adults, which increases their risk of alcohol-related difficulty. On the average, teenagers who drink can become alcoholics twelve times faster than adults who drink. Alcohol intoxication is identical to the effects of barbiturates. Technically, alcohol is classified as a depressant; however, the effects of alcohol may vary with the individual. In terms of food value, alcohol has nothing to support its use except that of calories devoid of vitamins and minerals. Its prolonged use can cause brain damage, cancer, heart disease, pancreatic tumors, liver damage, and ulcers.[15] Why, then, do some teenagers (and preteenagers) drink? It appears that one of the principal reasons is to emulate adults. Children are growing up faster in terms of social activities. The automobile and the media foster a greater sense of sophistication among young people. Because drinking is a socially accepted and encouraged activity among adults, it is logical that young people will adopt the same view. Alcohol also is a tool to relieve tension, to relax, to feel more socially acceptable, or to get high. In a recent survey of over 200,000 eleventh and twelfth graders conducted by the National Parents' Resource Institute for Drug Education (PRIDE), almost half of the students said they drank liquor, and one third said that they try to get "bombed."[16]

In recent years, public attention has focused on teenage drinking, but little has been done to combat it. Gallup Polls, during their 25-year history, have indicated the use of drugs as one of three major school problems. Presidents Bush and Clinton, in their respective administrations, also listed drug-free schools among their national education goals, but community effort remains uncoordinated. Two well-regarded programs, however, are receiving much attention. Projects DARE (Drug Abuse Resistance Education) and SPECDA (School Program to Educate and Control Drug Abuse) use local police officers to educate fifth through seventh graders about the dangers of drug use. Resistance to peer pressure is a key element in both programs, which focus on the dangers of alcohol, drugs, and tobacco.[17]

To deal more specifically with the question of the school's role in alcohol education, several points are germane:

1. Alcohol use among young people is a community problem and therefore must be confronted on that basis. All social agencies, schools, police, media, and so on, must cooperate to help educate the community, as well as to prevent and treat this malady.
2. Schools can serve as a leader in organizing community support. Task forces can discuss the pervasiveness of alcohol-related problems in both the community and school and recommend strategies.
3. Multiple approaches are best in dealing with alcohol education. Textbooks, field trips, resource persons, and materials supplemented by skills developed in the affective domain can do much to build student self-respect.
4. Teachers and counselors educated in alcohol education are vital to the success of such a program. Educators who can recognize symptoms and offer specific advice in regard to treatment are instrumental.[18]

Child Abuse

Another noncurricular social issue to be discussed in this chapter is that of child abuse, "the battered child syndrome" as it has been called. For centuries, children have been abused physically and emotionally in a variety of ways, as well as neglected in regard to their basic needs. Children historically have had few rights. Now that child abuse has been formally identified, its components are analyzed as scientifically as possible, and careful records are being kept by experts on the problem. Educators, technically, are involved because it is their legal responsibility to report instances of abuse to appropriate authorities. In a broader and preventive sense, however, educators can play an important role in saving many children before such trauma occurs.

Child abuse traditionally had been thought of mainly as excessive physical punishment, but this view in recent times has been enlarged considerably. Child abuse is now regarded as any of the following:

1. Nonaccidental injury or pattern of injuries without reasonable explanations, such as burns, bites, or beatings

2. Neglect in regard to food, clothing, shelter, or medical care
3. Sexual molestation of a child for the gratification of an adult, such as rape, incest, fondling of the genitals, or exhibitionism
4. Aggressive or excessive emotional deprivation or abuse, or verbal assault to force the child to meet unreasonable demands[19]

Some principal reasons emerge among the many possible explanations about why an adult might commit child abuse. An adult who has the potential for such cruelty is one who was probably mistreated as a child. Further, the abusive adult usually has low self-esteem; cannot cope with a crisis very effectively, which often triggers abuse, cannot tolerate the child's level of specific performance and, consequently, demands more; or views the child differently from other children. Abusers generally are normal people in that most love their children. They also cannot be classified objectively because they are from all socioeconomic levels, races, and ethnic and religious groups. Such abuse is usually not a single occurrence of violence or deprivation but rather a pattern of behavior. This pattern, however, may not characterize the total relationship the adult has with the child, but it is serious enough to warrant intervention by appropriate individuals. Alcohol abuse is a significant factor in almost all child abuse cases.

Child abuse estimates range between one to 2 million cases per year. Additionally, a sad commentary on the reported cases is that even though two-thirds of the victims were school-age children, educators reported fewer than one-third of the cases.[20] The major reasons for the low involvement on the part of educators were varied. Educators reported only serious injuries, partly because they believed they lacked appropriate diagnostic skills. Additionally, educators failed to become seriously involved for fear of legal retaliation by parents and, even more basically, they believed that such reports were ineffective.

The fact of the matter is, however, that legally educators in all states must report cases of child abuse. States vary concerning who should report as well as what kinds of cases should be reported. Yet in regard to the types of cases, there is unanimity concerning physical abuse. In every state, such offenses must be reported. Educators have state statutes on their side regarding immunity from civil or criminal liability, as long as the report is done in good faith. Some states have even indicated in their immunity provisions that good faith is inherent automatically. This legal support should be somewhat comforting when educators are faced with the decision to report on reasonable grounds a suspected case of child abuse.[21]

There are a number of obvious clues which, in combination, might help teachers in identifying abused children. These clues are the following:

1. A fearful or withdrawing manner
2. Evidence of unusual bruising, lacerations, or fractures
3. Frequent "accidental" injuries
4. Looking to strangers randomly for attention
5. Indifference to parents in regard to relief from discomfort
6. Excessive anxiety

7. Truant or runaway behavior, or lingering after school
8. Inconsistency between observed injury and its causation as expressed by the parent
9. Denial by child that any problem exists
10. Self-deprecating comments by the child
11. Destructive or cruel behavior[22]

The role of the school in ameliorating this problem of abuse is complex. First, teachers and principals, especially, need training in dealing with suspected abuse. Administrators need to inform faculty and staff about the procedures for reporting actual and suspected cases. Second, periodic workshops for school personnel are crucial in disseminating vital information on the entire subject of child abuse. Third, a knowledgeable person on the staff should be assigned the role of liaison between the school and pertinent community agencies and parents.[23]

In sum, the caring and observing teacher is again the link between the child in need and the appropriate assistance. As in the situations of youthful suicide and alcohol abuse, the teacher can make a difference.

Violence and the School

The escalating disregard for life in American society is, in many schools, destroying the social cohesion needed to foster effective teaching and learning. No social problem has justifiably drawn as much attention in recent months as has violence inside and outside the school building. In 1992, one study reported that, of twelfth graders surveyed, 19 percent had been injured by or threatened with a weapon during their last school year. In grades eight, 10, and 12, 25 percent of the students surveyed reported that they had carried a gun, knife, or club to school within the previous school year.[24]

Although these statistics seem startling, elementary school children (during their total elementary experience) have watched on television about 8,000 murders and over 100,000 other acts of violence.[25] Given this fact, it should not be surprising that many children perceive violence as a normal act. In 1991, it was reported that guns were the fifth leading cause of accidental death of children 14 years of age and younger. In addition, 1.2 million latch-key children have access to guns at home.[26] About 20 percent of all students from ninth through twelfth grades carry a weapon regularly. Black, male teenagers are particularly vulnerable in that nearly half of their deaths in 1988 were by firearms.[27]

Currently, schools have probably no greater challenge than trying to provide a safe environment for all concerned—students, teachers, and administrators. An "antigang, antiviolence" curriculum must be initiated. School must be a refuge from harm. A discipline code regarding weapons and drugs and a consistently enforced behavior policy involving a reporting system, when necessary, to social workers, and police must exist. Parents, police, and social workers must be involved in the process. Simultaneously, teachers must reflect respect for individuals, must maintain a sense of humor, and should seldom threaten students.[28]

Young people are generally less violent if they participate in meaningful relationships and if they find varied opportunities at school to express themselves. The more teachers can collaborate with families about school life and can be consistent and structured in their involvement with students, the more positive students may be about school.[29] Schools are becoming informed centers of conflict resolution and mediation because many students do not know how to react to insults, failure, and so forth except by violence. Consequently, in over 5,000 schools nationwide, conflict resolution programs are being offered in an attempt to reverse the trend of violence in society at large. "Peer mediation" seems to be the most popular form. In this plan, a core of trained students helps "disputants" work through conflicts without imposing solutions; however, solutions must be expressed in writing and are signed by those involved and honored by school officials. These agreements, like the mediation process, cannot deal with illegal problems, but the opportunity to engage in discussion may prevent harmful conflict.[30]

Summary

Numerous social forces emanating outside the school have a powerful impact upon every aspect of the educational program. In a direct sense, these forces are noncurricular, but in an indirect manner they affect the extent to which children learn and the climate or well-being of the school and community, and they certainly have a relationship to the future welfare of children. The representative social forces included in this chapter were school racial desegregation, youth suicide, alcohol abuse among young people, child abuse and violence. The school can play an instrumental role in the direction of each of these forces.

The quest for greater educational opportunity in the United States has been an ongoing struggle for well over a century. Early U.S. Supreme Court decisions dealt with the concept of racial "separate but equal" educational opportunity. The Court finally overturned the doctrine of statutory *de jure* segregation in its famous *Brown* decision of 1954. Since that case, courts have been struggling with intentional *de jure* and accidental *de facto* segregation as applied to public education. *Brown* is the moving force in these judicial decisions.

Public schools have complied in a variety of ways with judicial and statutory mandates to desegregate racially. The phrase "with all deliberate speed" has been a relative term in regard to the manner in which school districts have implemented desegregation plans. Several of these methods were discussed in this chapter. In addition to these good-faith plans of action, it is imperative that school districts also implement multiethnic education in their total program.

There are other representative social forces outside the public schools that influence educational programs. These forces are also noncurricular in origin, but their impact becomes educational, particularly as schools attempt to help other social agencies remove either the causes of these forces or mitigate the effects on young people. Schools are social institutions. What happens outside usually affects what goes on within. The more schools are knowledgeable about the significance of these forces, the better the learning climate and future for young people.

Implications for Future Teachers

Social forces, such as teenage drinking and violence, have a profound effect upon the well-being of the school. Teaching and learning can occur only when students are ready to learn. Given present social conditions, students are seldom able to focus energies upon cognitive matters.

Teacher education is more realistic if prospective teachers become cognizant of sociological factors that enhance or impede learning. It is meaningful for a teacher to know his or her subject matter if it is in context of an awareness of the attendant social baggage that students bring to or acquire in and around school. The university and the public school are sources of knowledge regarding the context in which young people will learn.

Discussion Questions

1. Many social forces in the community greatly affect the public school. Racial desegregation is one such force on the social continuum which can enhance equality of educational opportunity. What is meant by the term "equality of educational opportunity"?
2. Cite the significance of both U.S. Supreme Court cases, *Plessy* v. *Ferguson* (1896) and *Brown* v. *Board of Education* (1954). How were the public schools affected by these decisions? What has happened judicially since *Brown* to enhance educational opportunity?
3. What is multiethnic education? How can it be encouraged?
4. Youthful drinking, teenage suicide, violence, and child abuse are examples of community problems that adversely affect the well-being of the school. What role can the school play in helping other social agencies to improve each of these representative social forces?

Notes

1. Doc. no. 252, The Civil Rights Act, April 9, 1866. *Documents of American History*, vol. 1 (to 1898), Henry Steele Commager, ed. (New York: Appleton-Century-Crofts, 1968), 464–5.

2. R. Freeman Butts, *Public Education in the United States: From Revolution to Reform* (New York: Holt, Rinehart and Winston, 1978) 143, 335–6.

3. *Jones v. Alfred H. Mayer Co.*, (1968) 392 U.S. 409.

4. S. Alexander Rippa, *Education in a Free Society: An American History,* 7th ed. (New York: Longman, 1992), 145.

5. "Student Diversity Varies Widely," *NEA Today,* 12 (December 1993): 8.

6. Theodore R. Sizer, "Education and Assimilation: A Fresh Plea for Pluralism," *Phi Delta Kappan,* 58 (September 1976): 35.

7. "Federal Indian Reservations and Trust Lands," *The World Almanac and Book of Facts, 1993.* (New York: World Almanac, 1993), 459.

8. Patricia Locke Flying Earth and Dean Chavers, "The Status of Indian Education," *Journal of Thought,* 19 (Fall 1984): 32–4.

9. Lisa Jennings, "Experts Hope Report Returns Youth-Suicide Issue to Front Burner," *Education Week,* IX (September 20, 1989): 1 & 20.

10. "Teenage Suicide," *Education Week,* IV (October 31, 1984): 1.

11. Cynthia Pleffer, "Suicide Behavior of Children," *Exceptional Children,* 48 (1981): 170–2.

12. Carl L. Tishler and Patrick C. McHenry, "Parental Negative Self and Adolescent Suicide Attempts," *Journal of American Academy of Child Psychiatry,* 21 (1982): 404–8.

13. "Teenage Suicide," 12; also Suzanne Harper, A Review of *Suicide Intervention in the Schools* by Scott Poland in *School and Safety,* 38 (Spring 1990): 38.

14. *Teen Suicide.* (St. Louis: Life Crisis Services, 1986), n.p.

15. Health Consequences of Alcohol Use, "Care Unit Hospital of St. Louis Special Outreach IMPACT Conference, October 10–14, 1983, n.p.; also, Enoch Gordis, M.D., "Alcohol: A Special Risk for Youth," *The Challenge* 4 (November/December 1989): 4.

16. *What Policies Can Reduce Teen Drug Abuse?* San Diego, CA: Opposing Viewpoints Pamphlets, Greenhaven Press, Inc., 1990, 127.

17. *Ibid.,* 108–13.

18. Lowell Horton, *Adolescent Alcohol Abuse.* Fastback 217 (Bloomington, IN: Phi Delta Kappa Educational Foundation, 1985): 34–40.

19. *Questions and Answers on Child Abuse.* National Committee for Prevention of Child Abuse, 1977, 1.

20. Bruce Beezer, "Reporting Child Abuse and Neglect: Your Responsibility and Your Protections," *Phi Delta Kappan,* 66 (February 1985): 435.

21. *Ibid.*

22. *Child Abuse is Scary,* Parents Anonymous, 1977, 4.

23. *Beezer,* "Reporting Child Abuse," 436.

24. T. Toch, T. Guest, and M. Guttman, "Violence in the Schools," *U.S. News and World Report* 115 (November 8, 1993): 31–7.

25. *Ibid.,* 34.

26. Annette Kessler, "Peaceful Solutions to Violence," *Principal* 73 (November 1993): 11.

27. Millicent Lawton, "Why Are Children Turning to Guns?" *Education Week,* XI (November 6, 1991): 14.

28. Robert P. Cantrell and Mary Lynn Cantrell, "Countering Gang Violence in American Schools," *Principal* 73 (November 1993): 6–9; K. S. Trump, "Tell Teen Gangs: School's Out," *American School Board Journal* 180 (July 1993), 39–42.

29. Lorraine B. Wallach, "Helping Children Cope With Violence," *Young Children,* 8 (May 1993): 7–11.

30. "Schools Test New Ways to Resolve Conflict," (Association for Supervision and Curriculum Development) *ASCD Update,* 35 (December 1993): 4–6.

Recommended Readings

Bennett, William J. *What Works: Schools Without Drugs.* Washington, D.C.: U.S. Department of Education, 1987.

Borman, Kathryn M. and Joel H. Spring. *Schools in Central Cities.* New York: Longman, 1984.

Chase, Naomi F. *A Child is Being Beaten.* New York: Holt, Rinehart and Winston, 1975.

Frady, Marshall. *To Save Our Schools, To Save Our Children.* Far Hills, N.J.: New Horizon Press, 1986.

Giovacehini, Peter. *The Urge to Die: Why Young People Commit Suicide.* New York: Macmillan Co., 1981.

Gollnick, Donna M. and Philip C. Chinn. *Multicultural Education in a Pluralistic Society.* 2nd ed. Columbus, OH: Charles E. Merrill, 1986.

Gutek, Gerald L. *American Education in a Global Society.* New York: Longman, 1993.

Katzelson, Ira and Margaret Weir. *Schooling for All: Class, Race, and the Decline of the Democratic Ideal.* New York: Basic Books, 1986.

Kierstead, Fred D. and Paul A. Wagner, Jr. *The Ethical, Legal, and Multicultural Foundations of Teaching.* Madison, WI: Brown and Benchmark, 1993.

Kincheloe, Joe L., Teresa Scott Kincheloe, and George H. Staley, guest eds. *Journal of Thought,* 19 (Fall 1984), 171 pp. on "Indian Education, 1984."

Kotlowitz, Alex, *There Are No Children Here: The Story of Two Boys Growing Up in the Other America.* New York: Doubleday, 1991.

Lender, M.E. and J.D. Martin. *Drinking in America: A History.* New York: The Free Press, 1982.

Lickona, Thomas. "Drugs and Alcohol," *Educating for Character; How Our Schools Can Teach Respect and Responsibility.* New York: Bantam Books, 1991, Chapter 19, pp. 375–95.

"Native Americans," *National Forum,* LXXI (Spring 1991): 2–36.

Tower, Cynthia C. *Child Abuse and Neglect: A Teacher's Handbook for Detection Reporting, and Classroom Management.* Washington, D.C.: National Education Association, 1984.

Towers, Richard L. *How Schools Can Help Combat Student Drug and Alcohol Abuse.* Washington, D.C.: National Education Association, 1987.

Whitman, Mark, ed. *Removing a Badge of Slavery: A Record of Brown v. Board of Education.* New York: Markus Wiener Publishing, Inc., 1993.

Willie, Charles V., Antoine M. Garibaldi, and Wornie L. Reed, eds. *The Education of African-Americans.* New York: Auburn House, 1991.

Selected U.S. Supreme Court Cases:
  Plessy v. *Ferguson* (1896) 163 U.S. 537.
  Gaines v. *Canada* (1938) 305 U.S. 337.
  Sweatt v. *Painter* (1950) 339 U.S. 629.
  McLaurin v. *Oklahoma State Regents* (1950) 339 U.S. 637.
  Brown v. *Board of Education* (1954) 347 U.S. 483.
  Brown v. *Board of Education* (1955) 349 U.S. 294.
  Green v. *County School Board* (1968) 391 U.S. 430.
  Alexander v. *Holmes County Board of Education* (1969) 396 U.S. 19.
  Swann v. *Charlotte-Mecklenburg Board of Education* (1971) 402 U.S. 1.
  Keyes v. *School District No. 1* (1973) 413 U.S. 921.
  Milliken v. *Bradley* (1974) 418 U.S. 717.
  Milliken v. *Bradley* (1977) 433 U.S. 267.

Chapter 10

Policy Development in Public Education

Free and universal elementary and secondary education is one of America's unique and distinguishing characteristics. Most citizens recognize this system of education as our greatest safeguard of freedom and our best guarantee for economic and social growth.

The school as an institution receives its mandate from the society it serves. However, the school is only one of many institutions. Government, the family, and the church are also vital to the health and development of our society. All these institutions have complementary purposes. Each, in its own right, provides for the needs of society in general and the individual citizen in particular. The educational programs of the school would be ineffective if not for the supporting role played by government, the family, and the church.

A hallmark of all these institutions is change. The National School Public Relations Association makes a dramatic point concerning this phenomenon as it impacts education:

> *Calculators, cable television, microcomputers, video discs, satellites, teleconferencing—the list of new technologies arriving on the scene almost daily is growing and becoming more important to our lives. Only a decade ago, the idea of computers being as common in the home as the television was looked upon as an idea as farfetched as man walking on the moon was in the middle of this century.*
>
> *No one will deny that the . . . [present] is the age of technology, an age as dramatic as the industrial revolution in its capacity to change the way we live. Students today will have their future, and much of their present, dominated by electronic wizardry. And unless they have an understanding of and the ability to use the new technology, they will be as illiterate as persons who cannot read or write.*[1]

This statement highlights the responsibility of the school to adapt educational programs to the advances of technology. However, it is equally important for the school to remain flexible to assimilate new understandings concerning human communication and behavior. This adaptive responsibility by no means negates the school's obligation to transmit to students those principles contained in the U.S. Constitution and Bill of Rights; rather, it underscores the dynamic rather than the static nature of the school as an institution.

The inevitable question rising from this treatment is, "How does all this happen?" The answer is twofold—through policy development and administration. This chapter will explain educational policy while Chapter 11 treats educational administration. Policy development occurs at the federal, state, and local levels.

Role of the Federal Government in Setting Educational Policy

The United States Constitution is conspicuous in its omission of a provision or specific reference to education. The Tenth Amendment to the Constitution, ratified in 1791, states, "The powers not delegated to the United States by the Constitution, nor prohibited by it to the States, are reserved to the States respectively, or to the people." Thus, education from the very beginning of our country has been considered to be a state function.

Experience shows, however, that the federal government has been involved. Through the legislative branch, Congress provides funds to the states and school districts for special services and programs. The United States Office of Education, a cabinet-level agency in the executive branch of the government, administers programs established through congressional legislation. The many Supreme Court decisions affecting education testify to the influence of the judicial branch of the federal government on our schools. The National School Boards Association issued a publication in 1982 entitled *The Federal Role in Education: A Foundation for the Future* that analyzes why the federal government becomes involved with public education. The following summarizes the major issues that have fostered federal involvement.

Economy The connection between public education and the nation's economic well-being is now stronger than ever before. New technologies are quickly changing the work place. Federal assistance is needed to identify national labor market trends and to develop career awareness to meet the needs of the nation's changing work force.

Poverty Poverty is an ever-increasing national problem. In 1980, 29.3 million people, or 13 percent of the U.S. population, were below the poverty line. The path out of poverty for millions of disadvantaged students is compensatory education. According to the author, the need for a strong federal role in educational solutions is as great as ever because of the magnitude of the problem, the human cost of ignoring the problem, and the historical movement of poor people across state lines.

Defense   As weapons and support systems become more technological, the military needs more trained workers. The armed forces currently spend over $12 billion per year on manpower training programs, in many cases to teach fundamental technical skills to relatively short-term employees. These fundamentals could be taught in the public schools if appropriate programs were supported.

Civil Rights   Although much racial discrimination in education was eliminated during the 1960s, federal data collection and enforcement are still needed today to maintain this progress. Education plays a central role in attaining the benefits of a democratic society. Therefore, Congress plays a legitimate function when it identifies and corrects cases of discrimination based on race, gender, disabling condition, or English deficiency.[2]

A relevant example of influence exerted upon education by the executive branch of the federal government is the timely report issued by the National Commission on Excellence in Education. On August 26, 1981, Secretary of Education T. H. Bell created the commission. He directed the commission to examine the quality of education in the United States and to draft a report for him and the nation within eighteen months. Bell was prompted to create the commission because of the widespread perception that something was seriously remiss in our educational system.

The commission's charter contained specific areas to be investigated and analyzed, including the following:

1. Assessing the quality of teaching and learning in the nation's public and private schools, colleges, and universities
2. Comparing American schools and colleges with those of other advanced nations
3. Studying the relationship between college admissions requirements and student achievement in high school
4. Identifying educational programs that result in notable student success in college
5. Assessing the degree to which major social and educational changes in the last quarter century have affected student achievement
6. Defining problems which must be faced and overcome if we are to pursue successfully the course of excellence in education[3]

The commission members relied on five sources of information in making their analysis:

1. Papers commissioned from experts on education
2. Testimony from administrators, teachers, students, representatives of professional and public groups, parents, business leaders, public officials, and scholars
3. Existing analysis of issues in education
4. Written communications from citizens, teachers, and administrators
5. Descriptions of notable programs and promising approaches in education[4]

The recommendations of the Commission are based upon the following assumptions. First, everyone has the capability to learn. Second, everyone is born with the desire to learn, which can be nurtured through formal education. Third, a solid high school education is within everyone's reach. Fourth, lifelong learning will help people develop the necessary skills for new careers and for citizenship.

The report of the commission is entitled *A Nation at Risk: The Imperative for Educational Reform* and has particular significance for all educators, including those preparing to become teachers. Many states have begun implementing the recommendations of the commission.

President George Bush released a long-range plan for achieving national educational goals on April 18, 1991 titled *America 2000: An Education Strategy.* This established the following national goals:

1. By the year 2000, all children in the United States will start school ready to learn;
2. By the year 2000, the high school graduation rate will increase to at least 90%;
3. By the year 2000, American students will leave grades four, eight, and twelve having demonstrated competency in challenging subject matter including English, mathematics, science, history, and geography; and every teacher in the United States will ensure that all students learn to use their minds well, so that they may be prepared for responsible citizenship, further learning, and productive employment in our modern economy;
4. By the year 2000, U.S. students will be first in the world in science and mathematics achievement;
5. By the year 2000, every adult American will be literate and possess the knowledge and skills necessary to compete in a global economy, and exercise the rights and responsibilities of citizenship;
6. By the year 2000, every school in America will be free of drugs and violence and will offer a disciplined environment conducive to learning.

The U.S. Secretary of Education, Richard W. Riley, stated in a speech at the 1993 National School Boards Association's convention that there are three "overarching principles" in President Clinton's administration: 1. improving teaching and learning; 2. creating opportunity and responsibility in the school; 3. building partnerships with other agencies.[5]

Role of the State Government in Setting Educational Policy

This involvement of the federal government, however, does not supplant the jurisdiction of state governments, but rather complements and enriches state efforts. The authority of the state to create and govern public schools is embodied in every state constitution and exercised through each state legislature. These legislatures have delegated certain aspects of their authority to local boards of education. To ensure some control over these boards, most state legislatures have established minimum educational program requirements that each board must implement in order to receive state financial aid. In addition, most states have retained the authority to license teachers and administrators.

The educational administrative arm of many state legislatures is a state department of education, which, in turn, is usually governed by a board and administered by a commissioner or state superintendent. Figure 10-1 visualizes the jurisdictional relationship between the legislature and a state educational agency.[6]

In 1950 the National Council of Chief State School Officers issued a statement that properly described the state's educational responsibility and the state's relationship to local and federal agencies. This statement is as relevant today as it was when it was first published.

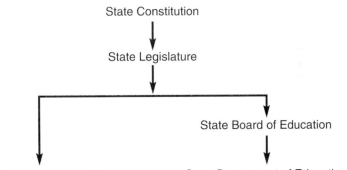

FIGURE 10-1   Jurisdictional Flow Chart

Source: R. W. Rebore, *Personnel Administration in Education: A Management Approach*, 2nd ed. (Englewood Cliffs, N.J.: Prentice Hall, 1987), p. 5. Used with permission.

Our system of constitutional government makes the states responsible for the organization and administration of public education and for general supervision of nonpublic schools. Each state has in practice delegated authority to organize and operate schools to various types of local administrative units of its own creation (Boards of Education). Within its general unity, our system of education leaves room for diversified programs among states and local administrative units.

Local, state and federal governments all have a vital interest in education. Each can contribute most effectively only if there is appropriate allocation of responsibility among them and only if relations among them are properly defined. Initiative and responsibility must be encouraged in the local units which operate most of the schools. The states must insure organization, financial support and effective administration of education programs of suitable quality and make certain these programs are available to every child. The federal government has an obligation to provide supplementary assistance to the states in accord with the national interest in universal education.

Local school boards and other state education authorities represent the public in the administration of education. Working with their professional staffs, these authorities are responsible for carefully planned programs of education and for obtaining the participation of the people in planning the kinds of schools and education they need and want.[7]

Role of the Local Board of Education in Setting Educational Policy

School districts are perhaps the most democratically controlled of all government agencies. The citizens of a local community elect school board members who are charged with formulating policies for the organization and administration of the schools. While state departments of education exercise regulatory authority to assure that every school district will provide a minimum educational program, the citizens of local districts maintain direct control over their schools through locally elected boards.

As the duties and responsibilities of school board members are described, it is very important to keep in mind that education is a state function. The courts have consistently upheld this position. By virtue of the authority delegated from a state legislature to school boards, the members represent the state even though they are locally elected. Board members, as individuals, have no authority outside a legally constituted board meeting. Policies can be agreed upon only at an official board meeting, and individual members cannot bind the board to any action except as authorized by the board at an official meeting.

In governing a school district, the board of education should elicit guidance from the superintendent and his or her staff before formulating policies. There are many more influences in our contemporary society that affect board decisions than there were even five years ago. Thus, the professional staff can and should become a continual resource to board members as they formulate policies. After the board of education establishes a policy, it is the responsibility of the superintendent and his or her staff to implement that policy.

Who is the typical school board member? What is the age, gender, religious affiliation, educational level, and so on, of this individual? There is no such person; there is no typical school board member! People campaign for election to the board of education for a variety of reasons; all are so personalized that they defy classification. However, once a person is elected to the board, he or she immediately assumes a mandate to govern the educational experience of children and young people, the effects of which are pervasive. It has always been recognized that membership on a school board is one of the most important governmental positions in our community.

School Board Policy Development

In exercising their authority to govern schools, boards of education must engage in the task of creating policies. This most important responsibility cannot be successfully accomplished without guidance from the professional educational staff and, at times, an attorney. There are many influences that affect policy construction, these are illustrated in Figure 10-2. Board policies must not conflict with the U.S. Constitution, federal laws, and federal court decisions. In like manner, policies must not conflict with the appropriate state constitution, state statutes, or state court decisions. Regulations issued by a state department of education should be considered by a board in creating policies but may be ignored. However, penalties such as loss of state aid make it impractical for a school board to create policies in conflict with such regulations. Local traditions, opinions, and goals also should be taken into consideration because policies objectionable to the local community will weaken citizen support. In addition, blatant disregard by board members for the wishes of a community often results in their political demise.

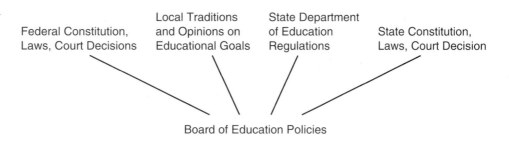

FIGURE 10-2   Board of Education Policies

Source: R. W. Rebore, *Personnel Administration in Education: A Management Approach,* 2nd ed. (Englewood Cliffs, N.J.: Prentice Hall, 1987), p. 7. Used with permission.

Advantages for developing policies have been outlined in *The School and Community Relations* and provide a rationale for their creation.

> *Policy facilitates the orientation of new board members regarding relations between the school and community.*
>
> *Policy facilitates a similar orientation on the part of new employees in the school system, both professional and nonprofessional.*
>
> *Policy acquaints the public with the position of the school and encourages citizen involvement in educational affairs.*
>
> *Policy provides a reasonable guarantee that there will be consistency and continuity in the decisions that are made under it.*
>
> *Policy informs the superintendent what he may expect from the board and what the board may expect from him.*
>
> *Policy creates the need for developing a detailed program in order that it may be implemented.*
>
> *Policy provides a legal reason for the allocation of funds and facilities in order to make the policy work.*
>
> *Policy establishes an essential division between policy making and policy administration.*[8]

School board policies should not be confused with administrative rules and regulations that constitute the detailed manner by which policies are implemented. Rules and regulations delineate who does what, when, and where. In fact, many rules and regulations may be required to implement one policy.

A properly conceived and phrased board of education policy has the following characteristics:

> *It is stated in broad, general terms but it is clear enough to allow for executive direction and interpretation.*
>
> *It reveals the philosophy of the board of education as members understand the desires of the community.*
>
> *It provides purpose and rationale for the subject about which a policy is being made.*
>
> *It suggests how the matter is to be carried out.*
>
> *It is never executive in substance or tone.*
>
> *It covers situations which are likely to occur repeatedly.*
>
> *It is always subject to review by the board with the objective of improvement in accordance with changing conditions.*

Also, the policy should:

> *Provide support and authority for all school programs and activities.*
>
> *Be brief, clear, concise, and complete.*

Be stable even during personnel changes.

Have adequate provisions for review and amendment.[9]

The policies of a school board are usually incorporated into a manual format in order to be easily consulted by administrators, teachers, and citizens.

The administrative staff under the supervision of the superintendent generally has the responsibility of codifying and developing the policy manual. After the manual has been completed, a continuous concern is keeping it updated. Many districts update their policy manual once a year using the board of education meeting minutes as a resource document.

There are four popular formats used in writing policies. The most common format is the resolution style on which the school board votes to take action. Equal Employment Opportunity and Affirmative Action policies are usually adopted in this resolution style. A second format sets forth the rationale for the policy and establishes broad goals. The third style incorporates an identification of who is responsible for implementing the policy. This is a common practice in formulating policies that address a specific function such as collective bargaining (see Box 10-1). The policy might identify the "Director of Employee Relations" as the chief negotiator for the school board and establish the confines within which he or she will function. A fourth format is used when the school board wishes to eliminate possible misunderstanding about how the policy is to be implemented. This type of style, therefore, incorporates administrative rules and regulations.

School Board Procedures and Operations

The laws of most states define school boards as corporate entities and, therefore, the board as a board exists only when its members are meeting in a legally constituted session. The board as a whole, and not individual members, conducts school district business.

Of course, the jurisdiction of the board extends only to governing the educational experience of children living within the legally constituted boundaries of the school district.

The School Board Meeting

The effective governance of a school district requires the board of education to meet on a regular basis, usually once a month. Most boards have a policy establishing the time and place of regular meetings. Special meetings are called from time to time for the purpose of handling problems and issues that cannot wait until the regular meeting or that would be better dealt with apart from the regularly scheduled meeting. Usually special meetings are called by the president of the school board or when a majority of the school board members request a special meeting. The task of notifying board members concerning the purpose, time, and place of special meetings is the responsibility of the superintendent of schools.

BOX 10-1   Model Board of Education Policy on Collective Negotiations

The board of education finds that joint decision making is an effective way of governing and administering the school systems. If school district employees have the right to share in the decision-making process affecting salaries, fringe benefits, and working conditions, they become more responsive and better disposed to exchanging ideas and information concerning operations with administrators. Accordingly, management becomes more effective.

The board of education further declares that harmonious and cooperative relations between itself and school district employees protects the patrons and children of the school district by assuring the orderly operation of the schools.

This position of the board is to be effectuated by:

1. Recognizing the right of all school district employees to organize for the purpose of collective negotiations;

2. Authorizing the director of employee relations to negotiate with the duly elected employee representatives on matters relating to salaries, fringe benefits, and working conditions;

3. Requiring the director of employee relations to establish administrative policies and procedures for the effective implementation of the negotiations process. This is to be accomplished under the supervision of the assistant superintendent for personnel who, in turn, is directly responsible to the superintendent of schools.

Upon successful completion of the negotiations process, the board of education will enter into written agreements with the employee organizations.

Source: Ronald W. Rebore, *Personnel Administration in Education: A Management Approach,* 2nd ed. (Englewood Cliffs, N.J.: Prentice-Hall, 1987), p. 294. Used with permission.

The board of education usually meets at the central administrative office building or in a school. It is common practice for the president of the board to ask visitors in attendance at a meeting if they wish to address the board. This usually occurs at the beginning of the meeting.

Most states have a statute that provides for public bodies to meet in a closed executive session about certain issues. While the variety of provisions makes classification difficult, the following are the most common reasons for the holding of an executive session:

1. The hiring, terminating, or promotion of personnel
2. A proceeding involving student discipline such as probation or expulsion
3. Litigation involving the school district
4. The lease, purchase, or sale of property

The School Board Meeting Agenda

As the chief executive officer of the school board, the superintendent is usually charged with preparing the agenda for the meetings. The agenda ensures that the ordinary business of the school district will be timely addressed. School board members, however, may request that the superintendent add items to the agenda for discussion or action. In fact, most superintendents contact individual board members before the agenda is prepared for this very purpose. The agenda with minutes from the preceding meeting, accompanied by pertinent reports and explanatory materials, is usually sent to each board member before the meeting. This gives each member sufficient time to properly prepare for the meeting.

The order of business at the board meeting will be dictated by the items to be dealt with. However, the following order will be followed at most meetings.

1. *Call to order.* The president of the board calls the meeting to order. If the president and vice president are both absent, the secretary presides and then the treasurer in the secretary's absence. A quorum is necessary to transact business and is usually defined as two-thirds of the members.
2. *Scheduling visitors' presentations.* It has become common practice in recent years for boards of education to allow visitors to address the board about their concerns. The board may limit the number of individuals allowed to speak and may set a time limit on presentations.
3. *Approval of the agenda.* The members may change the agenda by adding or deleting items.
4. *Approval of the warrant.* The board of education must approve paying the bills of the district and the payroll. The warrant is a listing of the checks by numbers; to whom the checks are written; and the purpose for which each check is to be issued. After the board approves the warrant list, the checks may be signed and mailed. It is common practice for the signatures of the president and treasurer to appear on the checks.
5. *Unfinished business.* If the board of education did not complete a previous board agenda, this is the appropriate time when such items are addressed.
6. *New business.* The superintendent, upon the request of the president, may make preliminary remarks about the items to be discussed and acted upon.
7. *Superintendent's report.* Many superintendents present information to the school board about educational programs and issues as a part of each board meeting. The actual report may be given by other administrators, teachers, or staff members. A budget operating summary is a very important report which is a regular part of such a section. Other reports range from an explanation of curricular programs to the district's standardized testing program, or any other aspect of the school district's operation.

Minutes of the Board Meetings

The minutes of the board meetings are the formal and legal medium by which the board of education communicates and documents its decisions. Courts have traditionally accepted the minutes of board meetings as relevant in litigation involving the actions of school boards. Thus, the secretary of the board must diligently oversee the accurate recording of the board's decisions.

The minutes of the board meetings are public documents and, therefore, may be reviewed by all interested citizens. Most school districts keep the minutes at a central office and in a place or container that is fireproof, secure, and safe from vandalism. Some school districts microfilm the minutes and keep the microfilm in a different place from the original records, thereby adding a significant degree of security against possible loss of the minutes.

Most states have statutes which permit the minutes of executive sessions to be a closed record from public inspection.

The contents of the minutes usually include the following:

> *First, identification data which include the time and place of the meeting; the board members and staff members in attendance; the approval of minutes from the preceding meeting; and the purpose of the meeting, if it is a special meeting or executive session.*

> *Second, identification of who made the motions at the meeting; who seconded the motions; a record of how each member voted by name unless it was a unanimous vote; and a statement indicating if the motion passed or failed.*

> *Third, identification of all other matters brought before the school board and the disposition of these matters if the board did not take action.*

Officers of the School Board

State statutes usually provide for how the school board must be organized. There are differences from state to state. However, a few generalizations may be made that apply to all boards of education. First, a president or chairperson is elected by the board members. He or she presides at the board meetings and acts as the spokesperson for the entire board when it is necessary to make a public statement concerning an issue facing the board. The president also has the duty of signing the official documents of the school district, including contracts; and a facsimile of the superintendent's signature usually appears on all school district bank drafts. A vice president or vice chairperson is also elected who assumes the duties of the president/chairperson in his or her absence.

A treasurer of the school board is elected and is charged with the responsibility of monitoring the financial affairs of the school district. This does not mean that the treasurer conducts the daily business operations of the district; that is an administrative responsibility. A facsimile of the treasurer's signature usually appears on all school district bank drafts.

The secretary of the school board, who is also elected by the other board members, is responsible for monitoring the accurate recording of school board meetings; safekeeping the official school district records; and attesting by signature to the accuracy of official school district reports. The secretary also attests to all contracts by signature. A recording secretary, who is an employee of the district, is responsible for handling the mechanics of the secretary's duties.

School Board Consultants and Advisory Committees

Our contemporary society is very complex and, therefore, so are the issues and problems facing boards of education. It has become common practice for school boards to hire consultants who have an expertise that can be used by the board. These consultants fall into two broad categories—those providing continuous services and those providing occasional services. Every school board will need the assistance of an attorney and a certified public accountant, both of whom are usually employed on a continual basis because it is beneficial to the district for these professionals to acquire an in-depth and ongoing understanding of school district operations.

When the school district is in need of occasional services from other professionals such as a property appraiser or an architect, the board will advertise for such services and review the credentials of interested individuals before making a choice.

Valuable information and a great deal of good public relations is obtained by soliciting the assistance of citizens and patrons of the school district. Citizens advisory committees have been utilized to study and collect data for boards about such issues as student discipline, homework, and drug abuse.

Board-Staff Relations

Members of school boards are elected public officials and as such are subject to all the political pressures that confront other public officials. Teachers, administrators, and staff members as well as students, parents, and other citizens are concerned about the potential decisions of school boards and how these decisions will affect them. Teacher unions, in particular, are very politically active in many school districts.

It should not be surprising, then, that school board members and newly elected members are contacted by employees, not only about policy issues, but also concerning problems they face in their work. They will want the board members to intervene on their behalf. The most appropriate response for the board member is to refer the employee to his or her immediate supervisor in order to resolve the problem. The board member should also encourage the employee to use the chain-of-command in appealing an unresolved problem.

A sympathetic response and the fact that a board member listened to an employee's concern may ease his or her anxiety. The cliche is true, "There are two sides to every story." It is not, however, the responsibility of a board member to listen to both sides but rather to refer the person to the proper administrator. School board members must always remember that they have no jurisdiction as individuals and can act only at a legally called board meeting. Further, the board of education is a policy-making body and should not interfere with the administration of the district.

Summary

Our system of free and universal public education is a unique characteristic of American society. The school as an institution receives its mandate to educate children from society. Our educational programs must address the fundamental principles of individual freedom, individual responsibility, and democracy but with flexibility to incorporate new developments and conditions.

Implementing the educational goals of society is the responsibility of the individual states. The mandate to create and govern public schools is embodied in state constitutions. The state legislature is the avenue through which this authority is exercised. The administrative arm of the state legislature is the department of education that is usually governed by a board and administered by a commissioner or state superintendent. The legislature also delegates certain aspects of its authority to local boards of education. The state department of education maintains some control over local boards by establishing minimum educational program requirements and teacher certification requirements and by providing funds to help finance education.

The federal government has had an ongoing influence on education by congressional acts that provide funds for special programs, by the regulations of the United States Office of Education, and by Supreme Court decisions. A relevant example of influence exerted upon education by the executive branch of the federal government is the report *A Nation at Risk: The Imperatives for Educational Reform* issued by the National Commission on Excellence in Education. However, the federal government's power and influence in education are adjunct to the authority of the state.

School districts are some of the most democratically controlled agencies of government. The citizens of a local community elect school board members who are charged with the governing of the school district. There is no typical school board member. People make decisions to seek election to the board of education for a variety of reasons, all of which are so personalized that they defy classification. Membership on a school board is one of the most important governmental positions in our community, state, and nation. Our American society understands that freedom and our economic system demand an educated citizenry.

School boards are corporate entities and, as such, can function only at a legally constituted board meeting. Board members have no authority as individuals. The responsibility of the school board to govern the school district is exercised in three major areas: creating policies, evaluating programs, and supervising the superintendent.

In exercising their authority to govern schools, boards of education formulate and adopt policies. School board policies should not be confused with administrative rules and regulations, which are detailed procedures that implement board policies. The policies of the school board are usually incorporated into a manual format.

Most boards of education meet on a regular basis, usually once a month. Special meetings may be called from time to time for the purpose of handling problems and issues that cannot wait until the regular meeting or that would be better dealt with in a special meeting. Most state statutes have provisions allowing public bodies to meet in executive session about certain issues, usually dealing with personnel, property, law suits, and student discipline.

Board meetings are generally organized around a formal agenda which includes the following:

1. Call to order
2. Approval of the agenda
3. Visitor presentations
4. Approval of warrants
5. Unfinished business
6. New business
7. Superintendent's report
8. Adjournment

All official actions of the school board must occur at a board meeting. The minutes of the board meeting are the formal and legal medium by which the board communicates and documents its actions. The minutes of the board meetings are public documents and must be open to review by all interested citizens.

Most states have statutes that require the school board to elect officers who are charged with carrying out school board operations. The most typically designated offices are, of course, president, vice president, treasurer, and secretary.

School boards will need the assistance of regular and occasional consultants. An attorney, certified public accountant, auditor, property appraiser, and so on, are hired to provide expertise that the board can use in governing the district. Valuable assistance is also obtained by many boards through citizens advisory committees.

Members of the school board are often contacted by school district employees who want the board members to intervene on their behalf because of a problem at work. Experienced board members will refer these individuals to their immediate supervisors. Furthermore, the board member may encourage the persons to appeal their grievances through the chain-of-command all the way to the board if the problem is not resolved.

Implications for Future Teachers

There are two major implications in the area of policy development. First, teachers need to understand the difference between the policy role of the board of education, and the management role of the administration. Teachers will often approach school board members with issues and problems that can only be effectively handled by the building principal or superintendent of schools. Going outside the chain of command by bringing issues and problems to school board members can place the teacher in conflict with a principal or the superintendent.

Second, teachers need to understand the role of federal and state governments if they are going to effectively lobby Congress and state legislators for passage of legislation that will benefit education and teaching. Since there are so many teachers in our country, the influence on legislation can be stronger than any other group of professionals.

Discussion Questions

1. Compare and contrast the role of the federal government with the role of the states in setting educational policy.
2. What variables affect the development of local board of education polices?
3. Describe the order of business that normally would be followed at a board of education meeting.
4. Why would a board of education commission advisory committees?
5. Describe the role and function of local boards of education.

Notes

1. National School Public Relations Association, "New Challenge for Schools: Age of Information," *Education USA* 24, no. 19 (January 4, 1982): 141.

2. Educational Research Service, "Federal Role in Education," *ERS Bulletin* 10, no. 2 (October, 1982): 4.

3. The Commission on Excellence in Education, *A Nation at Risk: The Imperative for Educational Reform* (Washington, D.C.: Government Printing Office, 1984), 1–2.

4. Ibid., 2–4.

5. National School Boards Association, "Riley Advocates 'Goals 2000' Legislation," *School Board News,* 13, no. 6 (April 1993), p. 5.

6. Ronald W. Rebore, *Personnel Administration in Education: A Management Approach, 2nd ed.* (Englewood Cliffs, NJ.: Prentice-Hall, 1987), 5.

7. The National Council of Chief State School Officers, *Our System of Education* (Washington, D.C.: The Council, 1950), 5–6.

8. Leslie W. Kindred, Dan Bagin, and Donald R. Gallagher, *The School and Community Relations* (Englewood Cliffs, N.J.: Prentice-Hall, 1976), 30.

9. Missouri School Board Association, *A Manual for Missouri School Board Members* (Columbia, Mo.: The Association, 1981), H-3.

Recommended Readings

American Association of School Administrators. *Goal Setting and Self Evaluation of School Boards.* Arlington, Va: The Association, 1985.

American Association of School Administrators. *Holding Effective Board Meetings.* Arlington, Va: The Association, 1985.

American Association of School Administrators. *Roles and Relationships: School Boards and Superintendents.* Arlington, Va: The Association, 1985.

Kowalski, Theodore J. "Why Your Board Needs Self Evaluation," *The American School Board Journal* 168, no. 7 (July 1981): 21–23.

National School Public Relations Association. "Boards In Transition," *Education USA* 27, no. 32 (April 1985):241.

National School Boards Association. "Boards Need Education, Too!" *Updating School Board Policies* 19, no. 5 (May 1988):1–2.

National School Boards Association, *The Federal Role in Education: A Foundation for the Future.* Washington, D.C.: The Association, 1982.

The Commission on Excellence in Education. *A Nation at Risk: The Imperative for Educational Reform.* Washington, D.C.: Government Printing Office, 1984.

Thomas, M. Donald. "A Prominent School Chief Reflects on What Makes a Board Member Exemplary," *The American School Board Journal* 172, no. 4 (April 1985):31–44.

Underwood, Kenneth E., Wayne P. Thomas, Tony Cooke, and Shirley Underwood. "Portrait of the American School Board Member," *The American School Board Journal* 167, no. 1 (January 1980):23–25.

C h a p t e r *11*

Administration of Local Public Schools

The enriched lifestyle enjoyed by U.S. citizens is a result of free public education. Business and industry, the arts, and government continue to need well-educated people for the growth and development of this lifestyle. There is, therefore, an expectation that the quality of education will increase and that more citizens will have the opportunity to attain higher levels of education. Further, it does not require much elaboration to see how the microchip has revolutionized our daily life, and how important it is that schools prepare children to maximize the benefits offered by microcomputers. Education has gradually evolved into a very complex process because of the expectations of the American people and because of technological advances. Thus, effective education can occur only within an organization that is capable of analyzing the needs of future generations and that is capable of creating delivery systems that will meet these needs. What follows, therefore, is a brief treatment of the school as an organization and a more detailed treatment of educational administration.[1]

The Nature of Public School Districts

In every organization there is a central issue that is the foundation upon which the organization is built. That issue can be reduced to a major question, "What is the mission of the organization?" To the casual observer, this question might appear easily answered, but, in reality, it is most difficult. The difficulty lies in the fact that "mission" is an organic concept that is subject to periodic change.

For school districts, the obvious answer is, "to educate children, adolescents, and young people." So far so good! However, what does "to educate" really mean? Does educate mean providing transportation and food service to children or does it mean just providing classroom instruction in the "basics"? Should statistics be a part of the high school mathematic curriculum? Should foreign language be taught in elementary school? Should all students be given the opportunity to use microcomputers? Obviously, there are no pat answers to these questions! However, "mission" is the only justifiable reason to create and maintain public school districts.

Therefore, a school district, as an organization, must devise a process by which its mission is continually under review for the purposes of refining and defining the nuances of that mission. This mission is put into operation by developing detailed and specific goals that direct the governance and management functions of the school district. For example, a common goal in all districts is to provide a sequential learning experience in grades kindergarten through twelve in order to provide each student with the opportunity to acquire reading and language skills commensurate with each student's ability. A second goal might be to provide each student living over one mile from school with transportation services and pick-up/departure points within one-half mile from his or her home. Of course, it is desirable for school board members to enunciate the mission of their school district through policy statements that are readily available to the constituents of the district.

The Nature of Public School Management

For some unknown reason, educators prefer to speak about *administration* rather than *management* when referring to the functions and tasks performed by superintendents, central office administrators, and principals. Perhaps educators believe that *management* as a term is more appropriately applied to business and industry, while *administration* is better applied to the educational enterprise. This treatment will use the terms interchangeably because the current literature tends to blur this distinction.

What is meant by the term "management"? Since the Egyptians built the pyramids, people have attempted to define what it is that someone does who is in command that results in a desired outcome. Well, that theorizing is precisely the definition of management; it is controlled action that leads to a desired outcome.

Management in school districts can be viewed from this same perspective but with a little elaboration. It is controlled action because the mission of a school district can only be achieved through well-conceived action. From the viewpoint of an administrator, controlled action usually takes place in the following sequence:

First, a decision must be made by the administrator about what he wants the professionals, whom he supervises, to do.

Second, he must make a decision about which professionals he wants to perform certain functions and tasks.

Third, the administrator must establish a standard of performance that he wants the professionals, whom he supervises, to reach.

Fourth, the administrator must review the performance of the professionals he supervised to determine if the mission of the organization is being realized.

Fifth, the administrator must develop controls on how functions are to be implemented by creating appropriate processes and procedures.

Sixth, rewards and incentives must be developed by the administrator if he or she hopes to increase the level of performance of his or her subordinates.

The desired outcome of management in school districts is to provide educational services to children. This is the imperative of educational administration.

Competency Model

Proper and effective management requires competent administrators. Competency means that an administrator has the knowledge and skills necessary to manage the people and resources (what people need to fulfill their responsibilities) to attain a desired outcome. Good intentions and being a successful teacher may not necessarily mean that a person will be a competent administrator.

The knowledge necessary to be an administrator has been interpreted in most states to mean completing a set of courses or a graduate program in educational administration.[2] The coursework usually centers around three areas: management (school law, finance, personnel administration, collective negotiations, buildings and sites, and so on); the supervision of professional personnel; and courses in curriculum development.

To be an effective educational administrator, a person must have the ability to control his or her behavior, to supervise other people, and to manage operational functions.

In the final analysis management is an *art*. Yes, scientific knowledge is a necessity; yes, learned skills are necessary. However, no one can be an effective administrator through the application of a set formula. The art of management is the ability that an administrator possesses to analyze and interpret the variables of a decision and to make that decision because of past personal experience and experience in practicing management. Inherent in the analysis and interpretation of variables is the ability to foresee the various consequences that different decisions will create and to choose the consequence that will produce the most desired effect.

The Dynamics of Leadership

There are multiple levels and degrees of leadership that a superintendent of schools, a principal, or another administrator can achieve based upon the parameters of the job and the individual's desire to become a "high performer." "Leadership" in the latter case is not a characteristic to be acquired but rather the outcome or result of performance. A person can become a leader in his or her community because of his or her achievements in serving the community; in like manner, a principal can become a leader in education because of his or her recognized achievement in administration. Thus, an individual's high degree of performance is what gives him or her a position of leadership.

The very basic level of leadership is derived from the job position. The superintendent of schools is in a leadership position by reason of his or her authority and responsibility. The decisions the superintendent makes can have an effect upon every student in the school district and upon every teacher and staff member. Leaders by reason of high performance are individuals who are easily recognized. They outperform their colleagues because of the way in which they set goals for themselves, the way in which they solve problems, how they manage stress, and how they take risks. Research has proliferated in psychology in the last decade about why some individuals outperform others. In Russia the Soviets called this research "anthropomaximology." Most teachers will readily recognize the type of leadership exercised by the superintendent and principal for whom they work.

The Organization of the Central Office

Historically, boards of education have delegated the responsibility for implementing school policies to a chief executive officer—the superintendent of schools. Thus, the superintendent assumes full control of all operations. As pupil enrollment increases, however, it usually becomes necessary to develop specialized central office functions.

The Superintendent of Schools

No position within education has received more attention in the news media and press over the past decade than the superintendency. "The job is much more political than ever before" appears to be the reason why there is such a tremendous turnover rate among superintendents; indeed, the turnover rivals that of losing baseball managers.[3] Declining enrollment, teacher layoffs, dwindling financial resources, labor union strikes, and failing pupil achievement test scores constitute some of the major problems facing contemporary public schools. The individual who is often singled out as contributing to these problems rather than solving them is the superintendent of schools. He becomes the tangible target for hurled criticism when the real culprits are too elusive to be found.

The superintendent of schools acts as the chief advisor to the board of education on all matters that affect the school system. Thus, the superintendent is responsible for providing board members with reports, data, and other information that will help them in their decision making. The superintendent should provide such information not only at the request of the board but also when he believes that the information would help board members.

As the chief executive officer of the school board, the superintendent is responsible for the following:

1. Formulating and recommending policies to be adopted by the board of education
2. Establishing administrative rules and regulations that are necessary to carry out the policy decisions of the board
3. Preparing and submitting an annual budget to the board of education
4. Expending the board-approved budget in accordance with school board policies
5. Recommending candidates for employment to the board of education
6. Formulating and administering a program of supervision for the instructional program
7. Submitting an annual report to the board of education on the operations of the school district

The superintendent of schools is also responsible for assuming a leadership role with other professional educators at the local, state, and national levels. This will help the superintendent to be informed about current issues facing education, which he or she in turn should communicate to the board of education and the local school community.

This description of the role and function of the superintendent clearly establishes the significance of his position as the chief executive officer of the school board. He is not by position the "head teacher" or the "lead administrator" or the "instructional leader" of the school district. He is first and foremost the chief executive officer of the board. This does not imply that the superintendent cannot function as an instructional leader or be identified with the teaching and administrative staff. The ideal superintendent fulfills all of these roles.

The Administrative Team

The superintendent of schools is responsible for the overall management of the school district. Obviously, it is impossible for the superintendent to manage all the major functions himself except in the very smallest of school districts. Functions such as personnel management, secondary school management, elementary school management, curriculum services management, and administrative support services management are usually delegated to assistant superintendents in most districts.

These assistant superintendents, along with other administrators, constitute the administrative team. The concept of team management refers to participation of all administrators in setting administrative policy (not to be confused with board of education policies) and of translating these policies into administrative strategies. Administrative policies are goals that management believes are necessary to fulfill the mission of the school district as reflected in the board of education policies. Administrative strategies constitute the "game plan" on how the goals can be achieved. The strategies are implemented through processes and procedures that address daily operations.

Thus, the superintendent conferring with the assistant superintendents at a "cabinet meeting" about a new board of education policy on affirmative action might ask the assistant superintendent for personnel to draft a list of appropriate goals on recruiting minority candidates for job vacancies. At a subsequent cabinet meeting when these goals are presented, each assistant superintendent could discuss how the goals (administrative policies) can be achieved (their strategies) in their respective areas of management. The assistant superintendent for personnel would then meet with his staff and discuss how the strategies can be realized. In other words, what procedures can be initiated in the recruitment process to attract minority candidates? Perhaps contacting college and university job placement offices that have a large representation of minorities could be one procedure, while a second could be advertising in newspapers of general circulation. Notification of vacancies in all internal divisions of the school district could be a third procedure. The assistant superintendents managing these divisions might have decided at the cabinet meeting that they would encourage minorities (women, blacks, the handicapped) working under their supervision to apply for promotions when vacancies occur.[4]

This team management approach is applicable to each level within the school district. An assistant superintendent should formulate and establish division policies and strategies with his staff members.

The team management concept is also very effective at the building level where assistant principals constitute the "principal's cabinet." The assistant principals could set up the same situation with staff members from the departments in the school that they manage.

The advantages to the team management approach are obvious. First, team management makes good use of the talent present in all school districts. Second, change is more likely to be implemented with minimal resistance if decisions are cooperatively made. Third, all levels within the district are forced to identify administrative policies and strategies that are compatible and have the same ultimate objectives.

Because there is a need in all school districts to identify various echelons in the administrative organization, it is common practice that the title of director or coordinator be attached to administrative positions responsible to an assistant superintendent in charge of a particular function. Figure 11-1 represents a possible central office organization that incorporates a line authority from superintendent to assistant superintendents (cabinet positions) to directors and coordinators. The number of central office administrators listed suggests that this could be the organizational structure for a school district with a pupil population of ten thousand to twenty thousand. It is designed as a model exemplifying the possible scope of central office administrative positions. Smaller school districts would compress central office responsibilities into fewer positions. For example, a school district with two thousand students might be administered by a superintendent and an assistant superintendent who share all of the responsibilities.

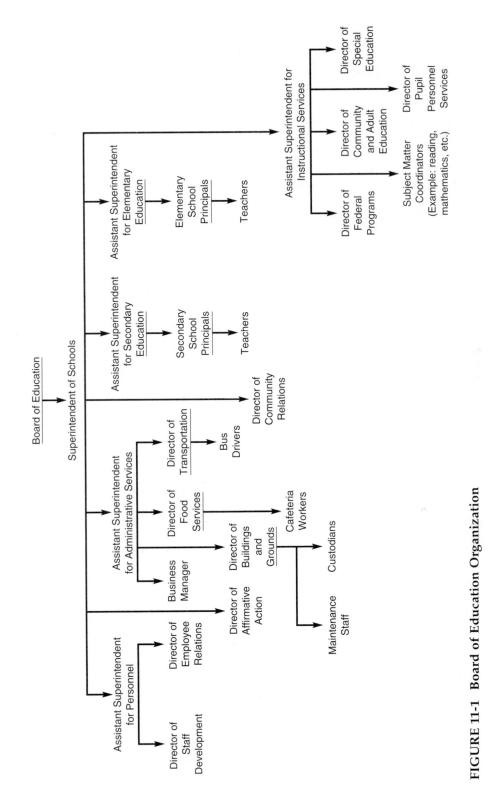

FIGURE 11-1 Board of Education Organization

Source: R. W. Rebore, *Educational Administration: A Management Approach* (Englewood Cliffs, N.J.: Prentice-Hall, 1985), p. 4. Used with permission.

Individual School Building Organization

During the early years of our country's development, one-room school houses were staffed by teachers who were responsible not only for instruction but also for performing all tasks related to the maintenance and upkeep of the buildings. This situation gradually changed during the 1800s as education developed into a profession. By the beginning of the 1900s, education had advanced to the point where instructional materials, teaching techniques, and licensing requirements highlighted the expertise of the teacher. One aspect of that expertise is the capability of the teacher to take a body of knowledge and organize it into instructional units or lessons. A second aspect is the skill to present the lessons in such a way that students learn the content.

This specialization of the teacher's role was the catalyst that caused the creation of the modern-day principalship. During the evolutionary period of the teacher's role, many forms appeared as precursors to the present-day function of the building principal. As schools expanded and employed more teachers, one was usually chosen as the headmaster or headmistress. This was a title brought over from England and, as the word itself indicates, the "head" teacher had charge of the school.

The contemporary public school is composed of an administrative staff, instructional staff, professional support staff, and classified staff. Each of these categories of employees performs a vital service. However, teaching has always held a preeminence because it constitutes the primary mission of the school.

Elementary Schools

Figure 11-2 is an organizational chart for an elementary school with an enrollment between four hundred and seven hundred pupils. The pattern of grade-level organization could be kindergarten through grade five, through grade six, or through grade eight, depending upon the organizational pattern of the secondary school program. The curriculum organization could be nongraded or traditional with team teaching or with undivided classroom teacher units. The school building, in like manner, could have an architectural design utilizing the open space concept or the self-contained classroom model.

The principal is the administrative executive in the elementary school building. It is his or her responsibility to provide the leadership necessary for the effective execution of the school's mission, that is, of course, to educate the children in his or her school. The primary skill of the principal is to manage the human and material resources available in such a manner that the school's objective is realized. The role of the elementary school principal, therefore, revolves around performing the following tasks:

1. Formulating building-level policies to define clearly the duties and responsibilities of the professional staff, classified staff, students, and parents in the school's attendance area

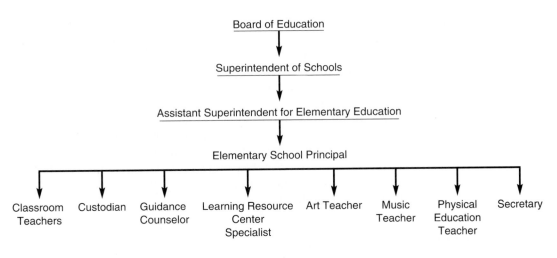

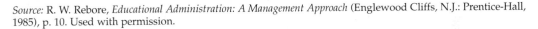

FIGURE 11-2 Elementary School Organization

Source: R. W. Rebore, *Educational Administration: A Management Approach* (Englewood Cliffs, N.J.: Prentice-Hall, 1985), p. 10. Used with permission.

2. Developing a personnel planning forecast to ensure that the right number of staff members with the most appropriate credentials are available to carry out the mission of the school
3. Conducting an ongoing projection of pupil enrollment that will be the basis used in personnel planning and budgeting
4. Developing a building-level budget for supplies, materials, and equipment
5. Initiating an ongoing facility maintenance and operations plan to ensure that the building is energy efficient and in proper condition

The principal as administrative executive is a rather new concept in many school districts but has become a necessity, given the complexity of our contemporary society. Traditionally, the principal evaluated teacher performance and handled chronic pupil disciplinary problems. This concept does not nullify the traditional role of the principal but rather expands the scope of his responsibilities.

The instructional staff is responsible, of course, for teaching the basic skills to students. In the elementary school program, the expertise of the teacher lies in his or her ability to take the material to be taught and organize it and present it to the children in such a way that learning occurs. Academic freedom for an elementary school teacher usually consists of the right to organize and present the curriculum in the manner that he or she finds to be most effective with students. Determining *what is to be taught* is the prerogative of the board of education. Of course, the professional staff acts as a resource group to the board in this endeavor. The elementary school teacher should be well-educated in child development theory and the psychology of learning because it is upon these bases that effective learning depends.

Other professional staff members are charged with helping teachers in the instructional process. In the model presented in Figure 11-2, these professionals include the guidance counselor, learning resource center specialist, and fine arts and physical education teachers. All these professionals, along with the classroom teachers and building principal, are responsible for pupil discipline and effective communication with parents.

The classified staff includes building secretaries and custodians. These individuals also provide a vital service in every elementary school. The tasks they perform relieve professional staff members so they can concentrate on the instructional-learning process. In addition, parents and students are constantly interacting with classified staff members, making these individuals valuable public relations agents of the school district.

Secondary Schools

Figure 11-3 is an organizational chart for a junior high school, middle school, or high school. The enrollment could be from fifteen hundred to two thousand students. The pattern of grade-level organization might be (1) junior high school (grades 7–9) and high school (grades 10–12) or (2) middle school (grades 6–8) and high school (grades 9–12). Middle schools have become the subject of much research within the last decade and have proven to be an effective method of organizing the curriculum. Child development theory appears to substantiate that sixth-grade students are closer in maturity to seventh- and eighth-grade students than to fifth graders. In like manner, ninth-grade students are closer in maturity to tenth graders than they are to eighth-grade students. The emphasis in middle school, like that in an elementary school, should be on learning as it relates to child development and the acquisition of basic skills, rather than on mastering the rudiments of a subject area.

Junior high schools are structured to provide the student with a transition period to high school and more closely resemble high schools in curriculum and instructional philosophy. It is important, however, for teachers and administrators to guard against making a junior high school into a miniature senior high school. The emphasis should be on *preparing* the student for his high school experience.

Much of what has been said about the role and function of the building principal, instructional staff, professional support staff, and classified staff can be applied to secondary school personnel. The principal, as the administrative executive of a secondary school, is responsible for developing building-level policies, for personnel planning, for pupil enrollment projecting, for budget preparation, and for facility management. The major difference is that the secondary school principal usually shares these responsibilities with an administrative team composed of assistant principals who are assigned to specific areas of management. Figure 11-3 assigns administrative services to one assistant while curriculum and instruction are assigned to a second assistant principal. Of course, pupil discipline and communicating with parents are the responsibilities of all

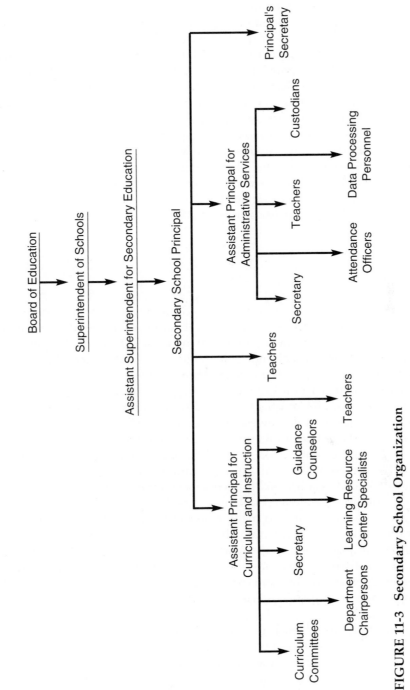

FIGURE 11-3   Secondary School Organization

Source: R. W. Rebore, *Educational Administration: A Management Approach* (Englewood Cliffs, N.J.: Prentice-Hall, 1985), p. 12. Used with permission.

staff members. Teacher evaluation is a most important responsibility and is such a time-consuming process that most principals divide the number of teachers to be evaluated between him- or herself and the assistant principals.

The instructional staff is organized into departments with chairpersons assuming much of the responsibility for helping assistant principals in scheduling and budgeting for their departments. While child development and the psychology of learning are important in all instructional situations, the emphasis in a high school is on content mastery. Other building-level professions such as guidance counselors, learning resource center specialists, as well as district-wide professionals such as social workers and psychometrists, assist secondary school teachers with problems and issues that might affect classroom instruction.

The size of the classified staff is larger in the secondary school and includes not only secretaries and custodians but also attendance officers and data processing specialists. Their services are essential if the contemporary secondary school is going to be effective.

Summary

Providing educational services has evolved into a very complex process because of the expectations of the American people and because of advances in technology. Instruction, as the key component of these educational services, can be effectively provided to children only within an organization charged with the delivery of these services. That organization is the local school district.

Each school district must devise a process by which its mission is continually under review for the purpose of refining and defining the nuances of that mission. This mission is viewed in practice as the detailed and specific goals that direct management functions of the school district. Thus, "management" may be defined as controlled action that leads to an outcome. This function requires "competent" administrators. Competency means that an administrator has the knowledge and skills necessary to manage people and the resources toward attaining the desired outcome. The knowledge requirement has been interpreted in most states to mean completing a set of courses or a graduate program leading to administrator licensing. The skill requirement means that the administrator can manage himself, other people, and operational functions. In the final analysis, administrator competency rests on the theory that management is an art; an administrator must possess the ability to analyze and interpret the variables of a decision and make that decision based upon past experiences.

There are multiple levels of leadership that an administrator can attain. The basic level is derived from a person's job position. Successive degrees of leadership are attained because of the level of performance that an individual achieves. Leadership is a necessary characteristic of an educational administrator.

Team management refers to participation by administrators at all levels within a school district in setting administrative policy and in translating that policy into administrative strategies. This approach makes good use of available personnel talent, reduces resistance to change, and forces continuity of purpose.

Functions are performed by administrators within a given organizational framework. The superintendent, as the chief executive officer of the school board, has full control of all school operations. These operations are so complex that his efforts must be augmented by a central office administrative team. This team is usually composed of assistant superintendents who administer the major functions of the school system. These assistant superintendents usually form a *cabinet* which helps the superintendent formulate strategies and shares in the decision-making process. Directors and coordinators perform administrative tasks which support the major functions of a district, and they generally report to assistant superintendents.

The individual schools in our contemporary society are composed of an administrative staff, instructional staff, professional support staff, and classified staff. Each of these categories of employees performs a vital service toward the accomplishment of the school's mission—to educate children and young people.

In addition to performing the traditional responsibilities of evaluating teacher performance and handling chronic pupil disciplinary problems, the building principal performs an executive function. The role of the principal has expanded in scope to include formulating building policies, developing personnel planning forecasts, conducting pupil enrollment projections, preparing a building budget, and managing the school plant.

The instructional staff is responsible for teaching the curriculum. This includes organizing instructional materials and deciding on the most appropriate method of instruction to be used. Other professional personnel, including counselors and learning resource center specialists, provide valuable services which support the efforts of the classroom teachers. Maintaining good pupil discipline and open communications with parents are responsibilities not only of the building principal but also of the entire professional staff.

Classified personnel, which includes secretaries and custodians, perform tasks that free the professionals to concentrate on the instructional-learning process.

Implications for Future Teachers

School districts are very complex organizations that are not always understood by teachers. Knowing and understanding the nature of school district and school building administration, will make it easier for teachers as they address issues and problems. For example; if a teacher needs particular instructional materials which are not in the budget, the building principal might be able to remedy the situation. A telephone call from the teacher to the central office purchasing office will not usually be effective.

Further, when both teachers and administrators understand and appreciate each other's responsibilities, the atmosphere within a school can be positive, cooperative, and supportive. This in turn produces the milieu within which effective instruction and learning can take place.

Discussion Questions

1. What is the "mission" of local school districts?
2. Describe the competencies required of school administrators in our contemporary society.
3. Explain the concept "team management" as it relates to school district administration.
4. Explain the various degrees of "educational leadership."
5. Describe the role and function of the building principal.

Notes

1. Peter Drucker, "Quality Education: the New Growth Area," *The Wall Street Journal* (July 19, 1983),24.

2. American Association of School Administrators, *Guidelines for the Preparation of School Administrators* (Arlington, Va.: The Association, 1979), 3–10.

3. National School Public Relations Association, *Education USA* 22, no. 47 (July 21, 1980):347.

4. American Association of School Administrators, *Profiles of the Administrative Team* (Arlington, Va.: The Association, 1971), 11.

Recommended Readings

Johnson, James H., *Total Quality Management in Education.* Eugene, Oregon: Oregon School Study Council, 1993.

McLeod, Willis B., Brenda A. Spencer, and Leon T. Hairston, "Toward a System of Total Quality Management: Applying the Deming Approach to the Education Setting," *Spectrum: Journal of School Research and Information,* 10, no. 2 (Spring 1992), pp. 34–42, Arlington, Virgina.

Morphet, Edgar L., Roe L. Johns, and Theodore L. Reller. *Educational Organization and Administration: Concepts, Practices, and Issues.* 4th ed. Englewood Cliffs, NJ.: Prentice-Hall, 1982.

Parks, A. Lee. "RX for Managers: The Management Styles of Well-Run Businesses Can Be Applied by School Execs." *American School and University* (April 1985):33–35.

Rebore, Ronald W. *Educational Administration: A Management Approach.* Englewood Cliffs, NJ.: Prentice-Hall, 1985.

Robbins, Stephen P. *Organization Theory: The Structure and Design of Organizations.* Englewood Cliffs, N.J.: Prentice-Hall, 1983.

Sergiovanni, Thomas J., Martin Burlingame, Fred D. Coombs, and Paul W. Thurston. *Educational Governance and Administration.* Englewood Cliffs, N.J.: Prentice-Hall, 1980.

Chapter 12

The Financing
of Public Education

Local and State Financing of Public Education

Public schools have historically been financed through the levying of property taxes at the local level. In fact, many school districts receive over 50 percent of their revenue from the property tax. The states also share in the responsibility to finance education. The manner in which the states fulfill this obligation differs widely. However, for the most part, the states appropriate a portion of their "general revenue" to help finance the schools. General revenue is generated through consumption taxes and income taxes. Thus, state taxing systems usually do not earmark a certain tax for the support of education. This chapter will explain the taxing mechanisms used by boards of education and the states in carrying out their responsibility to provide a free education to all children and youth of our country. Further, this chapter will discuss (1) the role of the federal government in financing education and (2) the budgeting processes used by most school districts.

Major Types of Taxes

In general, taxes are levied either on the monetary flow derived from the production of goods and services in our economy or on the property assets of individuals and corporations. The most common types of taxes levied on the monetary flow derived from production are individual income taxes, corporation income taxes, and consumption taxes. Thus, the production of goods and services produces wages and profits which, in turn, are used to purchase household goods and market goods. Most states place the revenue collected from income and consumption taxes into their general revenue.

The tax on the property assets of individuals and corporations is considered a tax on wealth. Most states have statutes which give local school boards the authority to levy such a tax.[1]

Property Tax

Usage of the term "property tax" extends not only to taxes on real property but also to taxes on personal property. "Real property," of course, refers to land and buildings. "Personal property" refers either to tangible personal property (furniture, automobile, farm animals, and so on) or intangible personal property (stocks, bonds, and so on).

The primary source of revenue for local school districts is derived from a real property tax. This has been the situation from the very beginning of our free public school system. The real property tax is also commonly referred to as an *ad valorem* tax because it is levied on a percentage of the value of the property.

The tax levied on property is usually expressed in terms of "mills." A mill is a monetary unit equalling .001 of a dollar. Therefore, a tax rate of 500 mills equals 50 cents. This tax rate, however, being an *ad valorem* tax, is levied on only a percentage of the fair market value of the property. For example, the state of Missouri appraises all residential property at approximately 20 percent of its fair market value for the purpose of levying property taxes. Further, Missouri levies the property tax against this appraisal in units of $100. Therefore, if a certain house has a market value of $100,000, it would be appraised at $20,000 for tax purposes. This $20,000 is then divided by 100 units and multiplied by the tax rate. If the tax rate is 500 mills, this home owner would pay $100 in taxes.

The property tax continues to survive despite criticism that has been publicly voiced beginning with Adam Smith in his book *Wealth of Nations*. A contemporary criticism of the property tax centers on the issue of tax administration. There are inequities in many states in the procedures that are used not only in assessing property but also in collecting taxes. Reform in the administration of the property tax has occupied the attention of many state legislatures in recent years, but there is still a considerable number of abuses to be eradicated.

The property tax laws in most states require property to be assessed at a uniform percentage of full and fair market value. These same laws, however, often allow property assessors to be elected rather than appointed. This has two disparaging effects: First, political considerations might take precedence over accurate assessments; second, elected assessors may not have the proper training and background to arrive at fair property values. Another criticism of property tax systems results from the time span between reappraisal or reassessment in many states. Property values are constantly changing. If there is a significant period of years between reassessments, property values may significantly increase or decrease.

Because the property tax is the primary source of revenue supporting the education of children in most school districts in most states, the wealth of those districts will depend upon the assessed valuation of the property located within the boundaries of each district. Consequently, school districts with a great deal of commercial or industrial property will receive more revenue than those districts with big concentrations of residential property. Further, those districts with considerable residential property will probably be required to educate more children with less money than those districts with a large amount of commercial and industrial property.

Business and industry, of course, will pass on to the consumer the dollars paid to school districts in taxes. In the end, therefore, the consumer not only pays his residential property taxes but also the costs levied against business and industry. In this next section, it will also become clear that the consumer ultimately pays for that part of education financed through consumption taxes.

Consumption Taxes

Consumption taxes are levies placed upon either commodities or transactions which are paid by consumers for goods and services. The most common forms of consumption taxes are excise, sales, use, and gasoline. Of these four taxes, the sales tax produces the largest amount of state general revenue, a portion of which is used for education.

Consumption taxes are economical and convenient to collect. Further, consumption taxes provide an immediate cash flow to states and are a relatively stable source of revenue.

In recent years, the sales tax has been used by many states in their attempts to find new sources of revenue to finance the rising costs of government. Sales tax has been used in two major ways: First, as a tax on selected items such as gasoline or tobacco; second, as a general retail tax on all goods. The varied uses of the sales tax by the states defy classification but the tax has become a major source of revenue used to provide education.

The primary criticism of consumption taxes is their regressive nature or inequity. The sales tax, for example, absorbs a higher percentage of income from the poor than from the wealthy! The actual amount of money levied, however, is somewhat insignificant in terms of severely hindering anyone's buying power or lifestyle. Some states, however, have attempted to exempt low-income persons from some consumption taxes by providing for a credit against state income tax in the amount paid in relation to state averages. Other states provide a cash refund to those not liable to pay income taxes, while still others exempt food and medicines from sales tax.

Income Taxes

The federal government and all the states levy an income tax on individuals and corporations. These taxes account for the highest percentage of revenue from a single source to both the federal and state governments, supplying about 50 percent of budget receipts.

The income tax is a progressive tax because the more income a person or corporation earns, the more each will pay in taxes. All the income tax systems have percentage or incremental tax brackets that are used to calculate the amount of tax paid in relation to income. For example, a person earning $25,000 could pay ten percent of this income in state taxes, equalling $2,500. A person with an income of $50,000 might pay 20 percent of this amount in taxes, equalling $10,000. For a corporation, the basic method of determining taxable income is obtained by subtracting the costs of doing business from gross income to calculate net income. This net income is then subject to taxation. It should be kept in mind that income taxes constitute part of the general revenue for the federal government and the states. Congress and the state legislatures are responsible for determining what portion of this revenue will go to support education.

Constraints on Taxation

In recent years, a number of issues have arisen that have led to constraints on the scope of taxation. Proposition 13 symbolized the "taxpayers revolt." In California on June 6, 1978, an amendment to the state constitution was passed that limited local property tax rates and made it difficult for local governments to increase other taxes. The effect of Proposition 13 was a 23 percent reduction in governmental revenues. Many other states followed with similar legislation.

Every state has statutes which set forth a maximum tax rate that can be levied by school districts without voter approval. Similar legislation deals with improving property assessment ratios and granting tax exemptions. Exempting business and industry as a method of attracting them into a local area can be devastating to a school district.

Finally, "full disclosure laws" have served as a control on school districts. Under this type of law, if a school board wants to increase a tax rate, the board must advertise and hold a public hearing before the rate can be set. Education, therefore, has many constraints placed on its major sources of revenue both at the local and state levels.

Public Borrowing for Capital Projects[2]

Capital projects usually refers to building schools, furnishing schools, remodeling schools, replacing roofs, buying boilers, and purchasing large, expensive equipment such as school buses.

Capital projects have traditionally been financed through public borrowing for three reasons. First, such projects are usually nonrecurring expenditures that should not be financed with funds generated through the operating tax levy. The operating levy is meant for paying salaries, fringe benefits, utilities, routine maintenance, and other ongoing expenses. Secondly, the large dollar outlay for capital projects would seriously affect the monies available for continuing daily operations if the funding were taken from the operating levy. Finally, the burden for financing capital projects should be spread out over many generations because more than one generation will benefit from such capital projects.

Capital projects are financed through the sale of municipal bonds. School districts receive the authority to sell bonds through a bond issue election. Therefore, the citizens who are registered voters in a local school district are the sole authority for authorizing the financing of capital projects through the sale of bonds. Thus, a distinctive characteristic of public borrowing is its voluntary nature. If the citizens of a school district do not wish to bind themselves and future generations to paying taxes for the retirement of the district's bonded indebtedness, they simply vote no in the bond issue election.

Each state has statutes which carefully regulate bond issue elections and the sale of bonds that is known as the process of flotation.

Bonds are formal IOUs. When a bond issue is passed, the taxpayers in essence have said that the school board may sell bonds. The money received from this sale is used to pay for the capital project, such as building a school. By passing the bond issue, the taxpayers also have said to those who bought the bonds that they will pay back the money received plus interest until the entire debt is repaid. The money to pay back the debt plus interest is generated through a special tax usually known as a debt service or debt retirement levy.

The debt service levy may be five cents, seven cents, twenty-five cents, or whatever is needed to pay back the principal and interest for a given year. That amount may change depending on the schedule for the redemption of the bonds. Like the operating levy, the debt service levy is applied against the assessed valuation of the property in the school district.

State Grants-in-Aid

The various levels of federal and state government that collect taxes do not spend all the money they receive on managing their affairs. In fact, the principle underlying the concept of "grants-in-aid" makes the assumption that the federal and state governments will spend less than they receive while local governments will spend more. Thus, local school districts should receive grants-in-aid from their respective state governments. The manner in which this state aid is distributed to local school districts is the focus of this section.

Because education is a responsibility of state government, the allocation of grants-in-aid to local districts not only provides a method of fulfilling this obligation but also becomes a lever that the state can use in requiring districts to meet certain educational standards. More importantly, the state aid program should provide for the equalization of educational opportunity. This is partially accomplished by equalizing the financial resources of school districts. It is important for the state to ensure that a child's education does not depend on the wealth of the district in which he or she lives. This obligation of the state also requires recognition of the variation in per pupil costs associated with providing specialized education needed by some students. Thus, vocational education, agricultural education, education of the handicapped, and education of the gifted must be a consideration in the state aid program. Finally, the state must recognize the per pupil cost differential in local districts associated with such factors as density of population, which would result in a need for more pupil transportation in rural areas. In like manner, the higher cost of living in some metropolitan areas would affect teacher salaries in urban school districts. These are a few of the many variables that affect the equitable allocation of state funds to local school districts.

There are many models for allocating state grants-in-aid. No two states have exactly the same formula. Each year there is also a possibility that a given state legislature may alter its state aid formula.

In general, however, state allocation formulas may be divided into two broad categories: flat unit grants and equalization grants. Flat unit grants usually have either a uniform or variable characteristic. The uniform method allocates a certain amount per pupil, per teacher, or per some other unit. The variable method allocates a certain amount per some unit but allows for variation in need. For example, the allocation per pupil could be larger for high school students than for elementary school students because the costs of equipment, books, and supplies are greater in high school.

The equalization grant model provides for allocation of funds to local school districts in direct proportion to the local district's taxpaying ability. In other words, a wealthy school district should receive less per pupil, per teacher, or per some other unit than a poorer school district. Like flat grants, the per unit allocation could be uniform or variable. The most common equalization grant models are the Strayer-Haig-Mort Foundation Program, the percentage equalization program, and the district power-equalizing program.[3]

The Strayer-Haig-Mort Foundation Program has become the model in over half the states. Box 12-1 presents the state aid formula for Missouri. It is an excellent example of a model patterned after the Strayer-Haig-Mort Foundation approach. This Missouri formula is under review by both the judicial and legislative branches of government. The major concern is equalizing state aid without causing severe financial injury to those school districts which have received substantial state aid up to the present time. This is a phenomenon occurring in many states across the country.

Role of the Federal Government in Financing Public Education

The fact that education is a responsibility of each state has been discussed previously in this book. The federal government, however, has a long history of providing financial assistance to education. Although there is no accurate accounting of all the federal funds that have been expended for education, it is safe to estimate that almost every agency of the federal government has at one time or another expended monies for education.

BOX 12-1   State Aid Formula

Minimum Guarantee

1. (Number of eligible pupils) 1,050 × (75% of
   State Expenditure Factor) $1,517   = $1,592,850
2. (Aid to Dependent children + orphans)
   84 × .25 × (75% of State Expenditure Factor) $1,517   =   31,857
3. Minimum guarantee (line 1 plus line 2)   =   1,624,707

Deductions

4. Equalized Assessed Valuation
      Railroad and utilities = $30,000,000
     Assessed Valuation   = $13,000,000
     Total applicable
     Assessed Valuation   = $43,000,000 × (57% of State Expenditure Factor)
     (Pupil-weighted levy × income factor) ($1.45 × .9 = $1.305)   =   561,150
5. Intangible tax receipts (57% of school purposes)   =   11,500
6. Fines, forfeitures, and escheats (57% of school purposes)   =   13,200
7. Sales tax (57% of one-half of sales tax revenue)   =   119,700
8. Total deductions (sum of lines 4, 5, 6, and 7)   =   705,550
9. Basic entitlement (line 3 minus line 8)   =   919,157

Guaranteed Tax Base (GTB) Add-On

  [(GTB) $63,861 – (District applicable Assessed Valuation per pupil)
  $40,953]   =

10. (22,909 + 100 = $229.09) × [(District adjusted operating levy)
    $2.74 – (57% of pupil-weighted levy × income factor)
    ($1.45 × .9 = $1.305) = $328.744] × (number of
    eligible pupils) 1,050   =   345,181
11. District entitlement [line 9 plus line 10 × (Cost of Education 1.21)]   =   1,529,849
12. (Dist. entitlement per pupil $1,457 – (previous year's
    apportionment per pupil) $985.91   =   471.09
13. 25% of line 12 = $117.77 + $985.91 = $1,103.68 × (number of
    eligible pupils) 1,050   =   1,158,864
                                                             (limited apportionment)

Eligible pupils is determined by adding the average daily attendance (ADA) of resident pupils the preceding year to one-half of a two-count membership taken on the last Wednesday in September and January and dividing the sum by two:

$$\frac{\text{ADA} + \text{membership}}{2}$$

Districts may elect to use the number of eligible pupils for the last preceding year, the average number for the last three preceding years, or an estimate of the number for the current year.

Aid to dependent children is the number of children on the rolls of Aid to Dependent Children—ages 5 to 17 years—who are enrolled in the public schools, as certified by the State Division of Family Services, plus the number of orphan children enrolled in the public schools.

Continued

BOX 12-1 *Continued*

Equalized assessed valuation is determined by multiplying reported assessed valuation times .3333 and dividing the product by the effective ratio for the county.

Railroad and utilities state-assessed valuation for each district is determined by prorating the assessment according to the portion of September membership in the county in each district.

$$\frac{\text{District September membership}}{\text{September membership of county}} \times$$

(Valuation of state-assessed railroad and utilities properties) = district railroad and utilities assessed valuation.

Income factor is determined by dividing the district average adjusted gross income per return by the state average adjusted gross income per return—adding one to the result and dividing by two.

Sales tax revenue results from an increase of one percent in the statewide tax. This revenue is earmarked for distribution to the public school districts of the state.

State expenditure factor is determined by dividing the state total current expenditures for the second preceding year by the total number of eligible pupils in the state during that year.

Weighting factor applicable to ADC and orphan children eligible for consideration for state aid.

Pupil-weighted levy is determined by adding the product of the number of eligible pupils times the adjusted operating tax levy for the second preceding year for each district and dividing the aggregate total by the number of eligible pupils for the state.

District adjusted operating levy is determined by multiplying the sum of the teachers, incidental, and building funds rates by the effective ratio for the county and dividing the product by .3333.

Guaranteed tax base is the total equalized assessed valuation per pupil of the district containing a specified (90th) percentile of all pupils in the state from a ranking of districts of the state—ranked from low to high according to the total equalized assessed valuation per pupil.

Cost of education (C.O.E.) is a proportional relationship between a statistically predicted teacher's salary for each district and a statistically predicted teacher's salary for the state.

Source: Missouri Department of Elementary and Secondary Education, *State Aid Formula* (Jefferson City, Mo.: The Department, 1982). Used with permission.

The following are examples of federal assistance to education that documents the ongoing involvement of the federal government.

Land Grants Before our Constitution was adopted the Ordinance of 1785 declared, "There shall be reserved the lot number 16 of every township for the maintenance of public schools in each township." This policy was made operational by the Ordinance of 1787, which also contained wording that expresses— even today—the underlying purpose for much of federal financial aid: "Religion, morality and knowledge being necessary to good government and the happiness of mankind, schools and the means of education shall be forever encouraged."

Congress modified certain aspects of the land grant policy. However, it is significant that the land grants were instituted in the hope that the sale of this property would provide for most of the cost of public schools. Also, the federal government exercised no control over the public schools established through the sale of the granted land. In subsequent congressional acts, appropriations for public education would be granted for specific purposes and the federal government would exercise considerable control over how local school districts expended the funds. This had remained the policy down to the 1980s.

The Morrill Act   Enacted by Congress in 1862, this act granted 30,000 acres to each state for each senator and representative in Congress at that time. The land was sold and the proceeds were used for the "endowment, maintenance, and support of at least one college where the leading object shall be, without excluding other scientific and classical studies and including military tactics, to teach such branches of learning as are related to agriculture and the mechanic arts in such manner as the legislature of the states may respectively prescribe."

When the Morrill Act was passed, most colleges emphasized the classics and were not interested in preparing individuals for careers. Therefore, this act clearly demonstrated the federal government's interest in education, and it demonstrated that the government would take action if educational institutions were not providing effectively for the general welfare.

The Smith-Lever Act.   Enacted by Congress in 1914, it provided for extension services by county agricultural agents, 4-H leaders, and other specialists in agriculture and homemaking. The act also provided for home demonstration agents; this was a significant service because these agents brought families the latest developments in agriculture and family living. Finally, the Smith-Lever Act made funds available for the professional education of teachers in the areas of agriculture and homemaking.

The Smith-Hughes Act   In 1917 Congress enacted this act to provide funds for vocational education at the high school level. These vocational programs included agriculture, the trades, and homemaking. In addition, like the Smith-Lever Act, this act provided funds for the professional education of teachers in these fields. The Smith-Hughes Act called for matching funds by the states and local school districts receiving such aid. This matching fund provision adversely affected the developing of vocational education in less wealthy states and school districts.

The Smith-Hughes Act was modified, supplemented, and broadened by the following acts: the George-Reed Act, 1929; the George-Ellzey Act, 1935; the George-Deen Act, 1937; the George-Barden Act, 1946; the Vocational Education Act, 1963, and subsequent amendments to this act.

Veterans Training Programs   The first federal act for veterans was Public Law 178. It was passed in 1918 and provided vocational training for disabled veterans from World War I. Public Law 16 was passed in 1943 to provide similar training for disabled veterans from World War II.

Perhaps the most important congressional act providing education to veterans was Public Law 346, more commonly called the GI Bill of Rights. This act provided for the payment of reasonable allowances for books, tuition, and subsistence. It was very broad in application and gave veterans the opportunity to receive an education in almost every discipline. Veterans of the Korean War were allowed similar benefits by Public Law 550 passed in 1952; those serving in the armed forces during the cold war were provided benefits by Public Law 385 in 1966. Veterans serving after December 31, 1976, are assisted by Public Law 95-502. The benefits entitled by this act are substantially less than those of previous acts.

The National School Lunch Act, 1946   The federal government has been intricately involved in providing assistance to local districts for school lunches by this act, which was supplemented by a school milk program.

Public Laws 815 and 874   School districts providing an education to children whose parents or guardians work on federal installations may receive funds for the construction, maintenance, and operation of school facilities under these acts passed in 1950.

The National Defense Education Act   This act was passed in 1958 as a reaction to the launching of the first manmade satellite, Sputnik, by the Russians. Many citizens blamed the public schools for not keeping pace with world technology in the teaching of mathematics and the sciences. Congress viewed the situation from a broader perspective and enacted legislation that provided funds for the following:

1. Loans for college tuition
2. Equipment and the remodeling of facilities used to teach mathematics, science, and foreign language
3. Guidance and testing services to identify and encourage students to study mathematics, science, and languages
4. Development of area vocational programs
5. Research in the use of audiovisual media in teaching

Manpower Development and Training Act   The advances of technology had made the skills of some workers obsolete. Congress passed this act in 1962 to retrain these workers, and it also provided funds for the testing and selection of 16-year-old students who received occupational training under this same act. In 1966, the act was amended to include services for persons forty-five years of age and older.

The Elementary and Secondary Education Act   This has been, to date, the most important congressional act affecting education in this country. Passed in 1965, the purpose of this act was to strengthen education by providing financial assistance for programs under the following five broad categories:

Title I—assistance for educational programs designed to help children from families with low incomes

Title II—funds for libraries, textbooks, and audiovisual equipment and materials

Title III—funds for supplementary education to children in both public and private schools

Title IV—funds for regional educational research and training laboratories

Title V—funds for the strengthening of state departments of education

Public Law 94-142 Enacted by Congress in 1975, this act provides grants to states for the establishment and development of programs for children with disabilities from preschool through secondary school. In 1990 it was revised (see p. 56).

Refugee Act Congress enacted this act in 1980; it provides grants for special programs in bilingual education, English as a second language, or intensive English instruction for refugee children. In addition, this act provides funds for special tutoring programs in the basic skills of reading, language arts, and mathematics.

Education Consolidation and Improvement Act The purpose of this act was to streamline the administration of federal programs and to give the states greater flexibility and autonomy in handling federal funds. Many individual programs were folded into block grants. This act was passed in 1981 and has two major components, Chapter one and two. Chapter one provides funds to local school districts to implement special and supplemental instruction to students with low achievement records, living in attendance areas with a high concentration of low-income families. The programs are limited to remedial instruction of the basic skills of reading, language arts, and mathematics. These programs may function during the regular academic year, during the summer, or both.

Chapter two, the block grant, provides funds to be used at the discretion of the local school district for approximately forty program purposes that were outlined in the antecedent legislation. For example, the funds may be used for the following:

1. The improvement of instruction in the basic skills
2. Professional staff development
3. Curriculum development
4. The acquisition of school learning resources and instructional equipment
5. Guidance counseling and testing programs
6. Programs for gifted students
7. Programs for early childhood and parent education
8. Programs to reduce racial isolation

This act ushered in a significant change in the federal government's public policy toward education. It is reminiscent of the land grants in the sense that the federal government exercises minimal control over the block grants and the funds are provided for a broad range of purposes.

Omnibus Education Act   Congress approved an $8.3 billion re-authorization bill of federal aid to elementary and secondary schools in 1988. This legislation retained both the compensatory and block grant programs initially passed in 1981, with few modifications. Thus, the following have been re-authorized: Compensatory Education (Chapter one), Block Grants (Chapter two), Mathematics and Science Grants, Satellite Technology Grants, Magnet Schools Grants, Drug Education Grants, and Special Programs.

The Federal Budget and Education

The U.S. Congress has allocated approximately two percent of annual budget expenditures for education during the 1980s. This accounts for approximately eight percent of the states' and local school districts' budgets.[4] Constructing the U.S. budget is a political process that is significantly influenced by the philosophy of the current administration. Even a neophyte in politics can appreciate the difference among the Carter, Reagan, and Clinton administrations in their respective policies toward education.

In recent years there has been a great deal of interest in reforming education. The funding of reform, however, has been left to the states for the most part. Federal funding has decreased as much as $1 billion annually from previous eras. This situation could change with subsequent administrations. The only certitude is that the federal funding of education will continue to be organic in nature, changing in kind and amount from time to time.

School District Financial Management[5]

The financial management of school districts includes many interrelated functions, which ultimately demonstrate that the revenue and expenditures of the district support the best educational program possible, given the fiscal resources available.

The major components of financial management include: (1) budgeting procedures; (2) financial-accounting procedures; (3) purchasing, warehousing, and distribution procedures; (4) investing procedures; and (5) auditing procedures. This chapter will address only budgeting procedures because teachers will be involved in such procedures; the others are strictly administrative responsibilities.

The school district's budget is a plan for delivering the educational program and for projecting the district's revenues and expenditures that will support this program. The last twenty years have seen many management innovations that addressed the budget construction process, including Program Planning Budgeting System (PPBS), Zero Based Budgeting, and Performance Budgeting. These and many other approaches to budgeting seek a process to serve as a useful management tool while providing the school board with a method for prioritizing needs. No system of budgeting will satisfy all the needs of a school district. Modifications, therefore, will be introduced that address the particular character of each school district.

There are four basic steps to an effective budgeting process. First, the budget is not an entity unto itself but rather a vehicle for accomplishing a purpose. The purpose of a school district is to educate children. This purpose is further refined by establishing goals and objectives. The board of education is responsible for setting these goals after receiving input from teachers, administrators, parents, students, and other school district patrons.

Second, these goals and objectives should be translated into a curriculum and, finally, set forth in terms of educational requirements. The professional staff under the direction of the superintendent of schools can then begin the process of attaching dollar amounts to educational requirements. For example, a school board may believe that a secondary school remedial reading program is needed. The superintendent, along with the building principals, teachers, and other central office administrators, will perform an assessment of needs to identify the number of secondary school children who require remedial reading. The superintendent and staff should then proceed to calculate the personnel, supplies, material, and other costs needed to introduce this program effectively.

Third, the business manager will make a revenue projection, which will be combined into a budgetary document that presents the proposed expenditures to make the goals of the school district operational.

Finally, the board of education must approve the budget. The school board can certainly challenge the budget submitted by the superintendent before approving it. In fact, the school board may wish to make changes in the expenditures, based upon the board's perception of the district's needs.

The actual budget document may take various forms but should include the following:

1. A budget message by the superintendent describing the important features of the budget and major changes from last year's budget
2. Projected revenue from all local, state, and federal sources, with a comparison of revenue for the last two years listed by fund and source
3. Proposed expenditures for each program, with a comparison of expenditures from the last two years listed by fund, object, and function
4. The amount needed to pay the principal and interest for the redemption of the school district's bonds maturing during the fiscal year
5. A budget summary

Box 12-2 demonstrates program goals established by a school district. Figure 12-1 illustrates how programs are broken down to identify total costs.

BOX 12-2   Statement of Goals for a School District Budget

Foreign Language Program for Elementary and Middle-School Students

To work with each child to help him learn the basic intellectual skills of linguistic flexibility in thought and tongue through a foreign language. To develop fluency in a foreign language to such a degree that an eighth-grade student could visit a foreign country and understand and converse with a native speaker on an elementary level, partially comprehend a publication in that language, and make himself understood in writing and language.

Objective Statement and Evaluative Criteria

At the end of eighth grade: That 75 percent of the students should be able to communicate in the language of instruction at an elementary level with a native speaker of that language as evaluated by the teacher.

That 50 percent of the students should be able to read a magazine or newspaper article in the language of instruction and state in that language a brief summary of an article as measured by the teacher. That 80 percent of the students should be able to easily write a dictation exercise in Spanish or French based on

previously studied material from the text based on a teacher-prepared dictation test.

That 75 percent of the students will give a five-minute oral report in the language of instruction on a topic of the student's choice to the teacher's satisfaction. That 70 percent of the students will pass the vocabulary test provided in the text with 85 percent accuracy.

Program Description

The foreign language program covers the four years of fifth, sixth, seventh, and eighth grades in the subjects of Spanish and French. There are six teachers in the program, three in each subject. The fifth- and sixth-grade students receive 150 minutes of instruction weekly; the seventh-grade students receive 135 minutes of instruction weekly, and the eighth-grade students receive 110 minutes of instruction weekly. Instruction is provided in a classroom environment using textbooks, and includes both written and oral work. Teachers may use other instructional materials such as songs, plays, magazines, newspapers, flashcards, etc. A language laboratory is available containing records, tape recorders, and filmstrips.

Source: National School Public Relations Association, *PPBS and the School: New System Promotes Efficiency, Accountability* (Arlington, Va.: The Association, 1972), p. 21. Used with permission.

Summary

Public schools are financed primarily through the levying of property taxes at the local level. The states also share in the responsibility to finance education. The states fulfill this responsibility by appropriating a portion of their general revenue to assist local school districts. General revenue is generated through consumption taxes and income taxes.

In general, taxes are levied either on the monetary flow derived from the production of goods and services in our economy or on the property assets of individuals and corporations.

The term "property tax" extends not only to taxes on real property but also to taxes on personal property. Real property, of course, refers to land and build-

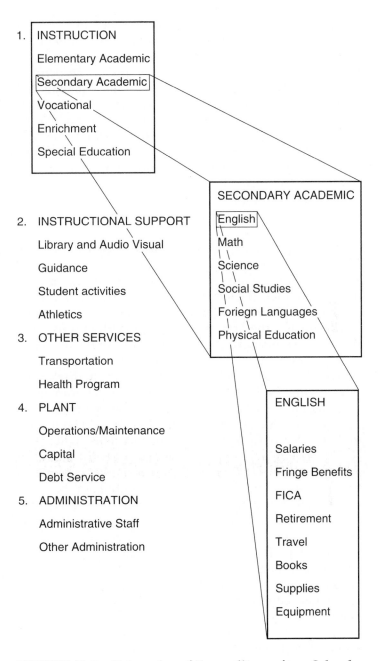

**FIGURE 12-1   Categories of Expenditures for a School
District Budget**

Source: National School Public Relations Association, *PPBS and the School:
New System Promotes Efficiency, Accountability.* Arlington, Va.: The
Association, 1972. Used with permission.

ings. Personal property refers either to tangible personal property (furniture, automobiles, farm animals, and so on) or intangible personal property (stocks, bonds, and so on). The primary source of revenue for local school districts is derived from a real property tax. The tax on property is usually expressed in terms of "mills," which is a monetary unit equaling .001 of a dollar. The real property tax is levied on only a percentage of the fair market value of property. The property tax has survived despite criticism which has been continually voiced, beginning with Adam Smith in his book *Wealth of Nations*. The contemporary criticism of the property tax centers on the issue of tax administration. There are inequities in many states in the procedures that are used not only in assessing property but also in collecting taxes.

The most common types of taxes levied on the monetary flow derived from production are individual income taxes, corporation income taxes, and consumption taxes.

Consumption taxes are levies placed upon commodities or transactions that are paid by consumers for goods and services. The most common forms of consumption taxes are excise, sales, use, and gasoline. Of these four taxes, the sales tax produces the largest amount of state general revenue, a portion of which is used for education. Consumption taxes are economical and convenient to collect. Further, they provide the states with immediate cash flow and are relatively stable. The major criticism of consumption taxes is their regressive nature.

The federal government and all the states levy an income tax on individuals and corporations. These taxes account for the highest percentage of revenue from a single source to both the federal and state governments.

In recent years, a number of issues have arisen that have subsequently led to constraints on the scope of taxation. The most significant constraints limit local property tax rates and place rigid requirements on the process of increasing taxes.

Capital projects refers to building, furnishing, and remodeling schools, replacing roofs, buying boilers, and purchasing large, expensive equipment such as school buses. Capital projects have traditionally been financed through public borrowing because these types of projects are nonrecurring, because they would seriously affect the operating funds, and because the burden for financing these projects should be spread out over future generations that will benefit from them.

Capital projects are financed through the sale of municipal bonds when authorized through a bond issue election. The district pays back the principal and interest on each bond with monies generated by a debt service levy.

Because education is a responsibility of state government, the allocation of grants-in-aid to local districts not only provides a method of fulfilling this obligation but also becomes a lever that the state can use in requiring districts to meet certain educational standards. More importantly, the state aid program must provide for the equalization of educational opportunity. This is partially accomplished by equalizing the financial resources of school districts. It is important for the state to ensure that a child's education does not depend on the wealth of the district in which he or she lives. There are many variables that affect the equalization of educational opportunity, including the special educational needs of students and the geographical location of individual districts.

There are many models for allocating state grants-in-aid. In general, state aid formulas may be divided into two broad categories: flat unit grants and equalization grants. Flat grants and equalization grants usually have either a uniform or variable characteristic. The most common equalization grant models are the Strayer-Haig-Mort Foundation Program, the percentage equalization program, and the district power-equalizing program.

The federal government has a long history of providing financial assistance to education. The following are examples of federal assistance: Land Grants, 1785 and 1787; Morrill Act, 1862; Smith-Lever Act, 1914; Smith-Hughes Act, 1917; Veterans Training Program Acts, 1918, 1943, 1952, 1966, 1976; National School Lunch Act, 1946; Public Law 815 and 874, 1950; National Defense Education Act, 1958; Manpower Development and Training Act, 1962; Public Law 94-142, 1975; Refugee Act, 1980; Education Consolidation and Improvement Act, 1981; and the Omnibus Education Act, 1988.

The U.S. Congress had allocated approximately two percent of annual budget expenditures for education during the 1980s. This accounted for approximately eight percent of states' and local school districts' budgets.

The financial management of school districts includes many interrelated functions which ultimately demonstrate that the revenue and expenditures of the district support the best educational program possible, given the fiscal resources available. The major components of financial management include budgeting procedures; financial-accounting procedures; purchasing, warehousing, and distribution procedures; investing procedures; and auditing procedures. The school district's budget is a plan for delivering the educational program and for projecting the revenue and expenditures that support it.

Implications for Future Teachers

Teachers must gain a working knowledge of not only how public education is financed, but also how their local school districts budget. Without this knowledge, teachers will be unable to answer the questions of parents about financial resources that underpin the teaching/learning process. Teachers also are the ambassadors, not only of education in general, but also of their school district. The more informed they are, the better they will represent their profession.

Discussion Questions

1. What is meant by the term "property tax"? How do local school districts derive revenue from this tax?
2. What are the major sources of revenue that a state receives?

3. Identify a few models that a state might use in allocating funds to local school districts.
4. What is the purpose of state grants-in-aid?
5. What is the purpose of the two most recent U.S. congressional acts providing funding to education?
6. Identify the interrelated functions that comprise the financial management of school districts.

Notes

1. Roe L. Johns, Edgar L. Morphet, and Kern Alexander, *The Economics and Financing of Education*, 4th ed. (Englewood Cliffs, NJ.: Prentice-Hall, 1983). 94–95.
2. Ronald W. Rebore, *Educational Administration: A Management Approach* (Englewood Cliffs, N.J.: Prentice-Hall, 1985), 116–19.
3. Johns, Morphet, and Alexander, *The Economics and Financing of Education*, 242–43.
4. National Education Association, *The Federal Education Budget* (Washington, D.C.: The Association, 1982), 13.
5. Rebore, *Educational Administration*, 141–42.

Recommended Readings

Break, George F. *Financing Government in a Federal System.* Washington, D.C.: Brookings Institution, 1980.

Guthrie, James, ed. *School Finance Policies and Practices.* Cambridge, Mass.: Ballinger Publishing Co., 1980.

Johns, Roe L., Edgar L. Morphet, and Kern Alexander. *The Economics and Financing of Education.* 4th ed. Englewood Cliffs, N.J.: Prentice-Hall, 1983.

Morphet, Edgar L., Roe L. Johns, and Theodore L. Reller. *Educational Organization and Administration: Concepts, Practices, and Issues.* 4th ed. Englewood Cliffs, N.J.: Prentice-Hall, 1982.

Rebore, Ronald W. *Educational Administration: A Management Approach.* Englewood Cliffs, N.J.: Prentice-Hall, 1985.

U.S. Department of Education. *Catalogue of Federal Education Assistance Programs—1985* (published annually). Washington, D.C.: Government Printing Office, 1985.

Chapter 13

Selection, Placement, and Induction

Selection

The objective of the selection process in school districts is to hire individuals who will be successful administrators, teachers, and other employees.[1] Although this purpose may appear self-evident, its implementation requires a thorough process. The cost of selecting employees is a major expenditure for most school districts. If the process does not produce effective employees, the cost to the district is often incalculable because of inadequate performance.

The minimum cost to hire any new employee has been calculated at $1,000. This cost includes advertising the position; printing and mailing applications; and the personnel time required to review applications, interview candidates, and check references. This presupposes that many routine tasks, such as writing job descriptions and establishing proper selection criteria, have already been accomplished. Training and orientating new employees is an additional cost directly related to the hiring process. Therefore, selecting individuals who will be successful and will remain with the school district for a reasonable period of time is an extremely important personnel process, significant not only because it fulfills the district's mandate to educate children but also because it affects the financial condition of the school district.

Selection takes place by a process which will minimize the chances of hiring individuals who are inadequate performers. Box 13-1 illustrates common aspects of the selection process.

BOX 13-1   The Selection Process

1. Write the job description.
2. Establish the selection criteria.
3. Advertise the vacancy.
4. Receive applications.
5. Select candidates to be interviewed.

6. Interview candidates.
7. Check references and credentials.
8. Select the best candidate.
9. Implement the job offer and acceptance.
10. Notify unsuccessful candidates.

Aspects of the Selection Process

The Job Description

A written job description is the end product of a process that is commonly referred to as "job analysis." This process gathers information about the position: what an employee does; why he or she performs certain tasks; how he or she does the job; what skills, education, or training are required to perform the job; the relationship the job has to other jobs; and what physical demands and environmental conditions affect the job. This information is also relevant to providing human resource planning, to creating job evaluation instruments, and to determining compensation programs.[2]

The job analysis is the vehicle for obtaining the necessary data to write a job description. The job description is an outline providing specific details concerning a job and the minimum qualifications necessary to perform it successfully.

No one format for writing a job description is universally acclaimed as most effective in each and every circumstance. However, certain elements are common to most job descriptions. These include the title of the job, duties that must be performed, the authority and responsibilities accompanying the job, and specific qualifications necessary for successful performance of the job.

Box 13-2 is a job description for a high school biology teaching position. This description begins with a summary of the job that outlines the overall responsibilities of the position. This is followed by a detailed explanation of specific job tasks and the relationship of the job to other positions in the school district. Finally, minimum qualifications for the position are listed.

The Selection Criteria

The second step in the selection process is establishing the criteria against which the candidates will be evaluated to determine who will be offered the job. Selection criteria are very different from the job description because the selection criteria delineate those ideal characteristics that, if possessed by an individual to the fullest extent possible, would ensure successful performance. Obviously, no one person will possess all the characteristics to the fullest extent, and not all characteristics have equal importance in determining who is the best candidate.

BOX 13-2   Job Description for a High School Biology Teacher

Job Summary

The high school biology teacher is responsible for teaching five periods of Biology I per school day with one noninstructional period for planning, grading papers, and individual conferences with parents and students. Teaching biology includes following the general curricular program established by the science department and approved by the building principal. The biology teacher accepts responsibility for the academic success of students when he or she is given reasonable control over those factors that contribute to such outcomes. He or she is responsible directly to the building principal.

Instructional Tasks

The high school biology teacher is responsible for promoting an effective instructional program in the classroom. This can be accomplished by evaluating the strengths and weaknesses of the curricular program and instructional materials; helping develop, implement, and evaluate new ideas, methods, and techniques for teaching biology; assisting in departmental budget preparation to insure the appropriateness of instructional supplies; recognizing that each student is an individual with different needs and abilities; utilizing a variety of instructional techniques; serving on

textbook committees; maintaining effective discipline and high academic standards; accepting constructive criticism; and recognizing the need for continuous self-evaluation.

General Professional Duties

In addition to specific instructional tasks, the high school biology teacher is also expected to maintain professional standards, including: keeping up-to-date in the subject area; serving on committees to advise on such nonacademic affairs as school discipline, honors awards, assemblies, etc.; serving on science curriculum committees; advising guidance personnel on matters relating to the science program; showing concern for the totality of the science program; and participating in local and national science and civic associations.

Job Qualifications

The high school biology teacher should possess the following minimum educational requirements:

A bachelor's degree with a major or minor in biological science

A State Secondary School Teaching Certificate with certification in high school biology.

Source: Ronald W. Rebore, *Personnel Administration in Education: A Management Approach,* 2nd ed. (Englewood Cliffs, N.J.: Prentice-Hall, 1987), p. 112. Used with permission.

The use of selection criteria is also a method of quantifying the expert opinion of those who will be interviewing candidates. Without criteria, each interviewer is left to his or her own discretion to determine if an individual will be able to perform the job.

Quantifying the opinions of interviewers also provides data to show that the best candidate was offered the position, thus demonstrating that the school district is an affirmative action and equal opportunity employer. The candidate with the highest score should be offered the position first; if he does not accept, then the candidate receiving the next highest score should be offered the position, and so on.

Appendix C on page 383 presents a sample of two selection criteria, one set for a high school English teacher and a second for an elementary school teacher. Each criteria instrument has been constructed so that particular characteristics may be rated and a final score obtained. The significant difference between the first instrument and the second is the weighting component on the second instrument. The compatibility of an applicant's educational philosophy with the school district's policies and curriculum is of primary importance, as indicated by the second instrument. Professional preparation is second, personal characteristics third, and experience the least important. The assumption underlying the second selection instrument is that an individual will best meet the needs of the school district if he or she has the proper attitude and philosophy. Experience will enrich an individual's performance, but one's philosophy is necessary to direct the benefits obtained by the experience. In like manner, an individual will grow in the job if his or her educational values are in harmony with those of the school district.

This method of evaluating candidates places responsibility on the interviewers to make a discriminatory judgment concerning the qualifications of each candidate. The interview itself is not the only source of information used to make a decision. The application, placement papers, transcripts, and letters of reference are also used by interviewers in determining an individual's qualifications for the job.

The Job Vacancy Announcement

The advertisement is an integral part of the selection process. It is based on the job description and should provide potential candidates sufficient information to make a decision on whether or not to apply for the position. Consequently, an advertisement must clearly identify the job title, major responsibilities of the job, the name and location of the school district, how to apply for the job, and the minimum qualifications for an applicant. It is common practice to allow at least a two-week period for receiving applications for teaching jobs.

Receiving Applications

A central office staff member, usually a secretary, is assigned to receive all the applications for a given job vacancy. As the applications come in, they are dated and placed in a designated file folder. This provides integrity to the process and establishes a method to monitor the progress toward filling the vacancy.

Many applicants will immediately have placement papers, transcripts, and letters of reference sent to the school district. These documents are also dated and attached to the appropriate applications.

After the deadline for receiving applications has been reached, a master list is compiled, with the names, addresses, and telephone numbers of those who have applied. The master list also includes by title the other documents that have been received in support of the applications, such as transcripts and letters of reference. The entire folder of applications, support documents, and the master list can then be assigned and given to a personnel administrator, who will perform the initial screening of the applications.

The master list of applicants should also be given to the administrator responsible for monitoring the affirmative action program. This person sends a letter to all those who have applied, asking them to identify if they belong to one or more minority groups listed on an enclosed form and to mail the form back to the school district. Because the purpose of the selection process is to hire the best candidate, this letter should state that filling out the form will have no bearing on who is hired for the position.

Selecting the Candidates to Be Interviewed

Screening the applicants is the next step in the selection process. The number of applicants to be interviewed will depend on the number of people who apply and on the nature of the position to be filled. If only five individuals apply for a vacancy and if each person meets the minimum qualifications, all five can be interviewed. This, of course, is not the norm except for those few job classifications where there is a shortage of qualified individuals, such as in the field of industrial arts. On the average, between five and ten applicants are selected to be interviewed for most teaching positions.

Interviewing the Candidates

Interviewing candidates is a shared responsibility between the personnel department and other school district staff members. The individuals who participate in the interviewing process are determined by the position to be filled. The supervisor of the new employee, along with those who have expert knowledge about the duties to be performed by the successful candidate, will usually interview the candidates. For example, candidates for a high school biology teaching position may be interviewed by the high school principal, the chairperson of the biology department, a biology teacher, a personnel administrator, and the assistant superintendent for secondary education.

Definition of an Interview   Essentially, an interview is a conversation between two individuals set up to generate information about the person being interviewed or other matters that are familiar to the respondent.[3] However, there are four characteristics of an interview that distinguish it from an ordinary conversation. First, an interview is a structured conversation with form and direction; it has a beginning, middle, and conclusion. Second, the interview is conducted by an individual who is prepared to move it in a direction dictated by the occasion. Third, both parties to the interview understand its purpose, which can only be accomplished through cooperation. Finally, the nature of the interview is clearly defined and specified.[4]

Types of Interviews   There are two basic types of interviews, the standardized interview and the open interview. The standardized interview follows a set of questions or procedures established to help ensure that the responses of the candidates can be readily compared. It is most effective in the initial interviewing of all candidates.

The open interview encourages the candidate to talk freely and at length about topics directed by the interviewer to suit the occasion. It is very helpful in the follow-up session with finalists for the job.[5]

In both types of interviews, the objectives are basically the same. The interviewer is attempting to gather facts from the respondent; to learn about the respondent's opinions, beliefs, and attitudes; and to experience the respondent as an individual.[6]

The Role of the Interviewer   The interviewer has an extremely important function. Not only does he or she direct the interview by asking questions, but he or she must also record the respondent's answers and give the respondent a favorable image of the school district. Through the interview process, the interviewer must evaluate and come to a conclusion about the suitability of each candidate. The selection criteria will quantify the observations of the interviewer, but, ultimately, the observations are subjective interpretations.

All interviews are more effective if they are conducted in a pleasant environment. This helps to put the candidate at ease and will facilitate the kind of exchange that gives the interviewer the most information about each candidate. Thus, the interviewer may use a room that allows the interview to be conducted without interruptions and may arrange the room in order to have eye contact with the candidate.

Legal Implications of Interviewing   Federal legislation and court decisions have had a significant impact on the types of questions that may be legally asked in an interview. For example, it was once common practice to ask a candidate if he or she had ever been arrested or spent time in jail. Because of a court case, *Gregory* v. *Litton Systems, Inc.*, school districts are now permitted to ask only about a candidate's record of criminal convictions.[7]

Below are a few of the more common enquiries that have legal implications:

1. *Marital and family status.* Questions to determine if a man or woman can meet specific work schedules are lawful; enquiries about being married, single, divorced, and so on, are unlawful.
2. *Race.* To request information about distinguishing physical characteristics is legal; to ask the color of the applicant's skin, eyes, and so on, is illegal if this directly or indirectly indicates race or color.
3. *Religion.* All inquiries are illegal.

4. *Sex.* Enquiries about or restrictions regarding sex are permissible only where a bona fide occupational qualification exists.
5. *Ethnic Background.* It is legal to ask which languages the applicant reads, writes, or speaks fluently; enquiries about the applicant's national origin are illegal.
6. *Credit Rating.* All questions about charge accounts or credit rating are unlawful.
7. *Name.* It is lawful to enquire whether an applicant has worked under a different name or nickname in order to verify work or educational records; it is unlawful to ask questions in an attempt to discover the applicant's ancestry, lineage, or national origin.
8. *Occupational Preference.* It is lawful to ask why an applicant wants to work for a particular company or institution; asking what kind of supervisor the applicant prefers is unlawful.
9. *Lifestyle.* Asking about future career plans is lawful; asking an applicant whether he or she drinks or takes drugs is also lawful.[8]

The Art of Questioning   The success of the entire interviewing process rests on the interviewer's skill in asking questions. It is a skill that is acquired through experience. However, a well-planned interview with a preestablished set of questions can be extremely useful to even the most experienced interviewer, and it is a necessity in the standardized interview. Appendix D on page 387 lists sample questions that are used in many interviews.

Group Interviewing   Some school districts prefer group interviewing, in which a number of staff members interview a candidate at the same time. Group interviewing can be very effective, and it certainly cuts down on the amount of time spent in this process. However, to be effective, one staff member usually serves as the group leader and takes responsibility for directing the interview.

Checking Credentials and References

A candidate's "credentials" include such items as a college or university transcript, a teaching certification or license, and a physician's verification of health. Transcripts and health verifications are usually not accepted if they are presented to the personnel department by the applicant; rather, they should be mailed directly to the school district by the respective college or university and physician.

It is common practice to request a health verification from a candidate only if he is chosen for the position. A contract or formal employment is usually not initiated until the health verification has been received in the personnel department. Letters of reference should be mailed directly to the personnel department and should include the applicant's current or last immediate supervisor.

Hiring a person who has a criminal record is a risk that has created concern for school districts across the country. School districts staff members and board members have become more aware of this possibility, because of recent news media notoriety given to educators previously convicted of child molestation.

Criminal background investigations are time-consuming, expensive, and also controversial. The National Education Association opposes fingerprinting as a condition of employment. Conducting the investigation and the extent of the investigation is dependent on school district policy, state statutes, and the discretion of the interviewing personnel administrator.[9]

The extent of an investigation is limited in most school districts to checking with local and state police to ascertain if the potential employee has been convicted of a crime. It is also possible to check with the Teacher Identification Clearinghouse (maintained by the National Association of State Directors of Teacher Education and Certification), a nation-wide clearinghouse with a database of all teachers denied certification, and whose certification has been revoked or suspended for moral reasons. The data are available only to states that have joined the clearinghouse. Individual school districts can neither join the Clearinghouse nor directly obtain information from it.

A school district wishing to check the fingerprints of an applicant against the files of the FBI can do so only if the state in which the school district is located has passed legislation authorizing this type of investigation. Further, the request must be processed by a law enforcement agency (such as the state police), that acts as the conduit through which the information is channeled to the school district.[10]

Selecting the Best Candidate

The personnel administrator responsible for implementing the selection process for a particular vacancy will organize all relevant data in such a manner that a choice may be made by the superintendent of schools. These data include the rank by scores on the selection criteria of those candidates who were interviewed by the staff, verified credentials and reference letters, and the application forms. The superintendent then selects the candidate who appears best qualified.

Implementing the Job Offer and Acceptance

The superintendent of schools may wish to interview the candidate he or she selects for the position or may wish to interview the top two, three, or five candidates before he or she makes a final choice. When the final decision has been made, the selected candidate will be formally offered the job. If this individual accepts the offer, a contract must be approved by the board of education and signed by the finalist.

Notifying the Unsuccessful Candidates

The final step in the selection process is to notify all applicants that the position has been filled. This is only initiated after the offer of employment has been accepted by the selected candidate, since there may be a need to offer the position to another candidate if the first refuses the offer.

The Employment Application Form

The first formal task in applying for a position is, of course, to fill out an application form, often a tedious activity enjoyed by few people. Two major reasons why most people dislike these forms is because some require information that seems irrelevant and some allot too little space for the requested information.

Appendix E on page 389 provides an example of a teaching application form that incorporates many elements commonly found on applications. The basic principle in constructing application forms is "Only ask for information you need to know!" Most information requested on applications falls under one of the following headings: personal data, education and/or professional preparation, experience, and references. Box 13-3 lists inappropriate questions for an application form because they are irrelevant or because they are illegal under civil rights and labor legislation.

Placement

The last phase in procuring a new employee for a school district is placing that individual in an assignment and orientating him or her to the school community.

BOX 13-3   Inappropriate Information Asked on Some Application Forms

Maiden name

Marital status

Name of spouse

Occupation of spouse

Number and age of children

Physical handicaps

Arrest record ("convictions" is appropriate)

Height and weight (unless these are bona fide occupational qualifications)

If applicant owns a home or rents

If applicant has relatives employed by the school district (A policy against hiring relatives of present employees is questionable.)

If the applicant has an automobile and a driver's license (unless this is a bona fide occupational qualification)

Where the applicant attended elementary and high school (Irrelevant on professional applications)

Religion

National origin

Race

Source: Ronald W. Rebore, *Personnel Administration in Education: A Management Approach,* 2nd ed. (Englewood Cliffs, N.J.: Prentice-Hall, 1987), p. 108. Used with permission.

Both aspects are interrelated; both are also continual processes because some staff members may be reassigned each year and will require a certain amount of induction. Placement and induction, therefore, should not be viewed as a one-time task but rather as an ongoing process.

Placement Policy

The following sample placement policy specifies how placement will be handled by a typical school district.

> *The placement of employees within the school system is the responsibility of the superintendent of schools. The superintendent may delegate the implementation to other appropriate administrators, but he or she retains ultimate jurisdiction over this task. In determining assignments, the wishes of the employee are taken into consideration if these do not conflict with the requirements of the district's programming, staff balancing, and the welfare of students. Other factors that will be taken into consideration in making assignments are educational preparation and training, certification, experience, working relationships, and seniority in the school system.*
>
> *A staffing survey form will be secured from each employee annually in February to assist in making assignment plans for the forthcoming school year.*
>
> *Professional staffing assignments will be announced by April 1. Teachers affected by a change in grade or subject assignments will be notified by their respective building principals. Teachers affected by a building transfer will be notified by an administrator from the personnel department.*[11]

This board of education placement policy clearly specifies the role of the superintendent in assigning all staff members to particular positions within the school system. The planning required in making assignments is very complicated, demanding the full attention of at least one personnel administrator in most school districts. Of course, it is to the school district's advantage to make assignments that are in harmony with the wishes of the employees. A significant cause of low morale among teachers is the assigning of individuals to schools, grade levels, and subject areas they find undesirable. The staffing survey is one method used by many districts in making assignments. (See Box 13-4.)

There are a number of variables to consider in trying to fulfill the wishes of employees in making reassignments due to maternity leave, resignations, retirements, deaths, or terminations. The most significant variables include staff balancing due to affirmative action requirements, the certification of professional employees, experience in an assignment, and working relationships.

For example, a teacher who is having difficulty accepting a certain principal's philosophy about how to handle children with behavioral problems might request reassignment to another school. The personnel department will determine if another position requiring the certification qualifications of that teacher is or

---

BOX 13-4   Staffing Survey

Name _____

Present job position assignment _____

Present building assignment _____

I wish to be considered for reassignment as follows:

Requested job position assignment _____

Requested building assignment _____

I understand that reassignment requests will be reviewed but are not guaranteed and that all decisions will be based on seniority, availability, and the best interest of the school district.

Signature _____

Source: Ronald W. Rebore, *Personnel Administration in Education: A Management Approach,* 2nd ed. (Englewood Cliffs, N.J.: Prentice-Hall, 1987), p. 130. Used with permission.

will become available. Furthermore, an analysis must be made to determine if such a reassignment would upset the balance in either school between experienced and inexperienced teachers, male and female teachers, and minority representation.

The welfare of students and implementation of the school district's instructional program are other primary considerations in making assignments. An industrial arts teacher who is also certificated as a physical education teacher might be denied reassignment to the physical education department because of the scarcity of applicants for industrial arts positions.

When there are a number of requests for reassignment, seniority is a common method used to make decisions after other variables are considered. Those employees with the most seniority in the school district should be given the first opportunity in reassignment. Involuntary reassignments are then given to those employees with the least seniority. Involuntary reassignments are also necessary, at times, because of reduction in force or unexpected vacancies.

Induction

Induction is the process designed to acquaint newly employed teachers with the school system and the relationships he or she must develop to be a successful employee. It is an administrative function that is often neglected or loosely organized in many school districts. The industrial and business communities place a high priority on induction; they have recognized for many years the cause-and-effect relationship of this process to employee retention and job performance.

An effective induction program should have well-defined objectives that reflect the needs of new employees and the specific philosophy of the school

Interviewing for a teaching position requires preparation.
(The University of Texas at Austin News and Information Service, photo by Larry Murphy)

system. Although the purpose of an induction program will vary with individual school districts, the following are common objectives in all programs:

1. To make the teacher feel welcome and secure
2. To help the teacher become a member of the "team"
3. To inspire the teacher toward excellence in performance
4. To help the teacher adjust to the work environment
5. To provide information about the community, school system, school building, faculty, and students
6. To acquaint the teacher with other staff members with whom he or she will be associated
7. To facilitate the opening of school each year

These objectives support the ultimate purpose of an induction program—to promote quality education for children. The teacher who is able to adjust in a reasonable period of time to a new position helps to accomplish this purpose.

Induction programs fall into one of two major categories: informational and personal adjustment programs. Informational programs are concerned with either initial material or updating information. Initial data consist primarily of information about the school system, the community it serves, and the particular school and community to which the new employee has been assigned. Updating informational programs are geared to the teacher who is reassigned; they concentrate on a particular school and community. Personal adjustment programs aim at helping the newly hired or reassigned teachers interact with principal, faculty, students, and parents of a particular school. The following is a detailed explanation of four major aspects of most orientation programs.

The School District

The personnel department is responsible for implementing the school district part of the induction program. The main thrust of this component is to convey an understanding of the school system's policies and services and to identify personnel such as assistant superintendents, program directors, and coordinators. All teachers are usually given a copy of the school board policies and a copy of the teacher's manual.

The employee benefits provided by the school district should be carefully explained to new teachers. Major medical and hospitalization insurance applications, retirement forms, government payroll withholding forms, and other enrollment documents are generally explained to new employees at the earliest possible time during the orientation process. Most insurance programs require a new employee to enroll a spouse or dependent within thirty days after commencing employment. If a spouse or dependent is enrolled after this time, he or she is usually required to take a physical examination, and the insurance company may deny coverage because of a medical condition. For example, a newly employed teacher who does not enroll his wife in the medical insurance program within thirty days may be denied coverage at a later date because his wife has a heart condition.

The Community

Orientation to the community is also the responsibility of the personnel department. Employees should be given information about the social, cultural, ethnic, and religious makeup of the community. How people make a living, customs, clubs and organizations, church denominations, museums, libraries, colleges or universities, and social services in the community are all appropriate topics for an orientation program.

Orientation to the community usually begins while candidates are still being selected, particularly during the interview. Candidates are told about the community and questioned about how they would respond to its various aspects if they were working for the district.

The School Building and Program

The building principal has responsibility for orienting new teachers to a particular school. First and most important is introducing new teachers to all other employees, both professional and classified, who work in the building. Explaining administrative procedures is also the responsibility of the building principal. It is essential for new teachers to know how to complete attendance forms, where to obtain supplies and materials, how to requisition audiovisual equipment, and how the school schedule operates. An initial conference with the building principal, the assistant principal, or a department head is one method used to acquaint new staff members to these procedures.

In some school districts a new teacher is assigned to an experienced teacher during the first year of employment. The new teacher will then have a person to call on when questions arise about the curriculum or building procedures. This has proven to be a successful technique because the experienced teacher does not pose a threat to the new teacher, whereas an administrator might.

Personal Adjustment

With the current emphasis on "team work" in all organizations, establishing good working relationships among colleagues is important if an organization is to achieve its objectives. In a service-rendering organization, such as a school district, this is even more critical because human relations are the basis for the effective delivery of services. When comfortable relationships are established, individuals become aware of different points of view, different practices, and common problems. Finally, forming relationships with other staff members helps an employee to develop pride and satisfaction in his or her work. Nothing is less rewarding than being isolated from colleagues or fellow employees in an organization.

The responsibility for helping new employees form meaningful relationships with existing staff members rests not only with the individual but also with the entire faculty and administration.

A highly effective orientation method for new employees is to organize activities that give them the opportunity to socialize with other staff members. Many districts make a practice of serving refreshments and allotting a certain amount of time for personal interaction either before or after school meetings. Holiday parties or dinners are also effective means of enabling teachers to meet each other on a social level. Service on faculty and school district committees is one method for teachers to become acquainted with each other, while providing the district with invaluable assistance in carrying out projects. Textbook selection committees, energy conservation committees, and principals advisory committees are becoming more common and successful in school districts.

It is important for professional staff members to become affiliated with local, state, and national teacher organizations. These are not only avenues for exchanging ideas but also sources of important and current information and services so vitally needed in our changing society. Their social activities, a regular feature of these organizations, help the individual form relationships with professionals in other school districts.

The Induction of First-Year Teachers

An area of special concern is the induction of first-year teachers. Douglas Hunt, who directs a project on the induction of beginning teachers, summarizes a common response about the plight of these teachers.

> *The importance of the proper induction and orientation of new appointees cannot be overestimated. Too many potentially capable teachers, including many who have devoted years of preparation to their careers, resign their positions and give up teaching because of an unnecessarily unpleasant and frustrating initial experience in a school that lacks an effective comprehensive orientation program. The consequence is unfortunate not only for the young teacher but also for society, which loses the valuable services of a trained teacher.*[12]

James Conant, the noted educator, was very vocal about this concern and recommended a number of suggestions he believed should be guaranteed by school boards to first-year teachers. They include the following:

1. Limited teaching responsibility
2. Aid in gathering instructional materials
3. Advice of experienced teachers whose own load is reduced so that they can work with the new teacher in his or her own classroom
4. Shifting to more experienced teachers those pupils who create problems beyond the ability of the novice to handle effectively
5. Specialized instruction concerning the characteristics of the community, the neighborhood, and the students[13]

The National Association of Secondary School Principals (NASSP) considers induction to be a continuation of teacher education and further postulates that a significant amount of learning by the new teacher will take place during the induction process. NASSP initiated a project to study the induction of first-year teachers, which basically elaborated on Conant's recommendations. The committee also developed a four-phase time period during which induction should occur. Phase I would begin during the summer months and would concentrate on orientating the new teachers to the school, school district, and community. Phase II, scheduled for the week before school opens, would emphasize procedures and identify support personnel. Phase III, during the first semester, would include daily meetings between a beginning teacher and a cooperating master teacher. They would review practical aspects of teaching, such as lesson planning, testing, grading, and disciplinary techniques. The second semester, the final phase, would gradually shift to a more theoretical approach to teaching. The new teacher would be encouraged to begin evaluating his or her performance and verbalizing his or her philosophy of education.

Great Britain recognized the difficulties encountered by first-year teachers and funded a pilot induction program during the 1970s in various schools throughout the country. This program provided newly employed teachers with released time for one day each week and a three-fourths teaching workload. Professional tutors were trained to help beginning teachers develop strategies in solving problems, and professional centers were organized to provide courses and seminars to improve the teacher's skills. The new teacher used his or her released time to attend the courses and seminars or to consult a tutor. Morale-boosting conferences were held in January and July, with an end-of-the-year seminar entitled "Have We Survived?"[14]

The education reform movement began with the publication of *A Nation at Risk* and has resulted in the enacting of legislation in over sixteen states calling for *mentoring* as an induction strategy for newly hired teachers. These states have mentoring programs that differ one from the other to some degree. However, the basic concept is the same in all of the programs, that is the pairing of an experienced teacher with a beginning teacher in order to provide the beginning teacher with support and encouragement. The experienced teacher can act as a role model for the beginning teacher, and through coaching, help the teacher develop his or her competencies, self-esteem, and sense of professionalism.

Summary

The objective of the selection process is to hire individuals who will be successful on the job. The cost of this process is a major expenditure for most school districts. It includes advertising the position, printing and mailing applications, interviewing candidates, and checking references. This process should be implemented in such a way that it will minimize the chances of hiring individuals who are inadequate performers. The following steps constitute the selection process:

1. *The job description.* The job description is the end product of a process known as the "job analysis." The job description outlines specific details of a position and establishes the minimal qualifications needed to perform the job successfully.
2. *The selection criteria.* Criteria instruments delineate those ideal characteristics that, if possessed by an individual to the fullest extent possible, will ensure the successful performance of the job. Selection criteria can also be used to quantify the expert opinions of those who will be interviewing candidates.
3. *The job vacancy announcement.* The advertisement is based on the job description and provides interested individuals with sufficient information to decide whether or not to apply for the position. The advertisement will identify the job title, major responsibilities, name and location of the school district, application procedure, and the minimal job qualifications.

4. *Receiving applications.* A central office staff member is usually assigned to receive all applications for a given vacancy. As the applications come in, they are dated and filed in a designated folder. This provides integrity to the process and establishes a method to monitor the progress toward filling the vacancy.

5. *Selecting the candidates to be interviewed.* The application form will usually contain a statement requesting applicants to have their placement papers, transcripts, and letters of reference sent to the personnel department. The form should provide sufficient information to evaluate each person against the selection criteria and against the minimum requirements for the job. Selected applicants are then interviewed for the position.

6. *Interviewing the candidates.* Interviewing candidates is a responsibility shared by the personnel department and other school district employees. Candidates will be interviewed not only by those who will supervise the new employee, but also by others who have expert knowledge about the duties to be performed by the successful candidate. An interview is essentially a conversation between two or more individuals conducted to generate information about the candidate.

7. *Checking references and credentials.* "Credentials" refers to such items as a college or university transcript, a teaching certification, and a physician's verification of health. These credentials along with letters of reference should be sent directly to the personnel department by the issuing source.

8. *Selecting the best candidate.* The personnel administrator who is responsible for implementing the selection process for a particular vacancy must organize all relevant data so that a choice can be made by the superintendent of schools.

9. *Implementing the job offer and acceptance.* For teaching positions, a contract must be approved by the board of education and signed by the finalist before this step is completed.

10. *Notifying the unsuccessful candidates.* This step is initiated only after the offer of employment has been accepted by the candidate because there may be a need to offer the position to another individual if the candidate selected refuses the offer.

The first formal task in applying for a position is filling out the application form. The basic principle in constructing application forms is "Only ask for information you need to know!" The information requested on most applications falls under one of the following headings: personal data, education and/or professional preparation, experience, and references.

The last phase in procuring a new teacher for the school district is the individual's assignment and orientation to the school community. The placement of employees within the school system is the responsibility of the superintendent of schools. The planning required in making assignments is a very complicated task, demanding the full attention of at least one personnel administrator in most school districts. It is to the school district's advantage to make assignments in harmony with the wishes of the teacher. A staffing survey is one method of systematically gathering information on the placement preferences of teachers.

Other variables that the personnel department must take into consideration in making assignments include staff balancing, certification requirements, experience, and working relationships. The welfare of students and implementation of the school district's instructional program are the primary consideration. When there are a number of requests for reassignment, seniority is a defensible criterion after the other variables are considered.

Induction is the process designed to acquaint a newly employed individual with the school system and the relationships he or she must develop to be a successful employee. An effective induction program will have well-defined objectives that will help the employee to feel welcome and secure, to become a member of the "team," to be inspired toward excellence in performance, to adjust to the work environment, and to become familiar with the school community.

Induction programs fall into one of two major categories: informational programs and personal adjustment programs. Informational programs are concerned with either imparting initial material or updating information. Initial data consist primarily of information about the school system, the community it serves, and the school where a new teacher will work. Updating informational programs are geared to the teacher who is reassigned; they concentrate on a particular school and community. Personal adjustment programs are designed to help the newly hired or reassigned teacher interact with the other people for whom and with whom he or she will work.

In effectively orienting new employees to the school district, policies and services must be thoroughly explained and systemwide personnel identified. Orientation to the community must convey to employees a knowledge and understanding of the social, cultural, ethnic, and religious makeup of the community. How people make a living, customs, clubs and organizations, church denominations, museums, libraries, colleges and universities, and social services are all appropriate topics for an orientation program.

Orienting new employees to a particular school and program begins by introducing new employees to their colleagues. A tour of the facility and an explanation of administrative procedures along with an orientation to the instructional program are also important aspects of this induction.

Personal adjustment orientation includes encouraging new employees to establish working relationships with their colleagues. Organized activities such as faculty meetings with time for socialization, holiday parties or dinners, serving on faculty and district committees, and membership in professional organizations are all effective ways of establishing desired relationships among the professional staff.

An area of special concern in the induction process centers around first-year teachers. Many potentially excellent teachers are lost to the education profession because they are not properly inducted. A number of suggestions and models have been developed. These recognize the importance of giving first-year teachers time to consult with colleagues and the opportunity to obtain feedback concerning their performance.

Implications for Future Teachers

Getting that first teaching position can be a traumatic experience if the selection process is not understood. Knowing who is responsible for what, the documents that are required, and the type of questions that can be asked in an interview can help to make this experience positive and rewarding.

Placement and induction can also be traumatic experiences if the new teacher does not know what is expected. The information in this chapter will provide new teachers with a benchmark he or she can refer to to know if the district and school administration are providing appropriate support.

Discussion Questions

1. Describe the selection process.
2. What variables must be taken into consideration in making staff assignments?
3. What are the special concerns of first-year teachers, and what can school district personnel do to help these teachers?
4. Describe the two major categories of induction programs.
5. Explain what information is inappropriate to ask on an employment application or in an interview.

Notes

1. The concepts in this chapter have been gleaned from Ronald W. Rebore, *Personnel Administration in Education: A Management Approach*, 2nd ed. (Englewood Cliffs, N.J.: Prentice-Hall, 1987), 95–154.

2. Redfern, George B. "Using Job Descriptions as an Administrative Tool," *Spectrum* (Winter 1984): 21.

3. Henry S. Dyer, *The Interview as a Measuring Device in Education* (Syracuse, N.Y.: ERIC Clearing House on Tests, Measurements, and Evaluations, 1976), 2.

4. Auren Uris, *The Executive Interviewer's Handbook* (Houston, Tex.: Gulf Publishing Co., 1978), 2.

5. Dyer, *The Interview as a Measuring Device in Education*, 2.

6. Uris, *The Executive Interviewer's Handbook*, 4.

7. "New Rules for Interviewing Job Applicants: Schools Ignore Them at Their Peril," *American School Board Journal* 164 (1977): 28.

8. Anna Nemesh, "The Interviewing Process," *Business Education Forum* 33 (1979): 19–20.

9. Sally Banks Zakariya, "How You Can Identify People Who Shouldn't Work with Kids," *The Executive Educator*, 10, no. 8 (August 1988), p. 17.

10. Zakariya, "How You Can Identify People Who Shouldn't Work with Kids," p. 17.

11. Rebore, *Personnel Administration in Education*, 137.

12. Jay E. Greene, *School Personnel Administration* (Radnor, Pa.: Chilton Book Co., 1971), 214.

13. James Conant, *The Education of American Teachers,* cited in Douglas W. Hunt, "Guidelines for Principals," Project on the Induction of Beginning Teachers (Arlington, Va: National Association of Secondary School Principals, 1969), 3.

14. Arline Kahn Julius, "Britain's New Induction Plan for First Year Teachers," *The Elementary School Journal* 76 (March 1976): 350–53.

Recommended Readings

Al-Rubaiy, Kathleen, "Five Steps to Better Hiring," *The Executive Educator,* 15, no. 8 (August 1993), pp. 21–23.

Dale, Jack, "Leave Hiring to the Experts," *The Executive Educator,* 13, no. 10 (October 1991), pp. 20–21.

Davis, Beverly Irby and Genevieve Brown, "Your Interview Image," *The Executive Educator,* 14, no. 6 (June 1992), pp. 22–24.

Fielder, Donald J., "Wanted: Minority Teachers," *The Executive Educators,* 15, no. 5 (May 1993), pp. 33–34.

Kowalski, Theodore J., Phillip McDaniel, Andrew W. Place, and Ulrich C. Reltzug, "Factors that Principals Consider Most Important in Selecting New Teachers," *Spectrum: Journal of School Research and Information,* 10, no. 3 (Summer 1992), pp. 34–39.

Odell, Sandra J., *Mentor Teacher Programs.* West Haven, Connecticut: NEA Professional Library, 1990.

Reinhartz, Judy, ed., *Teacher Induction.* West Haven, Connecticut: NEA Professional Library, 1990.

Sindelar, Nancy W., "Development of a Teacher Mentorship Program: High Professionalism and Low Cost," *Spectrum: Journal of School Research and Information,* 10, no. 2 (Spring 1992), pp. 13–18.

Strusinski, Marianne, "The Professional Orientation Program in the Dade County Schools," *Spectrum: Journal of School Research and Information,* 11, no. 2 (Spring 1993), pp. 10–16.

Tomlin, Michael E., "The Evolution of a New Teacher," *The Executive Educator,* 15, no. 3 (March 1993), pp. 39–41.

U.S. Department of Education, *Teacher Attrition and Migration.* Washington D.C.: OERI/Education Information Branch, 1993.

Vienne, Dorothy T., "Mentors with a Mission," *The Executive Educator,* 13, no. 8 (August 1991), pp. 32–34.

Witty, Elaine P., *Teacher Recruitment and Retention.* West Haven, Connecticut: NEA Professional Library, 1990.

Chapter *14*

Compensation, Performance Evaluation, and Staff Development

Compensation

Before engaging in any behavior, every human being consciously or subconsciously considers the same question, "What will I get out of this?"[1] Psychologists have recognized for a long time that satisfaction of needs is the motivation behind all actions. This satisfaction or reward might be money, a promotion, recognition, acceptance, receipt of information, the feeling that we are doing a good job, or any combination thereof.

This self-interest motive often carries a negative connotation, yet it is a reality of life. People act in ways they perceive to be in their own best interests. Whether or not a given act is truly in an individual's best interest is irrelevant if he or she believes it to be so. Even if an act appears to be irrational, such as handing in a resignation because of a minor misunderstanding at work, to the individual resigning, the act may be totally in keeping with what he or she believes to be in his or her best interest.

An interesting question related to human motivation is, "Does money stimulate an employee to put forth more effort?" The answer to this question is closely related to individual needs because money in itself is rarely an end but rather a means to "purchasing an end." A $2,000 raise for an employee making $20,000 a year would help that individual maintain the same standard of living in the face of inflation. That same raise would considerably improve the standard of living for an individual earning $10,000 a year, but it would have considerably less effect on the lifestyle of someone earning $40,000 per year. From this perspective, money does have a potential to motivate an individual if one is seeking to maintain or improve one's standard of living. In our social/economic system, we rarely find a person who is not concerned when his or her lifestyle deteriorates because salary increases are not keeping pace with inflation.

A classic study based on the responses of 157 professionals in an electronics company further supports the position that each dollar of merit increase has a value to the employee.[2] This research suggests that money is important to employees, regardless of the job level in the organization or the amount of salary that the individual earns. In addition, money has a great deal of symbolic value in our society, even though it has varying degrees of importance to individuals with different backgrounds and experiences.

If money is to motivate a teacher within a school district to greater performance, it must be very clear that such performance is indeed rewarded with more money. The behavior that is thus rewarded will be repeated, and the behaviors that are not rewarded will not be repeated. This, of course, is not the *modus operandi* of most school systems in the United States. The common position has been one of emphasizing intrinsic motivation. Teachers performed to the best of their ability because of the importance of educating children. The accountability movement, with taxpayers demanding a return on their dollar from teachers by way of increased student performance, and the increased number of teacher strikes for higher wages should dispel the myth that the performance of teachers is unaffected by money.

In addition to this experientially proven conclusion, statistical data support the position that money increases intrinsic motivation under the following two conditions: (1) Monetary rewards must closely follow performance in order to be reinforcing and (2) the employee must perceive the monetary rewards as being related to work behavior.[3]

A reasonable conclusion concerning the relationship of money to motivation is that money definitely affects performance under certain circumstances. Unfortunately, single salary schedules utilize the factor of seniority, which does not encompass performance but rather tends to reward an individual's survival for another year by advancing him or her to the next step on the schedule.

The previous observations concerning motivation as it relates to compensation have been reinforced by most state legislatures. In response to the National Commission on Excellence in Education report, almost every state has passed or is considering legislation calling for performance-based teacher evaluation and performance-related compensation. Because the public mood in the United States has set this course that will probably be followed until the end of the century, the orientation of this chapter is in keeping with the "performance model."

So far this discussion has centered upon the external reward of money as it relates to the quality of performance. It should be remembered, however, that most people are also motivated by intrinsic rewards, which are those that the employee receives from the job itself. The employee's satisfaction on the job is usually increased by the following: participation in the decision-making process, greater job discretion, increased responsibility, more challenging tasks, opportunities for personal growth, and diversity of activities. Industrial psychologists have long contended that rate of pay is not the most important determinant of job satisfaction. However, it is an indispensable part of every reward system.

Variables Affecting Compensation

The main purpose for establishing a compensation policy is to attract and retain qualified employees who will provide the type of service expected by the public. It is essential that employees understand the compensation structure and have confidence in the objectivity by which the system is implemented through the administration. Two major variables must be taken into consideration by the administration in constructing a compensation policy: performance and seniority.

Performance   The evaluation of performance is concerned with a basic question—Did you get the job done? To compensate individuals employed by the school district requires criteria for defining performance. The importance of using performance as a basis for rewarding employees is critical to all effective compensation systems.

School districts have required teachers to consider the effort generated by students as a determinant in evaluating performance. Even if effort does not directly influence a grade, some method should be available to indicate that a given student is putting forth his or her best effort. It is ironic, therefore, that school districts have long neglected effort by employees in their reward system. Yet, without such an orientation, a school district will fall prey to rewarding quantity rather than quality and the end rather than the means. There are also some situations in which performance is difficult to evaluate and effort becomes a primary determinant or reward. One such instance is cited by Stephen Robbins: A major eastern university was attempting to increase its research and had designated the objective of obtaining grants or funded research efforts as a critical benchmark toward that end. All faculty members were informed that rewards for the coming year would be based on performance in obtaining grants. Approximately 20 percent of the faculty made grant applications; however, after the first year of the program, none were approved. When the time came for performance evaluation and the distribution of rewards, the dean chose to give the majority of the funds available for pay raises to those faculty members who had applied for grants. Performance, defined in terms of obtaining funded research grants, was zero, so the dean chose to allocate rewards based on effort.[4]

This discussion is obviously concerned with a topic much debated in education: merit pay. There is no one best method for rewarding performance with money; however, the following comments will help to clarify this issue.

A merit pay system will be ineffective unless it has the following components:

1. Effective teacher evaluation procedures
2. Training programs for management and supervisory personnel who will implement the plan

3. School board and management commitment to the plan
4. Staff involvement in developing the plan
5. Teacher acceptance and satisfaction
6. Adequate financing
7. Rewards for all who meet the criteria
8. Plausible, fair, and equitable performance criteria
9. Valid and verifiable measures of results
10. Objectivity and consistency in applying assessment measures
11. Increased student learning promoted[5]

Seniority Length of time in a particular position plays a significant role in allocating rewards in the public sector. The civil service system of the United States is the best example of how seniority operates in a reward procedure.

The reason that seniority has been used by educational organizations to determine financial reward is because it can be applied so easily. A principal may evaluate a given teacher's performance either higher or lower than another teacher's performance; but if both teachers perform within the limits of what is considered satisfactory, both will get the same salary increase if they both have served the same number of years in the school system. This relieves the principal from converting his or her evaluation into a discrete reward and from recommending to the superintendent that each teacher receive a different dollar amount based on performance.

Nevertheless, seniority is a variable to be incorporated into a reward system because the basic purpose of establishing a reward policy is to attract and retain qualified employees. Seniority is ineffective only when it is the sole criterion for rewarding employees.

The necessity of retaining some form of seniority in a compensation plan that also rewards performance has lead to the establishment of what is commonly referred to as "career ladders." Two of the more frequently discussed programs are the Charlotte-Mecklenburg Schools Career Development Plan and the Tennessee Better Schools Program. The objective of these two, and most other programs, is to encourage teachers to direct their careers along a path that will lead to refined skills and higher levels of responsibility. For example, a person entering the education profession as an apprentice teacher must have met the following requirements:

1. Completed a teacher education program offered through an approved college or university
2. Attained a Bachelor's degree
3. Successfully completed student teaching
4. Successfully passed the National Teacher's Examination

This apprentice teacher could progress to subsequent higher levels of designation such as a teacher classified as Career Level I, II, or III. The path to these levels requires additional education and the assumption of more and more responsibilities. For example, a Career Level III teacher could be expected to serve as a curriculum specialist, seminar presenter in a staff development program, or a resource person to apprentice teachers. Each level of attainment could be rewarded with perhaps a more lucrative salary schedule. A bonus upon attaining each successive level would be another method of rewarding those reaching such level. Box 14-1 shows the career paths for teachers in Tennessee.

Direct Compensation: Salary and Wages

The basic philosophy underlying pay systems is "equal pay for equal jobs." However, the subjective nature of administrative judgments, collectively bargained agreements, state and federal pay guidelines, and salary rates in the public and private sectors have a definite influence on educational wage programs. To ensure external and internal equality, a school district must continually gather data on the wage and salary policies of other school districts and also on the wage and salary policies of private employers in the community and region. Most organizations are cooperative in sharing information concerning salary programs because they too understand that their system is influenced by others. Surveys by telephone and letter, governmental publications, and literature published by employee organizations and unions are also valuable resources in gathering information.

Public Disclosure of Salaries   Because school districts are public agencies, salary schedules and budget information have usually been disclosed not only to school district employees but also to the general public and at times to the media. However, many school districts consider the salaries of individual employees to be confidential. This situation brings up a number of concerns. First, in public agencies supported by tax money, the public has a right to know how its tax money is being spent and for what. Second, secrecy regarding salaries sometimes leads to misperceptions, which in turn may lead to dissatisfaction of employees with their pay.

Compensation Packaging   Because individual teachers have individual needs, no compensation program will satisfy everyone. A number of school districts, recognizing this fact, have developed compensation programs that allow each teacher to choose the combination of rewards most attractive to him or her. Thus, teachers are informed that their compensation is X dollars, and they can choose a mix of salary, life insurance, medical/hospitalization insurance, annuities, or other benefits suited to their particular situation. The concept underlying this approach is that teachers will be motivated toward higher performance if such performance carries a dollar value that can then be "spent" by the individual for rewards tailored to meet his or her needs.

BOX 14-1 Career Paths for Teachers

Apprentice Teacher (after probationary one-year period)

Entry Routes:
> Completion of a teacher training program and recommendation by an approved institution of higher education
>
> Trade shop personnel who meet appropriate standards

Qualifications/Requirements:
> Student teaching
>
> Successful completion of the National Teacher's Examination

Bachelor's Degree or
Employment standards required for trade shop personnel

Certificate:
> Three-year, nonrenewable

Contract/State Salary:
> Regular school term of 200 days
>
> State salary schedule based on training and experience

Career Level I

Entry routes:
> Three (3) years as an apprentice teacher
>
> Currently certified teachers with three (3) or more years of experience who wish to enter the new career paths

Qualifications/Requirements:
> Knowledge of subject matter
>
> Acceptable student achievement
>
> Participation in professional growth activities

Career Ladder Test*
Observation by evaluation team/teacher interview

Certificate:
> Ten-year, renewable

Contract/State Salary:
> Regular school term of 200 days
>
> State salary schedule based on training and experience plus state incentive pay supplement of $1,000

Career Level II

Entry Route:
> Currently certified teachers who have eight (8) or more years of appropriate experience

Qualifications/Requirements:
> Acceptable student achievement
>
> Participation in professional growth activities
>
> Observation by evaluation team/teacher interview
>
> Exceptional classroom practice
>
> Capability and willingness to assume additional duties

Career Ladder Test*
Evaluations by local and/or state supervisors and administrators

Certificate:
> Ten-year, renewable

Contract/State Salary:
> Contract for 10 months (200 days)—*current teachers only*—State salary schedule based on training and experience *plus* state incentive pay supplement of $2,000

BOX 14-1 *Continued*

Career Level III

Entry Route:
Currently certified teachers who have twelve (12) or more years of appropriate experience

Qualifications/Requirements:
Acceptable student achievement

Participation in professional growth activities

Observation by evaluation team/teacher interview

Classroom effectiveness

Capability and willingness to assume additional duties

Career Ladder Test*

Evaluations by local and/or state supervisors and administrators

Skill in supervising, evaluating and improving the performance of other teachers

Certificate:
Ten-year, renewable

Contract/State Salary:
Contract for 10 months (200 days)—*current teachers only*—state salary schedule based on training and experience *plus* state incentive pay supplement of $3,000

*Career Ladder certification, awarded after the Apprentice License, is optional and is in addition to the Professional License. Career Ladder certification provides salary supplements to Career Levels I, II, and III.

Source: Tennessee Better Schools Program (Nashville, Tenn.: Master Teacher-Master Administrator Act, 1983), p. 3; revised by Tennesee State Department of Education, 1993–94. Used with permission.

Salary Schedule. In public education, the traditional method in deciding the salaries of newly hired teachers is to place them on a salary schedule in relation to their academic preparation and experience. Many school districts do not give full credit for years of experience when hiring a teacher who has taught in another district. For example, a newly hired elementary school teacher with seven years experience in a neighboring school district might be placed on the fifth step of column 1 (bachelor's degree level—see Box 14-1). Thus, the steps on schedules do not necessarily represent seniority but rather levels within categories. There are distinct advantages to using this salary schedule approach in determining an individual staff member's salary. First, such a system easily demonstrates equality of salary between staff members with similar responsibilities. Thus, all teachers at all levels within the school system can be placed on the salary schedule. Because teachers have similar responsibilities whether they teach high school English or fourth grade, they are compensated without discrimination. Second, the salary schedule method can be used as a basis for determining compensation for meritorious performance. For example, teachers who perform at the "superior" level may be awarded a double step on the salary schedule. Third, the recruitment of personnel can become more effective if salary schedules are used by a school district. Potential teachers can readily see what their salary might be in the future.

A major question in establishing a salary is deciding on the appropriate number of steps to be included within each category. If the steps are too numerous, the salary increases received each year will be small. Usually teachers will be advanced one step each year if their performance is satisfactory. As mentioned above, multiple step increases can be given for superior performance and no step increase could be the outcome for an unsatisfactory performance by a teacher. If the steps are few in number, a teacher can reach the maximum in a category within a short period of time and, consequently, will have no place to progress over the long term.

Table 14-1 is an example of the type of salary schedule found in most school districts. There are five categories which correspond to the academic requirement necessary for placement in each category. The categories progress from the "bachelor's degree" level on through to level five. The steps in each category are listed down the left side of the schedule. Those teachers in category one could receive a step increase with satisfactory performance up through 15 steps. At that point they would not receive a step increase until they acquired 20 graduate hours of additional education in their subject area and thus would move to step 16 in

TABLE 14–1   Special School District of St. Louis County

TEACHER LEVEL
1993–1994 SALARY SCHEDULE

	BS 2 Yr Voc Cert	BS + 20 Hours 5 Yr Voc Cert	MA/5Yr Voc Cert + 10 Hr & 3 Yr Voc Teach	MA with 180 Hrs MA + 15 Hours/ 5 Yr Voc Cert + 25 Hours	MA + 30 Hours 5 Yr Voc Cert + 40 Hours
1	25,800	26,800	29,400	30,800	32,500
2	26,500	27,525	30,175	31,600	33,300
3	27,200	28,250	30,950	32,400	34,200
4	27,900	28,975	31,725	33,200	35,100
5	28,625	29,700	32,500	34,000	36,050
6	29,350	30,450	33,300	34,825	37,000
7	30,075	31,200	34,100	35,650	37,950
8	30,825	31,950	34,900	36,500	39,050
9	31,575	32,750	35,700	37,350	40,150
10	32,325	33,550	36,600	38,300	41,300
11	33,125	34,350	37,550	39,250	42,450
12	33,975	35,150	38,500	40,250	43,600
13	34,875	36,050	39,500	41,250	44,750
14	35,775	36,950	40,500	42,300	45,900
15	36,725	37,900	41,550	43,450	47,050
16		38,900	42,700	44,600	48,200
17			43,950	45,850	49,450
18				47,250	50,800
19					52,250

Note: An additional adjustment of $1000 will be added to the appropriate step on the MA+30 pay column for the doctoral degree.

category two. Therefore, this method encourages teachers to upgrade their knowledge and skills. Such is the case with all categories. There are categories that have experience requirements in addition to the academic ones.

It is important to note that most school boards will annually review their salary schedules and make adjustments by adding additional dollars to the schedules on an across-the-board basis because of inflation.

There are two processes that should be used to establish the basic wage for each salary schedule range. The preceding discussion of types of salary ranges illustrated the various methods used to calculate step increases but provided no indication of base salaries.

As previously stated, the first process centers on gathering salary data from other school districts and from the business/industrial community.

The second process involves gathering data from individual employees within the organization concerning the extent of their responsibilities, the tasks they perform, and their qualifications. The data can be analyzed and used to establish salaries as part of the annual review process. The data also provide a vehicle for reevaluating jobs to ascertain if they are properly assigned to the appropriate salary schedule and in the correct range.

Indirect Compensation: Fringe Benefits

Fringe benefits may be defined as benefits available to all staff members resulting from a direct fiscal expenditure. Because fringe benefits are available to all staff members and are not contingent upon performance, such services are not motivators but are more properly considered maintenance factors. Nevertheless, fringe benefits are commonly considered as an important part of an effective compensation program. Retirement programs, medical and hospitalization insurance, and life insurance are only a few of the many fringe benefits offered to staff members in school systems. Because these services are essential in our society, the quality of these and other fringe benefit programs can have a significant effect on the ability of a school district to attract and retain good teachers. Attracting individuals with excellent credentials and a desire toward excellence in performance from the outset will ultimately correct high turnover and absenteeism. Quality fringe benefits attract quality candidates for positions and will help to maintain employee commitment to the school district.

Types of Fringe Benefits Inflation continually eats away at real salaries and wages, which has been the reason for the rapid growth in wages over the last ten-year period. This same period has also produced a significant increase in the number of fringe benefits offered to employees of public school districts. The prediction made by John Sullivan in 1972 has come to pass.[6] The cost of fringe benefits in the United States has risen to approximately 35 percent of total salary and wages paid to employees.

School districts across the country are experiencing financial problems. Many districts have found that fringe benefit enrichment is an alternative when wage and salary increases are not feasible. As more school districts develop elaborate fringe benefit programs, greater pressure will be placed on competing school districts to develop similar programs in order to attract and keep teachers. There is also a growing recognition that fringe benefits are nontaxable, which has been another major stimulus toward their expansion.

Certain benefits must be provided by the school district: social security insurance, state retirement insurance, unemployment compensation, and workers' compensation. These benefits provide the employee with financial security and protection at retirement or termination; they provide for a staff member who is injured at school; and they provide survivors' benefits to dependents in the event of an employee's death.

Unemployment benefits are derived from a tax levied against employers calculated on a percentage of the employer's total wage payroll. Benefits received by unemployed workers are calculated from the individual's previous wage rate plus the length of previous employment. Unemployment benefits are provided on a limited basis, typically for a twenty-six week period.

Workers' compensation programs provide benefits to individuals injured or disabled while engaged in a job-related activity. Benefits paid to employees for injuries are based on schedules for minimum and maximum payments, depending on the type of injury sustained. For example, the loss of a hand is compensated with a higher dollar amount than the loss of a finger. Disability payments are calculated in a like manner based on the individual's current salary, future earnings, and financial responsibilities.

The funds for worker's compensation programs are borne entirely by the employer. While the programs are mandated by state laws, the method of obtaining worker's compensation insurance is usually left to the discretion of the employer, who may buy such protection from public agencies, private companies, or provide the protection through a self-insuring program. Like social security and unemployment insurance, worker's compensation is subject to the legislative process. Thus, requirements and benefits will certainly change with the passage of time.

Where mandated by state laws, retirement programs for teachers generally follow the prescriptions of these other protection programs. Contributions are calculated on the basis of an employee's wages and are usually matched by the school district. Benefits based on contributions are paid upon retirement with survivors' benefits available for the dependents of deceased teachers.

Voluntary Fringe Benefits   This category of benefits may be further divided into insurance programs, time away from the job, and services. Group insurance programs are available for almost every human need. Among the most common are major medical and hospitalization insurance, dental insurance, term life insurance, errors and omissions insurance, and optical insurance. The number of such programs available to employees depends on the fiscal condition of the school district and the demands of the employees. A school district is usually restricted by state statute to pay insurance premiums only for employees. Therefore, if an employee wishes to include dependents under such insurance programs, he or she must pay the additional premium for this coverage.

A fringe benefit that is often taken for granted by employees which, however, creates an additional expense to a school district is time spent away from work. Therefore, sick leave, vacation time, paid holidays, and sabbatical leave are, in fact, benefits provided at the discretion of the school system. In very large school districts, this can amount to a considerable expenditure of funds.

Most school systems provide employee services. Those most commonly found in public education are expenses paid for attendance at workshops, professional meetings, conventions, and tuition reimbursement. With the nationwide decrease in pupil enrollment leading to staff reduction, some districts are providing teachers with career counseling to help them prepare for jobs outside education.

Fringe benefits are certainly an important component of any compensation program, and they are important alternatives to large salary and wage increases.

Managed Health Care   Health care costs continue to increase at an alarming rate. If this *trend* continues, by the year 2000 health care expenditures will be approximately 16% of the Gross National Product. An alternative approach to the traditional insurance programs that is meant to maintain a high quality of care, but at a lower cost and in a more efficient manner, is *managed health care.*

Basically, managed health care coordinates services around the patient and thereby produces a more efficient delivery system. In order to accomplish this, school districts must employ *case management specialists* who evaluate cases that require extensive and/or expensive medical treatment. An alternative to hiring case management specialists, is contracting with a company specializing in *third party health care administration.* These case managers, or third party administrators, work with patients and physicians in order to identify alternatives that are medically sound yet cost effective. A common example is developing a plan that incorporates out-patient care after sufficient in-patient hospital care, rather than a prolonged hospital stay. Such specialists should also develop employee programs that encourage healthy life styles and thus the prevention of illness. It may be cost effective for a school district to offer mammograms, or diabetes testing, at a nominal cost to employees.

There are various levels of managed health care. *Utilization management* attempts to control costs through *catastrophic case management* and *utilization review.* When an employee suffers a catastrophic illness, the case manager begins the process of assisting the patient, and his or her physicians, to access the best treatment at the lowest cost. This could include care in a rehabilitation center, nursing home, extended care facility, or out-patient services in the patient's home. The case manager helps negotiate rates with these various facilities.

Utilization review usually includes the reviewing of all in-patient admissions, out-patient surgical procedures, in-patient substance cases, and in-patient psychiatric care. The purpose is to ascertain if such services are medically required. In addition, before a claim is paid, the case manager will review the charges for accuracy.

Another alternative to hiring case management specialists or contracting with a third party health care administrator, is for a school district to join a *managed care network*. Physicians who are members of the network have agreed to certain fee guidelines, and medical facilities that join the network have agreed to a certain quality of service and fee guidelines. The network provides the school district with efficient paperwork processing and also with cost information that will assist in the school district's financial planning.

There are many types of networks. One is called a *Preferred Provider Organization* (or PPO). Both hospitals and physicians belong to such a network. Physicians treat patients in their own offices. If a school district employee chooses a physician or hospital outside the network, most PPOs will pay a much smaller percentage of the bill. Hospitals and physicians outside the network cannot be monitored to insure quality care and cost containment.

A second type is a *Health Maintenance Organization* (HMO). In this arrangement, each patient is provided with a network primary care physician who controls access within the network to care for the employee and his or her dependents. A prepaid and fixed monthly fee for all services is another important feature of the HMO. Typically, HMOs are organized around four models: group, staff, individual practice, and point-of-service. In the group model, a group or groups of physicians provide care to patients at one or more locations. In the staff model, physicians are actually employed by an HMO and provide services at one or more locations. In the individual practice association model, an HMO contracts with physicians who practice out of their own offices. In point-of-service model, an HMO allows school district employees to chose physicians outside the network, but the employee will pay a higher percentage of the cost.

Many PPOs and HMOs have prescription drug plans whereby certain pharmacies within a network offer medication at a reduced cost. This kind of network can also be found outside of PPOs and HMOs.

Health Risks in the Workplace   A major issue facing many school districts is the rising cost of Workers' Compensation. In the early 1900s, an employee injured on the job had to pay for his or her own medical treatment and probably did not receive wages during the recovery period. An employee seriously injured requiring an extensive recovery period, would most likely not have a job if and when he or she was able to return to work. In 1910, individual states began to adopt various workers' compensation systems. This approach required employers to compensate employees injured on the job regardless of fault. In return, employees were not allowed to sue employers. The system has been beneficial for all parties concerned.[7]

Medical costs associated with workers' compensation have risen approximately 11% per year over the last ten years. Today employers pay approximately 60 billion dollars each year for workers' compensation, approximately $500 per employee.

For school district employees, there are three major categories of health risks that could require workers' compensation. Facility environmental risks are first. These include: radon gas, lead in the drinking water, asbestos in floor tile and other building materials, tobacco smoke, fungi, mold and spores, pesticides, cleaning materials, etc.[8] The second category is violence. Today, many teachers and staff members are working with students with a history of committing violent acts. The emergence of gangs is a contributing factor to the increasing number of violent acts committed against teachers and staff. Finally, there is the risk of infectious disease. Some special education teachers that work with physically impaired children risk back injuries lifting children from one position to another.

Family and Medical Leave Act, 1993[9]   President Clinton signed into law the Family and Medical Leave Act (P.L. 103-3) on February 5, 1993. The fundamental purpose of this act is to provide eligible employees as defined by section 3(e) of the Fair Labor Standards Act with the right to take twelve weeks of unpaid leave per year in connection with certain circumstances.

An employee may invoke this law in conjunction with the following:

1. The birth and first-year care of a child. This includes paternity leave.
2. The adoption or foster parent placement of a child. The entitlement ends when the child reaches age one or the twelve week period ends.
3. The illness of an employee's spouse, child, or parent. This includes a step-child, foster child, a child over eighteen years of age incapable of self care, and a step-parent.
4. The employee's own illness. This means a serious health condition that may result from not only illness but also injury, impairment, physical or mental condition. This may involve inpatient care or any incapacity requiring absence from work for more than three days and which involves continuing treatment by a health care provider. Also, this refers to any treatment for prenatal care.

The law became effective August 5, 1993. However, in those school districts that have a collective bargaining agreement with one or more bargaining units, the law became effective upon the termination of the master contract or on February 5, 1994 whichever occurred first. Because this is a labor law, the United States Department of Labor is the federal agency responsible for the development of implementation regulations.

All employees of private elementary and secondary schools and all employees of public school districts are covered by this Law.

Consolidated Omnibus Budget Reconciliation Act, 1986   This Federal Law requires school districts that provide group health plans for their employees and their dependents to offer an extension of the coverage on a temporary basis under certain conditions. An employee covered by the group health plan is eligible for continuation of coverage if his or her employment with the district is terminated (except in cases of gross misconduct), if he or she is laid-off for economic reasons, or if he or she is reduced to part-time employment and thereby would usually lose coverage.

Family members of an employee are also entitled to continued coverage under the following qualifying events: death of the employee; divorce or legal separation from the employee; medicare becoming the employee's primary health care coverage; termination, layoff, or part-time status of the employee; and ceasing to be considered a dependent child under the plan.

There are notification requirements under this law and the employee or family members must pay the premiums for the extended group health plan coverage. Extended coverage may last for eighteen, twenty-nine, or thirty-six months depending on certain qualifying conditions.

Performance Evaluation

Appraisal of performance in education is as old as pedagogy. However, for the most part, only three stages of historical development in American education during this century were concerned with the evaluation of teachers. During the 1920s, the efforts primarily focused on analyzing whether a given teaching style correlated with the philosophy and psychology of William James or John Dewey. The second stage was concerned with relating certain personality traits to excellence in teaching. The latest stage, which appeared in the 1960s and persisted throughout the 1970s, emphasized generic teaching behaviors that would be effective in all instructional settings. The research in this area coined such catch words as "structured" and "task-oriented" when reporting the types of teacher behavior that produced effective student outcomes.

In 1976 the National Institute of Education, in a request for proposals, called for a new approach to the definition of effective teacher training. This signaled the growth of a movement to license teachers on the basis of competencies and performance rather than on the completion of a teacher education program at an accredited college or university. Obviously, such an approach is predicated on a preconceived notion of what constitutes effective teaching.

The last decade has ushered in a dramatic change in the entire concept of evaluation. Parents and taxpayers are demanding, across the board, more accountability at all levels of performance.[10] School board members are also subject to accountability. This has led school employees, parents, and even organizations such as the National Education Association to support specific candidates in school board elections because of their dissatisfaction with the voting record of a particular board member.

The "systems" approach to management, which has been used extensively by industry and received a big boost in the early 1960s when Robert S. McNamara advocated its use in the U.S. Department of Defense, shifted the emphasis away from the traditional concept of teacher evaluation to the broader concept of employee appraisal management. Appraisal by objectives has become the touchstone phrase for the 1990s. This means that an employee can be effectively evaluated only within the context of attaining certain preestablished objectives. Establishing these objectives is part of the entire process of determining the organizational objectives of the school district.

Because of the integral relationship between all employees and because one employee's performance can affect the performance of other employees, all personnel must be evaluated. This begins with an evaluation of the superintendent of schools by the board of education and proceeds down through the chain of command, with each administrator evaluating those employees reporting to him. This process applies not only to teachers and administrators but also to classified employees. The performance of bus drivers, cooks, custodians, and secretaries should be evaluated by their immediate supervisors.

Although each position within a school district has a unique character, the following are universal reasons for appraisal, applicable to all school districts and all positions:

1. Appraisal fosters the self-development of each employee.
2. Appraisal helps to identify a variety of tasks that an employee is capable of performing.
3. Appraisal helps to identify staff development needs.
4. Appraisal helps to improve performance.
5. Appraisal helps to determine if an employee should be retained in the school district and how large a salary increase he or she should be given.
6. Appraisal helps to determine the placement, transfer, or promotion of an employee.

While parents and taxpayers are demanding increased accountability in employee performance, employees are also demanding accountability in the appraisal methods and techniques used in their evaluations. Administrators and supervisors are being asked to defend their evaluations and the procedures they used in making them. Consequently, it is extremely important to develop a consistent benchmark in establishing an appraisal process.

In the business and industrial community, that benchmark is the "job description" under which an individual was employed. Thus, an employee is evaluated in relation to his or her job description, which is the only defensible criterion against which performance should be measured.[11] Although this certainly does not mean that a job position will remain unchanged, it does imply that a revised job description may be necessary if a job has undergone considerable modification. Although job descriptions are seldom used as a component of evaluation in education, such use is a necessary prerequisite in establishing an effective appraisal process.

The Appraisal Process

The ultimate goal of all school districts is to educate children and adolescents. How this is accomplished depends upon a multitude of subordinate goals and objectives. It is not only organizationally appropriate but also legally wise for a school board to establish a policy statement on employee appraisal as one of these supportive objectives. Such a policy gives direction to the various administrative divisions of the school district in their development of organizational objectives. A policy statement might read thus:

> *Recognizing that quality education for the children and adolescents of this school district depends on the level of teacher, administrator, and staff member perform-ance, the board of education directs the superintendent of schools to develop and implement a process for employee appraisal.*
>
> *This process must address as its first priority the impartial and objective evaluation of individual employees in relation to the requirements of their positions within the school district and in how these positions help to actualize and support the instructional goals and objectives of this district.*[12]

In meeting the mandate of this policy, each organizational division within the school district is responsible for developing divisional objectives. The three major divisions in most school districts are personnel, instruction, and support services. For example, the instruction division of a school district might find it advantageous in a given year to concentrate on the development of an international cultures curriculum. Curriculum specialists, principals, and teachers would be enlisted to write course objectives that would incorporate cultural awareness from kindergarten through twelfth grade.

Each teacher would be required to develop personal objectives concerning how he or she plans to teach cultural awareness. For example, a high school home economics teacher could plan lessons highlighting the diet and manner of food preparation in specific countries. A fourth-grade teacher might invite people in the community who were born in a foreign country to visit his or her class to talk about their country. A middle school or junior high school language arts class might develop a minilesson introducing students to a series of foreign language phrases.

The next step in the appraisal development process is to decide on formal evaluation procedures. These procedures must be in writing and made available to the entire staff. A concern often voiced by teachers is that they were not adequately informed about the appraisal process. Because evaluation procedures are applicable to all school district teachers, a common practice is to incorporate them into the board of education policy manual that is distributed to all teachers when they are hired. Other school districts have handbooks that outline working conditions and specify the procedures and forms used in the appraisal process.

Developing the actual procedures is a task that is best performed by involving principal and teacher representatives. This committee approach produces a sense of involvement and accountability that helps to defend appraisal procedures in the face of possible criticism.

The procedures, of course, will be tailored to the needs of the individual school district. However, the following questions should be addressed in every set of procedures:

1. Who has the responsibility for making evaluations? (Example: principals evaluate teachers.)
2. In what settings will formal evaluations take place? (Example: a teacher will be evaluated in the classroom when he or she is teaching a lesson.)
3. On how many occasions will formal evaluations occur? (Examples: tenured teachers will be evaluated on one formal occasion each year; probationary teachers will be evaluated at a minimum on two formal occasions.)
4. In what setting will the results of formal evaluations be communicated to the person evaluated? (Example: in a conference immediately after the evaluation in the teacher's classroom.)
5. If a teacher disagrees with his or her evaluation, what grievance procedure should be available? (Examples: written rebuttal may be attached to the evaluation; appeal may be made to the superintendent.)
6. What effect will evaluation have on salary increases? (Example: a teacher with an excellent rating may receive a double step on the salary schedule.)

It is important to realize that appraisal of all employees is a continual and ongoing process. However, it is also important to have "formal" evaluations when a teacher can demonstrate his or her performance capabilities. Formal evaluation can apply to situations that involve interaction between an individual and a defined group. Teachers are subject to this process because of their interaction with students.

The final step in the appraisal process is analysis of the results that have been obtained through teacher evaluations to determine if these fulfilled instructional division objectives. If objectives have not been reached, and if they are still relevant to implementing the objectives and goals of the school board, the divisional objectives should be retargeted. This suggests that the teacher objectives apparently did not support the divisional objectives and should be realigned to support them. If both the divisional and teacher objectives have been realized, new objectives can subsequently be identified that will further the goals of the school district and the development of individual teachers. Figure 14-1 presents a schematic rendering of the appraisal process.

There are a number of popular evaluation techniques that have not been addressed in this section, such as self-evaluation, peer evaluation, and student evaluations. Such techniques should be encouraged and will certainly help a given teacher support his contention about the level of his performance.

Supervision and Evaluation of Staff   The primary responsibility of the principal is the supervision of teachers and staff members that is usually formalized

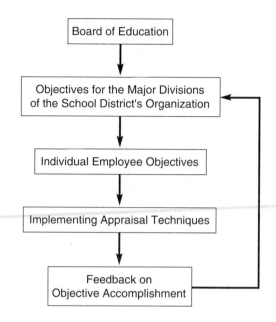

**FIGURE 14-1   Model for Developing
an Employee Appraisal
Process**

Source: R. W. Rebore, *Personnel Administration in
Education: A Management Approach,* 2nd ed.,
(Englewood Cliffs, N.J.: Prentice-Hall, 1987), p. 10.
Used with permission.

through the performance evaluation process. The purpose for supervising teachers is the improvement of instruction.

Individuals can become complacent without some outside intervention. Performance evaluation is the method by which the administration observes, analyzes, interprets, and makes suggestions for improvement in how teachers teach.

There are many different methods and evaluation instruments that can be used by the principal in carrying out this responsibility. Appendix F on page 393 presents an evaluation instrument with a philosophy and procedure that represents a traditional approach to teacher evaluation. The instrument identifies three major areas (teaching performance, professional qualities, and personal qualities) that are measured based upon the teacher's behavior. Appendix G on page 399 lists a number of indicators under each category and subcategory of the evaluation instrument that can be used to determine the quality of this behavior.

Different faculties in different communities have special needs that may not be met by the evaluation procedures and instruments presented in this discussion. The essence of the principal's responsibility is to develop a method and instrument that will produce a two-way communication between the teachers and principal which will result in the improvement of performance. In many school districts, the evaluation process and instrument is developed by the central office personnel department. In this case it is essential that the principals and representatives of the teachers be allowed to give input into the evaluation process. Also, it is critical that a grievance procedure be incorporated into the evaluation process so successive levels of management may be called upon to review an evaluation that a teacher believes to be a misrepresentation of his or her performance.

Evaluation Instruments As with the development of appraisal procedures, evaluation instruments are more appropriately constructed by the committee process. Many management consulting firms have developed appraisal forms that are easily adapted to the requirements of a school district. However, the construction of appraisal forms is not a difficult task, particularly with many prototypes available for the asking from neighboring school districts.

The basic format of an evaluation instrument has certain theoretical overtones. Most authors recognize two basic categories, trait forms and the result forms. In the trait approach the teacher is rated against a predetermined list of indicators in order to ascertain his or her level of performance. The results method compares the teacher's performance against objectives that were developed by the teacher and agreed to by his or her principal. In this latter method the teacher has the responsibility for documenting how the objectives were reached.[13]

This author believes that the most appropriate method of evaluating performance is to use a trait instrument to ascertain overall performance and to target objectives to specify improvement in performance. The results method also helps to ascertain if teacher objectives are supporting divisional and school board objectives. Teacher objectives can be developed more easily if overall performance has been measured. While the simultaneous use of trait instruments and objectives is not a common practice, the exclusive use of one or the other has never proven to be obviously superior.

Job descriptions also play an important role in constructing appraisal instruments and in developing objectives. The job requirements of a position are the legal parameters within which appraisal must be confined. A teacher performs these responsibilities to an acceptable, unacceptable, or superior level. To require a teacher to assume responsibilities that are not within his or her job description and to evaluate how he or she carries out these responsibilities is an example of inappropriate supervision and will not hold up in court if the teacher is dismissed on the basis of such performance.

Termination Procedures

A universal reason for evaluating an individual's performance is to determine the desirability of retaining the person as a staff member of the school district. A decision to dismiss a teacher, of course, is extremely difficult to make because of the importance of employment to a person's welfare and also because of the effects on the employee's dependents.

Employment counselors have seen the devastating financial and psychological effects that "getting fired" has on a person's life. In fact, the trauma usually centers on the individual's self-concept. Feelings of inadequacy, failure, self-contempt, and anger are common to people who have their employment terminated. Although most individuals are able to cope with such a situation, others never fully recover from the experience. Consequently, it is not only good personnel management but also a humane responsibility for school district administrators to develop termination procedures that are objective and fair, and that incorporate a due process to give a teacher the opportunity to modify or defend his or her behavior.

Due process is a right that has long been recognized as an integral part of our American legal system. It should also be noted that a legitimate objective of a staff development program is helping teachers to overcome deficiencies that affect their performance, which is the reason for including staff development in this chapter. Figure 14-2 presents a due process procedural scheme that exemplifies those found in most states.

Staff Development

Change is a constant condition of our human existence. Instant communication channels produced by technological advances place changes before student and teacher in the political, economic, scientific, and social milieu from within and outside our country. The mandate of public schools, of course, is to educate the children, adolescents, and young adults of our country in order to help them meet the challenges that tomorrow will bring because of these changes.

As an organization, a school district needs well-qualified administrators, teachers, and support personnel to fulfill this mandate. As the positions and job requirements within a school district become more complex, the importance of staff development programs increases.

Educating children once meant teaching reading, writing, and arithmetic in a self-contained classroom by a single teacher; teachers had little need to upgrade or alter their skills. However, rapid changes in our sophisticated society have created pressure on school districts to adapt by introducing new services, new instructional materials, and equipment.

Elementary and secondary schools budget approximately two billion dollars annually for instructional materials with about seventy million going for computer-based equipment. The projection for the 1990s is that computer spending will increase fourfold, to 300 million.

A Boston publishing company has introduced a computer system called "The Answer" which tests elementary school children in reading and mathematics, identifies areas where each child needs help, and then informs the teacher about remedial workbook exercises. These and other complex instructional aids, cou-

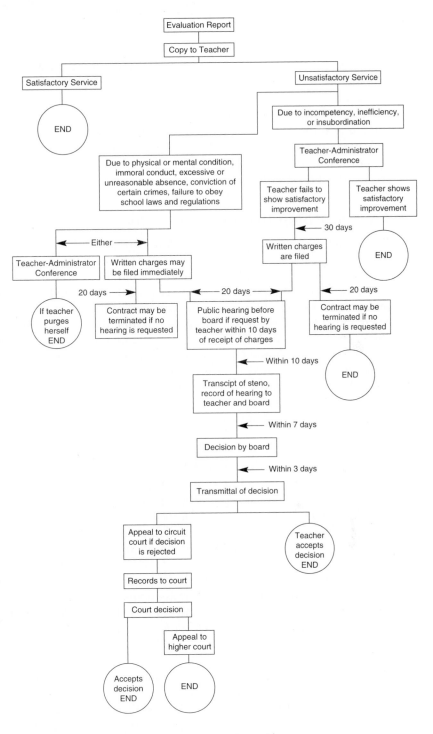

FIGURE 14-2   Teacher Evaluation Flow Chart

Source: Missouri Department of Elementary and Secondary Education, Jefferson City, Missouri. Used with permission.

pled with the need to upgrade interpersonal relationship skills and instructional methods as required by legislation, demand the creation of a staff development program.

It is absolutely impossible today for any teacher to enter the profession and remain in it for forty years with his or her skills basically unchanged. Therefore, staff development is not only desirable but also a necessary activity to which each school system must commit human and fiscal resources if it is to meet the changing needs of the community.

Creating a Staff Development Program

Experience has taught personnel administrators the folly of approaching staff development merely from the "let's have a workshop" model. This concept of what was and is still referred to in some school districts as "in-service training" has severe limitations not only in scope but also in effectiveness. Rather, the new-to-education but long-standing concept in the business community of "staff development" addresses the need to continually upgrade our knowledge and skills. The evolution of this approach is mirrored in all of our societal institutions. In the past, educational changes were implemented without giving teachers an opportunity to prepare for such changes. The Elementary and Secondary Education Act of 1965 and the Education Professions Development Act of 1968 funded many staff development projects. These funds have helped to foster the current interest in staff development. See Figure 14-3 for a model staff development program.

The Goals and Objectives of the School District   Educational goals and objectives, taken in the broadest sense, are similar across the country. Schools are concerned about educating children in the basic skills and developing those cultural values that will perpetuate our American heritage. How the various school districts adjust these goals and objectives to their particular situation accounts for the fact that no two staff development programs will be exactly the same.

The genesis of a staff development program, therefore, originates in educational goals and objectives. When these goals and objectives are formulated into written policies of the board of education, a staff development program has the necessary guidance to integrate the individual goals of employees with those of the school district.

Commitment to Staff Development   A major reason why some teachers perceive staff development activities as ineffective is because they receive little recognition for implementing newly acquired skills and ideas. Other conditions that affect the success of a staff development program include lack of appropriate program organization and lack of supervision during implementation. Clearly, these conditions are only symptomatic of a more fundamental problem—a lack of commitment.

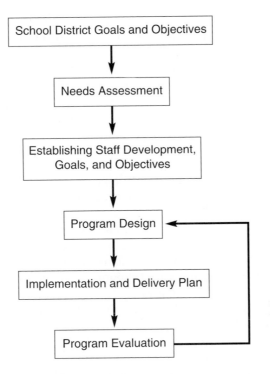

FIGURE 14-3   A Model for a Staff Development Program

Source: R. W. Rebore, *Personnel Administration in Education: A Management Approach,* 2nd ed., Englewood Cliffs, N.J.: Prentice-Hall, 1987), p. 10. Used with permission.

In delineating the tasks to be performed by the various levels of a school district, the board of education must set the stage by creating a positive climate for the program and by providing the necessary fiscal funding and appropriate policies for implementation. The central office administration, usually through the personnel department, is responsible for creating, managing, and supervising the staff development program. Building principals and supervisors are responsible for identifying the knowledge, skills, and abilities needed to carry out the goals and objectives of the school district. The teachers and staff members, in turn, are responsible for participating in the program. Consequently, the success of a staff development program depends on the commitment of each individual within each level of the school district organization.

Needs Assessment The primary purpose of a staff development program is to increase the knowledge and skills of teachers and staff members and thereby increase the potential of the school district to attain its goals and objectives. The process of assessing staff members' needs is essentially the process of determining the discrepancy between the existing and the needed competencies of the staff. This analysis must also consider projected personnel needs. Thus, a staff development program is concerned with both the abilities of individuals currently occupying a position and the abilities an individual will need to qualify for promotion to a position of more responsibility. The data obtained from the personnel planning inventories used in the personnel planning process along with needs assessment techniques and instruments provide the framework within which program goals and objectives can be established.

Staff Development Goals and Objectives Staff development goals and objectives will continuously change to meet the changing needs of individual staff members and the school district. A predominantly white suburban school district that begins to get an influx of black families might consider creating a program for the administrative, teaching, and support staff on the impact that the mingling of these two distinctive American cultures will have on the functioning of the school district. The introduction of computer-assisted instruction will create a need to instruct the teaching staff on the most effective use of this new equipment.

These examples of changes that affect the operation of the school district are more broadly formulated into goals and objectives. For example, a staff development goal involving integration might be stated as follows: To prepare the administration, teachers, and staff to address effectively the integration of black students into the school community. Objectives specifying this goal could be formulated as follows:

1. To develop a sense of appreciation for cultural differences on the part of teachers, administrators, and staff members.
2. To develop strategies for pupil behavior management should conflicts arise between students of different cultural heritages.

Program Design Designing a program involves more than finding a university professor who is interested in giving a workshop on a particular topic. Broadly conceived, program design is a process of matching needs with available resources through an effective delivery method.

There are a number of methods for delivering a staff development program. The National Education Association's Research Division lists nineteen methods used in program delivery:

1. Classes and courses
2. Institutes
3. Conferences
4. Workshops
5. Staff meetings
6. Committee work
7. Professional reading

8. Individual conferences
9. Field trips
10. Travel
11. Camping
12. Work experience
13. Teacher exchanges
14. Research
15. Professional writing
16. Professional association work
17. Cultural experiences
18. Visits and demonstrations
19. Community organization work

A variety of resource people enhances a staff development program. Among the most available and knowledgeable persons are teachers, senior staff members, college and university personnel, professional consultants, journal authors, teacher organization representatives, and administrators.

The Implementation and Delivery Plan A critical aspect in all staff development programs is the implementation and delivery phase. The very best of intentions and planning may result in failure unless attention is paid to providing staff members with appropriate incentives to participate and to make satisfactory time arrangements.

Time is a valuable commodity to all teachers and, thus, it is a key factor in organizing and encouraging them to participate in development programs. There is a growing trend to incorporate such programs as a part of the working day. Some school districts set aside a number of afternoons each month for development programs; others bring courses and lectures directly to the schools.

A common practice is to reimburse teachers for tuition and fees incurred in attending workshops or taking courses. Many school districts also pay for substitute teachers in order to facilitate program arrangements. The research on staff development programs generally agrees that incentives should be provided.

Program Evaluation Effective evaluation is the final phase in a staff development program. Some school districts see this as a rather complicated task involving multiple applications of statistics; others neglect it entirely. For most programs, a perception-based approach is both appropriate and effective. Participants are asked to rate the instructor conducting the program, the content of the program, how the program was organized, and the time and place where the program was presented.

When a particular program centers on skill or technique acquisition, it is appropriate to conduct a follow-up evaluation after the participants have had the opportunity to implement the techniques or to use their new skills. The evaluations are then used in future program design and will provide the necessary data to improve the entire staff development program.

Current Issues in Staff Development

During the first few decades of this century, boards of education encouraged teachers to earn a baccalaureate degree. From that time until the 1970s the thrust was on earning advanced degrees. The current trend, however, is to provide teachers with the opportunity to maintain a favorable outlook on teaching and to improve their effectiveness in the classroom. The following list summarizes the benefits that a staff development program can offer to the teacher:

1. *To update skills and knowledge in a subject area.* The knowledge explosion has created the need to reinterpret and restructure former knowledge. A teacher can no longer be assured that he or she understands the nuances of a subject area based on past learning.
2. *To keep abreast of societal demands.* Our society is continually changing. The teacher needs to understand and interpret the new demands society is placing on all its institutions and on the school in particular.
3. *To become acquainted with research on the instructional process and on new methods of teaching.* Like other professionals, teachers generally have good intentions of keeping up with the advances that are being made in their field. Available time often prevents them from carrying out these intentions, but a staff development program can meet this need.
4. *To become acquainted with the advances in instructional materials and equipment.* Educational TV, cable TV, and computer-assisted instruction are only a few of the many innovations that have potential for improving the quality of classroom instruction.

In the process of assessing teacher needs, the following sources of information can be of considerable help in designing a staff development program. First, the teacher needs-assessment survey has been a most effective technique. Most surveys take the form of a checklist containing many areas of possible needs and interests (see Appendix H on page 407).

A second source of information is the community survey which is administered to parents, usually through a school-based organization such as the Parent-Teacher Association. This survey may reveal parental concerns about a wide range of issues such as grading, student groupings, discipline, and drug use by students.

Third, certification requirements vary from state to state and occasionally change. The personnel department needs to keep all teachers and other certificated employees informed about requirements and should plan appropriate credit courses on both an off-campus and on-campus basis. The personnel master plan will also provide the personnel department with information about the future needs of the district for certain types of certificated employees.

The final source of information is research and curriculum studies. Staff development programs can be planned to correlate with future curriculum changes. Research leads to future skills and competencies that can be acquired and gradually introduced to ensure an even transition.

Summary

Psychologists have long recognized that satisfaction of needs is the primary motivation behind all human actions. In satisfying their needs, individuals will act in ways they perceive to be in their own best interest.

Two variables must be taken into consideration in a compensation program: employee performance and seniority. The rewarding of performance, however, must be the primary objective of a rewards program.

An effective program must include both intrinsic and extrinsic rewards. Intrinsic rewards pertain to the quality of the job situation; they may include participation in the decision-making process, increased responsibility, and greater job discretion. Extrinsic rewards are divided into direct and indirect compensation. Direct compensation is commonly referred to as salary or wages; indirect compensation is frequently referred to as fringe benefits. Two issues that have attracted considerable attention in regard to compensation program development are career ladders and merit pay.

An important question central to any pay policy is, "Does money motivate?" A reasonable conclusion, supported by experience and research, is that money does affect performance if it is clear the performance is rewarded by a salary increase.

A number of other issues in salary and wage management will have an effect on pay policy development: public disclosures of salaries, compensation packaging, and salary schedule construction.

Indirect compensation, or fringe benefits, may be defined as benefits available to all staff members. Fringe benefits help a school district attract and retain good employees. Certain fringe benefits are required by law; these include social security, state retirement programs, unemployment insurance, and workers' compensation.

Voluntary fringe benefits may be divided into insurance programs, time away from the job, and services. Group insurance programs are available for almost every human need including medical/hospitalization insurance, dental insurance, term life insurance, errors and omissions insurance, and optical insurance.

A fringe benefit employees often take for granted is time away from the job, which includes sick leave, vacation, paid holidays, and sabbatical leave. In like manner, certain services offered to staff members by school districts are in reality fringe benefits. These include paid expenses for attendance at workshops, professional meetings and conventions, and tuition reimbursement. When decreasing pupil enrollments cause staff reductions, many school districts offer career counseling services to teachers who will be looking for jobs outside education.

Because health care costs continue to increase at an alarming rate, many school districts are instituting managed health care programs that coordinate services around the patient. Another major issue facing school districts across the nation is the rising cost of workers' compensation resulting from the growing number of health risks in schools.

On February 5, 1993, President Clinton signed into law the Family and Medical Leave Act. The fundamental purpose of the Act is to provide eligible employees (as defined by section 3(e) of the Fair Labor Standards Act) with the right to take 12 weeks of unpaid leave per year under certain circumstances.

In 1986, the U.S. Congress passed the Consolidated Omnibus Budget Reconciliation Act (COBRA). This Federal law requires school districts that provide group health plans for their employees and their dependents to offer an extension of the coverage on a temporary basis under certain conditions.

There were three historical stages of development in American education during this century that concerned the evaluation of teachers. In the 1920s, efforts primarily focused on analyzing whether a given teaching style correlated with the philosophy and psychology of William James and John Dewey. The second stage was concerned with relating certain personality traits to excellence in teaching. In the 1960s the third stage emphasized generic teaching behaviors.

The last decade has ushered in a dramatic change in evaluation procedures. The traditional concept of teacher evaluation has been replaced by the broader concept of appraisal management. By this approach a teacher is evaluated within the context of attaining certain preestablished objectives.

The reasons that justify the establishment and implementation of an appraisal process for all staff members include these: to foster self-development, to identify a variety of tasks a teacher is capable of performing, to identify staff development needs, to improve performance, to determine if a teacher should be retained and what his or her salary increases should be, and to help in the proper placement or promotion of a teacher.

A significant aspect of an appraisal process is measuring a teacher's performance against his or her job responsibilities as outlined in a job description.

In developing an appraisal process, a board of education should establish a policy on staff appraisal to give direction to the various divisions within a school district. These divisions are responsible for developing objectives to implement the goals of the school board. Each employee is then responsible for developing personal objectives that further the divisional objectives. Consequently, staff member performance is measured against the degree to which each individual has attained his or her objectives. Feedback data are then available to analyze whether divisional objectives have been reached. The actual appraisal procedures for implementing this process are best developed by involving representatives of the staff members to be evaluated.

As with the development of appraisal procedures, evaluation instruments are more appropriately constructed by the committee process. There are two basic categories of evaluation instruments: trait forms and result forms. The trait approach rates an employee against a predetermined list of indicators to ascertain overall performance. The results approach involves comparing an employee's performance against objectives that were developed by the teacher and agreed to by the principal. Using both types of instruments helps to identify areas where improvement is needed.

Termination procedures, an aspect of the appraisal process that is seldom addressed, are extremely important. Because "getting fired" has a devastating effect upon the financial and emotional welfare of an individual, termination procedures must be fair and objective. Most states have statutory provisions outlining the due process that must be afforded teachers before termination. The education and welfare of students is the primary concern of a school district, but teachers also have rights that must be taken into consideration when developing appraisal procedures and dealing with dismissal.

Change is a constant condition of our American way of life. Improved communications place advances before students and educators in politics, economics, and science almost as soon as they occur.

School districts have a mandate to educate the youth of our country. To do so successfully, schools need well-qualified teachers, administrators, and support personnel. No staff member will remain competent in the face of accelerating change without some form of ongoing education. This is the impetus behind the recent emphasis on staff development programs.

Creating a staff development program consists of six separate but sequential processes:

1. Establishing school district goals and objectives, which become the foundation of the program;
2. Assessing the needs of school district staff members to determine if there is a discrepancy between the competencies of the staff and the requirements of the organization;
3. Establishing staff development goals and objectives;
4. Designing a program that will meet the staff development requirements;
5. Implementing the designed plan so that effective learning may occur; and
6. Evaluating the program to ascertain if it is meeting its objectives, which in turn will affect future program designs.

A staff development program for the instructional staff will focus on updating subject areas skills and knowledge, outlining societal demands and changes, presenting the findings of research on teaching methods and practices, and updating teachers on the advances in instructional materials and equipment.

In assessing the needs of teachers, four sources of information may be helpful: (1) the teacher needs assessment survey, (2) community surveys, (3) certification information coupled with the human resource master plan, and (4) research and curriculum studies.

Implications for Future Teachers

Although it is important to understand that adequate and appropriate compensation for teaching depends upon the resources of the school district, it is equally important to recognize the need for vigilance. Boards of education and administrators are constantly approached by special interest groups seeking a larger slice of the budget. Through membership in professional organizations and in the bargaining unit representing teachers, vigilance will be effective. Also, all teachers should continue to promote tax increases when necessary and should make state and federal legislators aware of teachers' economic needs.

The appraisal processes used in most school districts are adequate and fair. Every teacher, however, should become well-informed about this process along with its accompanying procedures if his or her employment rights are to be protected. The time to become informed is immediately after accepting employment in a school district.

Because of the continually changing and growing pool of information and knowledge and because of the many pressures placed on teachers, it is imperative for a school district to provide an appropriate staff development program. Teachers, however, must consider participation in such programs a professional responsibility.

Discussion Questions

1. Does "money" motivate teachers to higher levels of performance?
2. Describe the internal and external rewards of an effective compensation program.
3. Explain the purposes of the performance appraisal of teachers.
4. Name the six aspects of a staff development program.
5. Explain the concept underlying "merit pay" and "career ladders."

Notes

1. The concepts in this chapter have been gleaned from Ronald W. Rebore, *Personnel Administration in Education: A Management Approach*, 2nd ed. (Englewood Cliffs, N.J.: Prentice-Hall, 1987), 155–285.

2. Brian A. Giles and Gerald V. Barrett, "Utility of Merit Increases," *Journal of Applied Psychology* 55, no. 2 (April 1977): 103–109.

3. Fred Luthans, Mark Martinko, and Tom Kess, "An Analysis of the Impact of Contingency Monetary Rewards on Intrinsic Motivation," *Proceedings of the 19th Annual Midwest Academy of Management* (St. Louis, 1976): 209–211.

4. Stephen P. Robbins, *Personnel: The Management of Human Resources*, 2nd ed. (Englewood Cliffs, N.J.: Prentice Hall, 1982), 267.

5. Glen H. Tecker, *Merit, Measurement, and Money: Establishing Teacher Performance Evaluation and Incentive Programs* (Alexander, Va: National School Boards Association, 1985), 14.

6. John F. Sullivan, "Indirect Compensation: The Years Ahead," *California Management Review* (Winter 1972): 73.

7. Greg Steinmetz, "States Take on the Job of Holding Down Medical Costs of Workers' Compensation," *Wall Street Journal*, 3 March 1993, sec. B, B1.

8. Cathryn Ehrhardt, "Environmental Policy—a Priority for Schools in the 90's," *Updating School Board Policies*, 20, no. 8 (September 1989), 2–3.

9. U.S. Congress, *Family and Medical Leave Act*, Washington, D.C.: U.S. Government Printing Office, 1993.

10. Gregg W. Downey, "How to Get Rid of Your Bad Teachers and Help Your Good Ones Get Better," *American School Board Journal* (June 1978): 23.

11. Robbins, *Personnel: The Management of Human Resources*, 218–19.

12. American Association of School Administrators, *How to Evaluate Administrative and Supervisory Personnel*, vol. IX, AASA Executive Handbook Series (Arlington, Va.: The Association, 1977), 50.

13. James Lewis, Jr., *Appraising Teacher Performance* (New York: Parker Publishing Co., 1973), 25–28.

Recommended Readings

Abel, Gene B., "School District Health Care Expenses: Moderating the Escalating Rate of Growth," *School Business Affairs*, 57, no. 12 (December 1991), pp. 26–8.

Arnold, Jean B., "Family Leave: It's the Law," *The American School Board Journal*, 180, no. 10 (October 1993), pp. 31–4.

Brandt, Richard M., *Incentive Pay and Career Ladders for Teachers*. Albany, New York: University of New York Press, 1990.

Bridges, Edwin M. and Barry Groves, *Managing the Incompetent Teacher*. Eugene, Oregon: ERIC Clearinghouse on Educational Management, 1990.

Conway, James A., "Lessons for Staff Developers from an Organization Development Intervention," *Journal of Staff Development*, 11, no. 1 (Winter 1990), pp. 8–13.

Darling-Hammond, Linda and Jason Millman, eds., *The New Handbook of Teacher Evaluation: Assessing Elementary and Secondary School Teachers*. Newbury Park, California: Sage Publications, 1990.

Dickson, Lou Ann S., Mary Walton, and Virginia Guy, "Teacher Attitudes Toward a Career Ladder," *Spectrum: Journal of School Research and Information*, 10, no. 2 (Spring 1992), pp. 27–34.

Educational Research Service Staff, "Changes in Salaries and Wages for Public School Employees," *Spectrum: Journal of School Research and Information*, 11, no. 2 (Spring 1993), pp. 44–7.

Lieberman, Ann and Lynne Miller, eds., *Staff Development for Education in the '90s: New Demands, New Realities, New Perspectives*. New York: Teachers College Press, Columbia University, 1991.

Martini, Jr., Gilbert R., "Wellness Programs: Preventive Medicine to Reduce Health Care Costs," *School Business Affairs*, 57, no. 6 (June 1991), pp. 8–12.

Matlock, John, "Solving the Problem of Problem Employees," *The Executive Educator*, 14, no. 10 (October 1992), pp. 39–41.

Natale, Jo Anna, "Shopping for Health Benefits," *The American School Board Journal*, 179, no. 1 (January 1992), pp. 38–40.

O'Neil, I. Riley and David R. Adamson, "When Teachers Falter," *The Executive Educator*, 15, no. 1 (February 1993), pp. 25–32.

Pekoe Jr., Lawrence C., "Expert Evaluation," *The Executive Educator*, 13, no. 10 (October 1991), pp. 39–40.

Rossow, Lawrence F. and Jerry Parkinson, *The Law of Teacher Evaluation.* Topeka, Kansas: National Organization on Legal Problems of Education, 1991.

Southern Regional Education Board, *Paying for Performance—Important Questions and Answers.* Atlanta, Georgia: The Board, 1990.

Stein, Andrea R., "The Supervision Quandary," *The Executive Educator,* 14, no. 4 (April 1992), pp. 33–5.

U.S. Department of Education, *Teacher Salaries—Are they Competitive?* Washington, D.C.: OERI/Education Information Branch, 1993.

Chapter *15*

The Legal Liability of Teachers

Over the last decade, school districts have experienced an increase in litigation partially due to the fact that sovereign immunity has been abrogated by many state legislatures. Sovereign immunity is the common law principle that protects government officials from lawsuits resulting from the performance of their duties. School districts are governmental subdivisions of the state operating on the local level and, thus, school board members have been protected from such lawsuits. However, over 28 states have taken away this cloak of immunity and in the 1990s most of the remaining states may do the same.

The ripple effect from this situation has caused teachers to become more vulnerable to judicial review of their decisions and actions than teachers of a decade ago. Even if teachers act in good faith and with reasonable deliberation, they may find themselves defending their actions in court.

It is, therefore, imperative that teachers have a rudimentary understanding of the American judicial system and are capable of carrying out their daily responsibilities in such a manner that they can legally defend themselves if they are sued.

The following discussion is meant to provide teachers with a better understanding of their potential liabilities.

The American Judicial System

There are two systems of law. The first is known as "civil law" and is descended from Roman law; the rule of law in this system is established through statutes enacted by a legislative body. The second system is known as "common law" and is the basis of law in England. Under this system, the decisions rendered by a court become a guide or precedent to be followed by the court in dealing with future cases. The system of law found in the United States is a mixed system using both civil and common law principles.

Sources of Law

Three major sources of law form the foundation of our American judicial system: constitutions, statutes, and case law.

Constitutions are bodies of precepts that provide the framework within which government carries out its duties. The federal and state constitutions contain provisions which secure the personal, property, and political rights of citizens.

School districts have been continually confronted with constitutional issues, many of which have resulted in lawsuits. Some of these issues have dealt with the racial segregation of schools, education, academic freedom, the rights of students, and censorship of books.

Statutes are the enactments of legislative bodies more commonly called "laws." Thus the U.S. Congress or a given state legislature may enact a new law or change an old law by the passage of legislation. A statute is subject to review by the respective state or federal court to determine if it is in violation of the precepts set forth in a state and/or federal constitution.

The presumption is that laws enacted by legislative bodies are constitutional and that the burden of proving otherwise is determined only through litigation. Thus, if a state legislature passes a law requiring school districts to provide free bus transportation to parochial school children living within the boundaries of their respective districts, a citizen or group of citizens could initiate a lawsuit asking that state's supreme court to consider the constitutionality of the new law. The basis for the lawsuit might be a provision in the state constitution calling for the separation of church and state.

Because public schools are state agencies, the legislatures of every state have created statutes governing school districts. School operation, therefore, must be in compliance with such state statutes, and it is the responsibility of the board of education and the superintendent of schools to ensure compliance. Furthermore, the board of education cannot establish policies that are in conflict with state statutes or the acts of the U.S. Congress; in addition, the policies must not be in conflict with either the federal or state constitution. If a school board, for example, creates a policy prohibiting children with disabilities from attending school with other children, this policy would be in violation of the federal Public Law 94–142; it probably violates the due process guaranteed by the Fourteenth Amendment to the Constitution and maybe violates a given state constitution stipulating that an equal education must be provided for all children.

The third source, common law, is more properly called *case law* because it is derived from court decisions rather than from legislative acts. Past court decisions are considered binding on subsequent cases if the material facts are similar. This is the doctrine of "precedent." Lower courts usually adhere to the precedent (rule of law) established by higher courts in the same jurisdiction. The United States

Supreme Court and state supreme courts can reverse their own previous decisions and thereby change the rule of law. Thus, a state circuit court may apply a rule of law established by a state supreme court about what constitutes proper teacher supervision of children in a case alleging negligence that resulted in an injury to a child. In a later case the supreme court may redefine proper supervision and thus change the rule of law.

Two additional sources of law affect education even though they are not primary sources: administrative law and attorney general opinions.

Administrative law has developed through the creation of state and federal boards and commissions charged with administering certain federal and state laws. In carrying out their responsibilities, these boards and commissions establish rules and regulations. For example, school employees are likely to be affected by the regulations of the Social Security Administration, the Employment Security Administration, or the Workers' Compensation Commission. Of course, the actions of these boards and commissions are subject to review by the courts.

A second and frequently initiated legal procedure is to request an opinion from a state attorney general on the interpretation of a certain statute. In the absence of case law, this opinion can be used by educators in addressing legal issues.

Major Divisions of Law

Law may be divided into two major categories, civil law and criminal law. This distinction arises out of the rights protected under the law. Civil law protects those rights which exist between individuals, between corporations, or between an individual and a corporation. It is concerned with resolving disputes between these entities. The state or federal government is usually not a party to the dispute but, through the court system and the judge, acts as an impartial arbiter. There are many subdivisions of civil law that are readily familiar to most people and include the following: contracts, real estate, divorce, wills and estates, and torts.

For example, a dispute may arise because the employment of a tenured teacher was terminated by the board of education. The teacher may allege that the statutory due process was not followed in his or her dismissal. Because the school district is a state agency and because the dispute involved tenure, the lawsuit would be filed by the teacher's attorney in the state circuit court.

Criminal law protects the rights of society. An individual who commits a crime is violating a law enacted by Congress or by a state legislature to protect society. Thus, when a person is arrested and charged with committing a crime, the federal or state government prosecutes the individual. All the costs are borne by the government.

In certain cases, a civil and criminal wrong can exist at the same time. If a high school chemistry teacher is intoxicated and thus neglects to supervise his students properly as they perform a laboratory experiment which results in an explosion injuring certain students, the state may prosecute him for criminal negligence.

Furthermore, the parents of the injured children may bring a civil lawsuit against the teacher and the school district seeking damages for the injuries.

The Court Structure

The federal and state constitutions provide the framework for the establishment of our court systems. On the local level, municipal courts enforce city ordinances and handle such problems as traffic and housing code violations.

At the state level, the primary court is generally prescribed by the state constitution, which may also give the state legislature the power to create new and additional courts. Most states have four categories of courts: courts of special jurisdiction, circuit courts, courts of appeal, and a supreme court.[1]

Courts of special jurisdiction are limited and may hear only certain types of cases. Examples of these special courts include juvenile, probate, divorce, and small claims courts.

Circuit courts are usually considered to be courts of original jurisdiction. All major criminal and civil cases are tried before the circuit court. This court is of particular significance to teachers because most disputes involving contracts, tenure, and torts will be tried in a state circuit court. In like manner, because education is a state function, the state court system rather than the federal system has jurisdiction over the resolution of most disputes.

Appellate courts are found in all fifty states and are commonly referred to as "supreme court." In some states, there are intermediate courts of appeal that have jurisdiction to hear certain types of cases on appeal from circuit courts.

At the federal level, the United States Constitution provides for the establishment of a Supreme Court and gives Congress the authority to create inferior courts.[2] This power has been exercised by Congress to establish special jurisdiction courts, district courts, and the United States Court of Appeals. The federal courts of special jurisdiction, like the state courts of special jurisdiction, are limited to hearing certain types of cases. A few of these courts familiar to most people are tax court, court of claims, bankruptcy court, and court of custom and patent appeals.

The federal district courts, like the state circuit courts, are general courts of original jurisdiction. They are the trial courts, which hear litigation between citizens from two or more states, cases involving federal statutes, and cases involving the federal Constitution.

The decisions of a federal district court may be appealed to the United States Court of Appeals or, in certain cases, directly to the United States Supreme Court. The United States Supreme Court, of course, is the highest court in the country beyond which there is no appeal.

There is a distinction in the manner by which certain courts can hear cases that is important for educators to understand. Certain issues are traditionally tried in "equity" by the state circuit courts and federal district courts. The most familiar to teachers are injunctions. For example, a school board may go to a state circuit court to ask for an injunction directing a group of teachers to leave the picket lines and to return to the classrooms if there is a state statute prohibiting strikes by teachers. Obviously, if the parties named in an injunction fail to obey the court order, they are in contempt of court and may be punished by a fine or by jailing. Figure 15-1 illustrates the structure of courts.

Torts and Teachers

The term "tort" refers to a civil wrong, other than the breaking of a contract, that is committed against a person or a person's property.[3] Torts are so varied that it is difficult to categorize them. However, for the sake of demonstrating how tort litigation could affect both teaching and teachers, three types of torts will be explained.

Intentional torts are actions that a person takes that interfere with another person or that person's property. Such actions are usually crimes. Assault, battery, and defamation are the most common forms associated with personal interfer-

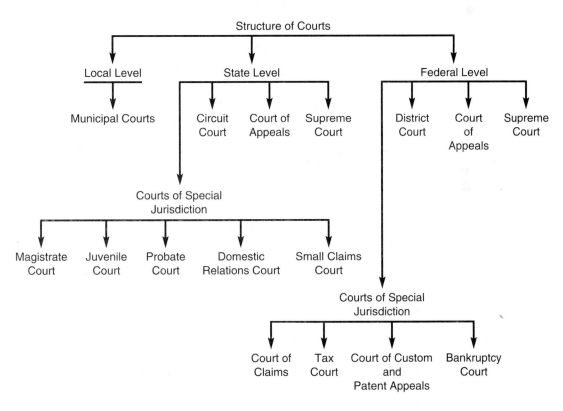

FIGURE 15-1   Structure of Court System

Source: R. W. Rebore, *Educational Administration: A Management Approach,* (Englewood Cliffs, N.J.: Prentice-Hall, 1985), p. 8. Used with permission.

ence. It is hoped that teachers will not be accused of an assault, which is a threat to physically harm someone, or a battery, which is the actual carrying-out of the threat. There are two situations, however, that teachers may find themselves involved with that may result in a lawsuit charging assault and battery. For example, two students are fighting and a teacher feels responsible to break up the fight. The physical encounter between the teacher and students might be such that an injured student could accuse the teacher of an assault and battery. The teacher in this case will have an easier time defending his actions if he followed the practice of using only that force necessary to restrain the two students.

The second situation involves the administration of corporal punishment. The common law principle of *in loco parentis* delegates to teachers the authority to discipline children placed under their supervision. The teacher, therefore, may administer reasonable corporal punishment for a breach of conduct. The teacher must not act out of malice or inflict lasting or permanent injury.

The concept of *reasonableness* is open to many different interpretations. The following four questions can act as a test of reasonableness by teachers as they establish guidelines for the administration of corporal punishment.

1. Was the rule being enforced a reasonable regulation?
2. Was the extent and form of corporal punishment reasonable in light of the breach of conduct?
3. Was the extent and form of corporal punishment reasonable in light of the student's age and known physical condition?
4. Did the teacher act to correct the behavior of the student or was he or she acting out of malice toward the pupil?[4]

The school district should also have a policy stating the purpose and manner in which corporal punishment may be applied. Such a policy should include the following provisions as a minimum:

1. Corporal punishment should be administered only in the presence of an administrator or teacher
2. Corporal punishment should not be applied by a teacher or administrator of the opposite sex as the child. Another administrator or teacher of the same sex as the child should be enlisted to carry out the punishment
3. The purpose for using corporal punishment should be to correct inappropriate behavior and not to harm the child

Defamation occurs when a person communicates something about another individual either by word of mouth (slander) or in writing (libel) that is false and brings hatred or ridicule to that person and also brings some other type of harm to him or her. Defamation is an area of potential litigation.

Teachers have access to records that contain extensive personal and academic information about their students. This information is privileged. In performing their responsibilities, however, teachers exchange a great deal of information about their students with other teachers, administrators, and parents. Under certain circumstances, teachers may also be requested to share information about students with agencies, institutions, or even prospective employers.

To avoid the allegation of defamation, teachers are well advised to observe the following guidelines in exchanging written or verbal information about students.

1. Information should be shared only with those who have a legal or professional right to such information.
2. Information should be communicated in good faith and without malice.
3. Information requested by an agency, institution, or prospective employer should be given only after receiving a signed release from the student or, if the student is a minor, from his or her parents or legal guardian.

It should be clear, therefore, that gossip or the idle sharing of privileged information with other teachers could result in a lawsuit.

A second classification of torts is usually referred to as "absolute liability." A self-evident example is when a person keeps a wild animal as a pet. If that animal escapes and injures someone, the owner is liable simply for having kept the animal in a residential area. Absolute liability is generally inapplicable to the instructional situation in elementary and secondary schools. However, a high school science teacher who brings a poisonous snake into the classroom as an exhibit for a lesson in herpetology would be unquestionably guilty of an absolute tort if the snake bites a student.

This example overlaps with the third category, negligence, in which a person's conduct falls below an established standard and results in an injury to another person. Four conditions must be present for a teacher to be negligent. First, the teacher must owe a duty to the students. The courts have held in numerous cases that teachers have three basic responsibilities: (1) adequate supervision of their students; (2) proper instruction; (3) maintaining the safety of the students while under a teacher's supervision. Second, the teacher must breach one or more of these responsibilities. Third, the teacher's conduct must be the probable cause of the injury. One of the basic questions, therefore, that will be asked in a tort lawsuit is if the teacher exercised *due care.* In other words, could the teacher have prevented the injury if he or she provided due care to the student? Thus, a causal relationship must exist between the breach of duty and the resultant injury or damage. Fourth, a tort exists only if there has been an actual loss or injury to a student. See Figure 15-2 for a classification of torts.

The following example will clarify how a teacher can demonstrate that he or she is carrying out instructional and supervisory responsibilities with regard to the safety of the students. A high school chemistry course requires students to perform laboratory experiments. Knowing that high school age students may be careless in carrying out experiments, a chemistry teacher could do the following:

1. Develop written guidelines on how to perform laboratory experiments safely
2. Require students to know the guidelines and practice safety procedures

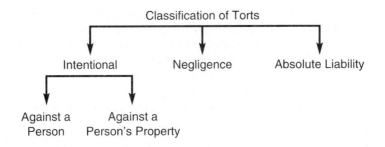

FIGURE 15-2   Classification of Torts

Source: R. W. Rebore, *Educational Administration: A Management Approach*
(Englewood Cliffs, N.J.: Prentice-Hall, 1985), p. 12. Used with permission.

3. Demonstrate the proper way to carry out experiments
4. Check to be certain that all chemicals are properly labeled and stored
5. Assign only that number of students that can be properly supervised as they perform the experiment
6. Directly observe the students as they perform experiments

In a tort liability lawsuit, if the question is one of negligence, the court will apply the principle of the reasonable person. This concept has a very specific application and definition. The reasonable person is someone who

1. Possesses average intelligence, normal perception, and memory
2. Possesses same superior skill and knowledge that the defendant has or purports to have
3. Possesses the same level of experience that the defendant has
4. Possesses the same physical attributes that the defendant has

Thus, the conduct of a teacher involved in the lawsuit is compared against the conduct of a mythical reasonable person. If a reasonable person could have prevented the injury, the teacher should be found negligent by the jury. The moral of the example is that all teachers should examine their professional responsibilities to determine if their conduct in fulfilling their responsibilities can withstand the test of the "reasonable person."

In a civil lawsuit that results in a decision for the plaintiff, the defendant will usually be required to pay actual damages, which is the amount of money that the injury cost. A broken arm could result in physician and hospital bills reaching thousands of dollars.

If it can be demonstrated in court that a person deliberately caused the injury, punitive damages may also be levied by the court against the defendant. This dollar amount is a punishment for intentionally bringing about the injury. In

Litigation is on the increase in public education.
(Marilyn Church)

some cases, punitive damages may equal or supersede the actual damages assessed by the court.

It should be clear from this presentation that every teacher must be protected by errors and omissions liability insurance. Sources for obtaining such coverage include professional teacher associations and insurance companies. Many school districts provide errors and omissions liability insurance for school board members, central office administrators, principals, teachers, and other employees. Finally, it should be remembered that most errors and omissions liability insurance policies do not cover punitive damages because this would amount to condoning an act that was deliberately perpetrated.

The Role of the Attorney in Tort Litigation

The selection of an attorney is the most important decision that a person will make as a defendant in a lawsuit. A common misconception about the attorney's role, however, is that the attorney will handle the litigation without much involvement from the defendant. On the contrary, the raw material that will be fashioned into a credible defense by the attorney is provided by the defendant.

Thus, an attorney performs basically three functions: first, analyzing the situations that led to the lawsuit in order to determine the facts and real questions involved; second, researching court cases and statutes for the purpose of deciding what "law" is involved; and finally, putting together a workable defense in relation to the material facts and the law.

A teacher who is being sued should select an attorney who has a proven track record in tort litigation. The judicial system is adversarial by design. There is always a winner and a loser in every lawsuit. The person with the most skilled attorney has the advantage in civil litigation.

Anatomy of a Lawsuit

Although lawsuits do not follow a set pattern, there is enough commonality in civil litigation to make a few general observations.[5]

A lawsuit is initiated when a person or persons files a petition with a court setting forth a cause that is an allegation. For example, the parents of a child who broke an arm from falling off playground equipment could allege that their child was not properly supervised by the teacher. A summons is then delivered by the court to the defendant, who in this case would be the teacher responsible for supervising the injured child during play periods. The teacher or the teacher's attorney will be required to appear in court on a given date for the purpose of answering the allegation set forth in the petition.

If the teacher denies being guilty of negligence, the next step involves clarifying the allegation and the material facts which support it. This may be accomplished by the taking of depositions, which is a formal procedure in which the parties to the lawsuit are required to answer questions posed by the respective attorneys. Written questions may also be required in lieu of or in addition to the taking of depositions.

The teacher's attorney may then file a motion to dismiss the case if the material facts do not appear to support the allegation. If the judge does not dismiss the case, a trial date is set. In civil cases involving such issues as tenure, or a tort, the defendant usually has the option of a jury trial or of having the judge render the decision.

If the decision is rendered in favor of the plaintiff, a remedy is assessed against the defendant that may involve a number of options depending on the nature of the case. In the tort liability case just described, the teacher may be required to pay the hospital bill and other related expenses for the child who was injured. Figure 15-3 illustrates the anatomy of a lawsuit.

Under certain circumstances the decision in a trial may be appealed to a higher court for review. The most common circumstances in which this may occur involve either a question of law or the impartiality of the trial proceedings. For example, a higher court could reverse the decision of a lower court because the higher court believes that a case law precedent was improperly applied by the

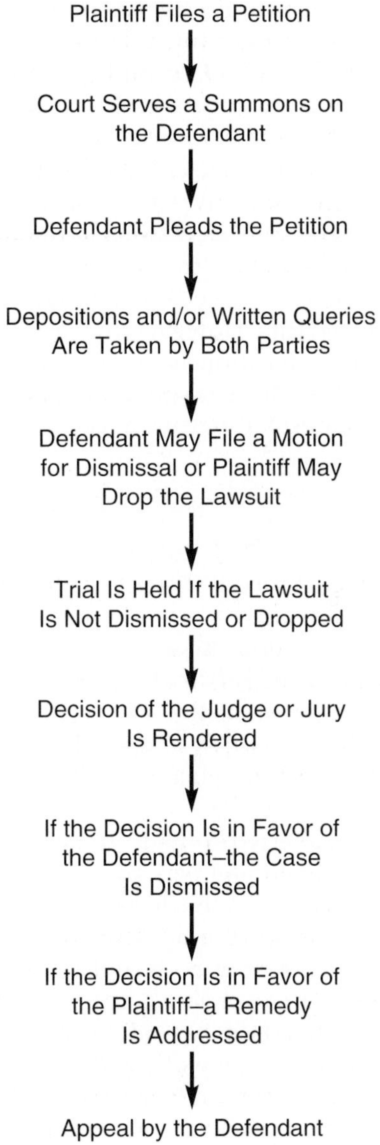

Plaintiff Files a Petition

↓

Court Serves a Summons on
the Defendant

↓

Defendant Pleads the Petition

↓

Depositions and/or Written Queries
Are Taken by Both Parties

↓

Defendant May File a Motion
for Dismissal or Plaintiff May
Drop the Lawsuit

↓

Trial Is Held If the Lawsuit
Is Not Dismissed or Dropped

↓

Decision of the Judge or Jury
Is Rendered

↓

If the Decision Is in Favor of
the Defendant–the Case
Is Dismissed

↓

If the Decision Is in Favor of
the Plaintiff–a Remedy
Is Addressed

↓

Appeal by the Defendant

FIGURE 15-3   Anatomy of a Lawsuit

Source: R. W. Rebore, *Personnel Administration in Education: A Management Approach,*
2nd ed., (Englewood Cliffs, N.J.: Prentice-Hall, 1987), p. 14. Used with permission.

lower court. In like manner, if the judge in the lower court demonstrated a prejudice against the defendant, a higher court may declare a mistrial.

The defendant in a civil lawsuit is determined by the nature of the case. In a tenure or teacher-contract dispute, the board of education as a corporate body is usually the defendant because the school board approves all personnel contracts. In a tort case, an individual such as a teacher may be named as the defendant. A more common occurrence over the last decade is for all individuals with line authority to be named as defendants. In the case of the child who was injured as a result of a fall from playground equipment, the teacher, the principal, the assistant superintendent for elementary education, and the superintendent may be named as defendants. However, the last decade has also witnessed the inclusion of the board of education as a defendant in most lawsuits including tort cases because the board, as the legal governing body of the school district, has greater resources at its disposal to pay damages.

Summary

Over the last decade, school districts have experienced an increase in litigation. In addition, teachers are far more vulnerable today to judicial review of their actions than teachers of a decade ago. It is imperative, therefore, that teachers have a rudimentary understanding of the American judicial system and are capable of making decisions that are legally defensible.

There are basically two systems of law. The first is called a civil law system, which attempts to establish all laws in the form of statutes enacted by a legislative body.

The second is referred to as a common law system, which is the basic approach used in England and was adopted in theory by most of the states in our country. Under this system, the decisions rendered by a court become a precedent to be followed by the court in dealing with future cases. The system of law in the United States is a mixture of both civil and common law.

Three major sources of law form the foundation of the American judicial system: constitutions, statutes, and court cases. Constitutions are bodies of precepts that provide the framework within which government carries out its duty. Statutes are the enactments of legislative bodies more commonly called laws. As stated above, common law emanates from the decisions of courts rather than from legislative bodies.

Two additional sources of law affect education even though they are not traditionally considered primary sources: administrative law and attorney general opinions.

Administrative law consists of those regulations set forth by agencies established by Congress and state legislatures. In the absence of case law, the state attorney general may be requested to render an opinion on the interpretation of a certain statute.

Law may also be categorized according to the rights being protected. Civil law attempts to protect those rights existing between individuals, between corporations, or between an individual and a corporation. Criminal law protects the rights of society.

The judicial system is composed of municipal, state, and federal courts. Most states have four categories of courts: courts of special jurisdiction, circuit courts, courts of appeal, and a supreme court. In like manner, there are four categories of federal courts: courts of special jurisdiction, district courts, the United States Court of Appeals, and the United States Supreme Court.

Our American judicial system also preserves the concept of equity. The state circuit and United States district courts may handle both law and equity issues. Certain issues are traditionally tried in equity, the most common being injunctions.

Tort litigation has become a serious consideration for teachers over the last decade. A tort is a civil wrong committed against a person or a person's property. There are three categories of torts: intentional torts, absolute liability, and negligence. Negligence involves conduct falling below an established standard that results in an injury to another person or persons. If the plaintiff receives a favorable judgment in a tort case involving an injury, the defendant will usually be required to pay the costs incurred by the injury. If it can be demonstrated in court that a person deliberately caused the injury, punitive damages may also be levied by the court against the defendant.

Litigation eludes a set pattern. However, there is enough commonality in civil lawsuits to allow teachers to make general observations that should be helpful as they carry out their responsibilities.

Implications for Future Teachers

The purpose of this chapter is to heighten the sensitivity of those preparing to become teachers to the potential risk of being sued. It is in no way meant to be all-inclusive. In addition, four implications for present and future teachers come forth from this treatment concerning legal liability.

First, ignorance of state and federal legislation and court decisions does not abrogate responsibility.

Second, teachers should attend workshops, seminars, and convention programs dealing with legal issues. The National Education Association, American Federation of Teachers, and other professional associations have convention programs and offer other services to educators that address the legal implications of teaching.[6]

Third, teachers must be active in promoting state and federal legislation that supports the educational goals of public education while protecting the rights of educators.

Fourth, it is imperative that teachers be protected through errors-and-omissions liability insurance.

Discussion Questions

1. What are the three major sources of law that form the foundation of the American judicial system?
2. What are the four basic categories of state courts?
3. Define what is meant by a "tort."
4. Describe the various aspects of a lawsuit.
5. What is the principle of the "reasonable person" as it is applied in tort litigation?

Notes

1. Kern Alexander, Ray Corns, and Walter McCann, *Public School Law: Cases and Materials* (St. Paul, Minn.: West Publishing Co., 1969), 9.

2. Ibid, 10.

3. Edward C. Bolmeier, *The School in the Legal Structure* (Cincinnati: The W.H. Anderson Co., 1968), 110.

4. Lawrence Kallens, J.D., *Teachers' Rights and Liabilities under the Law* (New York: Arco Publishing Co., 1971), 79.

5. Ronald W. Rebore, *Personnel Administration in Education: A Management Approach,* 2nd ed. (Englewood Cliffs, N.J.: Prentice-Hall, 1987), 330.

6. *Nation's School Report,* "Avoiding Personal Liability Suits" 7, no. 9 (May 1981), 1.

Recommended Readings

Alexander, Kern, Ray Corns, and Walter McCann. *1975 Supplement to Public School Law.* St. Paul, Minn.: West Publishing Co., 1975.

Delon, Floyd G., ed. *The Yearbook of School Law, 1974.* Topeka, Kan.: National Organization on Legal Problems of Education, 1974.

Hazard, William R. *Education and the Law.* 2nd ed. New York: The Free Press, 1978.

Hollander, Patricia A. *Legal Handbook for Educators.* Boulder, Col.: Westview Press, 1978.

Hogan, John C. *The Schools, the Courts, and the Public Interest.* 2nd ed. Lexington, Mass.: Lexington Books, 1985.

Jones, Thomas, and Darel Semler, ed. *School Law Update . . . Preventive School Law.* Topeka, Kan.: National Organization on Legal Problems of Education, 1985.

Kallens, Lawrence. *Teachers' Rights and Liabilities Under the Law.* New York. Arco Publishing Co., 1971.

McCarthy, M.M., and N.H. Cambron. *Public School Law.* Boston: Allyn and Bacon, 1981.

Menacker, Julius. *School Law: Theoretical and Case Perspectives.* Englewood Cliffs, N.J.: Prentice-Hall, 1987.

National School Report. "Avoiding Personal Liability Suits" 7, no. 9 (May 1981).

Rebore, Ronald W. *Educational Administration: A Management Approach.* 2nd ed. "Legal and Policy Issues in the Administration of Human Resources." Englewood Cliffs, N.J.: Prentice-Hall, 1987. 324–55.

The Bureau of National Affairs. *The United States Law Week.* Weekly publication. Washington, D.C.: The Bureau.

Updating School Board Policies. "Protecting against Personal Injury to Limit Your Liability" 16, no. 5 (May 1985).

Chapter 16

Equal Employment Opportunity and Public Education

Our contemporary American society is distinguished from prior historical periods by the tremendous number of federal laws and court decisions that delineate and more clearly define *civil rights.* This term is somewhat misunderstood and is often applied only to the constitutional rights of racial minority groups. However, it correctly refers to those constitutional and legislative rights that are inalienable and applicable to all citizens. Civil rights must be a consideration in the recruitment, selection, placement, promotion, and compensation of school district personnel. What institution besides the school can better provide continual leadership in respecting the personal rights of citizens?

What follows is an explanation of major pieces of federal legislation, executive orders, and court decisions that establish the scope of civil rights. It is not meant to be exhaustive because the legislative and judicial processes are organic in nature; therefore, modifications and change will undoubtedly occur. The underlying concept of equality, however, has timeless application.

As a prelude to this presentation, the important concept of affirmative action must be clearly understood because this is a requirement incorporated or implied in civil rights legislation and executive orders.

Affirmative Action

The often-quoted saying, "There can be justice for none if there is not justice for all," captures the intent of civil rights legislation; and the familiar yet authorless motto of many women that "in business we must all be like our fathers" depicts the purpose underlying affirmative action programs.

Affirmative action programs consist of detailed, result-oriented procedures, which, when carried out in good faith, should result in compliance with the equal opportunity clauses found in most legislation and executive orders. Affirmative action, therefore, is not a law unto itself but rather a set of procedures that organizations use to ensure compliance. An organization, therefore, cannot "violate" affirmative action; it violates the law.

Brief History of Affirmative Action

Although the term *affirmative action* is of recent origin, the concept of an employer taking specific steps to utilize fully and to treat equally minority groups can be traced to President Franklin D. Roosevelt's Executive Order 8802, issued in June 1941. Executive orders have the force of law in the federal government. This executive order established a policy of equal employment opportunity applying to companies that were awarded defense contracts. President Roosevelt issued a second order in 1943 extending the equal employment opportunity provision to all government contractors and for the first time mandating that all contracts must contain a clause specifically forbidding discrimination.

In 1953 President Dwight D. Eisenhower issued Executive Order 10479, which established the Government Contract Compliance Committee. This committee received complaints of discrimination against government contractors but had no power to enforce its guidelines.

The period of voluntary compliance ended in 1961 when President John F. Kennedy issued Executive Order 10925. This order established the President's Committee on Equal Employment Opportunity and gave it the authority to make and enforce its own rules by imposing sanctions and penalties against noncomplying contractors. Government contracts were required to have nondiscrimination clauses covering race, color, creed, and national origin.

In September 1965 President Lyndon B. Johnson issued a very important executive order that gave the secretary of labor jurisdiction over contract compliance and that created the Office of Federal Contract Compliance, which replaced the Committee on Equal Employment Opportunity. Every federal contract had to include a multiple-point equal opportunity clause by which the contractor agreed not to discriminate against anyone in hiring and during employment on the basis of race, color, creed, and national origin. The contractor had to further agree in writing to take affirmative action measures in hiring. President Johnson's Executive Order 11375 issued in 1967 amended Executive Order 11246 by forbidding discrimination on the basis of sex and religion. The secretary of labor issued Chapter 60 of Title 41 of the Code of Federal Regulations for the purpose of implementing Executive Order 11375. The secretary delegated enforcement authority to the Office of Federal Contract Compliance (OFCC), which reports to the assistant secretary of the Employment Standards Administration.

The OFCC provides leadership to government contractors in the area of nondiscrimination. The OFCC also cooperates with the Equal Employment Opportunity Commission (EEOC) and the Department of Justice on matters relating to Title VII of the 1964 Civil Rights Act as amended.

The EEOC was established by Title VII of the Civil Rights Act to investigate alleged discrimination based on race, color, religion, sex, and national origin. The EEOC was greatly strengthened in 1972 by the passage of the Equal Employment Opportunity Act. This act extended coverage to all private employers of 15 or more persons, to all educational institutions, to all state and local governments, to public and private employment agencies, to labor unions with fifteen or more members, and to joint labor-management committees for apprenticeships and training. The Equal Employment Opportunity Act also gave the commission the power to bring litigation against an organization that engages in discriminatory practice.

Equal Employment Opportunity Commission (EEOC)

A major failing of many school administrators is their lack of understanding about EEOC and its influence on school administration. This five-member commission has established, from time to time, affirmative action guidelines that, if adopted by school districts, can minimize liability against claims for discrimination. To further aid employers, on December 11, 1978, the EEOC adopted additional guidelines to be used to avoid liability arising from claims of "reverse discrimination" that could occur because of affirmative action programs designed to provide employment opportunities for women and for racial and ethnic minorities.

Following is a compilation from several sources that lists the requirements for affirmative action compliance by school districts.

First, the board of education must issue a written equal employment opportunity and affirmative action policy that commits the district to recruit, select, and promote for all job classifications without regard to race, creed, national origin, sex, or age (except when sex or age is a bona fide occupation qualification). The policy should also indicate that employment decisions will be based solely on an applicant's qualifications as they relate to the requirements of the position for which he or she is being considered. Finally, the policy should state that all personnel considerations such as compensation, fringe benefits, transfers, layoffs, recall from layoffs, and continuing education will be administered without regard to race, creed, color, national origin, sex, or age (*see* Box 16-1).

Second, the superintendent should appoint a top-level administrator to whom he or she can delegate the responsibility of implementing the equal employment opportunity and affirmative action policy. This person usually has the title "Affirmative Action Officer." In fulfilling the responsibilities, this officer should develop a detailed written affirmative action program. This program

---

BOX 16-1   Board of Education Policy on Equal Employment Opportunity and Affirmative Action

The board of education further recognizes that implementation of its responsibility to provide an effective educational program depends on the full and effective utilization of qualified employees regardless of race, age, sex, color, religion, national origin, creed, or ancestry.

The board directs that its employment and personnel policies guarantee equal opportunity for everyone. Discrimination has no place in any component of this school system. Therefore, all matters relating to the recruitment, selection, placement, compensation, benefits, educational opportunities, promotion, termination, and working conditions shall be free from discriminatory practices.

The board of education further initiates an affirmative action program to be in compliance with Title VII of the Civil Rights Act of 1964 and the Equal Employment Opportunity Act of 1972. This program shall insure: proportional minority and female representation and participation in all employment opportunities; that civil rights will not be violated, abridged,

or denied; that recruitment and selection criteria will be unbiased; that information relative to employment and promotional opportunities will be disseminated on an equal basis; and finally that every employee has a right to file an internal or external complaint of discrimination and to obtain redress therefrom based on the finding of facts that substantiate the complaint.

The following school district administrators are responsible for the effective implementation of the affirmative action program.

Superintendent of Schools. As the chief executive officer of the school system, the superintendent is directly responsible for exercising a leadership role in formulating and implementing procedures that are in keeping with this policy.

Director of Affirmative Action. Under the supervision of the superintendent, the director is responsible for the formulation and administration of the affirmative action program.

Source: Ronald W. Rebore, *Personnel Administration in Education: A Management Approach* (Englewood Cliffs, N.J.: Prentice-Hall, 1982), p. 51. Used with permission.

should include the establishment of internal and external methods of communicating the equal employment opportunity policy of the district. In addition, the affirmative action administrator is responsible for assisting other administrators in identifying potential problem areas involving equal opportunity; for designing and implementing equal opportunity auditing and reporting systems; for serving as the school district's liaison with government enforcement agencies; and finally, for keeping the superintendent informed of the latest developments in the area of equal opportunity.

Third, school districts should disseminate information about their affirmative action program to their internal and external publics. The board policy should be publicized through all internal media channels such as school meetings and on school bulletin boards. External dissemination might include printing the policy in brochures describing the district; notification of the policy to recruitment sources such as college/university placement offices; printing an equal opportunity and affirmative action statement on purchase orders, leases, and contracts;

sending the policy to minority organizations, community agencies, and community leaders.

Fourth, a survey should be made to analyze the number of minority and female employees in the school district by job classification. The percentage of minority and female employees currently working in each major job classification should be compared to the percentage of such groups present in the relevant labor market—that is, the geographical area in which the district can reasonably expect to recruit. This will determine "underutilization," which is defined as having fewer minorities or women in a particular job category than could be reasonably expected given the relevant job market; and "concentration," which is defined as having more of a particular minority or females in a job category than would be reasonably expected. A survey should also be conducted to analyze the number of females and minorities who have the necessary credentials to handle other positions in the district.

If "underutilization" is discovered, school district administrators can proceed to step 5, which is developing measurable remedial goals and developing a timetable indicating when such goals can reasonably be expected to be reached. Once long-range goals have been developed, it is relatively easy to establish specific and numerical targets for the hiring, training, transferring, and promoting of people to reach these goals within an established time frame. During this process, the causes of underutilization should be easily recognized by the administration.

Step 6, therefore, calls for developing and implementing specific programs to eliminate discriminatory practices. This is the ultimate objective of all affirmative action programs. Consequently, all individuals involved in the employee selection process must be trained to use objective standards in hiring that support affirmative action goals. Recruitment procedures must be analyzed and reviewed for each job category in order to identify and eliminate discriminatory barriers. For example, new recruitment procedures might include contacting educational institutions and community action organizations that represent minorities.

Reviewing the selection process to ensure that job requirements and hiring practices contribute to reaching affirmative action goals is a vital part of step 6. This includes making certain that job qualifications and selection standards do not screen out females and minorities. Job qualifications, therefore, must be directly related to job requirements. Nondiscriminatory standards can be developed!

Upward-mobility practices such as promoting and reassigning females and minority employees also play an important role in step 6. Through analysis of current promotion and assignment practices, existing barriers can be identified, and thus specific remedial programs can be initiated. These programs might include identifying those women and minority employees who have the necessary qualifications for upward mobility and providing training for those who do not have the qualifications.

Wage and salary structures, fringe benefits, and conditions of employment are other areas of potential discrimination. Title VII of the 1964 Civil Rights Act and the Equal Pay Act require wage and salary parity for all jobs requiring equal skill and having equal responsibility. Thus, a woman cannot be paid less than a man if she has skills and responsibilities equal to her male colleagues. All fringe benefits such as medical, hospital, and life insurance must be available on an equal basis to women and minorities who perform similar functions to other employees who have these benefits. Even in states that have "protective laws" barring women from hard and dangerous work, the courts have held that the equal employment requirements of Title VII supersede such state laws. Courts have also barred compulsory "maternity leave" and the firing of pregnant teachers.

Under federal affirmative action guidelines, the criteria for deciding when a person shall be terminated, demoted, disciplined, laid off, or recalled must be the same for all employees. Seemingly neutral practices should also be reexamined to see if they have a disparate effect on women and minority groups. Using seniority is, of course, a legitimate method to lay off employees including women and minorities when a school district is undergoing declining enrollment. However, job transfers and retraining of women and minorities might be necessary in order to sustain affirmative action goals.

Step 7 consists of establishing internal auditing and reporting systems to monitor and evaluate the progress being made in each aspect of the affirmative action program. Annual reports based on the data already mentioned should be available to all administrators, thus enabling them to see how the program is working and where improvement is needed. The keeping of records on employees by sex, race, and national origin can be a very sensitive issue. Such record keeping has been used by some school districts in the past as a discriminatory device prompting some states to outlaw the practice. In certain court cases, these records have even been used as evidence of discriminatory practices. On the other hand, these data will be demanded by federal government enforcement agencies; they are data that a school district can use to verify certain aspects of its affirmative action program. The EEOC suggests that such information be coded and kept separate from other personnel data.

Developing community support is the last step in an affirmative action program. This will probably include notifying institutions of higher education, community colleges, and business schools about future job requirements and encouraging women and minorities to prepare themselves academically for these jobs.[1]

Bona Fide Occupational Qualification

Discrimination by sex, religion, or national origin is allowed by the Equal Employment Opportunity Act under one condition, referred to in the law as follows:

> *Notwithstanding any other provision of this title, (1) it shall not be an unlawful employment practice for an employer to hire and employ employees, for an employment agency to classify, or refer for employment any individual, for a*

labor organization to classify its membership or to classify or refer for employment any individual, or for an employer, labor organization, or joint labor management committee controlling apprenticeship or other training, or retraining programs to admit or employ any individual in any such program, on the basis of his religion, sex, or national origin in those certain instances where religion, sex, or national origin is a bona fide occupational qualification reasonably necessary to the normal operation of that particular business or enterprise and (2) it shall not be an unlawful employment practice for a school, college, university, or other educational institution or institution of learning to hire and employ employees of a particular religion if such school, college, university, or other educational institution or institution of learning is, in whole or in substantial part, owned, supported, controlled, or managed by a particular religion or by a particular religious corporation, association, or society or if the curriculum of such school, college, university, or other educational institution or institution of learning is directed toward the propagation of a particular religion.[2]

Therefore, the director of personnel for a school district has the right to discriminate against women in hiring for the position of swimming instructor when part of the job description includes supervising the locker room used by male students. In like manner, a Roman Catholic school official may hire only those applicants who profess the Roman Catholic faith because the mission of the school is to propagate that particular faith.

In certain school districts the national origin of teachers is extremely important. One out of every twenty persons in the United States is now of Spanish-speaking origin, making this group the nation's second largest minority, after blacks.[3] Therefore, if a particular school has a pupil population consisting of mostly Puerto Rican students, being of Puerto Rican ancestry could be a bona fide job qualification for certain teaching positions in that school.

Judicial Review of Affirmative Action

Court decisions have further modified affirmative action guidelines and regulations. Although the courts will most likely continue to refine the interpretation of the Civil Rights Act and the Equal Employment Opportunity Act, certain basic conclusions have emerged and, thus, provide direction to school districts in their efforts to administer an affirmative action program.

First, discrimination has been broadly defined in most cases to apply to a class of individuals rather than a single person. Where discrimination was found to exist by the courts, remediation had to be applied to all members of the class to which the individual complainant belonged.

Second, it is not the intent but rather the consequences of the employment practice that determines if discrimination exists.

Third, even when an employment practice is neutral and impartially administered, if it has a disparate effect upon members of a protected class (those groups covered by a law) or if it perpetuates the effects of prior discriminatory practices, it constitutes unlawful discrimination.

Fourth, when statistics indicate that there is a disproportionate number of minorities or females in a job classification relative to their presence in the work force, this constitutes evidence of discriminatory practices. Where such statistics exist, the employer must show that this is not the result of overt or institutional discrimination.

Fifth, to justify any practice or policy that creates a disparate effect on a protected class, an employer must demonstrate a "compelling business necessity." The courts have interpreted this in a very narrow sense to mean that no alternative nondiscriminatory practice can achieve the required result.

Finally, court-ordered remedies not only open the door to equal employment but also require employers to "make whole" and "restore the rightful economic status" of all those in the affected class. In practice, the courts have ordered the hiring of certain applicants who were discriminated against.[4]

Filing a Charge of Discrimination with the Equal Employment Opportunity Commission

A charge can be filed by a person, on behalf of a person, or by any of the EEOC commissioners. This charge must be filed within 180 days of when the alleged discriminatory act occurred. In those states that have an employment discrimination law, the time may be extended to 300 days. First the EEOC must refer the charge to the appropriate state agency. Then the EEOC begins its investigation after the state agency concludes its procedures or after sixty days from the date of referral by the EEOC, whichever occurs first.

Some discriminatory practices are considered to be "continuing violations." A failure to promote because of a discriminatory system of promotions is an example of a continuing violation because it occurs each day the practice is followed. However, when an individual is denied employment because of discrimination, this constitutes a specific violation that occurred on a particular date. A continuing violation arises over a lengthy period of time. The time limit for filing a charge involving a continuing violation is 180 days after the cessation of the discriminatory practice. Therefore, as long as a practice continues, there is no time period for filing a charge.

If an individual is subject to a collective bargaining agreement and believes that he or she has been discriminated against, he or she may follow the grievance procedures set out in the master contract. This procedure in no way alters the time period during which a charge must be filed.

Investigation of the Discrimination Charge

It usually takes eighteen months after a charge is filed for an investigation to begin. The EEOC will demand broad access to an employer's records. An employer may object to the subpoena of records on the following grounds: The information is privileged; the compilation of information would be excessively burdensome; or the information sought is irrelevant to the charges.

The Determination

When the investigation has been completed, the EEOC will make a determination concerning the discrimination charge. This determination will take one of two forms: "reasonable cause," which means that the charge is meritorious and both parties (employer and charging party) are invited to conciliate the case; or "no cause," which means that the charge has no merit. If the charging party continues to believe that discrimination occurred, the court system is the next avenue of recourse.

The Process of Conciliation

This process begins when the employer or his authorized representative meets with the staff of the EEOC at one of the district offices to explore methods of conciliation. The usual methods employed are the following:

1. The employer and charging party may agree to a "conciliation agreement." The terms of this agreement are designed to eliminate the discriminatory practice and may include provisions such as back pay, reinstatement of the charging party if he or she was terminated, or establishing goals and a timetable for hiring and promoting minorities.
2. The employer may extend an offer, with the concurrence of the EEOC, to the charging party. If the charging party rejects the offer, the EEOC issues a "right to sue" notice, which gives the charging party 90 days to bring legal action against the employer.
3. The employer and charging party may agree to a settlement for a single individual. However, if the investigation by the EEOC reveals a discriminatory practice against a class of persons such as females or persons with disabilities, and if the employer along with the EEOC is unable to reach an agreement on a class determination, such is considered a "failure of conciliation" and the case is referred to the litigation division of the EEOC.
4. If the employer, charging party, and the EEOC are unable to reach an agreement, this is also considered a "failure of conciliation" and referral is made to the litigation division.

The Litigation Division

When conciliation fails, the litigation division evaluates the case to determine if there is a significant legal issue involved or if the cause could have a significant impact on systematic patterns of discrimination. If one or both of these conditions exist, the EEOC will most likely bring a lawsuit against the alleged discriminatory employer. The federal court system has jurisdiction in discrimination cases.

If a federal court rules in favor of the charging party, it may grant any relief it deems equitable. For example, the court may enjoin an employer to modify a promotion policy that does not follow affirmative action guidelines, or it may award an individual back pay up to two years prior to the date when the charge was filed with the EEOC.

Civil Rights Act (1991)

The passage of this new civil rights legislation, along with the Americans with Disabilities Act of 1990, embarked school districts on a new path for the 1990s. This is particularly true regarding the Civil Rights Act of 1991. The law for the first time extends punitive damages and jury trials to employees who have been objects of discrimination because of their race, national origin, gender, disability, or religion. School districts must be vigilant in developing and implementing proper procedures for the selection, discipline, and termination of employees.[5]

There are two significant procedural changes. First, the law allows compensatory and punitive damages. Before passage of this law and with few exceptions, plaintiffs could receive remedies limited to lost pay and benefits, reinstatement, and attorney's fees. Plaintiffs can now receive "compensatory damages," for emotional pain, inconvenience, and mental anguish. Further, if the plaintiff can prove that the employer acted with "malice" or with "reckless indifference," he or she may be awarded punitive damages. The customary remedies of remuneration of lost pay and benefits, reinstatement, and attorney's fees are still available, in addition to compensatory and punitive damages.

A major consideration for school administrators and board members is that they can be named as codefendants in an action brought against a school district under the Civil Rights Act of 1991. The law states that punitive damages cannot be levied against a school district because it is a governmental agency but that punitive damages can be levied against individuals such as administrators and school board members.

Limits on the amount of compensatory and punitive damages have been established as follows:

- Plaintiffs may be awarded damages up to $50,000 if the school district has at least 15 but not more than 99 employees.
- Plaintiffs may be awarded damages up to $100,000 if the school district has between 100 and 200 employees.
- Plaintiffs may be awarded damages up to $200,000 if the school district has between 200 and 500 employees.
- Plaintiffs may be awarded damages up to $300,000 if the school district has more than 500 employees.

There are two exceptions to these limits. For age discrimination, the limit is twice the amount of lost pay and benefits; no limit exists for race discrimination there. Another school district liability not previously available in relation to damages is reimbursement to the plaintiff of expert witness fees.

The second significant procedural change involves the right of a complainant to receive a jury trial in an employment discrimination case in which compensatory and/or punitive damages are sought. Jury trials were seldom allowed in employment discrimination cases before implementation of this law. The major consideration concerning this issue is not only the unpredictability of juries but also the perceived bias of juries against employers.

Because of this law, a significant substantive change has occurred in the way the school personnel function is managed. The Civil Rights Act of 1991 overruled several U.S. Supreme Court decisions that appeared to favor employers. Under the new law, the burden of proof in a discrimination case is clearly placed on the school district to justify an employment practice that, at face value, is neutral but that results in discrimination against a protected class.[6]

Equality for the Disabled

Title V of the Rehabilitation Act of 1973 contains five sections, four of which relate to affirmative action for disabled individuals, and one of which deals with voluntary actions, remedial actions, and evaluation criteria for compliance with the law. The congressional intent in enacting the Rehabilitation Act is identical to the congressional intent underlying other civil rights legislation such as the Civil Rights Act (prohibiting discrimination based on race, sex, religion, and national origin) and Title IX of the Education Amendments (prohibiting discrimination based on sex). However, the U.S. Department of Health, Education, and Welfare (HEW) emphasized in the Federal Register promulgating the law that it also contains a fundamental difference:

> *The premise of both Title VI (Civil Rights Act) and Title IX (Education Amendments) is that there is no inherent difference of inequalities between the general public and the persons protected by these statutes and, therefore, there should be no differential treatment in the administration of federal programs. Section 504 (Rehabilitation Act), on the other hand, is far more complex. Handicapped persons may require different treatment in order to be afforded equal access, and identical treatment may, in fact, constitute discrimination. The problem of establishing general rules as to when different treatment is prohibited or required is compounded by the diversity of existing handicaps and the differing degree to which particular persons may be affected.[7]*

Subpart B of Section 504 specifically refers to employment practices. It prohibits recipients of federal financial assistance from discriminating against qualified persons with disabilities in recruitment, hiring and job assignment/classification, and in their salaries and fringe benefits. Employers are further required to provide reasonable work environment accommodations for employees with disabilities unless employers can demonstrate that such accommodations would impose an undue hardship on their business. The law applies to all state, intermediate, and local educational agencies. Finally, all educational agencies that receive financial assistance under the Individuals with Disabilities Education Act must take positive steps to employ and/or promote qualified persons with disabilities to work in programs created under this act.

Reasonable Accommodations

The requirement that employers make "reasonable accommodations" in the work environment for applicants and employees with disabilities has created a great deal of confusion. Reasonable accommodations include: employee facilities that are readily accessible to and usable by persons with disabilities; job restructuring; modified work schedules; modification or acquisition of special equipment or devices; the providing of readers; and other similar actions.

Employment Criteria

The U.S. Department of Health and Human Services in concert with the guidelines on selection procedures developed by the EEOC prohibits the use of any employment test or other criteria that screens out or discriminates against persons with disabilities unless the test or selection criteria can be proven to be job-related. Therefore, in selecting and administering tests to an applicant or employee with a disability, the test results must accurately reflect the individual's job skills rather than the person's impaired sensor, manual, or speaking skills, except when these skills are required for successful job performance.

The term "test" includes measures of general intelligence, mental ability, learning ability, specific intellectual ability, mechanical and clerical aptitudes, dexterity and coordination, knowledge and proficiency, attitudes, and personality. The term also refers to formal techniques of assessing job suitability that yield quantified or standardized scores. Such techniques include specific qualifying or disqualifying personal history and background data, specific educational or work history, scored interviews, biographical information blanks, interviewer's rating scales, and scored application forms.

The Americans with Disabilities Act (1990)

President George Bush signed into law the Americans with Disabilities Act (ADA) on July 26, 1990. This legislation is the most comprehensive ever passed to protect the rights of individuals with disabilities. Within the first 11 months after its passage, the Equal Employment Opportunity Commission received 11,760 discrimination complaints, which represented about 15% of that agency's caseload.

During that period, aggrieved persons collected over 11 million dollars in awards.[8] From a practical perspective, however, the ADA is an extension of the Rehabilitation Act of 1973. This extension pertains to the private sector and to those local and state governmental agencies that receive no federal monies. Because almost every school district in the nation receives some federal financial assistance (either directly or indirectly), which is the threshold requiring adherence to the Rehabilitation Act, school districts in compliance with the Rehabilitation Act will have little difficulty complying with the ADA.

Equality for Women

The French writer Stendhal believed that granting women equality would be the surest sign of civilization and would double the intellectual power of the human race. Although he wrote over one hundred years ago, equality for women continues to be a significant issue in our society.

In school districts the question of equal employment opportunity for women has most often applied to a specific job classification—administration. It is obvious to all observers that women are well represented in teaching, food service, and school bus driving positions. Skilled trade jobs in school districts are still dominated by males. A female carpenter, electrician, or plumber is a rarity not only in school districts but also in the business/industrial community. The critical issue in education, however, is the need to have women better represented in the administrator ranks.

The legal mandate of equal employment opportunity for women emanates primarily from two federal laws: Title IX of the Education Amendments of 1972, which prohibits sex discrimination in educational programs or activities in those school districts receiving federal financial assistance; and Title VII of the Civil Rights Act of 1964, as amended in 1972, which prohibits discrimination on the basis of sex as well as religion, national origin, race, and color.

Potential Areas of Employment Discrimination Concerning Women

As a general rule, school districts are prohibited from establishing job qualifications that are derived from female stereotyping. The courts have uniformly required employers to prove how job restrictions are bona fide occupational qualifications.

Some of the most common forms of discrimination against women in the business/industrial community are even less defensible in educational organizations. For example, some women have been denied employment because of height and weight requirements. In such situations, if a woman can demonstrate that she is capable of performing the job-related tasks, she has clearly established case law precedent to bring the employer to court. However, discrimination is much harder to prove in another situation. For example, it still occurs that an exceptionally talented woman will not be hired for an administrative position because she is a "nice and petite" person who does not measure up to the image of a strong leader.

In addition, the EEOC prohibits discriminating against a woman because of her marital status, because she is pregnant, because she is not the principal wage earner in a family whereas a male applicant is, or because she has preschool-age children.

The preferences of customers and clientele also are not bona fide occupational qualifications. Thus the preference of parents, teachers, and even students for a male principal in a given school does not permit the district to discriminate against female applicants for such a position.

Maternity as a Particular Form of Discrimination

On October 31, 1978, President Carter signed into law a pregnancy disability amendment (P.L. 95–555) to Title VII of the Civil Rights Act of 1964. The law has the effect of prohibiting unequal treatment for pregnant women in all employment-related situations. The EEOC has issued guidelines for implementing this law, indicating that it is discriminatory for an employer to refuse to hire, train, assign, or promote a woman solely because she is pregnant; to require maternity leave for a predetermined time period; to dismiss a pregnant woman; to deny reemployment to a woman who was on maternity leave; to deny seniority credit to a woman on maternity leave; and to deny disability or medical benefits to a woman for disabilities unrelated to but occurring during pregnancy, childbirth, or recovery from childbirth.

Sexual Harassment

The issue of sexual harassment in the workplace reached national and even international attention in 1991 when the United States Senate Judiciary Committee held hearings on President Bush's nominee for the United States Supreme Court, Clarence Thomas. This was an especially painful drama for the nation because the proceedings were aired on public television during which the well-respected Judge Thomas was accused of sexual harassment by an articulate witness, law professor Anita Hill, who detailed graphic charges against Thomas. He was subsequently appointed to the Supreme Court.

In 1980, the Equal Employment Opportunity Commission declared sexual harassment to be a violation of Title VII of the Civil Rights Act of 1964. Basically, there are two types of sexual harassment: *quid pro quo* discrimination and hostile environment discrimination. The first type is obvious. *Quid pro quo* discrimination occurs when an employment or personnel decision is based upon an applicant's or employee's submission to or rejection of unwelcome sexual conduct. Thus, a *quid pro quo* personnel decision occurs when employment opportunities or fringe benefits are granted because of an employee's submission to the employer's or supervisor's sexual advances.

Hostile environment discrimination occurs when unwelcome sexual conduct interferes with the employee's job performance. The standard for deciding environmental discrimination depends on whether the sexual conduct substantially affected the job performance of a reasonable person. Factors to consider in investigating hostile environment discrimination are: the nature of the conduct (physical, verbal, or both); the frequency of the conduct; the position of the harasser, coworker or supervisor; involvement of other employees in the conduct; the number of persons against whom the conduct was directed; and the severity of the conduct (hostile or patently hostile).

It is also important to determine whether the sexual conduct was unwelcome. Did the person alleging sexual harassment indicate that the sexual advances were unwelcome by his or her conduct? In making this determination, the timing of the protest and whether a prior consensual relationship existed with the alleged harasser are significant factors.

School districts are liable for the actions of their administrators and supervisors when these individuals act as the "agent" of the school district at the time of the harassment. For *quid pro quo* discrimination, the administrator or supervisor always acts as the agent of the school district. For hostile environment discrimination, the school district is liable if the district knew or should have known of the sexual harassment by the supervisor.

For coworkers who sexually harass their colleagues, the school district is liable if the agents, administrators, and supervisors knew or should have known about the harassment. When sexual conduct becomes known, the appropriate administrator or supervisor must act to remedy the situation.

It is also the responsibility of administrators and supervisors to take appropriate action to protect employees in the workplace against sexual harassment by non-employees. This responsibility is present when school district agents knew or should have known about the harassment.

For a school district to show employees and the general public that sexual harassment will not be tolerated, the board of education should adopt a policy prohibiting such conduct, and administrative procedures should be developed to effectively address allegations. Further, all employees should be required to participate in a staff development program about the issue of sexual harassment.

The board of education's policy should set forth the commitment of the school district to address sexual harassment in an expeditious and effective manner. Administrative procedures to implement the policy should set forth the complaint process and should include the completion of a complaint form that must be signed by the complainant. The appropriate personnel administrator should inform all parties of their rights. Both the complaint and the investigation should be kept confidential. The procedures also should contain a time-line for completion of the investigation. The policy and procedures must be communicated to all staff members.

A staff development program about sexual harassment for all employees should contain the following components: an explanation of the board policy and administrative procedures; specific examples of sexual harassment; myths about sexual harassment; and the distinction between welcome, consenual, and illegal sexual harassment. Administrator and supervisor staff development should include the above components but should also stress the importance of monitoring workplace behavior and the importance of protecting the complainant against retaliation.[9] Exhibit 16-1 is a sample board of education policy on sexual harassment.

Equality by Age

Peter Drucker, the nationally recognized expert in management theory and practice, has made a significant observation about employee retirement. "Flexible retirement is going to be the central social issue in the U.S. during the next decade. It is going to play the role that minority employment played in the 1960s and women's rights played in the seventies."[10] Drucker's observation is, however, only one aspect of an even larger issue—we are rapidly becoming a nation whose population is, by percentage, mostly middle-aged.

The Age Discrimination in Employment Act of 1967, as amended, is taking on increasing importance for school districts. This act was passed by Congress to promote the employment of the older worker based on ability rather than age. Because of this act, the Department of Labor has continuously sponsored informational and educational programs on the needs and abilities of the older worker. The "Statement of Findings and Purpose" in the Age Discrimination in Employment Act sets forth a rationale for its passage that is also a true reflection of current societal trends toward older workers:

> *Sec. 2.(a) The Congress hereby finds and declares that 1) in the face of rising productivity and affluence, older workers find themselves disadvantaged in their efforts to retain employment, and especially to regain employment when displaced from jobs;*
>
> *2) the setting of arbitrary age limits regardless of potential for job performance has become a common practice, and certain otherwise desirable practices may work to the disadvantage of older persons;*
>
> *3) the incident of unemployment, especially long-term unemployment, with resultant deterioration of skill, morale, and employer acceptability is, relative to the younger ages, high among older workers; their numbers are great and growing; and their employment problems grave;*
>
> *4) the existence in industries affecting commerce of arbitrary discrimination in employment burdens commerce and the free flow of goods in commerce.*

Provisions of the Age Discrimination in Employment Act

The law protects individuals who are at least 40 years of age but less than 70. It applies to private employers of 20 or more persons, to federal, state, and local

---

EXHIBIT 16-1   Sexual Harassment Policy

The Board of Education is committed to providing a work environment that is free from sexual harassment by administrators, supervisors, coworkers, and non-employees.

It is a violation of this policy for the categories of employees and non-employees named above to engage in sexual harassment by making unwelcome sexual advances, unwelcome requests for sexual favors, and by other unwelcome verbal or physical conduct of a sexual nature.

It is a violation of this policy for an administrator or supervisor to make a decision affecting the employment of an individual on the basis of that person's submission to or rejection of sexual advances. If an administrator or supervisor offers an opportunity or fringe benefit to an employee on the basis of that person's submission to or rejection of sexual advances, it also is a violation of this policy.

Conduct of a sexual nature that unreasonably interferes with a person's job performance will be considered sexual harassment.

It is the duty of each administrator and supervisor to monitor his or her area of responsibility to maintain an environment free from sexual harassment. Further, it is the duty of each administrator and supervisor to protect from retaliation an employee who files a complaint of sexual harassment.

An employee or former applicant for employment who believes that he or she has been a victim of sexual harassment should file a complaint with the director of affirmative action as soon as possible after the incident. If the director of affirmative action is the alleged harasser, the complaint should be filed with the superintendent of schools. If the superintendent is the alleged harasser, the board of education should receive the complaint.

When the complaint is received, the director of affirmative action should initiate an investigation as soon as possible. If the complainant requests an investigator of the same gender, and if the director of affirmative action is not of the same gender, another person of the same gender as the complainant will be appointed by the director to conduct the investigation. After the investigation, a report of the findings will be presented to the complainant, the alleged harasser, and the superintendent of schools. Both the investigation and the report are to be considered confidential. An employee who is found to be in violation of this policy will be subject to disciplinary action up to and including termination of employment with the school district.

It is the responsibility of the superintendent of schools to develop administrative procedures to implement this policy and to initiate a staff development program concerning sexual harassment in the workplace, this policy, and administrative procedures. This program must be offered to every employee.

---

governmental units regardless of the number of persons employed. The law also applies to employment agencies and labor organizations having 25 or more members in an industry affecting interstate commerce. The law does not apply to elected officials or their appointees.

It is against the law for an employer to refuse to hire or otherwise discriminate against any person concerning compensation, conditions, or privileges of employment because of age; to limit, segregate, or classify employees so as to deprive any individual of employment opportunities or adversely affect that individual's status as an employee because of age. It is against the law for an employment agency to refuse to refer for employment or otherwise discriminate against an individual because of age or to classify and refer anyone for employment on the basis of age. It is against the law for a labor union to discriminate against anyone because of age by excluding or expelling that person from membership; to limit, segregate, or classify its members on the basis of age; to refuse to refer anyone for employment resulting in a deprivation or limitation of employment opportunity, or otherwise adversely affect an individual's status as an employee because of age; or to cause or attempt to cause an employer to discriminate against an individual because of age.

Furthermore, the provisions of the Age Discrimination in Employment Act prohibit an employer, employment agency, or labor union from discriminating against a person for opposing a practice that is unlawful because of this act; discriminating against a person making a charge, assisting or participating in any investigation, proceeding, or litigation under this act; and publishing a notice of an employment vacancy that indicates a preference, limitation, or specification based on age.

Enforcement of the Age Discrimination in Employment Act

The administration of this act passed from the Department of Labor to the Equal Employment Opportunity Commission on July 1, 1979. At that time the average number of complaints had reached 5,000 annually. The EEOC can conduct investigations, issue rules and regulations to administer the law, and enforce the provisions of the law through the courts when voluntary compliance cannot be obtained.

AIDS and Discrimination

There is no topic or issue which has focused the attention and concern of so many people during the last five years as the acquired immune deficiency syndrome (AIDS). Without going into a long discussion of the medical aspects of the disease, it is sufficient for this treatment to state that the disease can be transmitted to others and that it is always fatal.

The hysteria over this disease caused the surgeon general, Dr. C. Everett Koop, to send an explanatory brochure to all the households in the United States. All health officials are in agreement about the manner in which the disease may be transmitted. Sexual contact with an infected person and the sharing of drug needles or syringes are the most common ways that the disease is transmitted.

Health officials are also in agreement that the disease cannot be transmitted by casual contact with an infected person. In fact, ordinary and casual contact between family members where a member had AIDS verified that the disease cannot be transmitted this way.

The hysteria continues to exist, however, and has caused concerns in the workplace which has resulted in discriminatory practices by some individuals, companies, agencies, and organizations. A significant development occurred in 1987 which has been helpful in dealing with discrimination against people infected with the AIDS virus. In *School Board of Nassau* v. *Arline,* the United States Supreme Court ruled that an infectious disease could constitute a handicap under Section 504 of the Rehabilitation Act of 1973. In this case the infectious disease was tuberculosis. However, in that same year a federal circuit court of appeals in California applied the *Arline* decision to a case involving an Orange County teacher with AIDS. The court ordered the school district to reinstate the teacher to his previous duties.

A further development occurred in 1988 when the United States Justice Department reversed its earlier position on AIDS and declared that fear of contagion by itself does not permit federal agencies and federally assisted employers to fire or discriminate against workers infected with the virus.

This legal opinion is binding on federal agencies, government contractors, *school boards,* managers of federally subsidized housing projects, and other organizations receiving federal contracts or financial assistance. The opinion emphasized that each situation must be determined on a case-by-case basis in order to decide if an infected person poses a direct threat to the health of others in the workplace.

The Rehabilitation Act of 1973 requires an employer to make "reasonable accommodations" for people with disabilities, which now include AIDS victims. The accommodations must be made if the person with AIDS can still perform the essential requirements of his or her job.

If an employer can demonstrate that making such accommodations would pose an undue hardship, then that company, agency, or organization can be excused. However, the regulations governing undue hardship are very stringent.

A situation when the reasonable accommodation regulation probably would not apply is in the case of a school bus driver who has advanced symptoms of the disease. The effects of AIDS on the central nervous system would preclude that person from continuing to drive a school bus.

Summary

The obvious purpose of this chapter has been to provide information to future teachers concerning their equal employment opportunity rights. This presentation includes rather detailed explanations that might be confusing upon the first reading. However, particular attention to the contents of this chapter could be most valuable to the neophyte in search of employment. Equal opportunity should be a given in our society, but prejudice does continue to exist in some school districts. The most effective weapon against such injustice is, first, recog-

---

EXHIBIT 16-2   Sample AIDS Policy

The Board of Education is committed to providing a school environment free from health risks for all students and staff members. This policy has been developed using information from the Federal Centers for Disease Control. In particular, it has been written to protect the rights of school personnel who are infected with the human immunodeficiency virus (HIV), which causes the acquired immunodeficiency syndrome (AIDS) that, in turn, can cause AIDS-related complex (ARC).

Further, the development of this policy has been guided by medical information, which has documented that HIV cannot be transmitted by casual person-to-person contact.

Thus, the Board of Education sets forth the following provisions.

- Each case of HIV, AIDS, or ARC will be evaluated on an individual basis.
- The administration will provide an ongoing program of education on the subject of HIV, AIDS, and ARC to students, staff, and the community.
- Employees who have been diagnosed as infected with HIV, AIDS, or ARC are encouraged to report this to the superintendent of schools accompanied by a written

statement from a licensed physician reporting on the employee's medical condition and capability of continuing in his or her present position.

- This medical information will be confidential to the superintendent of schools. The superintendent will share this information with other employees only on a "need to know" basis, the determination of which will be made in consultation with the infected employee. Those staff members so informed will also be instructed by the superintendent on the legal and policy provisions that require this information to be confidential.
- The employee shall continue in his or her position unless a deterioration in the employee's health significantly interferes with the performance of his or her job responsibilities. The employee's physician may also determine that the employee's job responsibilities pose a threat to his or her health. In either situation, a reasonable effort will be made to place the employee in another position.
- The employee is guaranteed all the protections and safeguards available to other employees according to law and Board of Education policy.

---

nition of unequal treatment and, second, knowledge of the most effective method in dealing with this situation.

Our contemporary American society is distinguished from prior historical periods by the numerous federal laws and court decisions that delineate and more clearly define "civil rights." Incorporated or implied in all civil rights legislation is the important concept of affirmative action. Affirmative action is not a law itself but rather a set of guidelines that organizations may use to comply with legislation and executive orders.

The Equal Employment Opportunity Commission was established by Title VII of the Civil Rights Act to investigate alleged discrimination in employment and in other personnel practices based on race, color, religion, sex, and national origin. The five-member commission, from time to time, has also established affirmative action guidelines.

Alleged discrimination charges can be filed with any of the EEOC's regional or district offices. The process includes filing a charge, investigation of the charge, determination of the charge, and the process of conciliation.

Limited discrimination is allowed by the Equal Employment Opportunity Act under one condition: when there is a bona fide occupational qualification mandating the employing of an individual of a particular sex, religious affiliation, or national origin. Therefore, a school district personnel administrator has the right to employ a male rather than a female for the position of swimming instructor when part of the job description includes supervising the locker room used by male students.

The Rehabilitation Act of 1973 prohibits recipients of federal financial assistance from discriminating against qualified individuals with disabilities in recruiting, hiring, compensating, job assignment/classification, and providing fringe benefits. Employers are further required to provide reasonable accommodations for employees with disabilities.

Equality in employment opportunities for women has been a central issue of the 1990s. The legal mandate of equal opportunity for women has emanated primarily from two federal laws: Title IX of the Education Amendments of 1972, which prohibits sex discrimination in educational programs or activities, including employment, for a school district receiving federal financial assistance; and, of course, Title VII of the Civil Rights Act of 1964, as amended in 1972. In addition, President Carter in 1978 signed into law a pregnancy disability amendment to the Civil Rights Act. This law had the effect of eliminating unequal treatment of pregnant women in all employment-related situations.

The EEOC issued guidelines in November 1985 concerning sexual harassment in the workplace. These guidelines state that an organization is responsible for its acts and those of its agents and supervisory staff with respect to sexual harassment. "Sexual harassment" means physical or verbal sexual advances and even off-color jokes.

The Age Discrimination in Employment Act of 1967, as amended, promotes the employment of the older worker based on ability rather than age by prohibiting arbitrary discrimination.

There is no topic or issue which has focused the attention and concern of so many people during the last five years as the disease of AIDS. Health officials are in agreement that this disease cannot be transmitted by casual contact with an infected person. The hysteria, however, continues to exist and has caused concerns in the workplace which have resulted in discriminatory practices. A significant development occurred in 1987 which has been helpful in dealing with discrimination against people infected with the AIDS virus. In *School Board of Nassau* v. *Arline,* the United States Supreme Court ruled that an infectious disease could constitute a handicap under Section 504 of the Rehabilitation Act of 1973. Further, in 1988 the United States Justice Department reversed its earlier position on AIDS and declared that fear of contagion by itself does not permit federal agencies and federally assisted employers to fire or discriminate against workers infected with the virus. This legal opinion is binding on school boards.

Implications for Future Teachers

Teachers have civil rights that protect them from unlawful actions committed by school administrators and boards of education. Certainly, the vast majority of administrators and board members act in the best interests of teachers and students; however, the pressures of our contemporary society on school districts make it imperative for teachers to know their civil rights and to be dauntless in pursuing their own employment interests.

Thus, in applying for a teaching position, an applicant has a right to know how the school district implements the selection process and why he or she was or was not selected for a position. Further, every teacher has a right to know how a school district implements the federal laws outlined in this chapter. Most districts inform their staff members through an employee handbook about their rights. In those districts where this does not occur, a teacher should inquire about the district's policies and procedures.

Sexual harassment is a good example. The right time to ask who in the school district is responsible for investigating sexual harassment is before an incident occurs.

Discussion Questions

1. Explain the concept "affirmative action."
2. What is meant by a "bona fide occupational qualification"?
3. What is the function of the Equal Employment Opportunity Commission?
4. Name and explain the federal laws which specifically protect the equal employment rights of women.
5. Explain the provisions of the Age Discrimination in Employment Act.

Notes

1. The eight steps are a composite of those found in the Equal Employment Opportunity Commission's *Affirmative Action,* vol. I (Washington, D.C.: Government Printing Office, 1974), 18–64.

2. *The Equal Employment Opportunity Act of 1972* (Washington, D.C.: Government Printing Office, 1972), 4.

3. Carlos J. Orvando, "School Implications of the Peaceful Latino Invasion," *Phi Delta Kappan* 59 (December 1977): 230, 231.

4. Equal Employment Opportunity Commission, *Affirmative Action,* 4–12.

5. Joann S. Lublin, "Rights Law to Spur Shifts in Promotions," *Wall Street Journal,* 30 December 1991, sec. 2. B1.

6. *Education USA,* 35, no. 18 (1993), 5.

7. Department of Health, Education, and Welfare, "Nondiscrimination on the Basis of Handicap," *Federal Register* 41, no. 96 (May 1976).

8. *Wall Street Journal,* 27 July 1993, sec. 1, p. A1.

9. Equal Employment Opportunity Commission, *Guidelines on Sexual Harassment in the Workplace* (Washington, D.C.: U.S. Government Printing Office, 1991).

10. Peter F. Drucker, "Flexible-Age Retirement: Social Issue of the Decade," *Industrial Week* (May 15, 1978): 66–71.

Recommended Readings

Clelland, Richard. *Section 504: Civil Rights for the Handicapped.* Arlington, Va.: American Association of School Administrators, 1978.

Gittins, Naomi E. and Jim Walsh, *Sexual Harassment in the Schools: Preventing and Defending Against Claims.* Alexandria, Virginia: National School Boards Association, 1991.

Hayes, James L. "Affirmative Action in the 1980's: What Can We Expect?" *Management Review* 70 (May 1981): 4–7.

Lewis, John F., Susan C. Hastings, and Anne C. Morgan, *Sexual Harassment in Education.* Topeka, Kansas: National Organization on Legal Problems in Education, 1993.

Ornstein, Allan C., and Daniel U. Levine "Schools, Society, and the Concept of Equality." *Clearing House* 55 (November 1981): 127–31.

Pollard, William F. "The Role of Organized Labor in Achieving Equal Opportunity." *The Journal of Intergroup Relations* 12 (Spring 1984): 12–22.

Rebore, Ronald W. *Personnel Administration in Education: A Management Approach.* 2nd ed. Englewood Cliffs, N.J.: Prentice-Hall, 1987, 37–69.

Templer, Andrew J., and James M. Tolliver. "Affirmative Action—Making It Effective in the Public Sector." *Public Personnel Management Journal* 12 (Summer 1983): 211–17.

U.S. Congress, Senate Committee on Labor and Public Welfare. *The Equal Employment Opportunity Act* of 1972, p. 3. Committee report. 92nd Cong. 2nd sess., March 1972. Washington, D.C.: Government Printing Office, 1972.

U.S. Equal Employment Opportunity Commission. *Affirmative Action and Equal Employment,* vols. I and II. Washington, D.C.: Government Printing Office, 1974.

Walters, Ronald. "The Politics of Affirmative Action." *The Western Journal of Black Studies* 6 (Fall 1982): 175–81.

A p p e n d i x A

Educational Philosophy Self-Test
Supplement to Chapter 4

The following sixty-eight statements are a cross-section of views about all phases of schooling, arranged to reflect mainly *progressive* and *essentialist* viewpoints. These have been the two dominant attitudes underlying theory and practice, especially in public education. Note that one may believe in positions of both philosophies and still be consistent in view. This educational stance is called *eclecticism*, a combination of two or more viewpoints resulting in a new position. One can see some value or truth in many beliefs.

On a sheet of paper, write down the numbers of *only* those statements below with which you *strongly agree:*

1. Secondary school teachers have the moral and legal right to teach about sensitive issues despite community opposition.

2. Since parents help pay for schools, they should be consulted periodically about acceptable educational methodology.

3. In social studies classes, economic free enterprise should emerge as the right economic system.

4. Social criticism is a function of the public schools, especially at the secondary level.

5. The school's major societal function is to teach youth to read, write, and compute well at all grade levels.

6. Vocational education and the liberal studies are equally important.

7. Salable vocational skills must be a primary function of the school.

8. The school should not significantly focus on social problems.

9. Externally enforced, humane discipline leads to self-discipline.

10. Promotion to the next grade level is usually justifiable despite one's academic progress.

11. Report cards should reflect progress from many viewpoints: academic, social, emotional, and physical.

12. "Truth" is a relative concept.

13. "Truth" is absolute either in terms of divine revelation or the accumulated wisdom of the centuries.

14. The only social constant or absolute is change.

15. The relevance of subject matter is determined chiefly by present social problems or by the intellectual desires of learners.

16. "General science" is a more appropriate subject of study than physics, chemistry, and so on, for students who are non-majors in any of the sciences.

17. Since life is competitive, students should be evaluated by how well they compare with others in most subjects.

18. The usefulness of formal study may not be realized for years.

19. Students must be taught that learning is often painful.

20. Experiences in the child's life inside the school must be closely related to experiences outside the school.

21. Generally speaking, effort begets interest.

22. Generally speaking, interest begets effort.

23. The U.S. Constitution should be amended to allow voluntary prayer in the public school.

24. Until better housing and equal employment opportunities become a reality for all, the public school should not ambitiously attempt racial desegregation.

25. Critical thinking, as opposed to the memorization of facts, should dominate the approach in social studies textbooks in elementary schools.

26. The value of an idea can be measured only by its immediate usefulness.

27. Generally speaking, the required study of a foreign language for all college students is a waste of time.

28. If a public school budget must be severely reduced, driver education, home economics, and varsity sports, for example, should be curtailed before other reductions are made in the sciences or humanities.

29. Ability grouping is vital to provide gifted students with as much challenge as possible.

30. College admissions tests should be adjusted to permit more students to enroll.

31. With the exception of a few colleges and universities, most American institutions of higher education do not deserve such a label. They are chiefly centers of vocational study.

32. Most subjects of study in high school should be elective.

33. Teacher education at the elementary school level should place more emphasis on what to teach rather than on how to teach.

34. Reading is an educational activity without equal at any level of schooling.

35. There are many roads to the acquisition of knowledge; reading is certainly one important avenue among others.

36. The basic purpose of formal education is to transmit the cultural heritage.

37. The basic purpose of formal education is to assist in the complete development of the total personality.

38. The attempt to individualize instruction, especially from kindergarten through grade twelve, should be a primary educational goal.

39. Morality arises from the quality of mutually shared experiences.

40. Since both the definition and measurement of the "whole" child are vague, it is a meaningless concept.

41. If there is to be any indoctrination whatsoever in the public school, it must be indoctrination in the method of pursuing knowledge.

42. Whenever possible, the problem-solving or inductive method of learning should be employed.

43. The accumulated wisdom of the centuries should be studied differently. Instead of approaching it chronologically, it should be approached topically in light of its pertinence.

44. No matter how much public support vocational subjects receive, there will never be the same prestige associated with them as with mathematics and the sciences.

45. Students at all grade levels should be taught well the difference between work and play.

46. To use class time for instruction in areas such as family life and sex education, drug education, and consumer economics takes valuable time away from the teaching of the basic, core subjects.

47. Pupil conformity to classroom rules should be *jointly* determined by teacher and pupils.

48. The teacher should be a dominant authority figure in the classroom simply because she or he is morally and legally expected to be such.

49. Most students need to be directed by a strong humane authority figure.

50. Inner freedom or self-discipline comes from experience in group activities.

51. Corporal punishment (paddling) should be considered an inhumane method of classroom control.

52. Since there is a constant danger of the teacher losing a professional image with students, it is best he or she remains emotionally distant from them.

53. Within broad limitations, school discipline should be permissive in order to allow students to learn social skills through group involvement.

54. The purpose of individualized instruction may be a noble one, but very unrealistic in light of limited financial resources.

55. Teaching is more of an art than a science. It always has been and will continue to be.

56. If a pupil in the elementary school matures socially and emotionally but fails to make significant academic progress, the teacher can still believe he or she has had a successful year.

57. If a teacher and student reach an impasse on what should be learned in an independent study project, the teacher's will must prevail because of his or her greater experience and knowledge.

58. School counselors should exert no influence on the student that may undermine the teacher's authority.

59. School dress codes in the high school are necessary.

60. Generally speaking, a student's knowledge of the structure of the federal government will make him or her a better citizen.

61. The more a student learns to perform tasks automatically (memorization), the more he or she can think productively about similar but more complex topics.

62. An emotional conviction to a socially acceptable ideal can be a religious experience.

63. It matters little if one believes in moral absolutes and employs experimental methods in teaching.

64. As long as students like school and achieve, it matters little what approach the teacher employs.

65. It is tiresome to hear frequently how bad traditional educational methods have been. There is some truth in all points of view.

66. Individualized instruction arises primarily from a teacher's belief in improving instruction. Ethical beliefs may or may not be related to classroom methodology.

67. Progressive education was formally an early twentieth century reform movement. It helped to stimulate change. Hopefully, there will always be influential reformists on the educational scene to prevent stagnation.

68. Reporting student progress should combine, in a written form, both academic achievement based upon group norms and growth in social and emotional skills.

Now, looking at the key on the next page, place a "P" for progressivism or an "E" for essentialism next to the numbers of those statements with which you strongly agreed and add up the number of P's and E's accumulated. Although this examination is not standardized, the authors believe that if you compiled over twenty progressive or essentialist statements, you strongly lean toward that overall educational viewpoint. If your score does not reflect either conservative (E) or liberal (P) educational positions, then you may be an eclectic. This means you see some value in different approaches. The authors desire prospective teachers to be systematic and clear about their educational views. This applies to eclecticism as well.

Key to Educational Philosophy Self-Test

1. P	13. E	25. P	37. P	49. E	61. E
2. E	14. P	26. P	38. P	50. P	62. P
3. E	15. P	27. P	39. P	51. P	63. N
4. P	16. P	28. E	40. E	52. E	64. N
5. E	17. E	29. E	41. P	53. P	65. N
6. P	18. E	30. P	42. P	54. N	66. N
7. P	19. E	31. E	43. P	55. E	67. N
8. E	20. P	32. P	44. E	56. P	68. N
9. E	21. E	33. E	45. E	57. E	
10. P	22. P	34. E	46. E	58. E	
11. P	23. E	35. P	47. P	59. E	
12. P	24. E	36. E	48. E	60. E	

P, Progressivism; E, Essentialism; N, Neither.

Annotated Bibliography of National Reports and Studies on Education

Supplement to Chapter 5

1989

State Policies on Sex Education. New York: The Alan Guttmacher Institute, 1989.

Three national surveys in 1988 indicated that the AIDS crisis and early sexual activity have spurred widespread adoption of sex education curricula. Most sex education teachers offer content about birth control and sexual abstinence. Sixty percent of secondary school students take at least one such course before graduation. Inadequate parental and community support often impede instruction.

Smith, Edward E. *Report on the Homeless.* Washington, D.C.: Office for the Education of Homeless Children, U.S. Department of Education, 1989.

The Stewart B. McKinney Homeless Assistance Act of 1987 provided the stimulus for this report to encourage state and federal programs to assist homeless school-aged youth. About 600,000 youth are homeless and fewer than one-half of these youth attend school regularly.

Turning Points: Preparing American Youth for the 21st Century. Princeton, NJ: Carnegie Council on Adolescent Development, 1989.

This report focuses on the crucial years of early adolescence and offers a plan for correcting the "volatile mismatch" between the structure and curriculum of middle school grades and needs of students at this level. Better flexibility, teacher education, and community involvement can all assist in "recapturing millions of youth adrift."

A Common Destiny: Blacks and American Society. Washington, D.C.: National Research Council, 1989.

Segregation and differential treatment of blacks continue to be widespread in schools, which also do little to compensate for socioeconomic handicaps. Teacher behavior, school climate, and the content and organization of instruction can affect learning greatly despite low socioeconomic status.

1990

National Assessment of Educational Progress, *Learning to Read in Our Nation's Schools.* Princeton, NJ: National Assessment of Educational Progress, 1990.

This assessment, based upon 33,000 students in reading and writing classes in grades four, eight, and twelve, indicates that students spend little time reading or writing within or outside school. About one-half of the students read ten or fewer pages daily and wrote only a few paragraphs during a six week period of the study.

National Commission on the Skills of the American Work Force, *America's Choice: High Skills or Low Wages?* New York: National Commission on the Skills of the American Work Force, 1990.

A report, which among several recommendations, advocates that every teenager about age sixteen be required to qualify for employment or further training. Non-college bound youth especially need to fill the predicted "skills-void" in the labor force.

National Commission on Testing and Public Policy, *From Gatekeeper to Gateway: Transforming Testing in America.* Chestnut Hill, MA: National Commission on Testing and Public Policy, 1990.

This study highlights the point that despite increased reliance on standardized multiple choice tests, they are overused, imperfect, and can distort schooling and social policy. Assessment should be broader in scope and focus on performance, including standardized testing.

National Assessment of Educational Progress, *The U.S. History Report Card.* Princeton, NJ: National Assessment of Educational Progress, 1990.

A study of about 16,000 students in grades four, eight, and twelve. Indicates that these students have some rudimentary knowledge of history and civics; however, they fail to demonstrate an in-depth knowledge of either.

1991

Center for Civic Education and the Council for the Advancement of Citizenship, *Civitas.* Washington, D.C.: National Council for the Social Studies, 1991.

An eclectic report "reintroduces" civics education into the nation's schools throughout all grades by means of a curriculum authored by scholars from over twenty national groups. Civic knowledge, skills, and virtues are advocated.

National Assessment Governing Board, *Levels of Mathematics Achievement.* Washington, D.C.: National Assessment Governing Board, 1991.

This report indicated that fewer than 20 percent of American students in grades four, eight, and twelve can display mastery of challenging mathematical content.

National Education Goals Panel, *The National Education Goals Report: Building a Nation of Learners.* Washington, D.C.: National Education Goals Panel, 1991.

This first report card on the national education goals reflected only a few passing grades: high school completion rate, math and science performance, and lessened drug abuse among youth.

Boyer, Ernest L. *Ready to Learn: A Mandate for the Nation.* Lawrenceville. NJ: Princeton University Press, 1991.

In this report, sponsored by the Carnegie Foundation for the Advancement of Teaching, the Foundation's president, Ernest Boyer, focused on the need to help children enter school well prepared. Better health care and parent education are two key suggestions to help children overcome stressful pre-school environments.

1992

American Association of University Women (AAUW) *How Schools Shortchange Girls.* Annapolis, MD: AAUW, 1992.

Girls are "systematically" discouraged from pursuing studies that would foster productive future employment in science, technology, and engineering. Forty recommendations are cited which range from reducing sex discrimination to adopting "gender-fair" curricula.

Boyer, Ernest L., *School Choice.* Ewing, NJ: Carnegie Foundation for the Advancement of Teaching, 1992.

Even though 13 states and several school districts have adopted a variety of "choice" measures since 1987, this study indicates that 70 percent of parents of children in public schools want no other choice and oppose by a two-to-one margin any attempt to include private schools.

Center for the Assessment of Educational Progress. *Learning Mathematics* and *Learning Science.* Princeton, NJ: Educational Testing Service, 1992.

An international study of students nine and 13 years of age in 20 countries indicated that American students age 13 ranked low in math and science, whereas students age nine ranked high in science but low in math.

Center for the Study of Testing Evaluation and Educational Policy. "The Influence of Testing and Teaching Math and Science in Grades 4–12." Chestnut Hill, MA: Boston College, 1992.

Standardized and textbook tests, according to findings in this study, stress lower level thinking and knowledge and affect classroom instruction in a negative manner. Conceptual knowledge and problem solving abilities are underplayed in both kinds of tests and teachers are forced to "rush their instruction" to prepare students for testing.

Hechinger, Fred M. *Fateful Choices: Healthy Youth for the 21st Century.* Waldorf, MD: Carnegie Council on Adolescent Development, 1992.

Many adolescents adopt risky behaviors that will endanger their future. Of 28 million adolescents between 10 and 18, 7 million are being harmed by health and life-threatening activity. Another 7 million are at moderate risk. Better health care services and education, and safety in and around school are crucial to implement. Alcohol, drugs, sexual activity without condoms, and gang membership are serious obstacles to general well-being.

International Association for the Education of Educational Achievement (IDEA). *Education at a Glance.* Hamburg, Germany: International Coordinating Center, University of Hamburg, 1992.

American students (ages nine and 14) in this study involving 32 nations, out-performed their peers in reading literacy. Only students from Finland, France, Sweden, and New Zealand did better. Improved reading instruction, emphasizing literature and meaning have helped to raise American literacy.

National Assessment of Educational Progress (NAEP). *The 1990 Science Report Card.* Washington, D.C.: NAEP, 1992.

The findings of this study corroborate earlier studies related to poor performance by fourth, eighth, and twelfth graders in scientific content. Applying knowledge to interpret graphs and tables, designing experiments and expressing detailed scientific data are skills students generally do not possess.

National Assessment of Educational Progress (NAEP). *Reading In and Out of School.* Washington, D.C.: NAEP, 1992.

American students, according to this study, read very little anywhere. About 45 percent of fourth graders, 63 percent of eighth graders, and 59 percent of 12th graders read 10 pages or fewer per day for school. About 20 percent of all students say they read nothing elsewhere.

National Association for State Boards of Education (NASBE), *Winners All: A Call for Inclusive Schools.* Alexandria, VA: NASBE, 1992.

In this study, state school boards of education are strongly encouraged to adopt "full" inclusion policies for children with disabilities. Teacher licensure also should be awarded only on the basis of preparation to teach children, both with disabilities and without disabilities.

National Longitudinal Transition Study. *Youth With Disabilities: How Are They Doing?* Washington, D.C.: U.S. Department of Education, Office of Special Education, 1992.

Most graduates (69.4 percent) with disabilities find employment within four years; however, only 14 percent of students with disabilities receive any post-secondary training within two years.

National School Boards Association (NSBA), *States of School Desegregation: The Next Generation*. Madison, WI: University of Wisconsin Center for Demography, 1992.

> This study reveals data to show that Hispanic students are more segregated than blacks in American schools. About 63 percent of blacks attend schools that are less than half-white, but almost 75 percent of Hispanic students attend schools that are mainly minority.

New American Schools Development Corporation (NASDC). New American Schools Contest, Washington, D.C.: 1992.

> The corporation cited above (NASDC) was created in 1991 to raise $200 million for the design and implementation of a new era of "break the mold schools." Of 686 competitors, 11 were selected. Multi-age classrooms, focusing on self-paced instruction, characterize the winners.

1993

Committee for Economic Development, *Why Child Care Matters: Preparing Young Children for a More Productive America*. New York, NY: Committee for Economic Development, 1993.

> This report warns that gaps in the quality and accessibility of child care are hampering educational opportunities for young children. The authors of this report recommend financial restructuring by means of tax credits, vouchers to help especially low income families, and to ensure that Headstart begins to reach three and four-year-old children.

High/Scope Educational Research Foundation. *Significant Benefits: The High/Scope Perry Preschool Study Through Age 27*. Ypsilanti, MI: High/Scope Press, 1993.

> In this longitudinal preschool study, 58 children who, were three and four years of age and who are now age 27, have shown "striking social gains" by comparison with their peers (65 in a control group). These experimental subjects have committed fewer crimes, have higher earnings, and possess a stronger commitment to marriage. The implications of this study focus on the point that strong Head Start programs can make a difference.

Interstate New Teacher Assessment and Support Consortium. *Model for New Teachers* (Draft), Washington, D.C.: Council of Chief State School Officers, 1993.

> State policy makers and other educational leaders have developed a draft model of standards for beginning teachers that identifies a core of essential skills. The standards are organized around guiding principles, such as understanding one's academic discipline, adapting instruction to diverse learning styles, *etc.*

National Assessment of Educational Progress (NAEP) and the National Center for Education Statistics. *NAEP 1992: Mathematics Report Card for the Nation and the States*. Pittsburgh, PA: NAEP and Superintendent of Documents, 1993.

This report indicates that in 18 of the 37 states which participated in the NAEP's assessment, over 50 percent of the tested 8th graders tested showed significant mathematical gain since 1990; however, 75 percent of 4th graders failed to achieve "basic" mastery of such knowledge and skills. Only 50 percent of twelfth graders could solve problems using fractions, decimals, and percents.

National Catholic Education Association (NCEA). *Enrollment in Roman Catholic Schools, 1992–93.* Washington, D.C.: NCEA, 1993.

For the first time since 1963, enrollment in Roman Catholic schools has increased by one percent. From pre-K through grade 12, enrollment is 2,567,630, an increase of 16,767 students. Prekindergarten and kindergarten programs have grown the most.

National Performance Review, *From Red Tape to Results: Creating a Government That Works Better and Costs Less.* Pittsburgh, PA: Superintendent of Documents, 1993.

The recommendations of this task force focus on eliminating about 40 of the U.S. Education Department's 230 current programs. About 20 other programs should be consolidated; for example, employment and training programs and another 10 should be reorganized into flexible grants. The savings would be as much as $108 million over five years.

R.M.C. Research Corporation, *et al., National Study of Before and After School Programs.* Washington, D.C.: U.S. Office of Education, 1993.

In 1991, about 1.7 million children (K–8) were enrolled in a variety of before and after school programs, with about one-third of them enrolled in public school-sponsored programs. While these programs are providing a safe refuge for children, the tuition, high turnover of staff, and ineffective activities make such arrangements little more than custodial care. There is, however, excellent educational potential in these programs.

Toma's Rivera Center, *Resolving a Crisis in Education, Latino Teachers for Tomorrow's Classrooms.* Claremont, CA: Toma's Rivera Center, 1993.

In 1991, Hispanics composed 11.8 percent of the nation's students, but only 3.7 percent of this nation's teachers were Hispanic. In 1993, fewer than 2 percent of prospective teachers are Latino. States need proactive policies to encourage Hispanics to seek teaching as a career: loan forgiveness, flexible certification, internships, bilingual programs, etc.

1994

Rebecca A. Marcone, *After Six Years: The Preschool Impact,* Washington, D.C.: District of Columbia Public Schools, 1994.

In a study involving 461 children from 95 schools in Washington, D.C., two groups of pre-K and Head Start children (one group younger than the other) were studied to show academic growth over a seven year period. In general, "child initiated" learning and social development programs proved to have more lasting effects than programs with an academic emphasis. Parental involvement promotes success.

Kathryn Taaffe Young, *Starting Points: Meeting the Needs of Our Youngest Children.* Waldorf, MD: Carnegie Corporation of New York, 1994.

A Carnegie Corporation of New York task force highlighted research to show that the first three years of life are the most critical in a child's development, yet the most neglected by public policy. Chief among the recommendations are programs to encourage planning for parenthood and to promote a healthy environment. Parenthood education should begin in the elementary school.

National Education Commission on Time and Learning, *Prisoners of Time*, Washington, D.C.: U.S. Department of Education, Government Printing Office, 1994.

A two-year study was done by the above advisory panel to show the relationship between time and learning in the nation's schools. The panel recommended that high school students should spend about six hours daily in nine core academic subjects. Presently such students spend half that time daily compared with students in France, Germany, and Japan. A longer school year is recommended along with the dissolution of the Carnegie unit.

SRI International, *How Chapter 2 Operates at the Federal, State, and Local Levels,* Washington, D.C.: Planning and Evaluation Service, 1994.

This study is the basis for the Clinton Administration to eliminate the Chapter 2 block grant programs in favor of channeling money into more specific reform programs. Instructional materials and innovative programs receive most of the funding; however, results are difficult to measure in terms of student performance.

A p p e n d i x C

Selection Criteria

Supplement to Chapter 13

Selection Criteria for a High School English Teacher

Applicant _____ Date _____

A check on the scale is an indication of initial judgment. It is assumed that other sources of information may alter the interviewer's judgment about the applicant's suitability. 1 = inferior; 3 = average; 5 = superior.

Selection Criteria

	1	2	3	4	5

A. Personal characteristics and qualifications
    1. Personal appearance—neat, clean, and so on
    2. Poise/stability—knows self
    3. Ability to present ideas
    4. Voice projection
    5. Use of English language/speech
    6. Pleasant personality—not irritable
    7. Exemplifies leadership traits
    8. Demonstrates good judgment

Subtotal _____

B. Professional characteristics and qualifications
    1. Knowledge of subject matter
    2. Educational philosophy meets job needs

Source: Ronald W. Rebore, *Personnel Administration in Education: A Management Approach,* 2nd ed. (Englewood Cliffs, N.J.: Prentice-Hall, 1987), pp. 113–116. Used with permission.

	1	2	3	4	5

3. Concern for student differences
4. Enthusiasm for teaching
5. Interacts well in a group
6. Shows signs of creativity
7. Flexible—evidence of cooperation
8. Teaching methodology—shows variety
9. Pupil control techniques
10. Professional attitude
11. Knowledgeable about English curriculum
12. Willingness to sponsor activities
13. Undergraduate grades in English
14. Classroom management techniques
15. Job-related hobbies and/or special talents
16. Overall undergraduate grade-point average
17. Knowledge of teaching/learning process

Subtotal _____

	1	2	3	4	5

C. Experience and teaching
    1. Relevance of previous teaching experience
    2. Years of previous teaching experience
    3. Certification in English
    4. Certification in another area(s)
    5. Relevance of student teaching
    6. Grade received for student teaching
    7. Member professional organization

Subtotal _____
Total Score _____

The following is a general appraisal of this individual's promise for future success as an English teacher in our school district. Check one:

Should not be considered; poor applicant	Endorse with reservations; inferior applicant	Should be considered; average applicant	Good first impression; strong applicant	Exceptional potential; outstanding applicant

Additional comments:
Interview began _____ Interview ended _____
Interviewer _____

Selection Criteria for an Elementary School Teacher, Self-contained Classroom

Applicant _____ Date _____

Interviewer _____

SELECTION CRITERIA	*POSSIBLE POINTS*	*DESIGNATED POINTS*
1. Professional preparation—Does applicant hold the necessary college preparation and appropriate state certification?	25	
2. Experience—Was the applicant's past teaching experience or student teaching experience successful?	10	
3. Personal characteristics—Are applicant's manner and dress appropriate to the standards of the school district?	15	
4. Educational philosophy—Are the educational ideas and values of the applicant compatible with the school district's policies and curriculum?	50	

Comments: Possible 100   Total _____

Appendix D

Interviewing Questions
Supplement to Chapter 13

1. What unique qualities do you possess that we should consider?
2. What do you know about our school district?
3. Will you tell me about your hobbies?
4. What clubs and activities would you be willing to sponsor?
5. Please share with me your thoughts on:
   Traditional education
   Open education
   Team teaching
   Nongradedness
   Large-group instruction
   Small-group instruction
6. How do you feel about thematic (unit) planning?
7. In what ways would you provide for differentiated assignments?
8. How would you provide for the individualization of instruction?
9. What are your thoughts about PTA and other community organizations?
10. How many students can you adequately instruct in any given time?
11. What is your philosophy of education?
12. Please tell me about the methods of evaluation that you would use.
13. Why will our school district be better for having hired you?
14. Why would you like to teach in our school district?
15. Please give me your thoughts on some recent educational literature that impressed you.
16. How would you provide for a rich educational climate in your classroom?

Source: Ronald W. Rebore, *Personnel Administration in Education: A Management Approach,* 2nd ed. (Englewood Cliffs, N.J.: Prentice-Hall, 1987), pp. 117–18. Used with permission. Questions compiled by C. John Brannon, superintendent of South Side Area School District, Hookstown, Penn.

17. What is your conception of the way an instructional materials center should function in a school?
18. How would you utilize the services of the guidance and counseling staff?
19. What is wholesome about American education today?
20. What should be improved in American education as it exists today?
21. Do you feel you know yourself? Your hopes? Aspirations? Long-range goals?
22. What is your philosophy of life?
23. How does your area of certification relate to the other disciplines?
24. Please tell me about the artifacts you would regularly use in your instruction.
25. What is your concept of the role of the administration in relation to teachers? To students?
26. As a teacher in our district what would be your role in our community?
27. Are you familiar with the works of any of the educational philosophers?
28. Can you conceptualize educational programs and buildings of the year 2000? What might they be like?
29. In what way does your discipline (area of certification) lend itself to outdoor education?
30. Are you familiar with differentiated staffing? How would you relate to that eventuality in our district if you were teaching here?
31. Should students have any part in the evaluation of teachers? Why?
32. To what extent should students be involved in determining what should be taught and how it should be taught?
33. What constitutes an effective classroom? Study hall?
34. Are you familiar with the scientific method of investigation? To what extent should that method be utilized in your classroom?
35. How would you handle controversial issues as they come before your class?
36. Please react to the job description prepared for the position for which you are applying.
37. What are your plans for furthering your education?
38. What, in your opinion, are the best ways to communicate with parents?
39. Is it still applicable that teachers should be exemplars in the community? Why?
40. What rights and responsibilities do you feel students should assume?
41. Please evaluate this interview and tell me how you think it could be improved to better acquaint other candidates with our district and the position for which you are applying.

Teacher's Application, Goodville School District

Supplement to Chapter 13

Application

For office use only

Interview date _____

Interviewer _____ Date _____

Position _____ Social security number _____

I. Personal data:

Name _____

          Last   First   Middle

Date of birth _____ Age _____

Present address _____ Phone _____

                     Street City State Zip

Permanent address _____ Phone _____

                       Street City State Zip

General condition of health _____

Are you willing to take a physical exam? _____

II. Professional data:

List in order of preference the subjects or grades you are prepared to teach:

1. _____ **2.** _____ **3.** _____

List teaching certificates held: State retirement no. _____

Source: Ronald W. Rebore, *Personnel Administration in Education: A Management Approach*, 2nd ed. (Englewood Cliffs, N.J.: Prentice-Hall, 1987), pp. 120–22. Used with permission.

List teaching certificates held (other states):

_____

Membership in professional organizations _____

What co-curricular activities are you prepared to sponsor (secondary level)?

_____

III. Teaching and/or administrative experience:

List experience in chronological order (starting with first position held) and account for each school year since you began teaching.

NUMBER OF YEARS OF EXPE-RIENCE	INCLUSIVE DATES FROM TO	NAME OF SCHOOL	LOCATION CITY OR COUNTY, STATE	GRADES, SUB. OR POSITION	ANNUAL SALARY	NAME OF PRINCIPAL	PRESENT ADDRESS OF PRINCIPAL

Kindergarten ___ years   Junior High ___ years   Administrative ___ years

Elementary ___ years   Senior high ___ years   Other ___ years

Total teaching experience ___ years

Name of superintendent under whom you last taught _____

IV. Educational and professional training:

Total number of hours to date: ___ Undergraduate ___

Graduate ___ Major ___ Number of major hours ___

Minor ___ Number of minor hours ___

	NAME OF INSTITUTE ATTENDED	STATE	DATES ATTENDED FROM	DATES ATTENDED TO	TIME IN YEARS AND FRACTION OF YEARS	GRADUATION DATE	GRADUATION DEGREE	SUBJECTS MAJOR	SUBJECTS MINOR
A. College or University									
B. Graduate Work									
C. Additional Education									

IV. For both secondary and elementary major

Hours of student teaching		
Place of student teaching		Address
Name of coop. teacher		Address
Subject or grade level of student teaching		

V. Professional references:

Location of confidential placement file _____

It is the responsibility of the applicant to have his/her placement file and college/university transcripts sent to the school district.

Please list three people who have firsthand knowledge of your work performance.

Have these individuals send a letter of reference to the personnel department if references are not included in your placement file. One of the three reference letters must be from your current or last immediate supervisor.

NAME	OFFICIAL POSITION	PRESENT ADDRESS

Signature: _____

Teacher Evaluation Report

Supplement to Chapter 14

Lindbergh School District
4900 South Lindbergh Boulevard
St. Louis, Missouri 63126

Teacher _____ School _____ Year _____
Status of teacher: (   ) **Probationary**   (   ) **Tenured**

Philosophy

Evaluation is a means of improving the quality of instruction.

Purposes

1. To improve the quality of teaching and services to the students.
2. To enable the teacher to recognize his or her role in the total school program.
3. To assist the teacher in achieving the established goals of the curriculum.
4. To help the teacher identify his or her strengths and weaknesses as a personal guide for improvement.
5. To provide assistance to the teacher to help correct weaknesses.
6. To recognize the teacher's special talents and to encourage and facilitate their utilization.
7. To serve as a guide for renewed employment, termination of employment, promotion, assignment, and unrequested leave for tenured teachers.
8. To protect the teacher from dismissal without just cause.
9. To protect the teaching profession from unethical and incompetent personnel.

Source: Lindbergh School District, *Teacher Evaluation Report* (St. Louis: The District, 1985). Used with permission.

Implementation

The evaluation is to be made by the building principal, grade principal, assistant principal, or acting principal.

If a teacher does not agree with an evaluation, she or he may request an additional evaluation to be made by another administrator of her or his choice.

Evaluation of a probationary (non-tenured) teacher's services will be made semi-annually during the probationary period with one of the evaluations completed during the first semester, and both completed before March 15. Each evaluation must be preceded by at least one classroom visit.

Evaluation of a permanent (tenured) teacher's services will be made every year with the evaluation completed before March 15. Each evaluation must be preceded by at least one classroom visit.

Definition of Terms

1. Superior: consistently exceptional.
2. Strong: usually surpasses the standards of Lindbergh School District.
3. Average: generally meets standards of Lindbergh School District.
4. Improvement needed: occasionally does not meet standards of Lindbergh School District.
5. Unsatisfactory: does not measure up to standards of Lindbergh School District.

Rating of unsatisfactory or improvement needed must include a written comment describing the cause for the rating.

Note: The space at the end of this form marked "Principal's Comments" may be used to record the observations of the teacher's exceptional performances and/or to record the principal's recommendations for improvement.

The space at the end of this form marked "Teacher's Comments" may be used by the teacher to record any comment or comments which she or he wishes to make.

	1	2	3	4	5
I. Teaching Performance					
A. Plans and organizes carefully					
1. Lesson is well planned					
2. Sets definite goals including student participation					
3. Makes clear, specific assignments					
4. Is familiar with appropriate guide and adapts to the recommendations therein					
5. Provides for individual and group instruction					

	1	2	3	4	5

B. Is skillful in questioning and explaining
  1. Asks thought-provoking questions
  2. Gives clear explanation of subject matter
  3. Exposes students to varying points of view
  4. Is aware of both verbal and non-verbal acceptance or rejection of students' ideas, and uses this skill positively

C. Stimulates learning through innovative activities and resources
  1. Encourages class discussion, pupil questions and pupil demonstrations
  2. Uses a variety of teaching aids and resources

D. Displays knowledge of and enthusiasm for subject matter taught

E. Provides a classroom atmosphere conducive to good learning
Maintains a healthy and flexible environment

F. Keeps adequate and accurate records
Records sufficient quantitative and qualitative data on which to base pupil progress reports

G. Has wholesome relationship with pupils
  1. Knows and works with pupils as individuals
  2. Encourages relationships that are mutually respectful and friendly
  3. Uses positive language with students that is devoid of sarcasm

H. Initiates and preserves classroom and general school management and discipline
  1. Rules of pupil conduct have been developed and teacher requires observance of these rules
  2. Rules of safety have been developed and teacher requires observation of these rules
  3. Emphasizes importance of both developing and maintaining self-respect and respect for others

II. Professional Qualities
  A. Recognition and acceptance of out-of-class responsibilities
    1. Participates in the general and necessary school activities
    2. Sometimes volunteers for the "extra" duties
    3. Serves on school committees

	1	2	3	4	5

B. Intra-school relationships
Cooperates effectively and pleasantly with
colleagues, administration and non-professional
personnel

C. Public relations
1. Cooperates effectively and pleasantly with
parents
2. Practices good relationships between school
and community

D. Professional growth and vision
1. Accepts constructive criticism
2. Participates in conferences, workshops and
studies
3. Tries new methods and materials

E. Utilization of staff services
Makes proper use of available special services

F. Understands the growth patterns and behaviors
of students at various stages of development
and copes satisfactorily with situations as they
occur

G. Ethical behavior
1. Protects professional use of confidential data
2. Supports the teaching profession

Definition of Terms for Personal Qualities

S—Satisfactory: meets or surpasses standards for Lindbergh School District
teachers.

I—Improvement needed: does not measure up to standards Lindbergh School
District teachers meet.

	S	I

III. Personal Qualities
   A. Health and vigor
      1. Has a good and reasonable
attendance record
      2. Is cheerful
      3. Displays a sense of humor
   B. Speech
      1. Is articulate
      2. Can be heard and understood by
all pupils in the room

	S	I
C. Grooming and appropriateness of dress		
Practices habits of good grooming		
D. Promptness in meeting obligations		
1. Reports to classes on time		
2. Performs assigned tasks properly		
3. Completes reports on time		
4. Arrives in the building at the required time		

A copy of the written evaluation will be submitted to the teacher at the time of the conference following the observation(s). The final evaluation report form is to be signed and retained by the principal, and a copy is to be retained by the teacher. In the event the teacher feels the evaluation was incomplete, inaccurate, or unjust, she or he may put the objections in writing on the back of this form. Teacher's signature acknowledges that the conference has taken place.

Date of Observation(s) _____

Time of Observation(s) _____

Length of Observation(s) _____

Date Evaluation Made _____

Principal's Comments

Overall Evaluation _____

Principal's Signature _____ Date _____

Teacher's Comments

Teacher's Signature _____ Date_____

Indicators for the Teacher Evaluation Instrument

Supplement to Chapter 14

Indicators for the evaluation items in the Teacher Evaluation Instrument were developed by the administrators in the Lindbergh School District. The indicators are representative of the kind of teaching-learning techniques the evaluator will be looking for when observing a teacher in a classroom situation. It is expected that each teacher will perform the skill as listed but that the final evaluation will be based on the degree of performance.

I. Teaching Performance.
   A. Plans and organizes carefully.
      1. Lesson is well planned.
         a. Written plans are available and followed by classroom teacher.
         b. Lesson includes preview, statement of objective and review.
         c. Lesson fits within an allotted time frame.
         d. Lesson follows a logical sequence.
         e. Lesson meets the needs of the student group.
         f. Long- and short-range goals are clearly defined.
         g. Lesson indicates the teacher has used the concept of diagnosis and prescription.
         h. Lesson is flexible to permit spontaneous teaching.
         i. Plans and procedures are provided.
         j. Materials and equipment are readily available.

Source: Lindbergh School District, *Teacher Evaluation Report* (St. Louis: The District, 1985). Used with permission.

    2. Sets definite goals including student participation.

        a. Long- and short-range goals are clearly defined.

        b. Students are involved in the goal setting process when appropriate.

    3. Makes clear, specific assignment.

        a. Reasonable and clear assignments are given in written form.

        b. Adequate time is given for clarification and discussion of assignment.

    4. Is familiar with appropriate guide and adapts to the recommendation therein.

        a. Lesson reflects thorough knowledge of curriculum guide.

        b. Long-range planning for coverage of objectives in curriculum guide is indicated.

    5. Provides for individual and group instruction.

        a. Lesson provides for individual instruction.

        b. Lesson provides for group instruction.

        c. Type of instruction is suited to lesson presented.

B. Is skillful in questioning and explaining.

    1. Asks thought-provoking questions.

        a. Asks questions requiring more than a one-word answer.

        b. Questions stimulate critical and divergent thinking.

        c. Asks thought-provoking written questions.

        d. Questions asked stimulate a response from students.

    2. Gives clear explanation of subject matter.

        a. Obtains response indicating understanding before continuing further explanation.

        b. Presents ideas in a logical sequence.

        c. Consistently uses correct grammar and vocabulary suited to the student.

        d. Presents accurate and complete content information.

    3. Exposes students to varying points of view.

        a. Establishes a background of general information on the topic before presenting varying points of view.

        b. Presents varying points of view consistent with curriculum.

        c. Elicits from students their points of view.

    4. Is aware of both verbal and non-verbal acceptance or rejection of students' ideas, and uses this skill positively.

        a. Does not show rejection through verbal or physical expression.

        b. Does not allow peer-rejection.

        c. Praises, elicits and responds to student questions and answers before proceeding.

C. Stimulates learning through innovative activities and resources.

    1. Encourages class discussion, pupil questions, and pupil demonstration.

        a. Listens patiently to students' comments, questions and answers.

        b. Questions are asked according to students' ability to answer correctly.

        c. Gives each student an opportunity to participate.

    2. Uses a variety of teaching aids and resources.

        a. Looks for and uses models, manipulative materials, films, outside speeches, work-sheets, records, etc.

        b. Uses appropriate materials and resources for the lesson.

        c. Displays materials that are coordinated with the lesson.

D. Displays knowledge of and enthusiasm for subject matter taught.

    1. Displays knowledge of subject matter taught.

        a. Displays knowledge of content of textbook(s).

        b. Demonstrates competence and familiarity with subject matter.

        c. Has comprehensive knowledge of related disciplines and uses it when appropriate.

        d. Answers students' questions readily and thoroughly.

        e. Probes for knowledge of content presented (encourages questions and activities that are designed to stimulate critical thinking).

        f. Goes beyond the textbook to enhance the content (may be observed by use of films, resource persons, reference materials, charts, etc.).

    2. Enthusiasm.

        a. Students respond positively to the teacher. (Do the students appear interested? Are they listening to the teacher? Are they awake? Are they talking to other students? Do they appear bored?)

        b. Interest and enthusiasm is evidenced from the teacher's presentation.

        c. Responds positively to the students, both verbally and visually.

        d. Elicits enthusiastic response from the students to the questions and answers.

        e. Uses techniques which engender enthusiasm in students (a change of pace, voice inflections, body movement).

E. Provides a classroom atmosphere conducive to good learning.

    1. Maintains a healthy and flexible environment.

        a. Sets the tone for students to feel free to ask and to respond to questions (students are not intimidated).

        b. Classroom atmosphere is controlled but not dominated by the teacher (students interact within the environment).

        c. Differing views and values are allowed to be discussed.

        d. Positive interpersonal relationships are easily observed.

        e. Uses humor in proper perspective.

        f. Room reflects students' work.

    2. Observes the care of instructional material and equipment.

        a. Equipment in use is carefully supervised.

        b. Equipment or material not in use is properly stored.

  c. Equipment is properly maintained and/or reported to the office for repair.

  d. Desks are devoid of writing and graffiti.

  e. Promotes respect for instructional materials and equipment.

F. Keeps adequate and accurate records.

 1. Records sufficient quantitative and qualitative data on which to base pupil progress reports.

  a. Records the number of written assignments, tests scores, daily grades, and exam grades in the grade book (indicators of each student's performance).

  b. Quality of data recorded shows relationship between the objectives and grades.

  c. Daily attendance is correctly recorded.

G. Has wholesome relationship with pupils.

 1. Knows and works with pupils as individuals.

  a. Individual strengths and weaknesses of each student have been identified.

  b. Knows and calls each student by name.

  c. Listens carefully and politely to each student.

  d. Encourages student ideas and concentrates on their response.

  e. Students do not hesitate to ask for clarification.

  f. Students appear to be an active part of the class.

  g. Creative responses are encouraged.

 2. Encourages relationships that are mutually respectful and friendly.

  a. Encourages positive behavior by maintaining complete control of self.

  b. Words and actions are positive.

  c. Exhibits qualities of warmth toward students.

  d. Elicits student responses.

  e. Sets an example of respect.

  f. Is sensitive to students' moods.

  g. Behavior is consistent with all students and situations.

  h. Handling of misconduct centers on the conduct or behavior, not the student.

  i. Requires student attention and gives attention in return.

 3. Uses positive language with students which is devoid of sarcasm.

  a. Praises and elicits responses from students.

  b. Sarcasm is not used.

  c. Is positive in actions, voice tones, and movements.

  d. Tone of voice is moderate and even.

H. Initiates and preserves classroom and general school management and discipline.

 1. Rules of pupil conduct have been developed and teacher requires observance of these rules.

   a. Classroom incidents handled in order not to interrupt entire class.
   b. Pupils are aware of rules and regulations.
   c. Students understand and follow room routine readily without teacher's direction.
   d. Demonstrates behavior which is achievement-oriented or businesslike.
   e. Is consistent and fair in expectations of behavior.
   f. Students enter room quietly and take seats.
   g. Students ask and receive permission to change patterns.
 2. Rules of safety have been developed and teacher requires observance of these rules.
   a. Classroom behavior shows a concern for safety.
   b. Safety procedures are properly posted and followed.
   c. Horseplay is not tolerated.
   d. Plays an active and positive role in the supervision of halls, restrooms, lunchrooms, and pre- and post-class times as well as at assemblies.
   e. Classroom is free of hazards.
 3. Emphasizes importance of both developing and maintaining self-respect and respect for others.
   a. Encourages positive behavior by maintaining own self-control.
   b. Uses words and actions which are positive.
   c. Exhibits qualities of warmth.
   d. Elicits positive student responses.
   e. Sets an example of respect.
   f. Is sensitive to student moods.
   g. Uses consistent behavior with all students.
   h. Handles misconduct on the basis of the conduct and not the student.
   i. Requires student attention and gives attention in return.
   j. Consistently maintains self-control.
II. Professional Qualities
  A. Recognition and acceptance of out-of-class responsibilities.
   1. Participates in the general and necessary school activities.
     a. Performs assigned duties consistently.
     b. Follows the school time schedule.
     c. Attends and participates in school-related activities.
     d. Participates in assigned meetings.
     e. Plays an active and positive role in the supervision of halls, restrooms, lunchrooms, and pre- and post-class times as well as at assemblies.
   2. Sometimes volunteers for the "extra" duties.
     a. Accepts responsibilities other than those considered general or necessary.
     b. Initiates volunteer services to the overall school program.

   3. Serves on school committees.
      a. Serves on district and/or school committees.
      b. Attends school and district committee meetings.
      c. Participates in school or district level committees.
B. Intra-school relationship.
   1. Cooperates effectively and pleasantly with colleagues, administration and nonprofessional personnel.
      a. Relationships with other professionals indicate acceptance of differing views or values.
      b. Practices relationships that are mutually respectful and friendly.
      c. Shares ideas, materials and methods.
      d. Informs appropriate personnel of school-related matters.
      e. Cooperates fairly and works well with all school personnel.
      f. Is effective in providing a climate that encourages communication between the teacher and professional colleagues.
C. Public relations.
   1. Cooperates effectively and pleasantly with parents.
      a. Maintains good communication with parents.
      b. Keeps best interest of student in mind.
      c. Provides a climate of open communication between the teacher and parent.
   2. Practices good relationship between school and community.
      a. Enhances school involvement with communities.
      b. Encourages community involvement and attendance in school situations.
D. Professional growth and vision.
   1. Accepts constructive criticism.
      a. Asks positive questions.
      b. Responds pleasantly to criticism.
   2. Participates in conferences, workshops, and studies.
      a. Engages in activities which promote professional growth.
      b. Engages in professional activities which are not required.
   3. Tries new methods and materials.
      a. Uses new methods and materials at appropriate times.
      b. Modifies materials when needed.
      c. Understands new techniques before using.
E. Utilization of staff services.
   1. Makes proper use of available special services.
      a. Makes use of and cooperates with district service personnel (guidance, library, supervisory, specialists and classified staff members).
      b. Utilizes special school district services as appropriate.
      c. Makes student recommendations and referrals to appropriate staff members as needed.

F. Understands the growth patterns and behaviors of students at various stages of development and copes satisfactorily with situations as they occur.

    a. Uses a variety of techniques to achieve desired work and skills, and adjusts the techniques to the age and maturity of the student.

    b. Does not expect identical behavior from all students; allows for individual differences.

    c. Is understanding and sympathetic to students with special learning and behavior problems.

G. Ethical behavior.

    1. Protects professional use of confidential data.

        a. Confidential information about students, their parents or staff members is not discussed in the lounge, cafeteria or in the classroom.

        b. Respects confidential information.

    2. Supports the teaching profession.

        a. Positive attitude toward teaching.

        b. Uses positive statements regarding teaching, students, school, and profession.

III. Personal Qualities

A. Health and vigor.

    1. Has a good and reasonable attendance record.

        a. Absences are infrequent and justifiable.

        b. Places emphasis on assigned duties.

        c. Except in cases of extreme illness, is present at school and is prepared.

    2. Is cheerful.

        a. Allows occasional humorous interruptions.

        b. Can relax and joke with students.

        c. Laughs with, not at, others.

    3. Displays a sense of humor.

        a. Smiles easily.

        b. Has a friendly attitude.

B. Speech.

    1. Is articulate.

        a. Consistently uses appropriate grammar.

        b. Communicates clearly.

    2. Can be heard and understood by all pupils in the room.

        a. Consistently uses appropriate tone of voice.

        b. Is easy to hear and understand.

    3. Speaks on the level of pupils' understanding.

        a. Uses appropriate vocabulary and examples according to students' level of understanding.

C. Grooming and appropriateness of dress.
  1. Practices habits of good grooming.
    a. Is clean and neat.
    b. Clothes are appropriate for job task.
    c. Dress adds to rather than detracts from classroom performance.
D. Promptness in meeting obligations.
  1. Reports to classes on time.
    a. Arrives at classroom before students.
    b. Classroom is open and in readiness prior to students' arrival.
    c. Classroom preparations do not interfere with obligations.
    d. Arrives in the building at the required times.
  2. Performs assigned tasks properly.
    a. Tasks are completed on time.
    b. Tasks are completed to letter and in spirit of the assignment.
  3. Completes reports on time.
    a. Does not have to be reminded of reports which are due.
    b. Completes reports according to expectations of administrator.
  4. Arrives in the building at the required time.

A p p e n d i x **H**

Needs-Assessment Survey
Supplement to Chapter 14

Needs-Assessment Survey for Instructional Staff

Directions: Please check all items according to your degree of interest. Return this completed form to the administration office.

	Degree of Interest		
	None	Some	Much
1. Methods of motivating students	—	—	—
2. Behavior objectives	—	—	—
3. Dealing with individual differences	—	—	—
4. New grouping patterns (non-graded school, team teaching)	—	—	—
5. Teaching critical thinking skills	—	—	—
6. Programmed learning	—	—	—
7. Designing independent study projects	—	—	—
8. Work-study programs	—	—	—
9. Career education	—	—	—
10. Using performance objectives	—	—	—
11. Advanced placement	—	—	—
12. Linguistics	—	—	—
13. Teacher made tests and mechanical scoring	—	—	—
14. Modern math workshop	—	—	—

Source: Lincoln Intermediate Unit No. 12 School District, *Needs-Assessment Survey* (New Oxford, Penn.: The District, 1982). Used with permission.

	Degree of Interest		
	None	Some	Much
15. Elementary science (experiment and demonstration)	—	—	—
16. Seminar on literature	—	—	—
17. Computer programming (course of study)	—	—	—
18. Oral communication	—	—	—
19. Education for economic competencies	—	—	—
20. Developmental reading	—	—	—
21. English for junior and senior high teachers (develop a course of study)	—	—	—
22. Audiovisual aids workshops (teachers)	—	—	—
23. Audiovisual aids workshops (teacher's aides)	—	—	—
24. Black history workshop	—	—	—
25. Consumer education in the secondary curriculum	—	—	—
26. New directions in social studies	—	—	—
27. Outdoor education workshop	—	—	—
28. Ecology workshop	—	—	—
29. Minicourses (in your field)	—	—	—
30. Music for elementary teachers	—	—	—
31. Seasonal art projects for elementary classrooms	—	—	—
32. Public library resources	—	—	—
33. Selection and evaluation of audiovisual and other instructional media	—	—	—
34. Spanish for teachers	—	—	—
35. Math for first- and second-grade teachers	—	—	—
36. Learning disabilities (identification and remediation)	—	—	—
37. Social studies for fifth- and sixth-grade teachers	—	—	—
38. Art workshop	—	—	—
39. Field trips	—	—	—
40. Physical education specialties	—	—	—
41. School library	—	—	—
42. Industrial arts (all purpose)	—	—	—
43. Pupil services	—	—	—
44. Speech therapy	—	—	—
45. Driver training (rap sessions)	—	—	—
46. Learning center (elementary)	—	—	—
47. Teaching English composition	—	—	—
48. Modern economics	—	—	—
49. Medical seminar (nurses)	—	—	—
50. Math enrichment (elementary)	—	—	—
51. Retirement and Social Security (teachers of retirement age)	—	—	—

	Degree of Interest		
	None	Some	Much
52. New elementary math adoptions (primary)	—	—	—
53. New elementary math adoptions (intermediate)	—	—	—
54. Early childhood (kindergarten curriculum)	—	—	—
55. Teachers' legal limitations and liabilities in the school	—	—	—
56. Learning and behavior	—	—	—
57. Behavior and discipline in the elementary school	—	—	—
58. The open space school	—	—	—
59. Language arts (elementary)	—	—	—
60. Elementary library facilities	—	—	—
61. Parent-teacher relations	—	—	—
62. Involving the child in social studies (elementary)	—	—	—
63. Involving the child in science (elementary)	—	—	—
64. Personalizing math (elementary)	—	—	—
65. Music for secondary teachers	—	—	—
66. Orientations for new teachers	—	—	—
67. The psychology of the disadvantaged child	—	—	—
68. Classroom management	—	—	—
69. Behavior modification	—	—	—
70. Parliamentary procedure	—	—	—
71. Home economics	—	—	—
72. Special education on elementary level	—	—	—
73. Special education on secondary level	—	—	—
74. Guidance workshop	—	—	—
75. Seminar in your subject area	—	—	—
76. Adolescent psychology in the modern world	—	—	—
77. General trends in education	—	—	—
78. Newspaper in the classroom	—	—	—
79. Data processing seminar (student attendance and grade reporting)	—	—	—
80. Teacher-made training aids	—	—	—
81. Rap sessions in your subject area	—	—	—
82. Creative classroom (display and bulletin boards)	—	—	—
83. Individualized reading	—	—	—
84. Techniques of teaching slow children	—	—	—
85. Instructional materials	—	—	—
86. Instructional games	—	—	—
87. Physical education (elementary)	—	—	—
88. Constructive seatwork	—	—	—
89. Individualized teaching and learning (elementary)	—	—	—

	Degree of Interest		
	None	Some	Much
90. Involving the child in language arts (elementary)	——	——	——
91. Updating courses of study (in your field)	——	——	——
92. Community relations	——	——	——
93. Effective questioning	——	——	——
94. Interaction analysis	——	——	——
95. Metric measurement (international system)	——	——	——
96. Communications and drug abuse seminar	——	——	——
97. Instructional management systems	——	——	——
98. Other suggestions	——	——	——

Index